☆☆**Forbes**
TRAVEL GUIDE
Formerly Mobil Travel Guide

SOUTHWEST
2011

ACKNOWLEDGMENTS

We gratefully acknowledge the help of our representatives for their efficient and perceptive inspections of the lodgings listed. Forbes Travel Guide is also grateful to the talented writers who contributed to this book.

Some of the information contained herein is derived from a variety of third-party sources. Although every effort has been made to verify the information obtained from such sources, the publisher assumes no responsibility for inconsistencies or inaccuracies in the data or liability for any damages of any type arising from errors or omissions.

Neither the editors nor the publisher assume responsibility for the services provided by any business listed in this guide or for any loss, damage or disruption in your travel for any reason.

Front Cover image: ©iStockphoto.com
All maps: Mapping Specialists

ISBN: 9781936010950
Manufactured in the USA
10 9 8 7 6 5 4 3 2 1

CONTENTS

STAR ATTRACTIONS

If you've been a reader of Mobil Travel Guide, you will have heard that this historic brand partnered in 2009 with another storied media name, Forbes, to create a new entity, Forbes Travel Guide. For more than 50 years, Mobil Travel Guide assisted travelers in making smart decisions about where to stay and dine when traveling. With this new partnership, our mission has not changed: We're committed to the same rigorous inspections of hotels, restaurants and spas—the most comprehensive in the industry with more than 500 standards tested at each property we visit—to help you cut through the clutter and make easy and informed decisions on where to spend your time and travel budget. Our team of anonymous inspectors are constantly on the road, sleeping in hotels, eating in restaurants and making spa appointments, evaluating those exacting standards to determine a property's rating.

What kinds of standards are we looking for when we visit a property? We're looking for more than just high-thread count sheets, pristine spa treatment rooms and white linen-topped tables. We look for service that's attentive, individualized and unforgettable. We note how long it takes to be greeted when you sit down at your table, or to be served when you order room service, or whether the hotel staff can confidently help you when you've forgotten that one essential item that will make or break your trip. Unlike any other travel ratings entity, we visit each place we rate, testing hundreds of attributes to compile our ratings, and our ratings cannot be bought or influenced. The Forbes Five Star rating is the most prestigious achievement in hospitality—while we rate more than 5,000 properties in the U.S., Canada, Hong Kong, Macau and Beijing, for 2011, we have awarded Five Star designations to only 54 hotels, 23 restaurants and 20 spas. When you travel with Forbes, you can travel with confidence, knowing that you'll get the very best experience, no matter who you are.

We understand the importance of making the most of your time. That's why the most trusted name in travel is now Forbes Travel Guide.

STAR RATED HOTELS

Whether you're looking for the ultimate in luxury or the best value for your travel budget, we have a hotel recommendation for you. To help you pinpoint properties that meet your needs, Forbes Travel Guide classifies each lodging by type according to the following characteristics:

★★★★★These exceptional properties provide a memorable experience through virtually flawless service and the finest of amenities. Staff are intuitive, engaging and passionate, and eagerly deliver service above and beyond the guests' expectations. The hotel was designed with the guest's comfort in mind, with particular attention paid to craftsmanship and quality of product. A Five-Star property is a destination unto itself.

★★★★These properties provide a distinctive setting, and a guest will find many interesting and inviting elements to enjoy throughout the property. Attention to detail is prominent throughout the property, from design concept to quality of products provided. Staff are accommodating and take pride in catering to the guest's specific needs throughout their stay.

★★★These well-appointed establishments have enhanced amenities that provide travelers with a strong sense of location, whether for style or function. They may have a distinguishing style and ambience in both the public spaces and guest rooms; or they may be more focused on functionality, providing guests with easy access to local events, meetings or tourism highlights.

Recommended: These hotels are considered clean, comfortable and reliable establishments that have expanded amenities, such as full-service restaurants.

For every property, we also provide pricing information. All prices quoted are accurate at the time of publication; however, prices cannot be guaranteed. Because rates can fluctuate, we list a pricing range rather than specific prices.

STAR RATED RESTAURANTS

Every restaurant in this book has been visited by Forbes Travel Guide's team of experts and comes highly recommended as an outstanding dining experience.

★★★★★Forbes Five-Star restaurants deliver a truly unique and distinctive dining experience. A Five-Star restaurant consistently provides exceptional food, superlative service and elegant décor. An emphasis is placed on originality and personalized, attentive and discreet service. Every detail that surrounds the experience is attended to by a warm and gracious dining room team.

★★★★These are exciting restaurants with often well-known chefs that feature creative and complex foods and emphasize various culinary techniques and a focus on seasonality. A highly-trained dining room staff provides refined personal service and attention.

★★★Three Star restaurants offer skillfully prepared food with a focus on a specific style or cuisine. The dining room staff provides warm and professional service in a comfortable atmosphere. The décor is well-coordinated with quality fixtures and decorative items, and promotes a comfortable ambience.

Recommended: These restaurants serve fresh food in a clean setting with efficient service. Value is considered in this category, as is family friendliness.

Because menu prices can fluctuate, we list a pricing range rather than specific prices. The pricing ranges are per diner, and assume that you order an appetizer or dessert, an entrée and one drink.

STAR RATED SPAS

Forbes Travel Guide's spa ratings are based on objective evaluations of more than 450 attributes. About half of these criteria assess basic expectations, such as staff courtesy, the technical proficiency and skill of the employees and whether the facility is clean and maintained properly. Several standards address issues that impact a guest's physical comfort and convenience, as well as the staff's ability to impart a sense of personalized service. Additional criteria measure the spa's ability to create a completely calming ambience.

★★★★★Stepping foot in a Five Star Spa will result in an exceptional experience with no detail overlooked. These properties wow their guests with extraordinary design and facilities, and uncompromising service. Expert staff cater to your every whim and pamper you with the most advanced treatments and skin care lines available. These spas often offer exclusive treatments and may emphasize local elements.

★★★★Four Star spas provide a wonderful experience in an inviting and serene environment. A sense of personalized service is evident from the moment you check in and receive your robe and slippers. The guest's comfort is always of utmost concern to the well-trained staff.

★★★These spas offer well-appointed facilities with a full complement of staff to ensure that guests' needs are met. The spa facil ties include clean and appealing treatment rooms, changing areas and a welcoming reception desk.

TOP HOTELS, RESTAURANTS AND SPAS

HOTELS

★★★★★FIVE STAR

The Broadmoor
(Colorado Springs, Colorado)
The Little Nell (Aspen, Colorado)
Skylofts at MGM Grand,
(Las Vegas, Nevada)
Stein Eriksen Lodge
(Park City, Utah)
Tower Suites at Encore Las Vegas
(Las Vegas, Nevada)
Tower Suites at Wynn Las Vegas
(Las Vegas, Nevada)

★★★★★FOUR STAR

Bellagio (Las Vegas, Nevada)
The Brown Palace Hotel
(Denver, Colorado)
Encantado Resort
(Santa Fe, New Mexico)
Encore Las Vegas (Las Vegas, Nevada)
Four Seasons Hotel Austin
(Austin, Texas)
Four Seasons Hotel Houston
(Houston, Texas)
Four Seasons Hotel Las Vegas
(Las Vegas, Nevada)
Four Seasons Resort and Club Dallas
at Las Colinas (Irving, Texas)
Four Seasons Resort Scottsdale at
Troon North (Scottsdale, Arizona)
The Grand America Hotel
(Salt Lake City, Utah)

Hotel Granduca (Houston, Texas)
The M Resort Spa & Casino Las
Vegas (Las Vegas, Nevada)
Mandarin Oriental Las Vegas
(Las Vegas, Nevada)
Mokara Hotel & Spa
(San Antonio, Texas)
The Palazzo Resort Hotel Casino
(Las Vegas, Nevada)
The Phoenician
(Scottsdale, Arizona)
The Ritz-Carlton, Bachelor Gulch
(Avon, Colorado)
The Ritz-Carlton, Dallas
(Dallas, Texas)
The Ritz-Carlton, Phoenix
(Phoenix, Arizona)
Rosewood Inn of the Anasazi
(Santa Fe, New Mexico)
Rosewood Mansion on Turtle Creek
(Dallas, Texas)
The Signature at MGM Grand
(Las Vegas, Nevada)
St. Regis Aspen Resort
(Aspen, Colorado)
St. Regis Deer Crest
(Park City, Utah)
The St. Regis Houston
(Houston, Texas)
The Venetian Resort Hotel Casino
(Las Vegas, Nevada)
Wynn Las Vegas (Las Vegas, Nevada)

RESTAURANTS

★★★★★FIVE STAR

Alex (Las Vegas, Nevada)
Joel Robuchon (Las Vegas, Nevada)
Kai (Chandler, Arizona)
The Inn at Dos Brisas
(Brenham, Texas)
Penrose Room
(Colorado Springs, Colorado)

★★★★★FOUR STAR

Abacus (Dallas, Texas)
Aureole (Las Vegas, Nevada)
Bradley Ogden (Las Vegas, Nevada)
Fearing's (Dallas, Texas)
Flagstaff House Restaurant
(Boulder, Colorado)
The French Room (Dallas, Texas)

Geronimo (*Santa Fe, New Mexico*)
Glitretind Restaurant
(*Park City, Utah*)
Le Cirque (*Las Vegas, Nevada*)
The Mansion Restaurant
(*Dallas, Texas*)
Michael Mina (*Las Vegas, Nevada*)
Mirabelle at Beaver Creek
(*Beaver Creek, Colorado*)
Mix in Las Vegas (*Las Vegas, Nevada*)
Montagna (*Aspen, Colorado*)
Nana (*Dallas, Texas*)

Picasso (*Las Vegas, Nevada*)
Quattro (*Houston, Texas*)
Restaurant Guy Savoy
(*Las Vegas, Nevada*)
Restaurant Kevin Taylor
(*Denver, Colorado*)
Riverhorse on Main
(*Park City, Utah*)
Stephan Pyles (*Dallas, Texas*)
Talavera (*Scottsdale, Arizona*)
Twist by Pierre Gagnaire
(*Las Vegas, Nevada*)

SPAS

★★★★★FIVE STAR
The Spa at The Broadmoor
(*Colorado Springs, Colorado*)
The Spa at Encore Las Vegas
(*Las Vegas, Nevada*)
The Spa at Mandarin Oriental
Las Vegas (*Las Vegas, Nevada*)
The Spa at Wynn Las Vegas
(*Las Vegas, Nevada*)

★★★★★FOUR STAR
Aji Spa (*Chandler, Arizona*)
Allegria Spa at Park Hyatt
Beaver Creek (*Avon, Colorado*)
Alvadora Spa at Royal Palms
(*Phoenix, Arizona*)
The Bachelor Gulch Spa at the Ritz-
Carlton (*Avon, Colorado*)
Canyon Ranch SpaClub at The
Venetian & The Palazzo
(*Las Vegas, Nevada*)
The Centre for Well-Being at the
Phoenician (*Scottsdale, Arizona*)
The Mokara Spa (*San Antonio, Texas*)
Remède Spa, St. Regis Deer Crest
(*Park City, Utah*)
The Ritz-Carlton Spa, Dallas
(*Dallas, Texas*)

The Ritz-Carlton Spa, Denver
(*Denver, Colorado*)
The Sanctuary Spa at Sanctuary on
Camelback Mountain
(*Paradise Valley, Arizona*)
Spa Bellagio (*Las Vegas, Nevada*)
Spa Mio (*Las Vegas, Nevada*)
The Spa & Salon at the Four Seasons
Resort and Club Dallas at Las Colinas
(*Irving, Texas*)
The Spa at the Brown Palace
(*Denver, Colorado*)
Spa at Four Seasons Resort Scottsdale
at Troon North (*Scottsdale, Arizona*)
The Spa at Four Seasons Austin
(*Austin, Texas*)
The Spa at Four Seasons Hotel
Las Vegas (*Las Vegas, Nevada*)
The Spa at Omni Tucson National
(*Tucson, Arizona*)
The Spa at Stein Eriksen Lodge
(*Park City, Utah*)
The Spa at Trump
(*Las Vegas, Nevada*)
Trellis, the Spa at the Houstonian
(*Houston, Texas*)
Willow Stream Spa at Fairmont
Scottsdale Princess
(*Scottsdale, Arizona*)

YOUR QUESTIONS ANSWERED

WHAT'S THE BEST WAY TO SEE LAS VEGAS IN ONE DAY?

The Strip, a.k.a. Las Vegas Boulevard, is the engine that keeps Las Vegas chugging along, and it's a requisite if you have limited time in town. The four-mile street takes you around the world in a matter of hours. See a miniaturized version of New York City, catch views from Paris' most recognized landmark, and travel gondolier-style through the Italian renaissance.

Regardless of where you're staying, it's easiest to begin at one end of the Strip and make your way from there. Cabs are nearly as common as slot machines on Las Vegas Boulevard, so you'll have no trouble finding one (though you may have to go to a hotel entrance to get one to stop). For a cheaper option—albeit pricey as public transportation goes—the high-tech (driverless) monorail can get you through the Strip in less than 15 minutes.

Start at **Mandalay Bay Resort and Casino** and head north, taking the indoor walkway to Luxor. While you're there, enjoy a morning poker lesson before hopping on the monorail to **Excalibur**, which puts you Strip-central in no time. From here, pick and choose the casinos that appeal to you. High stakes gamblers will enjoy the enormous and extravagant mega-resorts such as **The Venetian Resort Hotel Casino, Caesars Palace** and **Wynn Las Vegas** (and the perks that accompany such invited guests). Whereas the smaller casinos, like **O'Sheas** (*3555 Las Vegas Blvd. S., South Strip, 702-697-2711; www.osheaslasvegas.com*) and **Slots-A-Fun** (*2890 Las Vegas Blvd. S., South Strip, 702-734-0410*) tend to have better payouts and lower minimums. Once you've gotten your gambling fix—and perhaps, come to understand that the house always wins—it's time for some exceptional people gawking. Where else can you watch showgirls mingle with card sharks, and bachelorettes dance the night away in little more than lingerie? For a bit of aromatic pleasure, meander through the **Conservatory and Botanical Gardens** at Bellagio or entice your inner child as you browse the perfectly polished **Ferrari-Maserati** collection at **Wynn Las Vegas**. Depending on what you're in the mood for, there are, of course, a slew of big-name restaurants to choose from for dinner. Cap off your Vegas day with a **Cirque du Soleil** show; with so many to choose from, you're unlikely to go wrong, but our vote goes to *O* at Bellagio Las Vegas. If you've got anything left by midnight, the tables are always open.

WHAT'S THE BEST WAY TO TOUR THE GRAND CANYON?

It can be difficult deciding how to tackle the immense Grand Canyon—the entire park measures 1,904 square miles. You can go at it on your own and hike the trails, but if you want some guidance, you have plenty of options. There are mule trips that bring you through the canyon. If you prefer equines, go horseback riding on the terrain. For an aerial view, try one of the helicopter (some of which leave from Las Vegas) or airplane tours. Those who want to take advantage of the 277 miles of the Colorado River that run through the Grand Canyon can go on rafting journeys. There are even places along the landscape where you can bring your car, though four-wheel drive is necessary to traverse some areas. Be sure to book your tours ahead of time to ensure your spot.

The optimal times to visit the Grand Canyon are the fall and spring, when the crowds thin out at the popular tourist attractions. If you plan on hiking a lot, it may be wiser to stay overnight rather than try to cram it all in one day. Camping is available, but for less rustic accommodations, stay at the canyon's El Tovar. You'll see amazing views from the hotel, which is just 20 feet from the edge of the South Rim, but still have necessary amenities like toilets and showers. Again, reserve your room early; the hotel fills up a year in advance.

WELCOME TO ARIZONA

HIKE THE GRAND CANYON. RELAX AT A SPA. HIT THE LINKS.

This rapildy growing—its population has more than tripled since 1940—offers all of this and more.

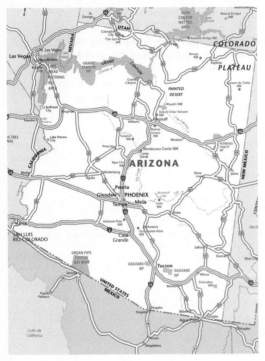

Arizona is known for its hot summers, mild winters and desert landscape. But the northern mountains, cool forests, spectacular canyons and lakes offer a variety of vacation activities, including fishing, whitewater rafting, hiking and camping. The northern, central part of the state is on a plateau at higher altitudes than the desert in the southern region of the state and has a cooler climate.

There are also meadows filled with wildflowers, ghost and mining towns, dude ranches and intriguing ancient Native American villages. The state has 23 reservations and one of the largest Native American populations in the United States. More than half of that population is Navajo. Visitors can scoop up craft specialties, including baskets, pottery, woven goods, jewelry and kachina dolls.

Arizona has scores of water parks, interesting museums, zoos and wildlife exhibits. And who says it doesn't snow in Arizona? There are several places for downhill skiing, including the Arizona Snowball in the north, Mt. Lemmon Ski Valley near Tucson and Sunrise Ski Resort in the east.

Of course, there is also plenty of what people have come to expect here. There are more than 300 golf courses across the state, making it home to several stops on the PGA Tour, most notably the Phoenix Open. You'll also find some of the best spas in the country. All of these add up to make Arizona one of the nation's favorite spots for recreation and relaxation.

HIGHLIGHTS

ARIZONA'S BEST ATTRACTIONS

GRAND CANYON

If there's one place to visit in Arizona, it's these stunning 277-mile-long canyons. After all, it is the Grand Canyon State. People come to hike the trails and traverse the area by mule just to see the breathtaking views.

PHOENIX

Amid the rocky, mountainous Southwestern landscape, Phoenix provides an urban oasis. Phoenix is the heart of Arizona, not to mention its capital. It's where you'll find all of the pro sports teams, top museums, best restaurants and more.

SCOTTSDALE

This beautiful city is known for two things: spas and golf. Scottsdale has some of the best spas in the country, so come here to unwind amid the gorgeous scenery and indulge in massages, facials, body wraps and more. Or hit the greens on one of the award-winning courses.

TOMBSTONE

To see remnants of Arizona's past as part of the Wild West, head to Tombstone. The town was filled with saloons and gunfights. In fact, the famous showdown at the O.K. Corral took place at this National Historic Landmark.

NORTHERN ARIZONA

The main reason to visit Northern Arizona is its gorgeous scenery. After all, it is home to one of the most breathtaking spots in the world, the Grand Canyon. But there's more to this vast area than those famous rocks. Head to the Grand Canyon's nearby city, Flagstaff, for a good place to see Navajo country, Oak Creek Canyon and Humphreys Peak, the tallest mountain in Arizona at 12,670 feet. If you're looking for more water activities, visit Page on the east end of the Glen Canyon Dam on the Colorado River. The dam forms Lake Powell, a part of the Glen Canyon National Recreation Area. The lake, 186 miles long with 1,900 miles of shoreline, is the second-largest man-made lake in the United States. Or you can check out Kayenta's surrounding area, which offers some of the most memorable sightseeing in the state, including the great tinted monoliths.

Another spectacular spot is Sedona, famous worldwide for the beauty of its surrounding red rocks. Sedona has grown from a pioneer settlement into a favorite film location. This is a resort area with numerous outdoor activities, including hiking, fishing and biking, which can be enjoyed all year. For a taste of Americana, hit the open road. Arizona's historic Route 66 begins at Seligman, and the tiny town (population about 500) has more Route 66 kitsch than you can imagine. If you're more interested in learning about the people and history of this region, the small town of Holbrook has a lot to offer. There you can find a wealth of information on the histories of the Navajo, Hopi, Zuni and White Mountain Apache tribes. Stop here on your way to the Petrified Forest National Park to learn about these unique tribes. To find out more about the Native Americans of this area, also check out Window Rock, the headquarters of the Navajo Nation. Go outside and find out what makes these Northern Arizona cities a playground for travelers.

WHAT TO SEE

FLAGSTAFF
ARIZONA SNOWBOWL SKI & SUMMER RESORT
6355 Highway 180, Flagstaff, 928-779-1951; www.arizonasnowbowl.com

It's all about skiing at this 50-acre resort. It has two triple and two double chair-lifts; a patrol, a school, rentals; restaurants, bars, a lounge; and lodges. Test out the 32 trails; the longest run is more than two miles and has a vertical drop of 2,300 feet. In the summer, jump on the Skyride, which takes you up to 11,500 feet for panoramic views atop an extinct volcano.

Mid-December-mid-April, daily. Skyride (May-September).

COCONINO NATIONAL FOREST
1824 S. Thompson St., Flagstaff, 928-527-3600; www.fs.fed.us

This national forest surrounds Flagstaff and Sedona. Outstanding scenic areas include Humphreys Peak—Arizona's highest point—as well as parts of the Mogollon Rim and the Verde River Valley, the Red Rock country of Sedona; Oak Creek Canyon (where Zane Grey wrote Call of the Canyon); and the San Francisco Peaks. Among the forest's extinct volcanoes and high country lakes, you can do some fishing, hunting, winter sports and camping.

Hours vary by season.

LOWELL OBSERVATORY
1400 Mars Hill Road, Flagstaff, 928-774-3358; www.lowell.edu

The dwarf planet Pluto was discovered from this observatory in 1930. Now it offers guided tours, slide presentations and telescope viewings. The telescope domes are unheated, so be sure to bundle up if you go during cold-weather months.

Daytime hours: November-February, daily noon-5 p.m.; March-October, daily 9 a.m.-5 p.m. Evening hours: September-May, Wednesday, Friday, Saturday 5:30-9:30 p.m.; June-August, Monday-Saturday 5:30-10 p.m.

HIGHLIGHTS

WHAT ARE THE TOP OUTDOOR ACTIVITIES?

CHECK OUT COCONINO NATIONAL FOREST
Nestled in this national forest is Humphreys Peak, Arizona's highest point. You'll also come across extinct volcanoes and beautiful vistas of the Mogollon Rim, the Verde River Valley and the Red Rock country of Sedona.

VISIT SUNSET CRATER VOLCANO NATIONAL MONUMENT
Between 1064 and 1065, a volcano erupted and left this area, a cone-shaped mountain of cinders and ash. Around the rim of that cinder cone are mineral deposits that give the crater its sunset coloring.

MARVEL AT THE GRAND CANYON
No trip to this part of Arizona would be complete without visiting the majestic Grand Canyon. Millions of people come to the canyon each year to see the desert landscape and those famous rocks.

SEE LOTS OF COLOR AT THE PETRIFIED FOREST NATIONAL PARK
This national park has one of the world's biggest and most colorful collections of petrified wood. In addition, the park offers historic structures, archeological sites and displays of over 200-million-year-old fossils.

EXPLORE THE NAVAJO RESERVATION
There are a number of sites to see at this Native American reservation, the largest in the U.S, including Canyon de Chelly National Monument and Navajo National Monument.

GET WET AT SLIDE ROCK STATE PARK
This park gets pretty busy, but that's because it's so fun to glide down the natural sandstone waterslide. The 43-acre park also offers swimming, fishing and hiking.

MORMON LAKE SKI CENTER

5075 N. Highway 89, Flagstaff, 928-354-2240

The terrain includes snowy meadows; huge stands of pine, oak and aspen; old logging roads; and turn-of-the-century railroad grades. There are also more than 20 miles of marked, groomed trails. The center offers a school, rentals, a restaurant, a ski shop and guided tours, including moonlight tours on full-moon weekends.

Daily 8 a.m.-5 p.m.

SUNSET CRATER VOLCANO NATIONAL MONUMENT

7133 N. US Highway 89, Flagstaff, 928-526-0502; www.nps.gov

Between the growing seasons of 1064 and 1065, violent volcanic eruptions built a large cone-shaped mountain of cinders and ash called a cinder cone volcano. Around the base of the cinder cone, lava flowed from cracks, creating the Bonito Lava Flow on the west side of the cone and the Kana'a Lava Flow on the east side. The approximate date of the initial eruption was determined by examining tree rings of timber found in the remains of Native American pueblos at Wupatki National Monument. This cinder cone, now called Sunset Crater, stands about 1,000 feet above the surrounding terrain. Mineral deposits around the rim stained the cinders, giving the summit a perpetual sunset hue. A 20-mile paved road leads to Wupatki National Monument. Do not attempt to drive off the roads; the cinders are soft and the surrounding landscape is fragile. The U.S. Forest Service maintains a campground (May-mid-September) opposite the visitor center, and park rangers are on duty all year. Guided tours and naturalist activities are offered during the summer.

Visitor center: daily.

RIORDAN MANSION STATE HISTORIC PARK

409 Riordan Road, Flagstaff, 928-779-4395; azstateparks.com

This 6-acre park features an Arts and Crafts-style mansion built in 1904 by Michael and Timothy Riordan, two brothers who played a significant role in the development of Flagstaff and northern Arizona. Peruse original artifacts, handcrafted furniture and mementos. Then have lunch in the picnic areas or go on a guided tour (reservations are recommended).

Admission: adults $6, children $2.50, children under 7 free. May-October, daily 8:30 a.m.-5 p.m.; November-April, daily 10:30 a.m.-5 p.m.

WALNUT CANYON NATIONAL MONUMENT

Walnut Canyon Road, Flagstaff, 928-526-3367; www.nps.gov/waca

The monument is a spectacular, rugged 400-foot-deep canyon with 300 small cliff dwellings dating back to around A.D. 1100. The dwellings are well preserved because they are under protective ledges in the canyon's limestone walls. There are two self-guided trails and an educational museum in the visitor center.

Daily.

HIGHLIGHT

Look out over the great expanse of the Grand Canyon and the awe-inspiring vistas reveal a spectacular desert landscape. Rocks in this great chasm change colors from sunrise to sunset and hide an ecosystem of wildlife. It's no wonder millions of people visit this world wonder every year.

They come here to hike the trails, travel down by mule, camp at the base or simply stare in awe from the rim. The entire park is 1,904 square miles, with 277 miles of the Colorado River running through it. At its widest point, the north and south rims stretch 18 miles across, with average elevations of 8,000 feet and 7,000 feet, respectively. The canyon averages a depth of one mile. At its base, 2-billion-year-old rocks are exposed.

The South Rim, open all year, has the greater number of services, including day and overnight mule trips through Xanterra Parks & Resorts, horseback riding through Apache Stables (928-638-2891) and air tours (both fixed-wing and helicopter) through several local companies.

In addition to these tours, there are a variety of museums and facilities on the South Rim. The Kolb Studio in the Village Historic District at the Bright Angel Trailhead features art displays and a bookstore. It was once the home and business of the Kolb brothers, who were pioneering photographers here. The Yavapai Observation Station, one mile east of Market Plaza, contains temporary exhibits about the fossil record at Grand Canyon.

The North Rim, blocked by heavy snows in winter, is open from mid-May to mid-October. Due to the higher elevation, mule trips from the North Rim do not go to the river. Trips range in length from one hour to a full day. For details, call Grand Canyon Trail Rides at 435-679-8665.

Fall and spring are the best times to trek into the canyon because it's less crowded. Don't plan to hike to the base and back up in one day—changing elevations and temperatures can exhaust hikers quickly. It's best to camp in the canyon overnight (plan on an additional evening if hiking from the North Rim). Fifteen main trails provide access to the inner canyon. Make reservations for camping or lodging facilities early.

Rafting the Colorado River through Grand Canyon National Park also requires reservations far in advance of your intended visit. Trips vary from three to 21 days and can be made through a commercial outfitter, a private river trip or a one-day trip (which may or may not be in Grand Canyon National Park). For one-day white-water raft trips, call Hualapai River Runners (928-769-2119). Half-day smooth-water raft trips are provided by Wilderness River Adventures (800-992-8022).

WUPATKI NATIONAL MONUMENT

6400 N. Highway 89, Flagstaff, 928-679-2365; www.nps.gov/wupa

The nearly 2,600 archeological sites of the Sinagua and Anasazi cultures were occupied between A.D. 1100 and 1250. The largest of them, Wupatki Pueblo, was three stories high, with about 100 rooms. The eruption of nearby Sunset Crater spread volcanic ash over an 800-square-mile area and for a time, made this an active farming center. The half-mile ruins trail is self-guided, but you can pick up books at its starting point for some background information. The visitor center and main ruin are open daily. Wupatki National Monument and Sunset Crater Volcano National Monument are on a 35-mile paved loop off of Highway 89. The nearest camping is at Bonito Campground (May-October; 520-526-0866).

GRAND CANYON NATIONAL PARK

DRIVE TO CAPE ROYAL

North Rim (Grand Canyon National Park), about 23 miles from Bright Angel Point over paved road; www.nps.gov

During this drive, you'll encounter several good viewpoints—many visitors say the view from here is better than from the South Rim. Archaeology and geology talks are given in the summer and fall.

DRIVES TO VIEWPOINTS

1 Main St., South Rim (Grand Canyon National Park); www.nps.gov

The West Rim and East Rim drives out from Grand Canyon Village are both rewarding. Grandview Point and Desert View on the East Rim Drive are especially magnificent. West Rim Drive is closed to private vehicles from early April to early October, but free shuttle buses serve the West Rim and Village area during this period.

GRAND CANYON IMAX THEATRE

Highways 64 and 180, Tusayan, 928-638-2468; www.explorethecanyon.com

This IMAX theater shows a 35-minute film that highlights features of the Grand Canyon.

March-October, daily 8:30 a.m.-8:30 p.m.; November-February, daily 10:30 a.m.-6:30 p.m.; movie is shown hourly on the half hour.

KAIBAB NATIONAL FOREST

800 Sixth St., Williams, 928-638-2443; www.fs.fed.us

The forest spans more than 1.6 million acres; one section surrounds Williams and includes Sycamore Canyon and Kendrick Mountain wilderness areas and part of National Historic Route 66. A second area is 42 miles north on Highway 180 (Highway 64) near the South Rim of the Grand Canyon; a third area lies north of the Grand Canyon (outstanding views of the canyon can be had from seldom-visited vista points in this area) and includes Kanab Creek and Saddle Mountain wilderness areas, the Kaibab Plateau and the North Rim Parkway National Scenic Byway.

MULE TRIPS INTO THE CANYON

South Rim (Grand Canyon National Park), 928-638-3283; www.nps.gov

A number of mule trips are scheduled, all with guides. You can choose among one-, two- or three-day trips. Reservations should be made several months in advance.

TUSAYAN MUSEUM
Desert View Road, South Rim (Grand Canyon National Park); www.nps.gov

Learn about prehistoric man in the Southwest at this museum. Exhibits include an excavated pueblo ruin circa 1185.

Daily 9 a.m.-5 p.m., weather permitting. Tours: daily 11 a.m.-1:30 p.m.

YAVAPAI OBSERVATION STATION
South Rim (Grand Canyon National Park); www.nps.gov

You can get a nice view of the canyon here, but the station will also explain how the formations came to be. In addition, the observation station features a small museum, geological exhibits and a bookstore.

Daily 8 a.m.-8 p.m.

HOLBROOK
NAVAJO COUNTY HISTORICAL MUSEUM
100 E. Arizona, Holbrook, 928-524-6558; www.ci.holbrook.az.us

This museum showcases displays on Navajo, Apache, Hopi and Hispanic cultures. There are also petrified forest and dinosaur exhibits.

Monday-Friday 8 a.m.-5 p.m., Saturday-Sunday 8 a.m.-4 p.m.

PETRIFIED FOREST NATIONAL PARK
1 Park Road, Holbrook, 928-524-6228; www.nps.gov

These 93,532 acres include one of the most spectacular displays of petrified wood in the world. The trees of the original forest likely grew in upland areas and then were washed down onto a floodplain by rivers. Subsequently, the trees were buried under sediment and volcanic ash, causing the organic wood to gradually fill with mineral compounds, especially quartz. The grain, now multicolored by the compounds, is still visible in some specimens. For more information, check out the visitor center at the entrance off Interstate 40 and the Rainbow Forest Museum (off US 180), which depicts the paleontology and geology of the Triassic Era. Prehistoric Pueblo inhabitants left countless petroglyphs of animals, figures and symbols carved on sandstone throughout the park. The park also contains a portion of the Painted Desert, a colorful area extending 200 miles along the north bank of the Little Colorado River. This highly eroded area of mesas, pinnacles, washes and canyons is part of the Chinle formation, a soft shale, clay and sandstone stratum of the Triassic. The sunlight and clouds passing over this spectacular scenery create an effect of constant, kaleidoscopic change. There are very good viewpoints along the park road. Picnicking facilities are available at Rainbow Forest and at Chinle Point on the rim of the Painted Desert; no campgrounds are provided. You'll find service stations and a cafeteria are at the north entrance.

Daily.

KAYENTA
CRAWLEY'S MONUMENT VALLEY TOURS
Kayenta, 928-697-3463; www.crawleytours.com

Take guided tours in backcountry vehicles to Monument Valley, Mystery Valley and Hunt's Mesa. You can choose between half- and full-day trips. Sunset tours are also available.

Daily.

NAVAJO NATIONAL MONUMENT
19 miles southwest of Kayenta on Highway 163, then nine miles north on paved road Highway 564 to visitor center, 928-672-2700; www.nps.gov

This monument comprises three scattered areas totaling 600 acres and is surrounded by the Navajo Nation. Each area is the location of a large and remarkable prehistoric cliff dwelling. You can see two of the ruins on a guided tour. Headquarters for the monument and the visitor center are near Betatakin, the most accessible of the three cliff dwellings. Guided tours, limited to 25 people (Betatakin tour), are arranged on a first-come, first-served basis (May-September; call for schedule). The five-mile round-trip hike, which includes a steep 700-foot trail, takes five to six hours. Betatakin may also be viewed from the Sandal Trail overlook—a 1½-mile, one-way, self-guided trail. The largest and best-preserved ruin, Keet Seel (Memorial Day-Labor Day, call for schedule), is 8½ miles one-way by foot or horseback from headquarters. A permit is required either way, and reservations can be made up to two months in advance. A primitive campground is available for overnight hikers. The horseback trip takes all day. Horses should be booked when making reservations (no children under 12 without previous riding experience). The visitor center has a museum and film program.

Daily.

NAVAJO RESERVATION
www.explorenavajo.com

The Navajo Nation is the largest Native American tribe and reservation in the United States. The reservation covers more than 25,000 square miles within three states—with the largest portion in northeastern Arizona and the rest in New Mexico and Utah. More than 400 years ago, the Navajo people (the Dine) moved into the arid southwestern region of the United States and carved out a way of life that was in harmony with the natural beauty of Arizona, New Mexico and Utah. In the 1800s, westward-moving settlers interrupted this harmonious life. For the Navajo, this conflict resulted in their forced removal from their ancestral land and the "Long Walk" to Fort Sumner, New Mexico. The plan was judged a failure and in 1868, they were allowed to return to their homeland. The Navajo continue to practice many of their ancient ceremonies, including the Navajo Fire Dance and the Yei-bi-chei (winter) and Enemy Way Dances (summer). Many ceremonies are associated with curing the sick and are primarily religious in nature. Visitors must obtain permission to view these events—photography, recording and sketching are prohibited. Some of the most spectacular areas in Navajoland are Canyon de Chelly National Monument, Navajo National Monument, Monument Valley Navajo Tribal Park (north of Kayenta) and Four Corners Monument. Accommodations on the reservation are limited; reservations are recommended months in advance.

PAGE

BOAT TRIPS ON LAKE POWELL

Lake Powell Resorts & Marinas, 100 Lakeshore Drive, Page, 928-645-2433, 888-896-3829; www.lakepowell.com

Hop aboard for one-hour to one-day trips, some of which include a stop at Rainbow Bridge National Monument. Houseboat and powerboat rentals are also available. Reservations are recommended.

GLEN CANYON NATIONAL RECREATION AREA

Highway 89, Page, 928-608-6200; www.nps.gov

This recreation area boasts more than 1 million acres, including Lake Powell. There's a campfire program (May-September), swimming, waterskiing, fishing, boating, hiking, picnicking, restaurants, lodges and camping. The visitors center on canyon rim, adjacent to Glen Canyon Bridge on Highway 89, has historical exhibits. In case you need some aid, there's a ranger station seven miles north of the dam at Wahweap.

Daily.

RAINBOW BRIDGE NATIONAL MONUMENT

Page, 928-608-6200; www.nps.gov

See the world's largest-known natural bridge, a breathtaking phenomenon that attracts more than 300,000 visitors a year.

WILDERNESS RIVER ADVENTURES

2040 E. Frontage Road, Page, 928-645-3296, 800-992-8022;www.riveradventures.com

This company specializes in multiday trips on the Colorado River in Glen Canyon in raft-like neoprene boats. Reservations are required.

April-October.

SEDONA

OAK CREEK CANYON

Slide Rock State Park, 6871 N. Highway 89A, Sedona, 928-282-3034; www.fs.fed.us

This spectacular gorge may look familiar to you—it's a favorite location for Western movies. The northern end of the road starts with a lookout point atop the walls and descends nearly 2,000 feet to the stream bed. The creek has excellent trout fishing. At the southern mouth of the canyon is Sedona.

RED ROCK JEEP TOURS

270 N. Highway 89A, Sedona, 928-282-6826, 800-848-7728; www.redrockjeep.com

Hop in a Jeep for a rugged two-hour back-country trip to scenic places like Bear Wallow Canyon and the Sedona vortices, or energy spots. Other tours also available.

Daily.

SLIDE ROCK STATE PARK

6871 N. Highway 89A, Sedona, 928-282-3034; www.www.azstateparks.com

This 43-acre day-use park on Oak Creek offers swimming, a natural sandstone waterslide, fishing, hiking and picnicking.

May-September, daily 8 a.m.-7 p.m.; October-April, daily 8 a.m.-5 p.m.

TLAQUEPAQUE

336 Highway 179, Sedona, 928-282-4838; www.tlaq.com

A Spanish-style courtyard, it consists of 40 art galleries and stores. Inside the arts and crafts village there are bronze sculpture, ceramics, blown-glass creations, paintings and weavings.

Daily 10 a.m.-5 p.m.

SELIGMAN

GRAND CANYON CAVERNS

Old Route 66, Peach Springs, 928-422-3223; www.gccaverns.com

This natural limestone cavern is 210 feet underground and is the largest dry cavern in the U.S. Take an elevator down (the temperature is around 55 degrees, so bring a sweater). Guided 50-minute tours are offered.

June-September, daily 9 a.m.-5 p.m.; November-February, daily 10 a.m.-5 p.m.

WINDOW ROCK

CANYON DE CHELLY NATIONAL MONUMENT

Highway 191, Window Rock, 928-674-5500; www.nps.gov

The smooth red sandstone walls of the canyon extend straight up as much as 1,000 feet from the nearly flat sand bottom. When William of Normandy defeated the English at the Battle of Hastings in 1066, the Pueblo had already built apartment houses in these walls. Many ruins are still here. The Navajo came long after the original tenants had abandoned these structures. In 1864, Kit Carson's men drove nearly all the Navajo out of the area, marching them on foot 300 miles to the Bosque Redondo in eastern New Mexico. Since 1868, Navajo have returned to farming, cultivating the orchards and grazing their sheep in the canyon. In 1931, Canyon de Chelly and its tributaries, Canyon del Muerto and Monument Canyon, were designated a national monument. There are more than 60 major ruins—some dating from circa A.D. 300—in these canyons. White House, Antelope House and Mummy Cave are among the most picturesque. Most ruins are inaccessible but can be seen from either the canyon bottom or from the road along the top of the precipitous walls. Two spectacular, 16-mile rim drives can be made by car in any season. Lookout points—sometimes a short distance from the road—are clearly marked. The only self-guided trail (2½ miles round-trip) leads to the canyon floor and White House ruin from White House Overlook. Other hikes can be made only with a National Park Service permit and an authorized Navajo guide. Only four-wheel drive vehicles are allowed in the canyons—and each vehicle must be accompanied by an authorized Navajo guide and requires a National Park Service permit obtainable from a ranger at the visitor center, which also has an archaeological museum.

Daily.

NAVAJO NATION MUSEUM

Highway 64 and Loup Road, Window Rock, 928-871-7941; www.navajonationmuseum.org

This museum was established in 1961 to preserve Navajo history, art, culture and natural history. Peruse the display of more than 250 handmade textiles by the Navajo Master Weavers of the Toadlena/Two Grey Hills region of New Mexico.

Monday-Tuesday, Thursday-Friday 8 a.m.-5 p.m., Wednesday 8 a.m.-8 p.m., Saturday 9 a.m.-5 p.m.; closed on tribal and other holidays.

NAVAJO NATION ZOOLOGICAL AND BOTANICAL PARK
Tse Bonito Tribal Park, Window Rock, 928-871-6573; www.navajozoo.com

The animals and plants in this tribally owned zoo are of historical or cultural importance to the Navajo people. Animal inhabitants include coyotes, golden eagles and elk.

Monday-Saturday 10 a.m.-5 p.m.

WINSLOW

HOMOLOVI RUINS STATE PARK
HCR 63, Winslow, 928-289-4106; www.pr.state.az.us

This park contains six major Anasazi ruins dating from A.D. 1250 to 1450. The Arizona State Museum conducts occasional excavations in June and July. The park also has trails, a visitor center and interpretive programs.

Daily.

METEOR CRATER
Winslow, 20 miles west on I-40, then five miles south on Meteor Crater Road, 928-289-5898, 800-289-5898; www.meteorcrater.com

The crater is one mile from rim to rim and 560 feet deep. The world's best-preserved meteorite crater was used as a training site for astronauts. Now it also has a museum and the Astronaut Wall of Fame. Peer through the telescope on the highest point of the crater's rim for excellent views of the surrounding area.

May-September, 7 a.m.-7 p.m.; October-April, 8 a.m.-5 p.m.

WHERE TO STAY

FLAGSTAFF

★★★INN AT 410 BED & BREAKFAST
410 N. Leroux St., Flagstaff, 928-774-0088, 800-774-2008; www.inn410.com

This charming bed and breakfast, located in an 1894 Craftsman house, offers fresh-baked cookies during afternoon teatime alongside seasonal beverages such as iced tea and hot cider. Of course, the free gourmet breakfast is the bigger culinary draw, with dishes such as the delicious banana-oatmeal pancakes with blueberry sauce, pecan-custard French toast and artichoke-potato frittatas served every morning. Each room has its own individual theme and is decorated with antiques. They all come with a private bath, a fireplace, a mini-fridge, complimetnary wireless Internet, DVD players and extensive movie libraries.

9 rooms. Complimentary breakfast. No children under five. $151-250

★★★LITTLE AMERICA HOTEL
2515 E. Butler Ave., Flagstaff, 928-779-2741, 800-865-1401; www.littleamerica.com

Sporty types will want to check into Little America Hotel. Located on 500 acres of pine forest at the base of the San Francisco Peaks, this hotel has its own private hiking trails. It also has sand volleyball and badminton courts as well as horseshoe pits. Take a dip in the heated outdoor pool for views of the mountains or relax in the hot tub. The spacious guest rooms include

WHICH HOTELS HAVE THE BEST VIEWS?

El Tovar:
This hotel isn't just in the Grand Canyon—it sits 20 feet from the South Rim. The amazing vistas have drawn guests such as Theodore Roosevelt and Albert Einstein.

Enchantment Resort:
Tucked inside Boynton Canyon, Enchantment provides an unusual look at the craggy scenery. It's smack-dab in the middle of the gorgeous red rocks.

Hilton Sedona Resort and Spa:
The hotel is located in Coconino National Forest. From the patios and balconies, you can admire the red-rock formations surrounding the hotel.

L'Auberge de Sedona:
You'll get nice views of Red Rock Canyon and Magenta Cliffs at this hotel. For even more eye candy, dine alfresco along the creek at the hotel's L'Auberge Restaurant on Oak Creek.

floor-to-ceiling windows and flat-screen TVs. Guests can enjoy complimentary hors d'oeuvres, which are served nightly.

247 rooms. Restaurant, bar. Business center. Fitness center. Pool. $61-150

GRAND CANYON NATIONAL PARK
★★★EL TOVAR
On the Canyon rim, 928-638-2631, 888-297-2757; www.grandcanyonlodges.com

The premier lodging facility at the Grand Canyon, El Tovar Hotel—named in honor of the Spanish explorer Don Pedro de Tovar, who reported the existence of the Grand Canyon to fellow explorers—opened its doors in 1905 and was said to be the most expensive log house in America. Just 20 feet from the edge of the canyon's South Rim, the building is charming and rustic. The hotel features a fine dining room, lounge and a gift shop highlighting Native American artists. With so much to do right at your doorstep—hiking, mule rides, train excursions, interpretive walks, cultural activities—El Tovar offers the best of the Grand Canyon, combining turn-of-the-century lodge ambience with friendly service. Advance reservations are recommended, especially during the summer, which is usually booked up a year in advance.

78 rooms. Restaurant, bar. $61-150

SEDONA
★★★AMARA HOTEL, RESTAURANT & SPA
310 N. Highway 89A, Sedona, 928-282-4828, 866-455-6610; www.amararesort.com

Located along the banks of Oak Creek, this chic, contemporary resort features well-appointed rooms and tranquil surroundings. For an additional dose of calm, take one of the hotel's free yoga classes, head to the spa for a body wrap or massage, or visit the heated saltwater pool and fire pit. Rooms try to provide a serene space as well with pillow-top mattresses, Italian linens and soaking tubs. If you need to squeeze in some work, the rooms also offer sleek work desks and complimentary wireless Internet access.

100 rooms. Restaurant, bar. Complimentary breakfast. Pool. Spa. $151-250

★★★EL PORTAL SEDONA
95 Portal Lane, Sedona, 928-203-9405, 800-313-0017; www.innsedona.com

This secluded hacienda-style inn is conveniently located in the heart of Sedona near more than 50 shops and restaurants and is adjacent to arts and crafts village Tlaquepaque. As befitting its surroundings, the adobe-walled hotel offers turn-of-the-century-style rooms with Arts and Crafts furnishings, high-beam ceilings and stained glass. There are some modern updates to the rooms as well, such as complimentary wireless Internet, whirlpool tubs, cashmere blankets and Egyptian cotton sheets. On Wednesday nights there's a cookout in the hotel's courtyard.

12 rooms. Restaurant. Pets accepted. $351 and up

★★★ENCHANTMENT RESORT

525 Boynton Canyon Road, Sedona, 928-282-2900, 800-826-4180; www.enchantmentresort.com

Located within Boynton Canyon, this resort offers spectacular views of the rugged landscape from just about everywhere, and you can soak it all in from your room, since each one has an outdoor deck. Enchantment is full of Southwestern charm, from the Native American furnishings and decorative accents in the rooms to the regional kick of the sensational dining. Tennis, croquet, swimming and pitch-and-putt golf are some of the activities available for adults, while Camp Coyote entertains kids daily with Native American-inspired arts and crafts and special programs. The Mii Amo Spa draws on Native American and Ayurvedic principles for its menu of treatments.

220 rooms. Restaurant, bar. Business center. Spa. Tennis. $251-350

★★★HILTON SEDONA RESORT AND SPA

90 Ridge Trail Drive, Sedona, 928-284-4040, 877-273-3763; www.hiltonsedona.com

This Southwestern-style resort is located amid the Coconino National Forest. The spacious guest rooms and suites are well decorated and have gas fireplaces, wet bars, sleeper sofas and patios or balconies with views of the Red Rock vistas. There are three pools from which to choose, a full-service fitness center, tennis and racquetball and the nearby Sedona Golf Resort, featuring a 71-par championship course. The spa is steps from the hotel's main building. The property's Grille at ShadowRock features a Southwestern menu, and with its earth tones and soft lighting, is the perfect spot for a romantic dinner. During the day, the restaurant's outdoor patio is a great place to have a hearty breakfast or a light lunch.

219 rooms. Restaurant, bar. Fitness center. Spa. Pets accepted. Golf. $151-250

★★★L'AUBERGE DE SEDONA

301 L'Auberge Lane, Sedona, 928-282-1661, 800-905-5745; www.lauberge.com

This secluded resort offers views of the Red Rock Canyon and Magenta Cliffs. Rooms are housed in cozy cottages with fireplaces (the staff lights a juniper-infused fire in your room nightly) and an inviting lodge. There's plenty to do at this resort. Gourmet dining is an integral part of the experience, and L'Auberge Restaurant is noted for its fine French food, special five-course tasting menu and award-winning wine list. Best of all, you can dine creekside. In the mornings, go to the Great Room to nibble on complimentary baked goods and sip coffee, and in the evenings you can go there to partake in the wine and hors d'oeuvres reception. On Fridays, a professional astronomer leads stargazing sessions at the hotel. If you still have free time, check out the world-class spa.

53 rooms. Restaurant, bar. Pool. Spa. $251-350

★★★LOS ABRIGADOS RESORT AND SPA
160 Portal Lane, Sedona, 928-282-1777, 800-521-3131; www.ilxresorts.com

This Spanish-style stucco and tile-roofed hotel is set among the buttes of Oak Creek Canyon. Rooms are spacious with kitchens and pullout sofas. Activities such as Jeep tours, hiking, biking and helicopter rides are nearby.

182 rooms. Restaurant, bar. Pool. Tennis. Pets accepted. $251-350

WHERE TO EAT

GRAND CANYON NATIONAL PARK
★★★EL TOVAR DINING ROOM AND LOUNGE
1 Main St., South Rim, 928-638-2631; www.grandcanyonlodges.com

Considered the foremost dining establishment at the Grand Canyon, this restaurant provides a memorable experience, thanks to the spicy regional cuisine and spectacular canyon views (try to get a table by the window). The atmosphere is casually elegant with native stone fireplaces, Oregon pine-vaulted ceilings, Native American artwork and Mission-style accents. Diners can select from a well-rounded menu that blends regional flavors and contemporary techniques. Try the grilled lamb chops with apricot chutney and mint jelly with garden cous cous, or the wild Alaskan salmon tostada with organic greens and tequila vinaigrette served alongside corn salsa, lime sour cream and roasted pistachio rice. The wine list is extensive, so you'll have plenty of pairing options.

Southwestern. Breakfast, lunch, dinner. Reservations recommended. Children's menu. $16-35

SEDONA
★★★HEARTLINE CAFÉ
1610 W. Highway 89A, Sedona, 928-282-0785; www.heartlinecafe.com

This intimate, cozy restaurant is in a cottage surrounded by an English garden and showcases unique daily specials. The menu is creative, with a variety of culinary influences and vegetarian options. Dishes include chive pappardelle pasta with roasted butternut squash, wild mushrooms and garlic butter, and pistachio-crusted chicken with pomegranate sauce. If you enjoy what you eat, swing by the Market, which is next door to the restaurant. There you can pick up local foods, such as cheeses and chocolates, for the road.

International. Lunch, dinner. Outdoor seating. Bar. $36-85

★★★L'AUBERGE
L'Auberge de Sedona, 301 L'Auberge, Sedona, 928-282-1661; www.lauberge.com

This hotel restaurant sets a sophisticated tone with imported fabrics and fine china in its dining room. A covered porch with large windows offers views of Oak Creek, and an outdoor patio area is a relaxing choice in good weather. Dine on French-inspired American cuisine like juniper-dusted duck breast and foie gras with creamy lentil ragout and duck confit, or roasted pork tenderloin with cider-glazed pork belly, mushrooms, potato purée and blackberry gastrique. For a real culinary treat, try the customizable tasting menu that includes at least five courses. Whichever you choose for your meal, be sure to pair it with some wine; the restaurant has an extensive wine program with more than 12,000 bottles in its cellar.

French, American. Breakfast, lunch, dinner, Sunday brunch. Reservations recommended. Outdoor seating. Bar. $36-85

★★★RENÉ AT TLAQUEPAQUE
336 Highway 179, Sedona, 928-282-9225; www.rene-sedona.com

Located in the Tlaquepaque shopping area, this local favorite has been a mainstay in Sedona since 1977, and it's a perfect place to retire after a day of perusing the neighboring arts and crafts shops. The menu is varied, offering selections such as venison tenderloin, grilled ahi tuna salad, sweet potato ravioli and the signature dish, Colorado rack of lamb. Dine in one of two separate areas, where tables are topped with green and white tablecloths and flower-filled vases. On Fridays and Saturdays, the restaurant brings in entertainment. Expect to hear the sounds of guitar, piano, saxophone or Native American flutes.

French. Lunch, dinner. Reservations recommended. Outdoor seating. Children's menu. Bar. $36-85

★★★SHUGRUE'S HILLSIDE GRILL
671 Highway 179, Sedona, 928-282-5300; www.shugrues.com

Great views of the Red Rocks can be seen from the large windows of this Old World restaurant with a modern take. Flame-broiled shrimp scampi, crispy duck with a sun-dried sweet cherry and brandy au jus, and herb-grilled rib-eye gorgonzola are among the specialty dishes. Light jazz entertainment is offered nightly, with a pianist and guitarist performing on alternate evenings. A nice outdoor seating area offers guests a picturesque dining experience.

American. Lunch, dinner. Reservations recommended. Outdoor seating. Children's menu. Bar. $16-35

PHOENIX

Phoenix is in the heart of Central Arizona, but this buzzing center is almost a region unto itself. The capital of Arizona is the home base for the state's sports teams, noted museums and amazing restaurants that aren't limited to Southwestern cuisine. People come to the Valley of the Sun to unwind, with golf courses, mega-resorts and spas in abundance. The busy city against the backdrop of Camelback Mountain gives it the best of both the urban and rural worlds.

WHAT TO SEE

ANTIQUE GALLERY/CENTRAL ANTIQUES
5037 N. Central Ave., Phoenix, 602-241-1174

More than 150 dealers showcase heirloom-quality antiques in this 30,000-square-foot space. Shop for period furniture, silver and more. Monday-Saturday 10 a.m.-5:30 p.m., Sunday noon-5 p.m.

ARIZONA CAPITOL MUSEUM
1700 W. Washington St., Phoenix, 602-926-3620; www.lib.az.us/museum

Built in 1899, this stately building first served as the capitol for the territorial government, then as the state capitol after Arizona was admitted to the Union in 1912. The state moved to an adjacent office building in the 1970s for more space, and the original structure has operated as a museum since its restoration in 1981. See the House and Senate chambers exactly as they looked during early statehood. Guided tours are offered daily at 10 a.m. and 2 p.m. A landscaped area includes a variety of native trees, shrubs and cacti.

Admission: free. Monday-Friday 8 a.m.-5 p.m., Saturday 11 a.m.-4 p.m.

ARIZONA CENTER

400 E. Van Buren St., 602-271-4000; www.arizonacenter.com

This park-like plaza, situated among palm trees, gardens and pools, includes kiosks and stores like clothing boutique Culture Fresh. There are also restaurants, bars and a movie theater.

Monday-Saturday 10 a.m.-9 p.m., Sunday 11 a.m.-5 p.m.

ARIZONA DIAMONDBACKS (MLB)

Chase Field, 401 E. Jefferson, Phoenix, 602-462-6000; arizona.diamondbacks.mlb.com

The 2001 World Champion D-backs call this baseball field home. Chase Field has a number of restaurants, a beer garden and even a swimming pool. You can check it all out during 75-minute tours of the ballpark, which are offered year-round thanks to the retractable roof.

Tour admission: adults $7, seniors and children 7-12 $5, children 4-6 $3, children under 3 free. Monday-Saturday 9:30 a.m., 11 a.m., 12:30 p.m.

ARIZONA MINING AND MINERAL MUSEUM

1502 W. Washington St., Phoenix, 602-771-1600, 800-446-4259; www.admmr.state.az.us

This museum showcases Arizona's history as a top mining state with more than 3,000 minerals, gems, petrified wood and mining artifacts on display. One of the collection's highlights is the exhibit of colorful minerals taken from the state's copper mines.

Admission: adults $2, children free. Monday-Friday 8 a.m.-5 p.m., Saturday 11 a.m.-4 p.m.

ARIZONA SCIENCE CENTER

600 E. Washington St., Phoenix, 602-716-2000; www.azscience.org

More than 300 hands-on exhibits on topics ranging from geology to healing make learning fun. Gaze up at the stars in the state-of-the-art planetarium and stare wide-eyed at science films in the theater with a five-story screen. Don't miss the "Evans Family SkyCycle," which puts kids 15 feet in the air to ride on a 90-foot cable. It teaches about the principles of counterbalance and center of gravity, but kids will just enjoy the thrill.

Admission: adults $12, seniors and children $10. Daily 10 a.m.-5 p.m.

BILTMORE FASHION PARK

2502 E. Camelback Road, Phoenix, 602-955-1963; www.shopbiltmore.com

Bring your oversized Louis Vuitton handbag to this outdoor shopping area with brick walkways and retailers such as Cartier, Escada and Saks Fifth Avenue.

Monday-Wednesday, 10 a.m.-7 p.m., Thursday-Friday 10 a.m.-8 p.m., Saturday 10 a.m.-6 p.m., Sunday noon-6 p.m.

HIGHLIGHTS

WHAT ARE THE TOP THINGS TO DO IN PHOENIX?

TAKE YOURSELF OUT TO THE BALL GAME AT CHASE FIELD

As the official ballpark of the champion Diamondbacks, Chase Field is a must-visit for any baseball fan. Be sure to bring your swimsuit; there's an in-ground swimming pool and slide over the right-field wall.

SEE SOME GREAT ART IN THE HEARD MUSEUM

This internationally regarded Native American museum features everything from fine art to kachina dolls. The harrowing "Remembering Our Indian School Days: The Boarding School Experience" is the most memorable exhibit.

UNCOVER MYSTERY CASTLE

While some dads build dollhouses for their daughters, one loving father constructed an 18-room castle for his little princess. And this isn't an ordinary castle; it's made of native stone and found objects.

CAMELBACK MOUNTAIN
East McDonald at Tatum Boulevard, Phoenix
Its distinctive hump makes this mountain a very visible local landmark—and a popular spot for hiking. Trails wind through desert flora and fauna. The two 1½-mile strenuous summit trails gain more than 1,200 feet in elevation. Two shorter ones at the base provide much easier trekking, with elevation gains of only 100 and 200 feet.
Daily dawn-dusk.

DESERT BOTANICAL GARDEN
Papago Park, 1201 N. Galvin Parkway, Phoenix, 480-941-1225; www.dgb.org
This 150-acre botanical oasis is home to one of the world's foremost collections of desert plants. Thousands of plants line the 1/3-mile main trail, including more than half the Earth's cactus, century plant and aloe species. Music in the Gardens features performances by local bands on Friday evenings from February through June, and Saturday evenings from October through mid-November.
Admission: adults $10, seniors $9, students $5, children $4, children under 3 free. October-April, daily 8 a.m.-8 p.m.; May-September, daily 7 a.m.-8 p.m.

ENCANTO PARK AND RECREATION AREA

2605 N. 15th Ave., Phoenix, 602-261-8991; www.enchantedisland.com

Pack up the family and head to this 222-acre park just minutes from downtown. Kids can fish in a small lake, feed ducks in a pond, ride in boats, cool off in the swimming pool, and hop aboard a train and eight other rides geared to 2- to 10-year-olds at the Enchanted Island amusement park. Two public golf courses (18 holes and nine holes) appeal to an older crowd.

Daily.

HEARD MUSEUM

2301 N. Central Ave., Phoenix, 602-252-8848; www.heard.org

Immerse yourself in the culture and art of the Southwest at this internationally acclaimed Native American museum. The 130,000-square-foot museum boasts 10 galleries (and a working-artist studio), all packed with items that attract nearly 250,000 visitors each year. Works include contemporary Native American fine art, historic Hopi kachina dolls, important Navajo and Zuni jewelry and prize-winning documented Navajo textiles. Be sure to check out "Remembering Our Indian School Days: The Boarding School Experience," a moving exhibit that reveals how the government forced Native American children into military-type boarding schools. The Heard also offers artist demonstrations, music and dance performances and free tours.

Admission: adults $12, seniors $11, students $5, children 6-12 $3, children under 6 free. Monday-Saturday 9:30 a.m.-5 p.m., Sunday 11 a.m.-5 p.m.

HERITAGE SQUARE

Heritage & Science Park, 115 N. Sixth St., Phoenix, 602-262-5071

Heritage Square is one of three sites that make up Heritage & Science Park. (The other two sites are the Arizona Science Center and Phoenix Museum of History.) Historic Heritage Park has eight turn-of-the-century houses, including the restored 1895 Victorian Rosson House (docent-guided tours: Wednesday-Saturday 10 a.m.-4 p.m., Sunday noon-4 p.m.; closed mid-August-September; fee) and Arizona Doll & Toy Museum (The Stevens House, Tuesday-Saturday 10 a.m.-4 p.m., Sunday noon-4 p.m.; closed early August-September). You'll also find the open-air Lath House Pavilion here.

Daily.

MYSTERY CASTLE

800 E. Mineral Road, Phoenix, 602-268-1581

This quirky, imaginative 18-room castle made of native stone and found objects was built by Boyce Luther Gulley for his daughter Mary Lou, who often leads tours.

Admission: $5. October-May, Thursday-Sunday 11 a.m.-4 p.m.

PAPAGO PARK

625 N. Galvan Parkway, Phoenix, 602-261-8318; www.phoenix.gov

This 1,200-acre park with sandstone buttes is flatter than many others in the area and has more than 10 miles of trails, appealing to novice hikers and mountain bikers. Families often come to enjoy its many picnic areas and fishing lagoon, while the golf course lures duffers. The park offers good views of the city, especially at sunset from the Hole-in-the-Rock Archaeological Site, a naturally eroded rock formation.

Daily 5 a.m.-11 p.m.

PHOENIX ART MUSEUM

1625 N. Central Ave., Phoenix, 602-257-1222; www.phxart.org

At more than 160,000 square feet, this is one of the largest art museums in the Southwest. There are more than 17,000 works here—about 1,000 of which are on display at any given time, in addition to major traveling exhibits. The museum sponsors Family Sundays every third Sunday of the month for children ages 5-12, which includes imaginative art projects and self-guided explorations of the galleries.

Admission: adults $10, seniors and students $8, children 6-17 $4, children under 6 free. Free Tuesday. Wednesday-Sunday 10 a.m.-5 p.m., Tuesday 10 a.m.-9 p.m. First Fridays: first Friday of every month 6-10 p.m.

PHOENIX COYOTES (NHL)

Jobing.com Arena, 9400 W. Maryland Ave., Glendale, 486-563-7825; www.phoenixcoyotes.com

Phoenix's professional hockey team hits the ice at this arena.

PHOENIX INTERNATIONAL RACEWAY

7602 S. Avondale Blvd., Avondale, 602-252-2227; www.phoenixintlraceway.com

If you've seen *Days of Thunder* with Tom Cruise, you've seen this high-octane speedway. Big-name drivers fire up their engines on six weekends throughout the year. More than 100,000 spectators pack the raceway for NASCAR Weekend in late fall. Other events include the Rolex Grand American Sports Car Series and the IRL Indy Car Series. No other speedway in Arizona is open to so many different classes of cars. PIR also hosts plenty of non-racing events, including a large Fourth of July celebration.

PHOENIX MERCURY (WNBA)

U.S. Airways Center, 201 E. Jefferson St., Phoenix, 602-252-9622; www.wnba.com

The city's professional women's basketball team plays hoops here. If you want to see the ladies in action, the season runs May to August.

PHOENIX SUNS (NBA)

U.S. Airways Center, 201 E. Jefferson, Phoenix, 602-379-7867; www.nba.com

The Suns, Phoenix's professional men's basketball team, play hoops at U.S. Airways Center. You can catch a Suns game from October to May.

PHOENIX ZOO

Papago Park, 455 N. Galvin Parkway, Phoenix, 602-273-1341; www.phoenixzoo.org

See more than 400 mammals, 500 birds and 500 reptiles and amphibians at the zoo. The Arabian oryx and desert bighorn sheep are especially popular. The zoo holds special events, educational programs and outdoor recreational activities. Walk, bike (rentals available) or take a train ride around the park to see the creatures.

Admission: adults $18, children 3-12 $9, children 2 and under free. November 5-January 11, daily 9 a.m.-4 p.m.; January 12-May, daily 9 a.m.-5 p.m.; June-September, Monday-Friday 7 a.m.-2 p.m., Saturday-Sunday 7 a.m.-4 p.m.

HIGHLIGHTS

WHAT ARE THE PHOENIX'S BEST CULTURAL OFFERINGS?

ARIZONA OPERA

4600 N. 12th St., Phoenix, 602-266-7464; www.azopera.com
Founded in 1971, the Arizona Opera performs everything from *The Mikado* to Wagner's complete *Ring Cycle*, the latter of which the company performed twice. The company produces five operas each year at the Phoenix Symphony Hall.
October-March, Friday-Sunday.

ARIZONA THEATRE COMPANY

Herberger Theater Center, 222 E. Monroe St., Phoenix, 520-622-2823; 602-257-1222; www.aztheatreco.org
This professional company performs classic and contemporary works. Originally founded in 1967 in Tucson, ATC later created this Phoenix outpost. The company has tackled playwrights from Shakespeare and Shaw to Stoppard and Fugard. That means audiences get to see a diverse range of shows, everything from the musical *Ain't Misbehavin'* to an adaptation of the acclaimed book *Kite Runner*.
October-May.

COWBOY ARTISTS OF AMERICA SALE AND EXHIBITION

Phoenix Art Museum, 1625 N. Central Ave., Phoenix, 602-257-1222; www.phxart.org
Members of Cowboy Artists of America—a select group who produce fine Western American art—are considered the most prestigious in the genre. At this annual event, they offer more than 100 of their new, never-before-viewed works for sale, some of which command six figures. If that's more than you can wrangle, all the painting, drawings and sculptures remain on exhibit for a few weeks so everyone can enjoy them before buyers claim them.
Late October-mid-November.

NEW WORKS FESTIVAL

Phoenix Theatre's Little Theatre, 100 E. McDowell Road, Phoenix, 602-258-1974
See plays and musicals staged in their early phases. Actors perform works-in-progress with books in hand and with minimal set decorations. Some get produced as part of Phoenix Theatre's regular season.
Late July-mid-August

PIONEER LIVING HISTORY MUSEUM

3901 W. Pioneer Road, Phoenix, 623-465-1052; www.pioneer-arizona.com

Experience city life as pioneers in the Old West did. On these 90 acres celebrating the 1800s, you can belly up to the bar in the saloon, check out the chiseling in the blacksmith shop, eye the vintage fashions in the dress store, say a little prayer in the community church and more.

Admission: adults $7, seniors $6, children 6-18 $5, children 4 and under free. October-May, Wednesday-Sunday 9 a.m.-5 p.m.; June-September, Friday-Sunday 8 a.m.-2 p.m.

PUEBLO GRANDE MUSEUM AND ARCHAEOLOGICAL PARK

4619 E Washington St., Phoenix, 602-495-0901, 602-495-0902, 877-706-4408; www.ci.phoenix.az.us

At the ruins of a Hohokam village, revisit the past and learn how these prehistoric people lived in Arizona 1,500 years ago. You'll see an old platform mound that the Hohokam probably used for ceremonies or as an administrative center, an excavated ball court, reproductions of adobe homes and irrigation canals used for farming. Make the rounds of this 102-acre park on your own or take a guided tour on Saturday at 11 a.m. or 1 p.m. or on Sunday at 1:30 p.m.

Admission: adults $6, seniors $5, children 6-17 $3, children under 6 free. October-April, Monday-Saturday 9 a.m.-4:45 p.m.; May-September Monday-Saturday 9 a.m.-4:45 p.m.

ROADRUNNER PARK FARMERS' MARKET

3501 Cactus Road, Phoenix, 623-848-1234; www.arizonafarmersmarkets.com

Thousands of people come to this outdoor market to stock up on fresh produce grown in the Arizona desert. As many as 60 vendors sell melons, onions, peppers, squash, tomatoes and other fresh-from-the-farm crops. A few sell arts and crafts.

Saturday 8 a.m.-noon.

SQUAW PEAK PARK

2701 E. Squaw Peak Lane, Phoenix, 602-262-7901

The views—and the hiking—at this park will take your breath away. The demanding, 1.2-mile trek up the Summit Trail will test you every step of the way. For an easier route, opt for the Circumference Trail.

Daily.

WHERE TO STAY

★★★ARIZONA BILTMORE RESORT AND SPA

2400 E. Missouri Road, Phoenix, 602-955-6600, 800-950-2575; www.arizonabiltmore.com

The Arizona Biltmore Resort and Spa opened to great fanfare in 1929, and it was one of the city's first resorts. The nice thing about it today is that it's not trying to remain great—it just is. The Frank Lloyd Wright-inspired architecture—the famed architect was a consultant on the project—as well as the photos of all the presidents and famous people who have stayed here, take you back to another time. Spend your days lounging at one of the eight pools, playing the adjacent golf course or relaxing in the 22,000-square-foot spa. The rooms have Mission-style furnishings and pillow-top beds.

738 rooms. Restaurant, bar. Pool. Spa. Pets accepted. Tennis. $251-350

WHICH HOTELS ARE THE BEST FOR FAMILIES?

Arizona Grand Resort:
At the Arizona Grand Resort, the whole family will be planted at Oasis Water Park, which is the largest in the state. There are water slides, a wave pool and more.

Pointe Hilton Squaw Peak Resort:
The family will fit comfortably in this all-suite hotel. Kids will be busy in camp, with art projects and cooking lessons, or at the old-fashioned ice cream parlor.

Pointe Hilton Tapatio Cliffs Resort:
This all-suite hotel caters to little ones with an outdoor adventure program, dive-in movies and eight pools, some of which have waterfalls.

★★★ARIZONA GRAND RESORT

7777 S. Pointe Parkway, Phoenix, 602-438-9000, 866-267-1321; www.arizonagrandresort.com

This upscale resort offers spacious suites and villas with high-quality furnishings and an endless list of things to do. The onsite Oasis Water Park is Arizona's largest, boasting an eight-story waterslide, a wave pool and a "river" for tubing. There are also six swimming pools, lighted tennis courts, water and sand volleyball courts, racquetball and croquet, an 18-hole golf course and horseback riding. When you exhaust all that, there's hiking and biking in South Mountain Preserve next door. Or retire to your room and enjoy the sunset from your private balcony or patio.

640 rooms. Restaurant, bar. Business center. Spa. Golf. Tennis. $251-350

★★★JW MARRIOTT DESERT RIDGE RESORT AND SPA

5350 E. Marriott Drive, Phoenix, 480-293-5000, 800-835-6206; www.jwdesertridgeresort.com

This resort has it all: four sun-kissed pools, two 18-hole golf courses designed by Arnold Palmer and Tom Fazio, an eight-court tennis center, miles of hiking trails, a renowned spa and five restaurants. In summer, families can watch favorite movies like *Charlotte's Web* at the pool. The rooms are a draw as well. Each one has its own private balcony or patio that offers a nice view of the Sonoran Desert.

950 rooms. Restaurant, bar. Pool. Spa. Golf. Tennis. $251-350

★★★POINTE HILTON SQUAW PEAK RESORT

7677 N. 16th St., Phoenix, 602-997-2626, 800-947-9784; www.pointehilton.com

This sprawling all-suite resort at the base of Squaw Peak is great for families. The 9-acre recreational area includes swimming pools with waterfalls, a huge water slide and an 18-hole miniature golf course. Kids will think they're in heaven after spending a day splashing around here and then hitting the old-fashioned ice cream parlor. Children can also join Coyote Camp, where they learn about the state's Western folklore, culture and geography through art projects, cooking lessons and more. For adults, there's a spa with salon and fitness center, tennis courts, shopping and hikes in the adjacent Phoenix Mountain Preserve. Accommodations range from two-bedroom suites to three-bedroom casitas.

563 rooms. Restaurant, bar. Fitness center. Pool. Spa. Tennis. $151-250

★★★POINTE HILTON TAPATIO CLIFFS RESORT

11111 N. Seventh St., Phoenix, 602-866-7500, 800-947-9784; www.pointehilton.com

This resort is situated among the peaks of the Phoenix North Mountains, offering dramatic views of the city and valley below. The resort boasts its own water playground and a total of eight swimming pools, some with waterfalls. There's also a 138-foot enclosed water slide. Children can make the most of the water activities with the Kids Korral, an outdoor adventure program that includes dive-in movies and other poolside fun. The Lookout Mountain Golf Club is an 18-hole championship course set along the border of an 8,000-acre Sonoran Desert park. A full-service spa offers a variety of pampering treatments. The two-room suites all have living rooms and two TVs.

584 rooms. Restaurant, bar. Spa. Pets accepted. Golf. Tennis. $151-250

★★★★THE RITZ-CARLTON, PHOENIX

2401 E. Camelback, Phoenix, 602-468-0700, 800-241-3333; www.ritzcarlton.com

The hotel is in the middle of the Camelback Corridor, the exclusive shopping, dining and financial district of Phoenix. The rooms, classically decorated with beds topped with luxury Egyptian cotton linens, all have views of the skyline or the Squaw Peak Mountain Range. Bathrooms have marble tubs and are stocked with plush terrycloth robes. Then, of course, there's the service. Concierges will offer tips on everything from the area's best golf courses to the tastiest cocktail to sip in the lobby lounge. If you need a place for dinner, head to the hotel's festive Bistro 24, where you'll find modern takes on French classics like steak au poivre with crisp frites. To take in some sun, go outside to the heated pool and the sundeck area, which is cooled with hydro-misters.

281 rooms. Restaurant, bar. Business center. Fitness center. Pool. $251-350

★★★ROYAL PALMS RESORT AND SPA

5200 E. Camelback Road, Phoenix, 602-840-3610, 800-672-6011; www.royalpalmsresortandspa.com

Constructed in the late 1920s as a private mansion, this hotel brings a bit of the Mediterranean to the Sonoran Desert. Palm trees line the entrance to this hideaway surrounded by fountains and citrus trees, where lavish casitas and guest rooms have fireplaces, balconies, comfy pillow-top mattresses and LCD televisions. Plan to make a stop at the dreamy open-air spa, which has treatment rooms with garden areas and a villa with stone-heated tables under overhead showers. For dinner, you needn't look further than the onsite T. Cook's, which serves Mediterranean-influenced cuisine. If you want to get active, the resort offers a pool, croquet and bike rentals.

119 rooms. Restaurant, bar. Fitness center. Spa. Pets accepted. Pool. $251-350

WHERE TO EAT

★★★AVANTI

2728 E. Thomas Road, Phoenix, 602-956-0900; www.avanti-az.com

A stark, Art Deco-inspired interior of black and white provides the backdrop for this romantic Italian restaurant specializing in fresh pasta with rich sauces. Try the lobster and seafood ravioli with vodka sauce or the cannelloni fiorentina, a pasta crêpe stuffed with chicken, veal and spinach and doused with béchamel. The restaurant gets especially lively on Fridays and Saturdays, when a pianist plays jazz, swing and classical in the lounge area and sprinkles some comedy into his act.

Italian. Lunch, dinner. Reservations recommended. Outdoor seating. Bar. $36-85

★★BISTRO 24

The Ritz-Carlton, Phoenix, 2401 E. Camelback Road, Phoenix, 602-468-0700; www.ritzcarlton.com

Located within the Ritz-Carlton, Bistro 24 serves classic dishes such as steak au poivre and grilled seafood such as butter-poached halibut. Or you can go all out and order a farm-to-table dinner. The restaurant is spacious and unpretentious with colorful murals and an outdoor patio, and the service is impeccable. Come for Bistro 24's happy hour, which features half-priced martinis and appetizers.

French. Breakfast, lunch, dinner, Sunday brunch. Reservations recommended. Outdoor seating. Children's menu. Bar. $36-85

★★★CHRISTOPHER'S

2502 E. Camelback Road, Phoenix, 602-522-2344; www.christophersaz.com

This French-influenced spot is strategically positioned in the ritzy Biltmore shopping center. Opened in May 2008, Christopher's aimed to "create a sexy and ultra-chic experience enabling the perfect setting for intimate encounters." The menu is American with a French twist, like a foie gras terrine, Armagnac date tart and brioche starter followed by an arugula, poached pear, and blue cheese salad before a truffle-infused filet mignon or duck confit, goat cheese and fig pizza entrée. Watch it all being prepared at the bar on the sidelines of the contemporary open kitchen. Groups of up to 10 can reserve the chef's table, which comes with the nightly tasting menu—just be sure that the chilled white chocolate-corn husk creation is included.

American, French. Lunch, dinner. Outdoor seating. Bar. $36-85

★★★LA FONTANELLA

4231 E. Indian School Road, Phoenix, 602-955-1213; www.lafontanellaphx.com

The Italian husband-and-wife team that runs this Phoenix gem serves up recipes from their homeland, including fresh pastas and grilled meats. Go for the half-moon ravioli stuffed with butternut squash and splashed with a walnut-cream sauce or the grilled chicken breast with spinach, pancetta and fontina cheese. Save room for desserts, all of which are made in-house, including the gelati.

Italian. Dinner. Closed two weeks in July. Reservations recommended. Bar. $36-85

★★★RUTH'S CHRIS STEAK HOUSE

2201 E. Camelback Road, Phoenix, 602-957-9600; www.ruthschris.com

Born from a single New Orleans restaurant, the chain is a favorite among steak lovers. Aged prime Midwestern beef is broiled at 1,800 degrees and served on a heated plate sizzling in butter with sides such as creamed spinach and au gratin potatoes.

Steak. Dinner. Reservations recommended. Outdoor seating. Bar. $36-85

★★★T. COOK'S
Royal Palms Resort and Spa, 5200 E. Camelback Road, Phoenix,
602-840-3610, 800-672-6011;
www.royalpalmsresortandspa.com

Located in the Royal Palms Resort and Spa, this
stylish restaurant has deep cherry-wood floors,
hand-painted Italian frescoes and floor-to-ceiling
windows with views of Camelback Mountain. The
Mediterranean menu includes dishes such as pan-
roasted duck with cauliflower purée, grilled baby
bok choy, rhubarb chutney, potato crisp and ginger-
infused duck demi, and butter-poached lobster with
sour cream ravioli, asparagus and a champagne-chive
butter sauce. Some dishes, like the Mediterranean
paella, are made in the restaurant's fireplace.
*Mediterranean. Breakfast, lunch, dinner, Sunday brunch. Bar.
$36-85*

★★★TARBELL'S
3213 E. Camelback Road, Phoenix, 602-955-8100;
www.tarbells.com

Celebrated chef Mark Tarbell—he beat out Cat
Cora on *Iron Chef America*—continues to dazzle
with fresh seasonal dishes such as house-made
ribbon pasta with pork sausage, crushed Compari
tomatoes, piquillo peppers, bread crumbs and olive
oil, and double-cut pork chops with white cheddar
grits and bacon-braised Tuscan kale. The sophisticated restaurant features blond wood, white tablecloths and an exhibition kitchen—and somehow
maintains a friendly neighborhood feel, perhaps
thanks to the large curved bar that's a focal point.
American. Dinner. Reservations recommended. Bar. $36-85

★★★VINCENT ON CAMELBACK
3930 E. Camelback Road, Phoenix, 602-224-0225;
www.vincentsoncamelback.com

This intimate restaurant, which combines hearty
Southwest flavors with elegant French cuisine,
helped build Phoenix's culinary reputation. The
flawless waitstaff and creative menu continue to
attract crowds. Dishes include grilled wild boar loin
with celery root purée and habañero sauce, and duck
confit with candied citrus sauce and sweet potato
gratin. A dessert specialty is the soufflé, which
comes in flavors such as Grand Marnier, tequila and
lemon crêpe.
French. Lunch, dinner. Closed Sunday. Bar. $36-85

WHICH PHOENIX RESTAURANTS HAVE THE BEST CONTEMPORARY AMERICAN FOOD?

Christopher's:
Some of the best food
in Phoenix is served
at Christopher's. The
restaurant, in the
Biltmore shopping
center, serves American
cuisine with a
French kick.

Tarbell's:
Chef Mark Tarbell
triumphed in his
appearance on the TV
show *Iron Chef America*.
Find out why at his
eponymous restaurant,
which turns out
seasonal fare.

Wright's at the Biltmore:
This restaurant uses
farm-fresh ingredients
for its meat-heavy menu
that includes dishes such
as Colorado lavender
lamb loin and
steak Diane.

★★★WRIGHT'S AT THE BILTMORE

Arizona Biltmore, 2400 Missouri Road, Phoenix, 602-381-7632; www.arizonabiltmore.com

A homage to Frank Lloyd Wright, this restaurant off the lobby of the Arizona Biltmore reflects the architect's penchant for stark angles and contrasts. Muted Southwestern colors fill the comfortable room and a large-paneled window frames excellent views. The American cuisine features the freshest ingredients from boutique farms across the country. Some of the herbs the kitchen uses are plucked from the chef's garden right next to the dining room. The menu changes weekly, but you'll find dishes such as aged buffalo with white cheddar and Yukon purée. Be sure to sample one of the tempting chocolate desserts.

American. Breakfast, lunch (Monday-Saturday), dinner, Sunday brunch. Reservations recommended. Outdoor seating. Bar. $36-85

SPAS

★★★★ALVADORA SPA AT ROYAL PALMS

Royal Palms Resort and Spa, 5200 E. Camelback Road, Phoenix, 602-840-3610, 800-672-6011; www.royalpalmshotel.com

Inspired by that region's native flowers, herbs and oils, this Mediterranean-style spa brings the outdoors in through its open-air design and plant-inspired therapies. The healing properties of water are a focal point here, whether you're soaking in a bath of grape seeds and herbs or floating in the Watsu pool with an eight-foot grotto waterfall shower in a private garden terrace. Indulge in the Mediterranean Wrapture, a body wrap using olive leaf, cilantro, juniper and lavender extracts. The stone therapy facial stimulates circulation and detoxifies the skin. After your treatment, you can take yoga, tai chi, meditation and mat Pilates classes in the 24-hour fitness center.

★★★REVIVE SPA AT JW MARRIOTT DESERT RIDGE RESORT

JW Marriott Desert Ridge Resort, 5350 E. Marriott Drive, Phoenix, 480-293-3700, 800-835-6206; www.jwdesertridgeresort.com

The serenity and beauty of the desert are the true inspirations behind this spa, where outside celestial showers for men and women, private balconies—ideal for outdoor massages—and a rooftop garden with flowing water add to the atmosphere. Indigenous botanicals influence most of Revive's body treatments. Mesquite clay and desert algae body wraps detoxify and purify. Prickly pear and lime-salt body scrubs soften skin. Recharge with a workout in the spacious and well-equipped fitness center. In addition to cardio machines and free weights, this facility offers several classes, including tai chi, water fitness, golf conditioning, flexibility, yoga and mat Pilates. After a workout, dine on calorie-conscious meals at Revive's Spa Bistro.

SCOTTSDALE

Scottsdale sits in Central Arizona, but like Phoenix, the city is a major urban center. It's a popular resort destination on the eastern border of Phoenix, and it's renowned for outstanding art galleries, excellent shopping and dining, lush golf courses and abundant recreational activities. One of the city's standouts is its world-class spas.

WHAT TO SEE

ACACIA COURSE AT THE WESTIN KIERLAND GOLF RESORT AND SPA
15636 Clubgate Drive, Scottsdale, 480-922-9285; 480-922-9283; www.kierlandresort.com

Part of the resort's 27 perfectly manicured holes, the Acacia was created by Scott Miller, who once designed for Jack Nicklaus. Combine these nine holes with Ironwood or Mesquite's nine holes for 18 holes of great golf in one of Arizona's most beautiful resorts.

ANTIQUE TROVE
2020 N. Scottsdale Road, Scottsdale, 480-947-6074; www.antiquetrove.com

More than 150 dealers sell everything from vintage mink jackets to colonial rocking chairs from the 1940s and claw-foot bathtubs.
Daily.

CANYON COURSE AT THE PHOENICIAN
6000 E. Camelback Road, Scottsdale, 480-941-8200, 800-888-8234; www.thephoenician.com

The Canyon is the last in the triumvirate of courses that make the Phoenician a celebrated resort. This nine-hole course can be combined with either of the other two courses (Oasis or Desert) to make a challenging yet enjoyable 18-hole trek through the picturesque desert.

CASINO ARIZONA AT SALT RIVER
524 N. 92nd St., Scottsdale; www.casinoaz.com

The Salt River Pima-Maricopa Indian community hit the jackpot when it opened this casino in a prime location off the 101 Freeway on the valley's east side. They promptly opened a second location just a few miles north, off the same freeway *(9700 E. Indian Bend Road)*. The original funhouse is larger and a notch more upscale with five restaurants, the best being the elegant Cholla Prime Steakhouse. The 250-seat cabaret-style showroom rocks with big-name entertainers.
Daily.

CRUISE NIGHT AT SCOTTSDALE PAVILIONS
9175 E. Indian Bend Road, Scottsdale, 480-905-9111; www.scottsdalepavilions.com

While Scottsdale Pavilions may be one of the largest and most attractive shopping centers in the country, Saturday nights bring more people to the parking lot than the shops. They come for the hot rods: muscle cars, custom cars, street rods, antique roadsters, vintage trucks, motorcycles and even a few finely tuned imports.
Saturday 4-8:30 p.m.

DESERT COURSE AT THE PHOENICIAN

6000 E. Camelback Road, Scottsdale, 480-941-8200, 800-888-8234; www.thephoenician.com

This golf wonder joins two other nine-hole courses (aptly named the "Oasis" and the "Canyon") to earn the luxe Phoenician hotel some major accolades.

GRAYHAWK GOLF CLUB

8620 E. Thompson Peak Parkway, Scottsdale, 480-502-1800; www.grayhawk.com

Grayhawk has two courses: Talon, designed by David Graham and Gary Panks, and Raptor, designed by Tom Fazio. Both are nice, but Talon deserves more attention. Built in the Sonoran Desert, the course features many shots over desert brush or sand, with some water worked in for good measure. The course is good enough to host international-caliber tournaments such as the World Championship of Golf. If your game needs work, schedule some time at the Kostis McCord Learning Center, whose instructors include the two CBS commentators.

IRONWOOD COURSE AT THE WESTIN KIERLAND GOLF RESORT & SPA

15636 Clubgate Drive, Scottsdale, 480-922-9283, 888-625-5144; www.kierlandresort.com

Designed by Scott Miller (once a designer for Jack Nicklaus), the Ironwood, like the other two nine-hole courses at this resort, offers a beautiful setting for birdies, bogies and maybe even a hole-in-one.

LEGEND TRAIL GOLF CLUB

9462 E. Legendary Lane, Scottsdale, 480-488-7434; www.legendtrailgc.com

Drive, chip and putt your way through the Sonoran Desert on this picturesque course. Even if you don't quite shoot par, you'll enjoy the gorgeous vistas and desert landscape.

MESQUITE COURSE AT THE WESTIN KIERLAND GOLF RESORT & SPA

15636 Clubgate Drive, Scottsdale, 480-922-9283, 888-625-5144; www.kierlandresort.com

Like its two nine-hole counterparts, this course was designed by Scott Miller, former designer for Jack Nicklaus. Combine the courses to challenge and delight duffers of all skill levels.

MONUMENT COURSE AT TROON NORTH GOLF CLUB

10320 E. Dynamite Blvd., Scottsdale, 480-585-5300; www.troonnorthgolf.com

Test your skills in the shadow of Pinnacle Peak at this beautiful 18-hole course.

NORTH COURSE AT TALKING STICK GOLF CLUB

9998 E. Indian Bend Road, Scottsdale, 480-860-2221; www.talkingstickgolfclub.com

This Scottish links course stands ready to challenge golfers with its fairway bunkers, so don't let the gorgeous setting distract you.

OASIS COURSE AT THE PHOENICIAN

6000 E. Camelback Road, Scottsdale, 480-423-2450, 800-888-8234;www.thephoenician.com

The Phoenician has earned praise from national critics and local fans alike. Don't miss an opportunity to swing your clubs at one of three 18-hole combinations, of which the Oasis makes up nine holes.

HIGHLIGHTS

WHAT ARE THE BEST GOLF COURSES IN SCOTTSDALE?

THE WESTIN KIERLAND GOLF RESORT
The Westin boasts three 18-hole courses—the Acacia, Ironwood and Mesquite—at one of the state's most beautiful resorts.

THE PHOENICIAN
The trio of courses at this hotel are named after their scenic surroundings, the Canyon, Oasis and Desert. Combine two of the courses for a day of desert golf.

GRAYHAWK GOLF CLUB
There are two courses here, but the better of the pair is Talon. If you need proof, the Sonoran Desert course hosts big-time tournaments like the World Championship of Golf.

LEGEND TRAIL GOLF CLUB
Can't get enough of driving your club in the desert? Legend Trail's Sonoran course offers gorgeous views of the desert landscape. Dame duffers will want to tee up here; the club prides itself on being female-friendly.

TROON NORTH GOLF CLUB
This lovely club offers two courses in the shadow of Pinnacle Peak. If you need help with your swing, PGA pro Doug Hammer is available for private lessons.

TOURNAMENT PLAYERS CLUB OF SCOTTSDALE
Superstars like Tiger Woods have hit the greens at this club. They favor the Stadium Course, which is also the first course in the state to be designated an Audubon International Cooperative Sanctuary System for its work in preserving wildlife and protecting natural resources.

PINNACLE COURSE AT TROON NORTH GOLF CLUB

10320 E. Dynamite Blvd., Scottsdale, 480-585-5300; www.troonnorthgolf.com

Named for Pinnacle Peak, the course is one of two you'll find at the Troon North Golf Club. After swinging your heart out on the green—and admiring the view—dine at the club's Grille.

RAWHIDE WILD WEST TOWN

5700 W. North Loop Road, Chandler, 480-502-5600, 800-527-1880; www.rawhide.com

Gallop into the Old West at Arizona's largest Western-themed attraction. Roam the range on the stagecoach or train, test your aim in the shooting gallery, ride the mechanical bull, pan for gold, go horseback riding and take in the shows—from stuntmen throwing punches and squaring off in gunfights to performances by Native American and Mexican dancers. The Steakhouse serves up mesquite-grilled cuts of meat. Browse through the many shops.

Admission: free. Daily.

TALIESIN WEST

12621 N. Frank Lloyd Wright Blvd., Scottsdale, 480-860-2700; www.franklloydwright.org

Take a guided tour of this amazing compound and see Frank Lloyd Wright's passion for organic architecture. In the late 1930s, Wright and his apprentices built this winter camp out of the Sonoran Desert, using rocks and sand they gathered from the rugged terrain. In true Wright fashion, the architect designed the various buildings with terraces, gardens and walkways that link the outdoors with the indoors. Taliesin West still functions as an architecture school.

Admission: varies. Tours daily.

TALKING STICK GOLF CLUB-SOUTH COURSE

9998 E. Indian Bend Road, Scottsdale, 480-860-2221; www.talkingstickgolfclub.com

Unlike its counterpart, which is a Scottish links course, this is a traditional American-style golf course, punctuated with cottonwood and sycamore trees, creeks and lakes.

TOURNAMENT PLAYERS CLUB OF SCOTTSDALE

17020 N. Hayden Road, Scottsdale, 480-585-4334, 888-400-4001; www.tpc.com

Follow in the footsteps of Tiger Woods, Vijay Singh and other big-name golfers and swing into action on the TPC's greens—home of the Phoenix Open. The club has two options: the Stadium Course (the one the pros shoot) and the Championship Course, both open for daily play.

WILD WEST JEEP TOURS

7127 E. Becker Lane, Scottsdale, 480-922-0144; www.wildwestjeeptours.com

Fasten your seat belts for these three- to four-hour guided desert Jeep tours. The year-round tours will bring you all over the desert, and you'll get a chance to explore an ancient ruin.

Daily.

WHERE TO STAY

★★★THE FAIRMONT SCOTTSDALE

7575 E. Princess Drive, Scottsdale, 480-585-4848, 800-257-7544; www.fairmont.com

The pink Spanish-colonial buildings of this hotel are spread out over 450 lush acres overlooking Scottsdale and the majestic McDowell Mountains. Golfers come here to play the two championship courses—one of which hosts the PGA Tour's Phoenix Open. The Willow Stream Spa is also a big draw. Kids will love the aquatic recreation area with two water slides. The spacious rooms and suites are a blend of Mediterranean design with Southwestern accents and neutral desert colors, and they offer fantastic views.

649 rooms. Restaurant, bar. Pool. Spa. Pets accepted. Golf. Tennis. $251-350

★★★FIRESKY RESORT AND SPA

4925 N. Scottsdale Road, Scottsdale, 480-945-7666, 800-528-7867; www.fireskyresort.com

A three-story sandstone fireplace flanked by hand-painted adobe walls is the centerpiece of this romantic resort's lobby. A traditional Western theme is reflected in the décor, while the grounds include a sandy beach pool surrounded by palm trees and flowers, a Mediterranean-inspired lagoon as well as cozy fire pits. You can relax on the lush grounds or kick back at the nightly gratis wine hour with a glass of vino. Rooms are stocked with small luxuries such as pillow-topped beds, in-room yoga programs and mats, fully stocked honor bars and complimentary travel essentials you may have forgotten. There's an onsite spa, but you can also have massages and other spa services delivered in the comfort of your own room.

204 rooms. Restaurant, bar. Pool. Spa. Pets accepted. Beach. $151-250

★★★★FOUR SEASONS RESORT SCOTTSDALE AT TROON NORTH

10600 E. Crescent Moon Drive, Scottsdale, 480-515-5700, 888-207-9696;www.fourseasons.com

Located on a 40-acre nature preserve in the foothills of Pinnacle Peak, rooms are spread across 25 Southwestern-style casitas, with views of the desert. Amenities include down duvets, CD players, DVD players and baths stocked with L'Occitane products and deep soaking tubs. Book a suite—you'll get a plunge pool, an alfresco garden shower and an outdoor adobe-style kiva fireplace. A veritable mecca for golfers, the resort grants priority tee times at Troon North's two courses, considered among the best in the world. The spa offers desert nectar facials and moonlight massages, plus salon services and a fitness center. Three restaurants serve cuisine that reflects the resort's Southwestern setting, including kiva-oven roasted pizza with carne asada, roasted peppers and jalapeño jack cheese.

210 rooms. Restaurant, bar. Fitness center. Pool. Spa. Pets accepted. Golf. Tennis. $351 and up

★★★HILTON SCOTTSDALE RESORT AND VILLAS

6333 N. Scottsdale Road, Scottsdale, 480-948-7750, 800-528-3119; www.scottsdaleresort.hilton.com

Warm shades of gold, blue and apricot complement the resort's natural wood décor, creating a warm and welcoming atmosphere for guests. Families should opt for the two-bedroom villas, which offer all of the amenities of home, complete with full kitchens, washers and dryers, three flat-screen TVs,

WHAT SCOTTSDALE HOTELS HAVE THE MOST UNIQUE DECOR?

Hotel Valley Ho:
While most Arizona hotels use the Southwestern desert landscape for decoration inspiration, Hotel Valley Ho bucks the trend and offers retro-cool rooms with Mid-century modern décor. You'll find Eames chairs in the Terrace Suites and Philippe Starck-designed tubs in the studios.

The Phoenician:
Calling this hotel a museum wouldn't be an exaggeration. The Phoenician decorates its main building with a $25 million art collection of French tapestries, marble sculptures and more. Take an audio tour of the works interactive fountain.

wood-burning fireplaces and private patios. Galleries, shops and restaurants of Old Town Scottsdale are within easy walking distance, or you can take advantage of the hotel's bike rental facility. The resort has three eateries, and Fleming's Prime Steakhouse and Wine Bar is a great spot for lamb chops and a glass or two of wine.

190 rooms. Restaurant, bar. Business center. Fitness center. Pool. Pets accepted. $61-150

★★★HOTEL VALLEY HO
6850 E. Main St., Scottsdale, 480-248-2000, 866-882-4484; www.hotelvalleyho.com

A mid-century modern showpiece, this quirky hotel revels in its Jetsonian glory. Retro rooms are updated with plasma TVs, luxury bedding, CD players, Red Flower bath products and glass walls that open up onto a patio. The rooms still feature reproductions of 1950s-era furniture and bright, cheerful hues. The huge circular outdoor pool has private cabanas for alfresco massages or simply sipping cocktails in private. During the summer, DJs keep the pool area hopping during the weekends. The VH Spa offers a full menu of treatments, from lomi lomi massages to Tibetan yogic bodywork (a mix of acupressure and massage). Restaurants include the retro-chic Trader Vic's.

194 rooms. Restaurant, bar. Fitness center. Pool. Spa. Pets accepted. $151-250

★★★HYATT REGENCY SCOTTSDALE RESORT AND SPA AT GAINEY RANCH
7500 E. Doubletree Ranch Road, Scottsdale, 480-444-1234, 800-554-9288; www.scottsdale.hyatt.com

Set against the backdrop of the McDowell Mountains, the resort is nestled on 560 acres filled with shimmering pools, trickling fountains and cascading waterfalls. Desert tones and regional furnishings create contemporary havens in the rooms and suites. Each room comes with a private balcony or patio, a 37-inch LCD television and complimentary wireless Internet access. There's plenty to do on the hotel grounds. Go a couple of rounds on the three nine-hole championship golf courses, play tennis or frolic on the water playground while the kids attend camp. For a more romantic adventure, take your loved one on a gondola ride through the resort while a classically trained gondolier serenades you.

492 rooms. Restaurant, bar. Business center. Spa. Beach. Golf. Tennis. $351 and up

★★★CAMELBACK INN, A JW MARRIOTT RESORT & SPA

5402 E. Lincoln Drive, Scottsdale, 480-948-1700, 800-582-2169; www.camelbackinn.com

Since the 1930s, the Camelback Inn has appealed to travelers seeking the best of the Southwest. This special hideaway is situated on 125 acres in the Sonoran Desert. The pueblo-style casitas feature wood-beamed ceilings, private patios and kitchenettes. Set at the base of Mummy Mountain, the spa is a peaceful retreat. Duffers will want to try out the two 18-hole golf courses at the resort, especially the Arthur Hills-designed Padre Course with challenging water holes. Five restaurants satisfy every craving, but the home-style regional cuisine at Rita's Kitchen and the cuts at BLT Steakhouse are the better bets at the hotel.

453 rooms. Restaurant, bar. Pool. Spa. Pets accepted. Golf. Tennis. $251-350

★★★MARRIOTT SUITES SCOTTSDALE OLD TOWN

7325 E. Third Ave., Scottsdale, 480-945-1550, 888-236-2427; www.marriott.com

Catering mainly to business travelers, this Old Town hotel is close to Scottsdale Road and a large shopping mall. Its suites come equipped with 32-inch high-definition TVs, wet bars, refrigerators and balconies overlooking the desert. The hotel has plenty of recreational facilities, including a pool and fitness center, to help you wind down at the end of the day after your meeting.

243 rooms. Restaurant, bar. Business center. Fitness center. Pool. $251-350

★★★MILLENNIUM RESORT SCOTTSDALE, MCCORMICK RANCH

7401 N. Scottsdale Road, Scottsdale, 480-948-5050, 800-243-1332; www.millennium-hotels.com

Situated on a 40-acre lake in the midst of the McCormick Ranch, this hotel's setting attracts couples on romantic getaways, business travelers making the most of the amenities and vacationers looking for a full-service resort experience. Proximity to the lake means easy access to paddleboats and sailboats. Or cool off with a dip in the pool and its 20-foot horizontal waterfall. The resort also offers volleyball, tennis, swimming as well as two 18-hole PGA golf courses. The individually decorated villas include 40-inch flat-panel televisions, gas fireplaces, laundry facilities and private patios with grills.

125 rooms. Restaurant, bar. Pool. Spa. Pets accepted. Tennis. $151-250

★★★★THE PHOENICIAN

6000 E. Camelback Road, Scottsdale, 480-941-8200, 800-888-8234; www.thephoenician.com

This resort, located at the base of Camelback Mountain, features rooms and suites with imported Italian linens and oversized bathrooms with Italian marble. Staff is always on hand to help or steer you toward one of a number of activities, including desert hikes. Be sure to take a walk through the cactus garden and get an audio device for a self-guided tour of the hotel's $25 million collection of art, which includes French tapestries, Navajo rugs and contemporary fiber art. A resort within a resort, the Canyon Suites at the Phoenician offers sprawling, luxuriously decorated rooms and a separate pool with private cabanas. Guests are assigned ambassadors who arrange everything from in-room aromatherapy baths to chauffeured trips into town in the resort's Mercedes. There's little reason to leave the elegant, comfortable suite, which have DVD players, flat-screen TVs and Italian linen-swathed beds. But the resort's golf courses and full-service spa serve as the primary temptations.

643 rooms. Restaurant, bar. Business center. Pool. Spa. Pets accepted. Golf. Tennis. $251-350

★★★SCOTTSDALE COTTONWOODS RESORT & SUITES

6160 N. Scottsdale Road, Scottsdale, 480-991-1414, 877-344-3430;
www.scottsdalecottonwoods.com

The lobby, with its Spanish-colonial Monk's Tower, is both the entrance to the resort's many amenities and a buffer against the commotion of busy Scottsdale Road, located next to the Borgata Shopping Center. Lush landscaping with plenty of grass and flowers separates the lobby from the single-story guest rooms and suites. Head to one of two pools for a relaxing swim, play shuffleboard or volleyball, make use of the putting green or jog along a trail that includes workout stations.

170 rooms. Restaurant, bar. Business center. Pool. Pets accepted. Tennis. $151-250

★★★SCOTTSDALE MARRIOTT AT MCDOWELL MOUNTAINS

16770 N. Perimeter Drive, Scottsdale, 480-502-3836, 800-236-2427;
www.scottsdalemarriott.com

This all-suites hotel is in north Scottsdale. The colorful, attractive public areas and well-furnished guest rooms are designed for both families and business travelers. The rooms' sleep-inducing beds have down duvets, six feather pillows and Italian throws. They also come with flat-screen TVs, wet bars and mini-refrigerators. Some rooms have views of the Tournament Players Clubs Scottsdale golf course.

270 rooms. Restaurant, bar. Business center. Pool. Pets accepted. $61-150

★★★THE WESTIN KIERLAND RESORT AND SPA

6902 E. Greenway Parkway, Scottsdale, 480-624-1000, 800-937-8461; www.westin.com

Located in northeast Phoenix, this handsome boutique-style resort is adjacent to the 38-acre Kierland Commons, where specialty shops and restaurants attract serious shoppers and diners. The spacious rooms and suites feature soothing earth tones and regional furnishings. The resort includes two 18-hole golf courses, tennis courts, beach and volleyball courts and six restaurants. In addition to a pool, the hotel has a water park with a 900-foot lazy river with a waterfall and a 110-foot waterslide. The expansive Agave Spa looks to the traditional therapies used by Native Americans for inspiration.

732 rooms. Restaurant, bar. Pool. Spa. Pets accepted. Beach. Golf. Tennis. $251-350

WHERE TO EAT

★★★BOURBON STEAK SCOTTSDALE

The Fairmont Scottsdale Princess, 7575 E. Princess Drive, Scottsdale, 480-513-6002;
www.bourbonsteakscottsdale.com

Just another notch on chef Michael Mina's belt, Bourbon Steak Scottsdale has received accolades since it opened in early 2008. This modern American steakhouse takes the classics and improves them. Think three types of beef—certified Angus, American Kobe and A5 Kobe—all prepared with Mina's special touch. He poaches red meat in butter, lamb in olive oil and pork in bacon fat before grilling. Other options include whole-fried organic chicken, truffled mac and cheese, Maine lobster pot pie, and tapioca-crusted yellowtail snapper.

Contemporary American, steak. Dinner. Closed Sunday-Monday. Reservations recommended. Outdoor seating. Children's menu. Bar. $16-35

★★★DESEO

The Westin Kierland Resort & Spa, 6902 E. Greenway Parkway, Scottsdale, 480-624-1000, 800-354-5892; www.kierlandresort.com

The open-display kitchen is the focal point of this Nuevo Latino restaurant located in Scottsdale's Westin Keirland Resort. You'll likely also notice the colorful paintings on the walls from Nelson Garcia-Miranda. The Cuban artist visits the restaurant Tuesday to Saturday evenings to paint live. While he gets to work, choose from a variety of mojitos and be sure to order one of the signature ceviches. Other dishes include foie gras and fig empanadas and Muscovy duck breast with Asian pear and mango.

Latin American. Dinner. Closed Monday (in summer). Reservations recommended. Outdoor seating. Bar. $36-85

★★★EDDIE V'S PRIME SEAFOOD

20715 N. Pima Road, Scottsdale, 480-538-8468; www.eddiev.com

The relaxed lodge-themed interior of this restaurant features murals, black leather chairs, crisp white table linens and brick walls. Diners are entertained nightly by a band or a vocalist, but the main draw here is the food. The Maryland-style all-lump crab cakes are a must for an appetizer, and the bananas Foster makes a memorable end to a meal.

Seafood. Dinner. Reservations recommended. Outdoor seating. Bar. $36-85

★★★IL TERRAZZO

6000 E. Camelback Road, The Phoenician, Scottsdale, 480-423-2530, 800-888-8234; www.thephoenician.com

The Phoenician's Italian eatery aims to capture the rich, indigenous flavors of Italy through classic, upscale cuisine that represents all regions of the country. Chef de cuisine Victor Casanova, who previously served as sous chef at New York's Ocean Grill, offers such dishes as pan-seared scallops with lemon risotto and black truffle and the signature Kobe burger with crispy onions, horserad-ish, pickles and black truffle ketchup.

Italian. Breakfast, lunch, dinner, Sunday brunch. Reservations recommended. Outdoor seating. Children's menu. $36-85

★★★MOSAIC

10600 E. Jomax Road, Scottsdale, 480-563-9600; www.mosaic-restaurant.com

Chef/owner Deborah Knight uses ingredients and cooking techniques from around the world to create her own brand of eclectic cuisine, which includes dishes such as tamarind-spiced prawns, Thai shrimp and coconut soup, and fennel and 12-mushroom risotto. Three types of five-course tasting menus are available to suit all tastes (Mosaic, Ocean and Vegetable). Local artwork punc-tuates the earth-toned dining room with color, and a beautiful, custom-made mosaic floor adds sparkle.

International. Dinner. Closed Sunday-Monday; mid-August-September. Reservations recom-mended. Outdoor seating. Bar. $36-85

WHAT ARE THE BEST STEAK HOUSES IN SCOTTSDALE?

Bourbon Steak Scottsdale:

Two-time James Beard Award-winning chef Michael Mina puts a twist on dishes: dry-aged burgers come with duck-fat fries and the N.Y. strip has a garlic-soy dipping sauce.

Remington's:

Deals are sealed over the filet mignon and rack of lamb at Remington's. But people also come to the steak house for the live jazz music that goes down almost nightly.

Talavera:

Set right near Pinnacle Peak, Talavera offers regional carnivorous cuisine like Arizona grass-fed tenderloin with savory chorizo bread pudding.

★★★PALM COURT

Scottsdale Resort & Conference Center, 7700 E. McCormick Parkway, Scottsdale, 480-991-9000, 800-548-0293; www.thescottsdaleresort.com

Although this restaurant is on the third floor of the main building at the Scottsdale Conference Resort, you'd never know it once you enter the elegant candlelit dinning room, where tuxedo-clad waiters serve lavish French fare like Dover sole amandine. A classical guitarist provides lovely background music.

French. Breakfast, lunch, dinner, Sunday brunch. Reservations recommended. Bar. $36-85

★★★RANCHO PINOT

6208 N. Scottsdale Blvd., Scottsdale, 480-367-8030; www.ranchopinot.com

Situated within the Lincoln Village Shops, Rancho Pinot offers American cuisine using the best ingredients, many of them from local farms. You might find dishes such as handmade pasta with summer squash, scallions, mint and Parmesan cheese on the frequently changing menu. Art and Southwestern décor adorn the walls, and an open kitchen allows guests to watch the chef at work.

American. Dinner. Reservations recommended. Outdoor seating. Bar. $36-85

★★★REMINGTON'S

The Scottsdale Plaza Resort, 7200 N. Scottsdale Road, Scottsdale, 480-951-5101; www.scottsdaleplaza.com

Carnivores will want to come to this steakhouse in the Scottsdale Plaza Resort for its New York strip, filet mignon and rack of lamb. But the Sonoran crab cake starter with chipotle remoulade sauce and the house-baked pretzel rolls are just as tasty.

Steak. Lunch (Monday-Friday), dinner. Outdoor seating. Bar. $36-85

★★★ROARING FORK

4800 N. Scottsdale Road, Scottsdale, 480-947-0795; www.eddiev.com

Executive chef Bryan Hulihee turns out Western American cooking, inspired by founding chef Robert McGrath's cuisine, at this rustic yet refined dining room filled with exposed brick and blond wood. An open display kitchen is featured, and some booths across the aisle provide great viewing. The adjacent J-Bar is a fun place to congregate for a drink.

American. Dinner. Outdoor seating. Children's menu. Bar. $36-85

★★★SASSI

10455 E. Pinnacle Peak Parkway, Scottsdale, 480-502-9095; www.sassi.biz

Sassi, which resembles a Tuscan villa, serves up authentic Italian cuisine including handmade pastas, fresh seafood and local organic produce. Try the orecchiette con salsiccia, pasta with house-made sweet spicy sausage, rapini and Pecorino. The extensive wine list offers many delicious complements. Enjoy live music Friday and Saturday evenings.

Italian. Dinner. Closed Sunday-Monday. Outdoor seating. Bar. $36-85

★★★★TALAVERA

Four Seasons Resort Scottsdale at Troon North, 10600 E. Crescent Moon Drive, Scottsdale, 480-515-5700; www.fourseasons.com

The surrounding Sonoran Desert is palpable in this restaurant, due to rich red loveseats, sand-colored walls and cactus-green chairs, as well as a cozy glass-enclosed fireplace. Opt to dine under the stars on the patio—all the better to behold the craggy Pinnacle Peak and the desert expanse. Start your alfresco dinner with the lobster bisque with tempura squash. For entrées, this steak-house offers raw choices (Wagyu beef tartare), Nebraska corn-fed prime cuts, and a list of fish and chicken meals. Go for regional dishes, such as Arizona grass-fed tenderloin with savory chorizo bread pudding. A great deal is the daily two-course tasting menu that changes weekly, which in the past has included standouts such as arugula dotted with pear and gorgonzola, halibut with tomato and couscous, and warm chocolate cake with caramel ice cream.

Steak. Dinner. Outdoor seating. Children's menu. $86 and up

★★★TRADER VIC'S

6850 E. Main St., Scottsdale, 480-248-2000, 866-882-4484; www.hotelvalleyho.com

This branch of the classic 1950s Polynesian-themed restaurant serves up potent punches in bamboo coolers and perfect mai tais, which it purports to have invented in 1944, plus pupu platters of egg rolls and crab Rangoon. Entrées include wok-fried Szechuan prawns and ginger beef, or crispy duck with moo-shu pancakes. The décor takes its cue from the tiki bars of the past, with plenty of rattan and a totem here or there, but is updated.

Asian Pacific Rim. Dinner. Outdoor seating. $16-35

★★★ZINC BISTRO

15034 N. Scottsdale Road, Scottsdale, 480-603-0922; www.zincbistroaz.com

A high-energy spot, Zinc Bistro is in the Kierland Commons shopping center. The Parisian-style space, decorated with a tin ceiling and solid zinc bar, serves up crêpes, omelets, steaks, onion soup and more bistro fare.

French bistro. Lunch, dinner. Outdoor seating. Bar. $16-35

SPAS

★★★★THE CENTRE FOR WELL-BEING AT THE PHOENICIAN

The Phoenician, 6000 E. Camelback Road, Scottsdale, 480-941-8200, 800-888-8234; www.centreforwellbeing.com

This spa always thinks big, which means services here are on the cutting edge. Want to be more Zen in the real world? Sign up for a private meditation session, where you can learn visualization and other stress-reducing techniques. Have to work 100 hours just to take a week off? The Jin Shin Jyutsu utilizes a series of holding techniques to alleviate tension blocked in the body. Tend to overdo it on the golf course? The neuromuscular treatment offers spot relief for injuries. Of course, you'll want to go home looking as great as you feel, and for that there's no shortage of wraps, facials and scrubs. Even the state-of-the-art gym is inviting.

★★★THE SPA AT CAMELBACK INN
Camelback Inn, 5402 E. Lincoln Drive, Scottsdale, 480-948-1700, 800-582-2169; www.camelbackspa.com

The Spa at Camelback Inn's sophisticated chocolate-brown woods, flagstone walls and expansive windows create an inviting, placid retreat. If the gas fireplace in the main relaxation room doesn't soothe your spirit, head outside to the solarium and let the sound of rippling water from a flowing fountain do the trick. Relax in your own private casita, while you choose from the menu of massages, facials and body treatments, many of which draw from Native American techniques and indigenous ingredients.

★★★★SPA AT FOUR SEASONS RESORT SCOTTSDALE AT TROON NORTH
Four Seasons Resort Scottsdale at Troon North, 10600 E. Crescent Moon Drive, Scottsdale, 480-513-5145, 888-207-9696; www.fourseasons.com

You're guaranteed to relax at this 12,000-square-foot spa located in the Sonoran Desert. The resort's moonlight massage is the perfect way to end the day. A masseuse will come to your balcony or terrace to knead away your stresses under the stars. You'll also find facials that feature local, seasonal ingredients, including saguaro blossom, the state flower, as well as the more common green tea and honey. For the ultimate in pampering, get the signature pinnacle facial, which starts with your back, hands and feet being exfoliated and massaged. Then comes a champagne and caviar collagen facial that almost sounds good enough to eat. Half-day and full-day packages are available. There is also a full-service salon and fitness center here.

★★★★WILLOW STREAM SPA
Fairmont Scottsdale, 7575 E. Princess Drive, Scottsdale, 480-585-2732, 800-908-9540; www.fairmont.com

The facilities at the Fairmont Scottsdale are top-notch—from championship golf courses to great restaurants—and the spa is no exception. Many of the treatments make use of the Havasupai Waterfall (inspired by the oasis of waterfalls in the Grand Canyon) on the spa's first floor. The Havasupai Body Oasis treatment combines warm eucalyptus and herbal baths with the healing power of the waterfalls. Other services also reflect local surroundings. The Desert Purification features a body mask of cornmeal, clay and oats. An ayate cloth (made from the cactus plant) is then used to exfoliate skin. Or keep it simple with a facial or massage, and then hit the beauty salon for a spa pedicure.

WHERE TO SHOP

KIERLAND COMMONS
Scottsdale Road and Greenway Parkway, Scottsdale, 480-348-1577; www.kierlandcommons.com

This 38-acre urban village has a traditional Main Street feel and pedestrian-friendly layout. The well-landscaped streets are lined with more than 50 upscale retailers, such as 7 For All Mankind and Juicy Couture, and restaurants, including Morton's Steak House and P.F. Chang's China Bistro.
Monday-Saturday 10 a.m.-9 p.m., Sunday noon-6 p.m.

SCOTTSDALE FASHION SQUARE
7014-590 E. Camelback Road, Scottsdale, 480-941-2140; www.fashionsquare.com

The largest shopping destination in the Southwest features more than 225 retailers, including Neiman Marcus, Nordstrom, Louis Vuitton, Sephora and Tiffany & Co. After hitting the shops, relax in one of the sit-down restaurants or one of the less-formal food court eateries, or catch a movie.
Monday-Saturday, 10 a.m.-9 p.m., Sunday 11 a.m.-6 p.m.

CENTRAL ARIZONA

Phoenix may be the heart of Central Arizona, but the region offers a lot more than the big city. In Carefree, the immense Tonto National Forest stretches to the north and east and the city has the largest and most accurate sundial in the Western Hemisphere. An affluent community close to Scottsdale in the Valley of the Sun, Fountain Hills offers distinct beauty and lots of opportunities for outdoor recreation, and a casino for those who'd rather stay indoors.

Mesa, Spanish for "table," sits atop a plateau overlooking the Valley of the Sun and is one of the state's largest and fastest-growing cities. Mesa offers year-round golf, tennis, hiking and water sports. It also provides easy access to other Arizona and Southwest attractions. Founded as a trading post by the father of former Senator Carl Hayden, Tempe is now the site of Arizona State University, the state's oldest institution of higher learning, but it also has several cultural hot spots. If you are eager to try out one of the famed Western dude ranches, head to Wickenburg. It's the oldest town north of Tucson and well known for its dude ranches.

WHAT TO SEE

CHANDLER
CASA PALOMA
7131 W. Ray Road, Chandler, 480-777-2272; www.shopcasapaloma.com

It's worth stopping at this upscale strip mall with shops like makeup store Philosophy and chains like Ann Taylor. After shopping, pamper yourself at Rolf's Salon at the Foothills or dine at one of five restaurants.

CHANDLER CENTER FOR THE ARTS
250 N. Arizona Ave., Chandler, 480-782-2680; www.chandlercenter.org

This 64,000-square-foot performance center is known for its superb acoustics.

HIGHLIGHTS

WHAT ARE THE TOP THINGS TO DO?

PLAY A HAND OR TWO AT FORT MCDOWELL CASINO

You'll want to hit the tables at this casino, which offers the largest card room in the state. If cards aren't your thing, take a chance in the 1,400-seat bingo hall, the keno lounge or the endless rows of slot machines.

WALK AMONG THE WILD AT THE WILDLIFE WORLD ZOO & AQUARIUM

This place has the only aquarium between Albuquerque and San Diego. Aside from the marine animals, you can see white tigers, African lions, red and gray kangaroos and more.

GET SOME LAUGHS AT THE TEMPE IMPROVISATION COMEDY THEATRE

The comedy theater and restaurant offers a mix of big-name comedians, like Bobcat Goldthwait and Jamie Kennedy, as well as local yuksters.

COOL OFF AT TEMPE TOWN LAKE

You can lay out along the shore of this 224-acre lake. Or you can rent a rowboat, pedal boat or kayak for more active pursuits. Kids will enjoy the popular Splash Playground water park on the premises.

The London City Opera, Jay Leno, Anne Murray, Rita Moreno, Bob Newhart and the Phoenix Boys Choir are among the performers who have helped the center earn its reputation for staging shows that bring audiences to their feet. The main auditorium seats 1,550 but can be subdivided into three separate halls for smaller shows.

WILD HORSE PASS CASINO
5550 W. Wild Horse Pass, Chandler, 800-946-4452; www.wingilariver.com
With nearly 170,000 square feet of gaming action, this casino offers lots of options. The card room is decked out with 19 poker tables, while the bingo hall has 1,200 seats. There's also a 24-hour live keno section, more than 500 slot machines, a hotel and plenty of restaurants and entertainment options from which to choose.

FOUNTAIN HILLS
FORT MCDOWELL CASINO
Fort McDowell Road and Beeline Highway, Fountain Hills, 800-843-3678;
www.fortmcdowellcasino.com
This casino boasts the state's largest card room, a 1,400-seat bingo hall with jackpots as high as $50,000, a keno lounge with million-dollar payouts and 475 slot machines that keep the decibel level high night and day. Spend some of your winnings in one of four restaurants or at the lounge, which offers live entertainment daily.

LITCHFIELD PARK
WILDLIFE WORLD ZOO & AQUARIUM
16501 W. Northern Ave., Litchfield Park, 623-935-9453; www.wildlifeworld.com
You'll see white tigers, African lions, camels and rhinos at this zoo. It boasts a large collection of exotic animals, about 3,000, representing nearly 600 species. Wildlife World has the only public aquarium between Albuquerque and San Diego.
Admission: adults $27.50, children 3-12 $14.25, children 2 and under free.
Daily 9 a.m.-5 p.m.

MESA
ARIZONA MUSEUM FOR YOUTH
35 N. Robson St., Mesa, 480-644-2467; www.arizonamuseumforyouth.com
The exhibits frequently change at this hands-on fine arts museum for children. The museum keeps an art area where kids can learn creative fundamentals like drawing and building.
Admission: $6.50, children under 1 free. Tuesday-Saturday 10 a.m.-4 p.m.,
Sunday noon-4 p.m.

ARIZONA MUSEUM OF NATURAL HISTORY
53 N. MacDonald St., Mesa, 480-644-2230; www.mesasouthwestmuseum.com
Learn about the Native Americans who lived here, see a replica of a Spanish mission and a hall dedicated to dinosaurs as you explore this 80,000-square-foot regional resource.
Admission: adults $10, seniors $9, students $8, children 3-12 $6, children under 3 free.
Tuesday-Friday 10 a.m.-5 p.m., Saturday 11 a.m.-5 p.m., Sunday 1-5 p.m.

TEMPE

ARIZONA HISTORICAL SOCIETY MUSEUM
Papago Park, 1300 N. College Ave., Tempe, 480-929-0292; www.arizonahistoricalsociety.org

Wander through this regional museum to learn more about 20th-century life in the Salt River Valley. The 28,000 items in its collection include about 14,000 pieces in a country store and 2,800 stage props and sets from the 37-year run of the locally loved *Wallace and Ladmo Show* on KPHO Television. Another exhibit focuses on the many ways World War II transformed Arizona.

Admission: adults $3, seniors $2, children $2, children under 12 free. Tuesday-Saturday 10 a.m.-4 p.m., Sunday noon-4 p.m.

BIG SURF
1500 N. McClintock, Tempe, 480-947-2477

Check out America's original water park, a 20-acre desert oasis with a Polynesian theme. Ride some big ones in the wave pool, whoosh down 16 slippery water slides and more.

June-mid-August, daily; late May and mid-late August, weekends.

PHOENIX ROCK GYM
1353 E. University Drive, Tempe, 480-921-8322; www.phoenixrockgym.com

Scale 30-foot walls at Arizona's largest climbing gym. Beginners receive brief video training and a hands-on orientation. Gear is available to rent.

Admission: adults $11, children $8. Daily.

TEMPE BICYCLE PROGRAM
Tempe, 480-350-2775; www.tempe.gov

This bicycle-friendly city has more than 165 miles of bikeways. Most major destinations provide bicycle racks, including some particularly eye-catching ones designed by local artists. Several bicycle shops offer rentals for as little as $15 per day and give free bikeway maps.

TEMPE IMPROVISATION COMEDY THEATRE
930 E. University Drive, Tempe, 480-921-9877; www.tempeimprov.info

Check out some of the country's best stand-up comedians at this improv theater. An optional dinner precedes the 8 p.m. shows.

Thursday-Sunday.

TEMPE TOWN LAKE
620 N. Mill Ave., Tempe, 480-350-8625; www.tempe.gov

Tempe Town Lake on the Rio Salado, near the Mill Avenue shopping and dining district, is a 224-acre, two-mile waterway that offers rowboats, pedal boats, kayaks and canoes for rent, along with chartered cruises. The nicely renovated 1931 Tempe Beach Park has shaded picnic groves, sandy play areas, a grassy amphitheater and the popular Splash Playground water park (late April-late September). Take the tour, or simply enjoy the shoreline.

WICKENBURG
DESERT CABALLEROS WESTERN MUSEUM
21 N. Frontier St., Wickenburg, 928-624-2272; www.westernmuseum.org

This museum houses a Western art gallery, a diorama room, a circa-1915 street scene, period rooms, a mineral display and a Native American exhibit. Exhibits have included Best of the West, a look at art depicting the landscapes and people of the West.

Admission: adults $7.50, seniors $6, children under 17 free. Monday-Saturday 10 a.m.-5 p.m., Sunday noon-4 p.m.

FRONTIER STREET
Wickenburg, 928-684-5479; www.wickenburgchamber.com

This historic street is preserved in early 1900s style. The train depot, which houses the chamber of commerce; brick Hassayampa building, a former hotel; and many other historic buildings may be toured.

THE JAIL TREE
Tegner Street and Wickenburg Way, Wickenburg, 928-684-5479; www.wickenburgchamber.com

This tree was used to chain rowdy prisoners from 1863 through 1890, until the first jail was built. Friends and relatives visited the prisoners and brought picnic lunches.

WHERE TO STAY

CAREFREE
★★★THE BOULDERS RESORT & GOLDEN DOOR SPA
34631 N. Tom Darlington Drive, Carefree, 480-488-9009, 888-579-2631; www.theboulders.com

Located in the foothills of the Sonoran Desert just north of Scottsdale, the Boulders Resort and Golden Door Spa blends perfectly with the surrounding rock outcroppings, ancient boulders and saguaro cactus plants. The adobe casitas are distinguished by overstuffed leather chairs, exposed beams and Mexican tiles, while one-, two- and three-bedroom Pueblo Villas are ideal for families. The resort boasts a first-rate tennis facility and an 18-hole championship golf course. There's also rock climbing, hiking and tours of Native American cave dwellings and ruins. Guided night hikes using night vision equipment are especially fun.

215 rooms. Restaurant, bar. Business center. Fitness center. Pool. Spa. Pets accepted. Golf. Tennis. $351 and up

CHANDLER
★★★CROWNE PLAZA SAN MARCOS GOLF RESORT
1 San Marcos Place, Chandler, 480-812-0900, 800-528-8071;www.sanmarcosresort.com

Built in 1912, this property was the first golf course in Arizona. Located just a few miles from companies such as Motorola and Intel, it's a great choice for business travelers. Families can enjoy tennis and horseback riding. Guest rooms go all out to help you catch some z's, offering eye pillows, ear plugs, lavender spray and sleep CDs.

295 rooms. Restaurant, bar. Business center. Pool. Pets accepted. Golf. Tennis. $61-150

★★★SHERATON WILD HORSE PASS RESORT & SPA
5594 W. Wild Horse Pass Blvd., Chandler, 602-225-0100, 800-325-3535;
www.wildhorsepassresort.com

This unique resort on Gila River tribal land blends the look and feel of the area with the amenities and service of a contemporary hotel. Each detail of the interior has been added for its significance to Native American traditions, including the petroglyph-engraved furniture. The destination resort also features two 18-hole golf courses, the 17,500-square-foot Aji spa, an equestrian center for riding lessons and trail rides, jogging paths and tennis courts. Be sure to plan on dinner at Kai Restaurant, where chef Michael O'Dowd creates contemporary American cuisine inspired by local ingredients. A two-mile replica of the Gila River runs through the property and offers boat rides to the Wild Horse Pass Casino or the Whirlwind Golf Club.

500 rooms. Restaurant, bar. Pool. Spa. Pets accepted. Golf. Tennis. $251-350

FOUNTAIN HILLS
★★★INN AT EAGLE MOUNTAIN
9800 N. Summer Hill Blvd., Fountain Hills, 480-816-3000, 800-992-8083;
www.innateaglemountain.com

This small boutique hotel sits on the 18th fairway with views of Red Mountain, overlooking Scottsdale and Arizona. The suites have kiva fireplaces, sitting areas and whirlpool tubs. Six of the rooms have a theme, ranging from the Frank Lloyd Wright-inspired décor in the Prairie suite to the cowboy items in the Wild West suite.

42 rooms. Restaurant, bar. Pool. $151-250

GOLD CANYON
★★★GOLD CANYON GOLF RESORT
6100 S. Kings Ranch Road, Gold Canyon, 480-982-9090, 800-827-5281; www.gcgr.com

Located on 3,300 acres in the foothills of the Superstition Mountains, this resort is a good choice for golfers who want a value-focused retreat. The resort features a golf school and many scenic holes. The accommodations include suites and private casitas, some with fireplaces or whirlpools.

101 rooms. Restaurant, bar. Fitness center. Spa. Pets accepted. Golf. $61-150

LITCHFIELD PARK
★★★THE WIGWAM GOLF RESORT AND SPA
300 Wigwam Blvd., Litchfield Park, 623-935-3811, 800-327-0396;www.wigwamresort.com

Once a private club for executives of the Goodyear Tire Company, the Wigwam Resort is one of Arizona's most storied hotels. The rooms and suites highlight authentic regional design with whitewashed wood furniture, slate floors and Mexican ceramic tiles. The property includes award-winning golf courses, nine tennis courts, two pools with a water slide and a Red Door spa. Five restaurants and bars serve everything from filet mignon to sandwiches and salads.

331 rooms. Restaurant, bar. Business center. Spa. Pets accepted. Golf. Tennis. $251-350

MESA

★★★ARIZONA GOLF RESORT HOTEL & CONFERENCE CENTER

425 S. Power Road, Mesa, 480-832-3202, 800-528-8282; www. azgolfresort.com

Tropical palms and beautiful lakes surround this East Valley resort occupying 150 acres. Guest suites are arranged in clusters with courtyards, barbecue grills and heated spas. There is a golf school for novices, but more experienced duffers will get excited about the 14th hole of the championship course, which requires a 175 yard-shot through the trees and over water.

187 rooms. Restaurant, bar. Business center. Pool. Pets accepted. Golf. $61-150

★★★HILTON PHOENIX EAST/MESA

1011 W. Holmes Ave., Mesa, 480-833-5555, 800-445-8667; www.phoenixeastmesa.hilton.com

This hotel is centrally located in the East Valley, allowing for easy freeway access to many attractions and businesses in all directions. Phoenix Sky Harbor airport is 12 miles away. Guest rooms are arranged around the large atrium lobby and are decorated in rich autumn colors with velvety textures. French doors lead to a balcony. Relax by the pool, go horseback riding or hit the links at one of the nearby courses. The Zuni Bar & Grill serves a breakfast buffet and Sunday brunch. The bar is a good spot to meet up and drink one of the micro-brewed beers or margaritas.

260 rooms. Restaurant, bar. Business center. Fitness center. Pool. $61-150

PARADISE VALLEY

★★★THE HERMOSA INN

5532 N. Palo Cristi Road, Paradise Valley, 602-955-8614, 800-241-1210; www.hermosainn.com

Built by cowboy artist Lon Megargee as his home and studio, this inn is a nice alternative to the bigger resorts. Situated on a half acre marked by olive and mesquite trees, towering palms and brilliant flowers, the accommodations range from cozy casitas to huge villas. Rooms feature authentic furnishings and original artwork painted by Megargee some 70 years ago. The onsite restaurant, LON's, is Arizona's last authentic hacienda.

35 rooms. Restaurant, bar. Complimentary breakfast. Fitness center. Pool. Pets accepted. Tennis. $151-250

WHAT ARE THE BEST BOUTIQUE HOTELS IN CENTRAL ARIZONA?

Inn at Eagle Mountain:
This small, cozy hotel overlooks Red Mountain. To add to the intimate vibe, the suites have kiva fireplaces, sitting areas and whirlpool tubs.

Hermosa Inn:
Cowboy artist Lon Megargee originally built this hotel as his home and studio. Some of his original artwork adorns the walls of the casitas and villas.

Sanctuary on Camelback Mountain:
The rooms at this hotel ooze contemporary desert chic with woodblock floors, glass-tiled dry bars and luxe bathrooms with travertine marble showers and separate tubs.

★★★INTERCONTINENTAL MONTELUCIA RESORT & SPA

4949 E. Lincoln Drive, Paradise Valley, 480-627-3200, 888-627-3010; www.icmontelucia.com

Nestled within the Camelback Mountains, Montelucia's grounds cover 35 sprawling desert acres. There is no shortage of luxury at this Mediterranean-inspired resort. The grounds are lush, the restaurants are premier and the guestrooms are spacious. Take a dip in one or all of the five serene swimming pools. Sprinkled throughout the property are hidden plazas—cozy spots to sit and take in the peaceful surroundings. Arcade walkways lead guests to the numerous "pueblos." Standard rooms have rich colors and deep wood, while suites have beautiful fresco ceilings, antiques and two even have their own fountains in their living room. The kid's club is top-notch and caters to a wide range of activities; an indoor game room has Wii and Guitar Hero. The Oasis village is like walking into a new resort. Only adults are allowed to stay in the rooms here and the pool is a peaceful enclave. For dinner, be sure to make a reservation at Prado, Chef Claudio Urciuoli's signature restaurant. The menu features master dishes such as the Colorado lamb t-bone with black olives and wild mint and a daily paella special that serves two. The spa is outstanding and includes every amenity one could desire.

285 rooms. Restaurant, bar. Business center. Fitness center. Pool. Spa. $351 and up

★★★SANCTUARY ON CAMELBACK MOUNTAIN

5700 E. McDonald Drive, Paradise Valley, 480-948-2100, 800-245-2051; www.sanctuaryoncamelback.com

This boutique hotel overlooking the valley from Camelback Mountain truly is a sanctuary. You won't find typical Southwestern décor here. Casitas are the essence of desert chic with their spectacular contemporary design. Mountain casitas have woodblock floors, glass-tiled dry bars and luxurious bathrooms with travertine marble. The multilevel spa casitas boast floor-to-ceiling windows and walk-in closets, while the spa suites have outdoor soaking tubs in case you just can't bring yourself to walk the short distance to the large infinity-edge pool. Elements restaurant offers American fare with an Asian influence, served in a contemporary, elegant setting.

105 rooms. Restaurant. Business center. Fitness center. Pool. Pets accepted. Tennis. $251-350

TEMPE

★★★THE BUTTES, A MARRIOTT RESORT

2000 Westcourt Way, Tempe, 602-225-9000, 888-867-7492; www.marriott.com

This secluded resort sits atop a bluff overlooking Phoenix and the surrounding mountains. Take a dip in the pool surrounded by a lush landscape and a waterfall, or enjoy one of the four hot tubs carved out of the mountainside. Relax in the Narande spa, play some sand volleyball or horseshoes, or get in a game of tennis on the resort's eight courts. The Top of the Rock restaurant is a great spot for dining and offers beautiful views.

353 rooms. Restaurant, bar. Pool. Spa. Tennis. $151-250

WHERE TO EAT

CAREFREE

★★★LATILLA

Boulders Resort & Golden Door Spa, 34631 N. Tom Darlington Drive, Carefree, 480-488-7316, 888-579-2631; www.theboulders.com

The cuisine at this glass-enclosed restaurant in the Boulders Resort & Golden Door Spa focuses on Southwestern-influenced food, such as mesquite grilled pork tenderloin with portabello mushrooms, sweet potato and linguiça hash, sunchoke purée and pasilla jus. The rustic, cozy dining room is decorated with Ocotillo branches called latillas, which means "little sticks" in Spanish. The outdoor patio, warmed by a blazing fire, is an ideal spot to have a drink after dinner.

Contemporary American, Southwestern. Dinner. Reservations recommended. Outdoor seating. Bar. $36-85

CHANDLER

★★★★★KAI

Sheraton Wild Horse Pass Resort & Spa, 5594 W. Wild Horse Pass Blvd., Chandler, 602-385-5726; www.whpdining.com

Located in the Sheraton Wild Horse Pass Resort, this sophisticated restaurant, under the helm of chef Michael O'Dowd, showcases locally grown produce and a surprisingly rich Arizona-made olive oil in recipes that merge contemporary tastes and time-honored Native American techniques. (Kai means "seed" in Pima.) The results include lobster tail, corn and avocado atop fry bread, and rack of lamb sauced with a mole made from American Indian seeds. The staff guides diners through the experience with a laidback but confident manner, and can aptly describe any of the hundreds of fine bottles of wine on the list.

Southwestern. Dinner. Closed Sunday-Monday. Outdoor seating. Bar. $36-85

PARADISE VALLEY

★★★ELEMENTS

5700 E. McDonald Road, Paradise Valley, 480-607-2300, 800-298-9766; www.elementsrestaurant.com

Situated on the grounds of the Sanctuary at Camelback Mountain, Elements is a sleek spot that adds a touch of sophistication to leisurely breakfasts, power lunches and romantic dinners. Its clean, minimalist décor features stone and wood accents and expansive floor-to-ceiling windows that offer spectacular views of the sunset over Paradise Valley. The kitchen uses fresh, seasonal ingredients to create the menu of Asian-influenced contemporary American cuisine, which includes dishes such as chilled sesame and lime noodle salad, chili-cured duck breast and braised short ribs with citrus-scented mushrooms. The Jade Bar is a great spot for a drink.

American, Asian. Breakfast, lunch, dinner, Sunday brunch. Outdoor seating. Bar. $36-85

★★★LON'S

The Hermosa Inn, 5532 N. Palo Cristi Road, Paradise Valley, 602-955-7878; www.lons.com

Built by Southwestern artist Lon Megargee in the 1930s, the inn's adobe design and rustic furnishings are a fitting setting for some of the best American comfort food in the Phoenix area. The chef grows many herbs, heirloom fruits and vegetables and grains in the onsite garden to use in fresh seasonal specials, such as pork tenderloin with prickly pear braised cabbage, green beans and mashed potatoes and roasted lamb with goat cheese herb grits.

American. Lunch, dinner, Sunday brunch. Reservations recommended. Outdoor seating. Children's menu. Bar. $36-85

★★★PRADO

InterContinental Montelucia Resort & Spa, 4949 E. Lincoln Drive, Paradise Valley, 888-627-3010; www.pradolife.com

The signature restaurant within the InterContinental Montelucia Resort & Spa is popular among locals and resort guests alike. Paintings of Flamenco dancers line the wall and antiques fill the space. Thursday through Sunday, a talented Spanish guitar trio plays at just the right volume in the bar. There's even an Italian "romance" host who excels at storytelling and entertains diners. The cuisine is rustic and authentic, drawing from local and seasonal ingredients. Pasta dishes may include ricotta and spinach raviolini with heriloom tomatoes and local baby zucchini; your second course might be a juicy rib eye steak with sweet potatoes, shishito pepper and a spicy pepper jelly. There's also a three-course tasting menu for $39 ($59 with wines). Wines come mostly from Italy, Spain and France. Specialty cocktails include pisco sours, caiparinhas and mojitos, all with their own unique twist.

Italian. Breakfast, lunch, dinner. Reservations recommended. Bar. $35-86

SPAS

CAREFREE

★★★GOLDEN DOOR SPA AT THE BOULDERS

The Boulders Resort, 34631 N. Tom Darlington Drive, Carefree, 480-595-3500, 888-579-2631; www.theboulders.com

This branch of the original California spa is the jewel in the crown of the Boulders Resort. Many treatments nod to the region's Native American history. Ancient Ayurvedic principles are revived in the mystical treatments of bindi balancing, where crushed herbs exfoliate and light oils moisturize your skin, and shirodhara, which begins with massaging warm oil into your scalp and concludes with a mini facial massage and a heated hand and foot treatment. The 33,000-square-foot spa also includes a meditation labyrinth inspired by Hopi medicine wheels and a movement studio, which offers yoga, tai chi, Pilates, kickboxing and more.

CHANDLER

★★★★AJI SPA

Sheraton Wild Horse Pass Resort & Spa, 5594 W. Wild Horse Pass Blvd., Chandler, 602-225-0100; www.wildhorsepassresort.com

This resort spa will transport you a million miles away. Traditional Native American healing therapies are the backbone of Aji Spa, such as the Ho'dai massage, which uses hot rocks to soothe muscles. You'll get a dose of culture along with your comfort, too—meditation sessions, medicinal massages and a one-of-a-kind healing treatment that combines massage and ancient Pima techniques are among the offerings that honor Native American traditions.

PARADISE VALLEY
★★★JOYA SPA
InterContinental Montelucia Resort & Spa, 4949 E. Lincoln Drive, Paradise Valley, 888-627-3010; www.joyaspa.com

This gorgeous Moroccan-themed spa is a world unto itself. The 31,000-square-foot space is lavishly designed with rich colors, tented ceilings and dark walkways. The spa has one of the most complete and luxurious locker rooms, beautiful suites (some with antiqued hammered copper tubs and day beds) and a private pool on the top floor that overlooks the Camelback Mountain. Treatments are equally fabulous. The spa features an authentic Hamman as well as a yoga and fitness studio with views of the mountain. Try the Joyambrosia massage, which uses organic oils including Morocco's "liquid gold" argan oil, Spanish citrus, Moroccan mint and spices applied with circular movements and gentle stretching. It's both aromatic and relaxing.

★★★★THE SANCTUARY SPA AT SANCTUARY CAMELBACK MOUNTAIN
Sanctuary Camelback Mountain Resort and Spa, 5700 E. McDonald Drive, Paradise Valley, 480-948-2100, 800-245-2051; www.sanctuaryoncamelback.com

Originally designed as a tennis club in the 1950s by Frank Lloyd Wright protégé Hiram Hudson Benedict, the resort still offers an understated elegance first defined by Benedict. The resort's spa seems to include practically every treatment under the sun, from standard facials to acupuncture. The spa menu includes several Asian-inspired treatments, including Thai massage and shiatsu. The resort retains its commitment to the championship tennis courts that defined it from the start, but the grounds are also ideal for yoga and meditation. Guided desert hikes are available.

TUSCON

Tucson offers a rare combination of delightful Western living, colorful desert, mountain scenery and cosmopolitan culture. It is one of several U.S. cities that developed under four flags. The Spanish standard flew first over the Presidio of Tucson, built to withstand Apache attacks in 1776. Later, Tucson flew the flags of Mexico, the Confederate States and finally, the United States. Today, Tucson is a resort area, an educational center, headquarters for the Coronado National Forest and a place of business for several large industries. The city has many shops, restaurants, resorts and attractions.

WHAT TO SEE

BIOSPHERE 2
32540 Biosphere Road, Oracle, 520-838-6200; www.bio2.com

An ambitious attempt to learn more about our planet's ecosystems began in

HIGHLIGHTS

WHAT ARE THE TOP THINGS TO DO IN TUCSON?

GO OUTDOORS AT CORONADO NATIONAL FOREST
Coronado National Forest's 2 million acres offer endless outdoorsy possibilities. Fishing, bird watching, hiking and horseback riding are just a few of your choices.

TAKE FLIGHT AT PIMA AIR & SPACE MUSEUM
Pima is one of the biggest air and space museums in the world. It houses a top-notch collection of more than 300 aircraft and spacecraft.

BLAST OFF AT THE TITAN MISSILE MUSEUM
This may be your only chance to tour an underground intercontinental ballistic missile site, which was used as a deterrent during the Cold War.

TAKE IN THE LOCAL ART AT THE TUCSON MUSEUM OF ART AND HISTORIC BLOCK
The Tucson Museum houses its collection in historic adobe homes. Check out the display of American West art, which examines the landscape and its people.

SEE THE CACTI IN SAGUARO NATIONAL PARK
The enormous saguaro cacti at this national park have become icons for the American West. This is one of the few places in the country where you can see them.

September 1991 with the first in a series of missions undertaken inside this 3½-acre, glass-enclosed, self-sustaining model of Earth. (The crew of researchers relies entirely on the air, water and food generated and recycled within the structure.) It contains more than 3,500 species of plants and animals in multiple ecosystems, including a tropical rain forest with an 85-foot-high mountain. Visitors are permitted within the biospherian living areas of the enclosure. Walking tours include multimedia introduction to Biosphere 2. *Daily 9 a.m.-4 p.m.*

CENTER FOR CREATIVE PHOTOGRAPHY
University of Arizona, 1030 N. Olive Road, Tucson, 520-621-7968;
www.creativephotography.org
This collection of art by more than 2,000 photographers includes the archives
of Ansel Adams and Richard Avedon.
Admission: free. Gallery: Monday-Friday 9 a.m.-5 p.m., Saturday-Sunday 1-4 p.m.

CORONADO NATIONAL FOREST
300 W. Congress St., Tucson, 520-388-8300; www.fs.fed.us
Mount Lemmon Recreation Area, part of this two-million-acre forest, offers
fishing, bird-watching, hiking, horseback riding, picnicking, skiing and
camping. Madera Canyon offers recreation facilities and a lodge. Pena Blanca
Lake and Recreation Area and the Chiricahua Wilderness area in the southeast
corner of the state are part of the 12 areas that make up the forest. The Santa
Catalina Ranger District, located in Tucson (*520-749-8700*), has its headquarters at Sabino Canyon, 12 miles northeast on Sabino Canyon Road; a ¼-mile
nature trail begins at the headquarters, as does a shuttle ride almost four miles
into Sabino Canyon.

FLANDRAU SCIENCE CENTER & PLANETARIUM
University of Arizona, 1601 E. University Blvd., Tucson, 520-621-7827; www.flandrau.org
The center features interactive, hands-on science exhibits and an extensive display
of minerals. Check out the sky shows and viewings with the 16-inch telescope.
Admission: $7.50 adults, children $5, children under 4 free. Monday-Wednesday 9 a.m.-5 p.m.,
Thursday-Saturday 9 a.m.-5 p.m., 7-9 p.m., Sunday 1-5 p.m.; planetarium shows (limited
hours). Nightly telescope viewing: Mid-August-mid-May, Wednesday-Saturday 6:40-10 p.m.;
mid-May-mid-August, Wednesday-Saturday 7:30-10 p.m.

INTERNATIONAL WILDLIFE MUSEUM
4800 W. Gates Pass Road, Tucson, 520-629-0100; www.thewildlifemuseum.org
The museum includes hundreds of wildlife exhibits from around the world,
hands-on interactive computer displays, videos and a café.
Admission: adults $7, seniors and students $5.50, children 4-12 $2.50, children 3 and under
free. Monday-Friday 9 a.m.-5 p.m., Saturday-Sunday 9 a.m.-6 p.m.

OLD TOWN ARTISANS
201 N. Court Ave., Tucson, 520-623-6024, 800-782-8072; www.oldtownartisans.com
Restored adobe buildings (circa 1850s) in the historic El Presidio neighbor-
hood serve as shops for handcrafted Southwestern and Latin American art.
September-May, Monday-Saturday 9:30 a.m.-5:30 p.m., Sunday 11 a.m.-5 p.m.; June-August,
Monday-Saturday 10 a.m.-4 p.m., Sunday 11 a.m.-4 p.m.

PIMA AIR & SPACE MUSEUM
6000 E. Valencia Road, Tucson, 520-574-0462; www.pimaair.org
The museum puts on aviation history exhibits with an outstanding collection of
more than 250 aircraft, both military and civilian. Walking tours are also available.
Admission: adults $14-16, children $12-13, children under 7 free. Daily 9 a.m.-5 p.m.

REID PARK ZOO
1030 S. Randolph Way, Tucson, 520-881-4753; www.tucsonzoo.org

Aside from seeing polar bears, giraffes and white rhinos, you'll also find a rose garden and outdoor performance center at the zoo.

Admission: adults $6, seniors $4, $2, children under 2 free. Daily 9 a.m.-4 p.m.

TITAN MISSILE MUSEUM
1580 W. Duval Mine Road, Sahuarita, 520-625-7736; www.titanmissilemuseum.org

A deactivated Titan II missile is on display, as is a UH1F helicopter and other exhibits. A one-hour guided tour begins with a briefing and includes a visit down into the missile silo. The silo may also be viewed from a glass observation area located at the museum level.

Tours: adults $8.50, seniors $7.50, children 7-12 $5, children 6 and under free. Daily 9 a.m.-5 p.m.

TOHONO CHUL PARK
7366 N. Paseo del Norte, Tucson, 520-742-6455; www.tohonochulpark.org

This 37-acre preserve has more than 400 species of arid climate plants, nature trails, a demonstration garden, a geology wall and an ethnobotanical garden. You'll find many varieties of wild birds visiting the park. There are also exhibits, galleries, a tearoom and gift shops in a restored adobe house on the grounds. Walking tours are available.

Admission: adults $7, seniors $5, children $2, children under 5 free. Daily 8 a.m.-5 p.m.

TUCSON BOTANICAL GARDENS
2150 N. Alvernon Way, Tucson, 520-326-9686; www.tucsonbotanical.org

The gardens include Mediterranean and landscaping plants, native wildflowers, a tropical greenhouse and xeriscape/solar demonstration garden.

Admission: $7, children 4-12 $3, children 3 and under free. Daily 8:30 a.m.-4:30 p.m.

TUCSON MOUNTAIN PARK
Ajo Way & Kinney Road, Tucson, 520-883-4200; www.co.pima.az.us

You'll see more than 18,000 acres of saguaro cactus and mountain scenery at this park. There are also picnic facilities provided.

TUCSON MUSEUM OF ART AND HISTORIC BLOCK
140 N. Main Ave., Tucson, 520-624-2333; www.tucsonarts.com

This art museum is housed in six renovated buildings within the boundaries of El Presidio Historic District (circa 1800). In it you'll find pre-Columbian, Spanish-colonial and Western artifacts; decorative arts and paintings; art of the Americas; contemporary art and crafts; and a number of changing exhibits.

Admission: $8, seniors $6, students $3, children under 12 free. Free first Sunday of the month. Tuesday-Saturday 10 a.m.-4 p.m., Sunday noon-5 p.m.

WHERE TO STAY

★★★ARIZONA INN
2200 E. Elm St., Tucson, 520-325-1541, 800-933-1093; www.arizonainn.com

This inn was built in 1930 by Arizona Congresswoman Isabella Greenway, and is still owned by her family today. Guests who stay here are treated to quiet comfort with spacious, individually decorated casita-style rooms. Each room comes with a refrigerator, coffee maker, flat-screen TV, DVD player and DVD library. But you may not get to watch any movies since you'll likely be busy walking along the 14 acres of landscaped lawns and gardens

95 rooms. Restaurant, bar. Pool. Tennis. $151-250

★★★HILTON TUCSON EL CONQUISTADOR GOLF AND TENNIS RESORT

10000 N. Oracle Road, Tucson, 520-544-5000, 800-325-7832; www.hiltonelconquistador.com

Duffers and tennis players will want to brush up on their games at the Hilton Tucson El Conquistador. This resort and country club has extensive golf and tennis facilities, with 45 holes of golf on three championship courses and 31 lighted tennis courts. Each of the rooms has a patio and balcony, which are perfect places for you to perch and admire the breathtaking Santa Catalina Mountains on 500 acres of high Sonoran Desert terrain. The spa offers a full range of treatments.

428 rooms. Restaurant, bar. Business center. Pool. Spa. Pets accepted. Golf. Tennis. $151-250

★★★THE LODGE AT VENTANA CANYON

6200 N. Clubhouse Lane, Tucson, 520-577-1400, 800-828-5701; www.thelodgeatventanacanyon.com

Located in the foothills of the Santa Catalina Mountains on a 600-acre desert preserve, the Lodge is a peaceful getaway for tennis players, golfers and those in pursuit of nothing more than a day at the pool. Two 18-hole Tom Fazio-designed golf courses wind their way through the landscape of wild brush and giant saguaros, while the resort's tennis pro can help you master your serve on one of 12 hard courts. Rooms have Mission-style furniture, fully stocked kitchens and old-fashioned freestanding bathtubs.

50 rooms. Restaurant, bar. Fitness center. Pool. Spa. Pets accepted. Golf. Tennis. $351 and up

★★★LOEWS VENTANA CANYON RESORT

7000 N. Resort Drive, Tucson, 520-299-2020; www.loewshotels.com

Set on 93 acres in the Sonoran Desert, this resort offers modern comfort with a Southwestern twist. The two award-winning Tom Fazio-designed 18-hole golf courses challenge duffers. The spa offers a full menu of treatments as well as a fitness center. Five restaurants and lounges give a taste of

---

WHAT ARE THE BEST GOLF RESORTS NEAR TUCSON?

Hilton Tucson El Conquistador Golf and Tennis Resort:
You'll have views of the Santa Catalina Mountains while playing on the three courses at the Hilton. If you need help with your swing, there's also a golf school onsite.

The Lodge at Ventana Canyon:
You will play among native Sonoran Desert vegetation and enormous saguaros in this hotel's two 18-hole Tom Fazio-designed courses.

Omni Tucson National Golf Resort:
The Omni Tucson National Golf Resort's golf courses have hosted more than 30 PGA Tour events. There's one parkland-style course and one desert-style one.

The Westin La Paloma Resort and Spa:
The Westin offers a 27-hole Jack Nicklaus signature golf course. It makes the most of the desert landscape, with cacti, yucca, palo verde and agave dotting the course.

every kind of cuisine in a variety of settings, from poolside cafés to refined dining rooms. The Flying V Bar & Grill delivers Southwestern steakhouse fare in a dining room overlooking a golf course.

398 rooms. Restaurant, bar. Business center. Fitness center. Pool. Spa. Pets accepted. Golf. Tennis. $251-350

★★★MARRIOTT TUCSON UNIVERSITY PARK

880 E. Second St., Tucson, 520-792-4100; www.marriotttucson.com

This hotel is a good choice for those visiting the University of Arizona's campus. It's right at the front gate and features rooms that are specifically designed for business travelers. In the rooms you'll find down duvet-topped beds and flat-screen TVs. For a little extra, upgrade to the concierge floor, where you'll receive a continental breakfast, turndown service and access to a lounge for free.

250 rooms. Restaurant, bar. Business center. Fitness center. Pool. $251-350

★★★OMNI TUCSON NATIONAL GOLF RESORT AND SPA

2727 W. Club Drive, Tucson, 520-297-2271, 888-444-6664; www.omnihotels.com

Located in the foothills of the Santa Catalina Mountains, the Omni Tucson National Golf Resort and Spa has been the home to countless PGA Tours. But there's more than just golf here. There are two pools, four tennis courts, sand volleyball, lots of biking trails and the spa, which boasts 13,000 pleasure-pursuing square feet. Sign up for the terzetto massage, where two therapists perform choreographed massage. The comfortable rooms have a Southwest décor and feature views of the course or mountains. Some rooms also have full kitchens, although most people leave the cooking up to the resort's talented chefs.

129 rooms. Restaurant, bar. Business center. Pool. Spa. Pets accepted. Golf. Tennis. $61-150

★★★THE RITZ-CARLTON, DOVE MOUNTAIN

1500 North Secret Springs Drive, Marana, 520-572-3111; www.ritzcarlton.com

The Ritz-Carlton at Dove Mountain takes the service a step further by doing an excellent job at utilizing and incorporating its unique surroundings, with the Sonoran Desert and Tortolita Mountains as a backdrop. Sign up for a guided hike led by natives who not only have vast knowledge of the area, but also a deep understanding of the local culture. Every night, a native performs just outside the hotel with his flute to announce the coming of another magnificent Arizona sunset. The relaxed nature of this exclusive property allows for guests to feel just as comfortable wearing their hiking gear as their resort casual threads for an elegant dinner at Core. The resort also has 27 holes of Jack Nicklaus Golf, which serves as host to the World Accenture Golf Championship in February each year. The Spa and Wellness Center is a destination within itself and offers a wide array of treatments, massage therapies, and salon services. This unique structure includes indoor and outdoor treatment rooms and an outdoor Serenity pool terrace where guests are able to view ancient Native American carvings in nearby rocks.

253 rooms. Restaurant, bar. Business center. Fitness center. Pool. Spa. Pets accepted. $251-350

★★★THE WESTIN LA PALOMA RESORT AND SPA

3800 E. Sunrise Drive, Tucson, 520-742-6000, 800-937-8461; www.westin.com

The large rooms here have warm, golden color schemes and feature patios or balconies and bathrooms with granite countertops and dual sinks. Golfers are drawn to the 27-hole Jack Nicklaus-designed course adjoining the resort. You'll also find tennis, pools—one with a 177-foot waterslide—and the Elizabeth Arden Red Door Spa onsite, as well as five restaurants.

487 rooms. Restaurant, bar. Business center. Spa. Pets accepted. Golf. Tennis. $151-250

★★★WESTWARD LOOK RESORT

245 E. Ina Road, Tucson, 520-297-1151, 800-722-2500; www.westwardlook.com

The Westward Look Resort combines top-notch facilities, gourmet dining and sumptuous spa treatments in a naturally beautiful setting. Set on 80 acres filled with giant cacti and blooming wildflowers, this resort is home to a variety of birds and wildlife. You can take advantage of the scenery by heading outdoors for activities like horseback riding, onsite tennis and nearby golf.

241 rooms. Restaurant, bar. Spa. Pets accepted. Tennis. $251-350

WHERE TO EAT

★★★CORE KITCHEN & WINE BAR

The Ritz-Carlton, Dove Mountain, 15000 N. Secret Springs Drive, Marana, 520-572-3000; www.ritzcarlton.com

Mohawk-sporting chef, Joel Harrington, is the main attraction at the Ritz-Carlton, Dove Mountain's signature restaurant CORE. Joel's self-titled True American cuisine is basically American comfort food supplemented by local organic produce with a Southwestern flair. The signature chili-lacquered New York Strip steak topped with Poblano sauce walks the line between innovative and approachable. The drink menu includes more than 40 wines by the glass, as well as cocktails that incorporate local Southwest themes and flavors (lemon-grass mojito, jalisco flower). The focal point of the restaurant is shared between the open kitchen and the stunning Tortolita Mountains. Those choosing the former view are able to sit in the spacious patio while those preferring to watch Harrington and his team in action can perch at the wraparound counter.

American. Breakfast, dinner. Reservations recommended. $35-86

★★★GOLD

Westward Look Resort, 245 E. Ina Road, Tucson, 520-297-1151; www.westwardlook.com

Set at the base of the Catalina Mountains in north central Tucson at the Westward Look Resort, Gold offers a contemporary menu by chef James Wallace. You'll find options such as pine nut-crusted chicken with ziti pasta, pancetta, tomato and olives; and pancetta-wrapped scallops with ravioli and an ale cream sauce. Wednesday night features a prix fixe three-course meal and Thursdays feature a Spanish guitar player to provide the soundtrack to your dinner.

American. Breakfast, lunch, dinner. Reservations recommended. Outdoor seating. Children's menu. $36-85

★★★THE GRILL AT HACIENDA DEL SOL

5601 N. Hacienda del Sol Road, Tucson, 520-529-3500;
www.haciendadelsol.com

Rustic Spanish-colonial architecture, fine pottery and
Mexican art adorn this beautifully restored Tucson
landmark. The contemporary American cuisine is
complemented by a spectacular wine list and excellent
service. The creative menu, which includes dishes
like pecan wood-grilled pork chop with housemade
chorizo, basmati rice, haricot vert, Swiss chard and
saffron-butter sauce, makes this one of Tucson's
favorite dining destinations.

American. Dinner, Sunday brunch. Reservations recommended.
Outdoor seating. Children's menu. Bar. $36-85

★★★JANOS RESTAURANT

The Westin Paloma Resort & Spa, 3770 E. Sunrise Drive, Tucson,
520-615-6100; www.janos.com

The legendary chef Janos Wilder presides over this
French-inspired Southwestern masterpiece inside
the Westin La Paloma Resort & Spa. The restaurant
features both tasting and à la carte menus, which
constantly change and are inspired by influences from
around the world. The emphasis is on ingredients from
the region, utilizing an established network of local
farmers. The romantic setting features original artwork
and views of the valley.

Southwestern. Dinner. Closed Sunday; and Monday June-August.
Reservations recommended. Outdoor seating. Bar. $36-85

★★★KINGFISHER

2564 E. Grant, Tucson, 520-323-7739; www.kingfishertucson.com

The popular spot serves up dishes like macadamia nut-
crusted Hawaiian fish; penne with spinach, tomatoes,
gold potatoes, lemon, basil, extra virgin olive oil and
garlic; and an oven-roasted half chicken with pineap-
ple-ancho barbecue sauce. There's also a full oyster
bar with 15 varieties of oysters. On Mondays and
Saturdays, the sounds of jazz and blues can be heard
until midnight.

American. Lunch, dinner, late-night. Reservations recommended.
Bar. $36-85

★★★MCMAHON'S PRIME STEAKHOUSE

2959 N. Swan Road, Tucson, 520-327-7463;
www.metrorestaurants.com

This local favorite is a perfect spot for a romantic
evening or special occasion. Original local artwork
adorns the walls and a pianist performs nightly. Entrées
worthy of your special occasion include filet mignon

with portobello mushrooms, garlic and aged Romano cheese, and New York sirloin with onions, mushrooms, garlic and cracked black pepper.
Steak. Lunch, dinner. Reservations recommended. Outdoor seating. Children's menu. Bar. $36-85

SPAS

★★★★THE SPA AT OMNI TUCSON NATIONAL
Omni Tucson National Resort, 2727 W. Club Drive, Tucson, 520-575-7559; www.omnihotels.com

The Spa at Omni Tucson National has a tranquil and picturesque location in the foothills of the Santa Catalina Mountains. Whether you have half an hour or an entire day, this spa has something to offer. In 25 minutes, the tension-reliever massage works its magic where you are most tense, while the business facial cleanses, tones, exfoliates and hydrates in just under 30 minutes. Other facials include aromatherapy, deep-cleansing, antiaging and deluxe hydration. Body masks smooth rough skin with a variety of ingredients, including seaweed, desert rose clay, rich mud from the Dead Sea, shea butter and aspara, a plant that grows by the beach and is recognized for its calming properties.

WELCOME TO COLORADO

COLORADO'S TERRAIN IS DIVERSE AND SPECTACULARLY
beautiful—and attracts those who want to venture outdoors. Throughout the
state there are deep gorges, rainbow-colored canyons, grassy plains, breathtaking alpine mountains and beautiful landmass variations carved by ancient glaciers and erosion. Colorado is the highest state in the Union, with an average elevation of 6,800 feet. It has 53 peaks above 14,000 feet.

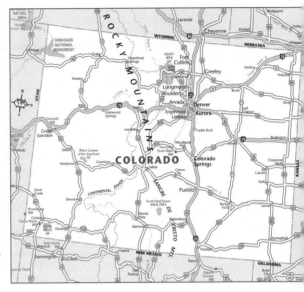

Whether you're visiting one of its booming big cities—Denver, Boulder or
Colorado Springs—or heading for the glitz of Vail or Aspen, Colorado beck-
ons people to spend more time outdoors. Hit the slopes, take a river-rafting
trip or drive up to the famous Pikes Peak. In between, take a trip back in time
by visiting historic homes, railroad depots and ghost towns.

Colorado has a rich history. When gold was discovered near present-day
Denver in 1858, an avalanche of settlers poured into the state. Then, when silver was discovered soon afterward, a new flood came. Mining camps—usually
crude tent cities on the rugged slopes of the Rockies—contributed to Colorado's colorful, robust past. Some of these mines still operate, but most of the
early mining camps are ghost towns today.

HIGHLIGHTS

WHAT ARE SOME OF THE BEST PLACES FOR OUTDOOR FUN IN COLORADO?

ASPEN
No other place better exudes that ski resort town vibe than Aspen. Travelers—including many celebrities—head here to take advantage of the great skiing, snowboarding and other outdoor pursuits.

COLORADO SPRINGS
To see some of the gorgeous scenery that Colorado is known for, take a trip to Colorado Springs. There, you'll find amazing rock formations at Pikes Peak and Pike National Forest. There are also hints of the area's Wild West past at places like the Museum of the American Cowboy.

DENVER
The state's capital is the center of it all. Here, you can find beautiful scenery at the Denver Botanic Gardens, animals at the Denver Zoo, juicy steaks in some of Colorado's best restaurants and most important, the Broncos' stadium.

VAIL
Vail rivals Aspen as the see-and-be-seen spot among resort towns. Like its nearby chic neighbor, Vail also boasts fantastic skiing and snowboarding. The town credits its legendary snow for making its slopes among the best in the country.

NORTHWESTERN COLORADO

Those who appreciate the more fabulous things in life vacation in the Northwestern region of Colorado. They come to ski and socialize in posh resort towns like Avon and Beaver Creek. Of course, the biggest resort town of them all is Aspen, named for its abundance of aspen trees. It's home to some of the most expensive real estate in the world and draws in the rich and famous with immaculate ski slopes, spectacular shopping and fine dining. A more affordable—and rowdier—alternative to Aspen is Breckenridge, the largest historic district in Colorado with 350 historic structures. More than 1 million skiers visit Breckenridge to hit the slopes.

Located on four interconnected mountains named Peaks 7, 8, 9 and 10, the terrain is revered by skiers but is especially popular with snowboarders. While Glenwood Springs may go down in history as the site where famous gunslinger Doc Holliday died in 1887, today it's a popular year-round health-spa destination, thanks to its famous hot springs. Grand Lake, on the northern shore of the largest glacial lake in Colorado, is one of the state's oldest resort villages. It boasts the world's highest yacht club, a full range of water recreation and horseback riding and pack trips on mountain trails. Snowmass Village, located at the base of a ski area and only eight miles from Aspen, is best known as the location of Snowmass Ski Area, a popular winter resort (but there's still plenty to do in the summer). The sport of ski jumping got its start at Steamboat Springs in 1913, when it was introduced by Norwegian Carl Howelsen. Since then, 10 national ski-jumping records have been set on Steamboat Springs' Howelsen Hill. The area has produced 47 winter Olympians. But it has more to offer than just ski jumping, with tons of summer activities and more than 100 natural hot springs in the area. No discussion of Northwestern Colorado resort towns is complete without Vail. Built to resemble a Bavarian village, it is the world's largest single-mountain ski resort. Known for having vast and varied terrain for every skill level of skier or snowboarder, Vail often tops ski resort lists and gets rave reviews for its legendary powder. Summer has also emerged as a prime recreation season on Vail Mountain, with mountain biking being the sport of choice. It doesn't matter which season you choose to visit these resort towns; there's plenty of action on and off the slopes all year round.

WHAT TO SEE

ASPEN
ASPEN HIGHLANDS
76 Boomerang Road, Aspen, 970-925-1220, 800-525-6200; www.aspensnowmass.com

The Aspen Highlands offers three quads, two triple chairlifts, a patrol, a school, rentals, five restaurants and a bar. There are 125 runs, the longest of which is three and a half miles with a vertical drop of 3,635 feet. Shuttle bus service runs to and from Aspen. Half-day rates are available.
Mid-December-early April, daily.

ASPEN MOUNTAIN
601 E. Dean, Aspen, 970-925-1220, 800-525-6200; www.aspensnowmass.com

This place has three quads, four double chairlifts, a gondola, a patrol, a school, restaurants and a bar. The property features 76 runs. The longest run is three miles with a 3,267-foot vertical drop. Shuttle bus service is available to Buttermilk, Aspen Highlands and Snowmass.
Mid-November-mid-April, daily.

BLAZING ADVENTURES
407 E. Hyman Ave., Aspen, 970-923-4544, 800-282-7238; www.blazingadventures.com

Take half-day, full-day and overnight river-rafting trips on the Arkansas, Roaring Fork, Colorado and Gunnison rivers. Trips range from scenic floats for beginners to exciting runs for experienced rafters. The brave ones can try out

HIGHLIGHTS

WHAT ARE SOME OF THE BEST PLACES FOR OUTDOOR FUN IN NORTHWESTERN COLORADO?

GO SKIING AND PEOPLE-WATCHING IN ASPEN

Aspen is known for its great slopes, so you can't go there without strapping on a pair of skiis and hitting the white stuff. This tony town is also a hot spot among celebrities, making it a prime spot for people-watching.

SNOWBOARD IN BRECKENRIDGE

If skiing isn't your thing, try its hipper cousin, snowboarding. Then follow the seasoned snowboarders to this spot, a less expensive and wilder resort town.

TAKE A DIP IN THE GLENWOOD HOT SPRINGS POOL

After a day of skiing, nothing will feel better than soaking your sore muscles in this toasty outdoor hot-spring pool. Its mineral waters supposedly have healing powers that will revive your achy body so that you can hit the slopes again tomorrow.

white-water rafting. Transportation is provided to the site. Bicycle, Jeep and hiking tours are also available.

BUTTERMILK MOUNTAIN
806 W. Hallam, Aspen, 970-925-9000, 888-525-6200; www.aspensnowmass.com
Here, you'll find two quads, three double chairlifts, a surface lift, a patrol, a school, rentals, a cafeteria, restaurants, a bar and a nursery. Buttermilk offers 44 runs, the longest of which is three miles with a vertical drop 2,030 feet. Snowboarding is available. Shuttle bus service runs from Ajax and Snowmass. *December-mid-April: daily 9 a.m.-3:30 p.m.*

INDEPENDENCE PASS
Highway 82 from Highway 24, Aspen, 970-963-4959;
Highway 82 through Independence Pass is a spectacular visual treat, not to mention an adrenaline rush—if you're afraid of heights, opt for another route. The winding road between Highway 24 and Aspen is among the nation's highest, reaching 12,095 feet at its rocky summit, and it offers beautiful vistas of Colorado's majestic forests and snow-covered peaks at every turn. Stop at the top for the views and a short trail hike. The pass is closed November to May.

AVON

BEAVER CREEK/ARROWHEAD RESORT

137 Benchmark Road, Avon, 970-476-9090, 800-842-8062; www.beavercreek.snow.com

There are 10 quad, two triple and three double chairlifts, a patrol, rentals, restaurants, a bar and a nursery. The longest run is two and a quarter miles with a vertical drop of 4,040 feet. If you want a break from skiing, you can go ice skating, do some snowmobiling or take a sleigh ride.

Late November-mid-April, daily. Cross-country trails and rentals: November-April. Chairlift rides: July-August, daily; September, weekends.

COLORADO RIVER RUNS

Rancho del Rio, 28 miles northwest of Highway 131, 970-653-4292, 800-826-1081; www.coloradoriverruns.com

Raft down the Colorado River. Tours depart from Rancho del Rio, just outside State Bridge, and last two and a half to three hours.

Admission: adults $36, children $30. May-September.

BRECKENRIDGE

BRECKENRIDGE SKI AREA

Ski Hill Road, Breckenridge, 970-453-5000, 800-789-7669; www.breckenridge.snow.com

This ski spot has seven high-speed quads, six double chairlifts, four surface lifts, eight carpet lifts, a school, rentals, four cafeterias, five restaurants on the mountain, a picnic area and four nurseries (from two months old). There are 112 runs on three interconnected mountains; the longest is three and a half miles with a vertical drop of 3,398 feet. There's also cross-country skiing, heli-skiing, ice skating, snowboarding and sleigh rides. Shuttle bus service is provided. Multiday, half day and off-season rates are available.

Ski: mid-November-early May, daily. Chairlift and alpine slide: mid-June-mid-September.

GLENWOOD SPRINGS

GLENWOOD HOT SPRINGS POOL

Hot Springs Lodge and Pool, 415 Sixth St., Glenwood Springs, 970-945-6571, 800-537-7946; www.hotspringspool.com

For centuries, visitors have traveled to the hot springs in Colorado to soak in their soothing—and many say healing—mineral-rich waters. Today, those same legendary springs feed this hot spring pool, the world's largest. The main pool, more than two blocks long, circulates 3.5 million gallons of naturally heated, spring-fed water each day. The complex includes lap lanes, a shallow play area, a diving area, two water slides and a therapy pool.

Late May-early September, daily 7:30 a.m.-10 p.m.; early September-late May, daily 9 a.m.-10 p.m.

SUNLIGHT MOUNTAIN RESORT

10901 County Road 117, Glenwood Springs, 970-945-7491, 800-445-7931; www.sunlightmtn.com

This resort offers two double chairlifts, a surface tow, a patrol, a school, rentals, a cafeteria, a bar and a nursery. Among the 67 runs, the longest is two and a half miles with a vertical drop of 2,010 feet. Half-day rates are available for snowmobiling.

Late November-early April, daily.

WHITE RIVER NATIONAL FOREST

900 Grand Ave., Glenwood Springs, 970-945-2521; www.fs.fed.us/r2/whiteriver

This forest's more than 2.5 million acres sit in the heart of the Colorado Rocky Mountains. Recreation is available at 70 developed sites with boat ramps, picnicking, campgrounds and observation points. To see nature in its true form, visit one of the wilderness areas that reside in the park, including Holy Cross, Flat Tops, Eagles Nest, Maroon Bells-Snowmass, Raggeds, Collegiate Peaks and Hunter-Frying Pan. (Check with local ranger for information before entering wildernesses or any backcountry areas.) Many streams and lakes provide trout fishing; there are also large deer and elk populations.

GRAND JUNCTION

ADVENTURE BOUND RIVER EXPEDITIONS

2392 H Road, Grand Junction, 970-245-5428, 800-423-4668; www.raft-colorado.com

Take a two- to five-day white-water-rafting trip on the Colorado, Green and Yampa rivers.

Admission: varies.

CROSS ORCHARDS HISTORIC FARM

3073 F Road, Grand Junction, 970-434-9814; www.wcmuseum.org

Costumed guides interpret the social and agricultural heritage of Western Colorado. Restored buildings and equipment are on display. There's also a narrow gauge railroad exhibit and a country store.

Admission: adults $4, seniors $3, children $2.50 and family groups $10. May-October, Tuesday-Saturday 9 a.m.-4 p.m.

KEYSTONE

KEYSTONE RESORT SKI AREA

1254 Soda Ridge Road, Keystone, 800-344-8878; www.keystone.snow.com

You'll find four ski mountains here: Arapahoe Basin, Keystone, North Peak and the Outback. The ski area has a patrol, a school and rentals. Snowmaking is available at Keystone, North Peak and the Outback. Cross-country skiing, night skiing, ice skating, snowmobiling and sleigh rides are on offer. Shuttle bus service is provided. There are combination and half-day ski rates as well as package plans. Summer activities include boating, rafting and gondola rides, as well as golf, tennis, horseback riding, bicycling and Jeep riding.

SNOWMASS VILLAGE

ASPEN SNOWMASS SKIING COMPANY

40 Carriage Way, Snowmass Village, 970-923-1220; www.aspensnowmass.com

This place has seven quads, two triple and six double chairlifts, two platter pulls, a patrol, a school, rentals, snowmaking, restaurants, a bar and a nursery. There are 91 runs; the longest is five miles with a vertical drop of 4,406 feet. There's 50 miles of cross-country skiing. Shuttle bus service runs from Aspen.

Late November-mid-April, daily.

BICYCLE TRIPS AND JEEP TRIPS

48 Snowmass Village Mall, Snowmass Village, 970-923-4544, 800-282-7238; www.blazingadventures.com

These bicycle and Jeep trips travel throughout the Snowmass/Aspen area. Transportation and equipment are provided.

June-September.

VAIL

COLORADO SKI MUSEUM & SKI HALL OF FAME

Vail Village Transportation Center, 231 S. Frontage Road E., Vail, 970-476-1876; www.skimuseum.net

Learn everything you ever wanted to know about skiing. The museum traces the history of skiing in Colorado back more than 120 years.

Admission: free. Daily 10 a.m.-5 p.m.; April-May until 5 p.m.

GERALD R. FORD AMPHITHEATER VILAR PAVILION/BETTY FORD ALPINE GARDENS

Ford Park and the Betty Ford Alpine Gardens, Vail, 970-845-8497, 888-920-2797;www.vvf.org

Enjoy top-notch entertainment under Vail's crystal-clear starlit skies at this open-air theater surrounded by the Betty Ford Alpine Gardens—a public botanical garden with more than 500 varieties of wildflowers and alpine plants. Performances throughout the summer normally include classical music, rock and roll, jazz, ballet, contemporary dance and children's theater.

June-August.

VAIL SKI RESORT

137 Benchmark Road, Avon, 970-476-9090, 800-503-8748; www.vail.com

This resort has a gondola, 14 high-speed quads, seven fixed-grip quads, three triple and five double chairlifts, 10 surface lifts, a patrol, a school, rentals, snow-making, cafeterias, restaurants, bars and a nursery. The longest run is four miles with a vertical drop of 3,450 feet.

Late November-mid-April, daily. Cross-country trails, rentals November-April; ice skating, snowmobiling, sleigh rides. Gondola and Vista Bahn June-August, daily; May and September, weekends.

WINTER PARK

DEVIL'S THUMB RANCH

3530 County Road 83, Tabernash, 800-933-4339; www.devilsthumbranch.com

Set on 3,700 acres at the foot of the Continental Divide, Devil's Thumb Ranch is a year-round resort with an abundance of activities in every season. In summer, visitors enjoy fly-fishing, horseback riding, river rafting, hiking, bird/nature walks and inflatable kayaking. Winter brings opportunities for cross-country skiing, sleigh rides, winter horseback riding, ice skating and snowshoeing.

DOG SLED RIDES

505 Zerex, Fraser, 970-726-8326; www.dogsledrides.com

Mush on these 30-minute, one-hour and two-hour rides on a sled pulled by eight Siberian and Alaskan huskies. Guides give talks on wildlife, trees and mountains.

FRASER RIVER TRAIL

Winter Park, one mile southeast off Highway 40, 970-726-4118; www.allwinterpark.com

This wide, flat, five-mile trail runs between the Winter Park Resort and the towns of Winter Park and Fraser, and is a haven for walkers, bikers and in-line skaters who want to enjoy the scenery without worrying about crosswalks or traffic lights. The route between Winter Park and Fraser has picnic tables.

WINTER PARK RESORT

85 Parsenn Road, Winter Park, 970-726-5514, 800-979-0332; www.skiwinterpark.com

In winter, skiers make full use of the resort's eight high-speed quad, five triple and seven double chairlifts and 143 runs—the longest is five miles, with a vertical drop 2,610 feet. A patrol, a school, equipment rentals and snowmaking, cafeterias, restaurants and bars are also on the property. There are NASTAR and coin-operated racecourses as well. In summer, the Zephyr Express chairlift takes mountain bikers and their two-wheelers to the top of a summit, where they can access the resort's 50-mile network of interconnected trails. Colorado's longest Alpine Slide brings riders on heavy-duty plastic sleds, equipped with hand-held brakes, 3,030 feet down the side of a mountain. An outdoor climbing wall, bungee jumping, disc golf (18 holes that wrap around the top of Winter Park Mountain) and miniature golf are also available.

STEAMBOAT SPRINGS

HOWELSEN HILL SKI COMPLEX

245 Howelsen Parkway, Steamboat Springs, 970-879-8499

This international ski jump complex includes a double chairlift, a Poma lift, a rope tow, five ski-jumping hills, a patrol, ice skating and snowboarding.
December-March, daily.

STEAMBOAT

2305 Mount Werner Circle, Steamboat Springs, 970-879-6111, 800-922-2722; www.steamboat.com

Steamboat has a high-speed gondola, four high-speed quads (two covered), six triple and seven double chairlifts, two surface tows, a patrol, a school, rentals, snowmaking, cafeterias, restaurants, bars and a nursery. Of the 142 runs, the longest is more than three miles with a vertical drop of 3,668 feet. Snowboarding and 14 miles of cross-country skiing are also on offer. Multiday and half-day rates are available.
Admission: varies. Late November-early April, daily. Gondola: Mid-June-mid-September.

STEAMBOAT LAKE STATE PARK

61105 Routt County Road 129, Steamboat Springs, 970-879-3922; www.parks.state.co.uss

The park offers swimming, water-skiing, fishing, boating, picnicking and camping.
Daily.

STRAWBERRY PARK NATURAL HOT SPRINGS

44200 County Road 36, Steamboat Springs, 970-879-0342; www.strawberryhotsprings.com

Mineral springs feed four pools, in which the water is cooled from 160 F to 105 F. There's a changing area, picnicking, camping and cabins.
Sunday-Thursday 10 a.m.-10.30 p.m., Friday-Saturday 10 a.m.-midnight.

HIGHLIGHTS

WHICH HOTELS ARE THE BEST FOR SKIING?

BEAVER CREEK LODGE
Skiers will appreciate that this European-style Lodge sits at the foot of the alpine heaven known as Beaver Creek Resort. It's also close to the Centennial and Strawberry Park chairlifts.

THE LITTLE NELL
The Little Nell has the unique distinction of being the only ski-in/ski-out hotel in Aspen. Plus, the hotel's coach service will transport you to and from any of the big local ski areas—Snowmass, Aspen Highlands, Buttermilk and Aspen Mountain.

PARK HYATT BEAVER CREEK RESORT AND SPA
This European-style hotel is in the heart of Beaver Creek Village. Avid skiers check into the Park Hyatt so that they have ski in/ski out access right from the lobby to Beaver Creek Mountain's nearly 150 runs.

THE ST. REGIS ASPEN RESORT
If you want to stay in Aspen and do some skiing, the St. Regis provides a convenient location at the base of Aspen Mountain. It sits between the gondola and lift, so that you'll have easy entry to some sweet ski spots.

STEAMBOAT SPRINGS HEALTH & RECREATION ASSOCIATION
136 Lincoln Ave., Steamboat Springs, 970-879-1828; www.sshra.org
Three hot pools are fed by 103-degree mineral water. A lap pool, saunas, exercise classes, massages, a weight room and summertime tennis courts are also available. *Daily.*

WHERE TO STAY

ASPEN
★★★ASPEN MEADOWS
845 Meadows Road, Aspen, 970-925-4240, 800-452-4240; www.aspenmeadowsresort.dolce.com
This 40-acre mountain retreat with its famous Bauhaus design is made of up six buildings and has hosted leaders from around the world since 1949, thanks to its state-of-the art conference facilities. The spacious guest suites include

study areas, wet bars and floor-to-ceiling windows with views of the mountains or Roaring Fork River.
98 rooms. Restaurant. Business center. Fitness center. Pool. Pets accepted. Tennis. $251-350

★★★HOTEL DURANT
122 E. Durant Ave., Aspen, 970-925-8500, 877-438-7268; www.durantaspen.com

This no-frills hotel offers wine and cheese après-ski and a rooftop hot tub and sauna to soak your depleted muscles. The 19 cozy—some more so than others—guest rooms are basic, but come with a complimentary continental breakfast in the morning. The location and relatively affordable rates are the primary pros here.

19 rooms. Complimentary breakfast. $151-250

★★★HOTEL JEROME
330 E. Main St., Aspen, 970-920-1000, 800-412-7625; www.hoteljerome.com

This downtown hotel was built in 1889 by Jerome B. Wheeler, co-owner of Macy's Department Store, and was one of the first buildings west of the Mississippi River to be fully lit by electricity. The boutique-style rooms here are magnificent, reflecting the hotel's Victorian heritage with carved armoires and beautiful beds. The service is superb: The ski concierge will take care of your every need, and guests are driven to the slopes in luxury SUVs. You also get access to the Aspen Club and Spa, a 77,000-square-foot exercise facility and spa. The dashing J-Bar is still one of the hottest places in town.

94 rooms. Restaurant, bar. Business center. Fitness center. Pool. Spa. Pets accepted. Golf. Tennis. $351 and up

★★★HOTEL LENADO
200 S. Aspen St., Aspen, 970-925-6246, 800-321-3457; www.hotellenado.com

In a town that's all about boutique and show, value doesn't get much better than this hotel. Fork over a fair rate (for Aspen) and you'll receive a cozy room with a four-poster hickory bed, Bose radio/CD player, down comforter and terry robes. Take advantage of your access to the rooftop deck and hot tub overlooking Aspen Mountain, heated boot lockers and daily ski storage. If that's not enough to make you happy, complimentary hors d'oeuvres and hot apple cider (lemonade in the summer) in the bar after 4 p.m. will hit the spot.

19 rooms. Bar. Complimentary breakfast. Pets accepted. $351 and up

---

WHICH HOTEL HAS THE BEST CONCIERGE?

The Ritz-Carlton, Bachelor Gulch: The hotel's concierge gets the top score not just for handling your luggage, but for also taking good care of your ski gear. The hotel's specially dedicated ski concierge will store your equipment and fetch it for you when it's time to hit the terrain. After a long day on the slopes, there's no need to worry about your messy gear; the ski concierge will clean it all.

★★★★★THE LITTLE NELL

675 E. Durant Ave., Aspen, 970-920-4600, 888-843-6355; www.thelittlenell.com

Tucked away at the base of a mountain, the Little Nell provides a perfect location either to hit the slopes or roam the streets in search of Aspen's latest fashions. The rooms and suites are heavenly cocoons that have been recently redecorated by famous interior designer Holly Hunt. They feature fireplaces, streamlined furnishings and luxurious bathrooms. Some suites have vaulted ceilings showcasing glorious mountainside views, while others overlook the charming former mining town. Enjoy the well-equipped fitness center, the outdoor pool and the Jacuzzi. Montagna restaurant is one of the most popular spots in town and serves inventive reinterpretations of American cuisine.

92 rooms. Restaurant, bar. Business center. Fitness center. Pool. Spa. Pets accepted. Closed late April-mid-May. $351 and up

★★★SKY HOTEL

709 E. Durant Ave., Aspen, 970-925-6760, 800-882-2582; www.theskyhotel.com

This hotel offers the convenience of being able to stumble upstairs from one of Aspen's trendiest bars, which is but a snowball's throw away from the rest of the city's nightlife. From the evening wine reception to the plush animal-print terrycloth robes, the Sky Hotel has taken your every vacation need into consideration. The rooms offer nice touches like L'Occitane bath products, iPod-compatible clock radios and humidifiers. Pets are welcomed with treats and their own beds and bowls in the room. The onsite ski shop will rent you equipment or store yours for free.

90 rooms. Restaurant, bar. Business center. Fitness center. Pool. Pets accepted. $351 and up

★★★★THE ST. REGIS ASPEN RESORT

315 E. Dean St., Aspen, 970-920-3300, 888-454-9005; www.stregis.com

Located at the base of Aspen Mountain between the gondola and lift, this hotel's upscale, Western atmosphere is the perfect respite from skiing, shopping and warm-weather activities such as fly-fishing and white-water rafting. The outdoor pool and accompanying lounge are ideal for whiling away warm after-noons, or you can relax in the lavish spa. Rooms are richly decorated in muted hues with bursts of color and oversized leather furniture. Expect complimen-tary water bottle service and a humidifier at turndown, as well as Remède bath amenities, bathrobes and slippers. The Restaurant serves American cuisine with Mediterranean inspirations in an elegantly relaxed setting with an exhi-bition kitchen, and Shadow Mountain Lounge is a popular gathering place to enjoy a cocktail.

199 rooms. Restaurant, bar. Business center. Fitness center. Pool. Spa. Closed late October-mid-November. $351 and up

AVON

★★★THE OSPREY AT BEAVER CREEK

10 Elk Track Road, Avon, 970-845-5990, 888-485-4317; www.vbcrp.com

Formerly the Inn at Beaver Creek, the Osprey underwent a $7 million renova-tion. It's all about location here: This ski in/ski out is just steps away from the Strawberry Park Express chairlift and is within walking distance of shops and eateries. The cozy and sophisticated guest rooms and suites offer an array of amenities, including plush robes, soaking tubs and ski boot heaters.

45 rooms. Bar. Fitness center. Pool. Ski in/ski out. Closed May, October. $251-350

★★★PARK HYATT BEAVER CREEK RESORT AND SPA

136 E. Thomas Place, Avon, 970-949-1234, 800-233-1234; www.beavercreek.hyatt.com

Situated at the base of the Gore Mountains, in the heart of Beaver Creek Village, the ski in/ski out resort is a classic mountain lodge, with rooms featuring oversized furniture, comfy quilts and marble bathrooms. The Performance Skiing Program helps guests improve their skiing within days. Afterward, visit Allegria Spa, which focuses on water-based treatments. In the summer, hit the links on the championship golf course. The resort has two restaurants and a café.

190 rooms. Restaurant, bar. Business center. Fitness center. Pool. Spa. Golf. Ski in/ski out. Tennis. $251-350

★★★THE PINES LODGE

141 Scott Hill Road, Avon, 970-845-7900, 866-605-7625; www.rockresorts.com

Nestled among towering pines, this resort offers views of the slopes of Beaver Creek Resort. The rooms include refrigerators, marble bathrooms, ski boot heaters and Starbucks coffee. After skiing, have a meal at the Lodge's elegant Grouse Mountain Grill.

60 rooms. Restaurant, bar. Fitness center. Spa. Pool. Golf. $251-350

★★★★THE RITZ-CARLTON, BACHELOR GULCH

130 Daybreak Ridge, Avon, 970-748-6200; www.ritzcarlton.com

Rugged meets refined at this resort, which sits at the base of the mountain at Beaver Creek. From the 10-gallon-hat-clad doorman who greets you to the great rustic room, this resort captures the spirit of the Old West while incorporating polished style. The rooms and suites are comfortable and fashionable, with leather chairs, dark wood furniture and wood-beamed ceilings. Iron chandeliers and twig furnishings adorn the public spaces. This family-friendly resort offers an abundance of activities, including fly-fishing, a horseshoe pit, two children's play areas, an outdoor pool, golf and skiing. If you want some company on a hike, make use of the hotel's Loan-A-Lab program and have the in-residence Labrador retriever, Bachelor, be your walking buddy. Have dinner in Wolfgang Puck's famous Spago restaurant, and afterward go to the Mountain Terrace's fire pit for the nightly marshmallow roast and live music.

180 rooms. Restaurant, bar. Business center. Fitness center. Spa. Pets accepted. Golf. Ski in/ski out. Tennis. $351 and up

BEAVER CREEK

★★★BEAVER CREEK LODGE

26 Avondale Lane, Beaver Creek, 970-845-9800, 800-525-7280; www.beavercreeklodge.net

Located at the foot of the Beaver Creek Resort, this European-style boutique hotel is close to the Centennial and Strawberry Park chairlifts. Curl up on the leather couch in front of the fireplace in one of the two-room suites, which feature kitchenettes. Condos have state-of-the-art kitchens, laundry facilities and master bedrooms with Jacuzzis.

72 rooms. Restaurant, bar. Fitness center. Spa. Ski in/ski out. $151-250

★★★THE CHARTER AT BEAVER CREEK

120 Offerson Road, Beaver Creek, 970-949-6660, 800-525-2139; www.thecharter.com

This lodge features hotel rooms, as well as one- to five-bedroom condos, that offer guests amenities like plush robes, Aveda bath products and high-speed Internet access. Each condo also includes a fully equipped kitchen, wood-burning fireplace, private bath and TV for each bedroom as well as maid service.

80 rooms. Restaurant, bar. Pool. Spa. Ski in/ski out. $151-250

BRECKENRIDGE

★★★ALLAIRE TIMBERS INN

9511 Highway 9/South Main, Breckenridge, 970-453-7530, 800-624-4904; www.allairetimbers.com

This charming log cabin bed and breakfast at the south end of Main Street is made from local pine. The innkeepers welcome guests with hearty homemade breakfasts, afternoon snacks and warm hospitality. Take the free shuttle from the inn to several chairlifts. After a day of activity, relax in the sunroom or retreat to the reading loft.

10 rooms. Complimentary breakfast. No children under 13. $151-250

★★★BEAVER RUN RESORT AND CONFERENCE CENTER

620 Village Road, Breckenridge, 970-453-6000, 800-265-3560; www.beaverrun.com

This large resort is popular with families in both winter and summer. The suites have full kitchens and the largest ones sleep up to 10 people. The property includes eight hot tubs and an indoor/outdoor pool, tennis courts and a spa with facials by Dermalogica. There's also a ski school for the kids, as well as miniature golf and a video arcade.

567 rooms. Restaurant, bar. Fitness center. Pool. Spa. Ski in/ski out. Tennis. $151-250

★★★GREAT DIVIDE LODGE

550 Village Road, Breckenridge, 970-547-5550, 888-906-5698; www.greatdividelodge.com

Just 50 yards from the base of Peak 9 and two blocks from Main Street, this lodge is excellent for winter or summer vacationing. The large guest rooms come with a wet bar, Starbucks coffee, Nintendo and wireless Internet access. Get around on the free hotel shuttle.

208 rooms. Restaurant, bar. Pool. $151-250

★★★SKIWAY LODGE

275 Ski Hill Road, Breckenridge, 970-453-7573, 800-472-1430; www.skiwaylodge.com

Individually designed rooms with mountain views and hearty, homemade breakfasts distinguish this Bavarian-style chalet from the rest. Plus, it's just blocks from Main Street. The inn offers ski-in/ski-out access.

9 rooms. Complimentary breakfast. No children under 10 years. Ski in/ski out. $61-150

EDWARDS

★★★THE LODGE & SPA AT CORDILLERA

2205 Cordillera Way, Edwards, 970-926-2200, 866-650-7625; www.cordilleralodge.com

The French-chateau architecture and beautiful mountaintop location make this one of the most exclusive resorts in the area. A lovely rustic style dominates the accommodations, where wood-burning or gas fireplaces add warmth and terraces offer views of the Vail Valley. The lodge also includes award-winning golf and a full-service spa. There are four restaurants on the premises. Try the traditional Irish fare at Grouse-on-the-Green, where even the interiors were constructed in Ireland.

56 rooms. Restaurant, bar. Business center. Pool. Golf. Tennis. $151-250

KEYSTONE

★★★KEYSTONE LODGE & SPA

22101 Highway 6, Keystone, 970-496-3000, 877-753-9786; www.keystonelodge.rockresorts.com

Keystone Lodge is a perfect Rocky Mountain getaway, thanks to a variety of activities, comfortable accommodations and enjoyable dining. The guest rooms and suites are the picture of mountain chic, with large windows framing unforgettable views of snow-capped peaks and the Snake River. You'll never be at a loss for something to do, with an onsite ice-skating rink, BMW driving tours, nearby skiing and golf and a complete fitness center. After an action-packed day, head to the Spa at Keystone Resort, which offers a number of soothing treatments.

152 rooms. Restaurant, bar. Business center. Fitness center. Pool. Spa. $251-350

STEAMBOAT SPRINGS

★★★SHERATON STEAMBOAT RESORT

2200 Village Inn Court, Steamboat Springs, 970-879-2220, 800-325-3535; www.starwoodhotels.com

This hotel is a great choice for families and business travelers—it's the only conference hotel in the area with ski-in/ski-out access. After a day on the slopes, enjoy the rooftop hot tubs or get a massage at the spa. The elegant and comfortable rooms include Sweet Sleeper beds. Ask for a slope-view room. The resort has boutiques and an art gallery.

239 rooms. Restaurant, bar. Business center. Fitness center. Pool. Spa. Golf. Closed mid-April-May, fall season. $151-250

★★★THE STEAMBOAT GRAND RESORT HOTEL

2300 Mount Werner Circle, Steamboat Springs, 970-871-5500, 877-366-2628; www.steamboatgrand.com

The accommodations here range from studios to private residences with Alder cabinets and granite countertops. The spa offers a menu of treatments, from hot-stone massage to herbal-hibernation body wraps. The fitness center has lots of equipment, but its best feature is the eucalyptus steam room, perfect after a day on the slopes. The Cabin restaurant has an extensive wine list and serves Midwestern beef aged at least 30 days in controlled cellars and native Colorado game.

327 rooms. Restaurant, bar. Fitness center. Pool. Spa. $251-350

SNOWMASS VILLAGE

★★★SILVERTREE HOTEL SNOWMASS VILLAGE

100 Elbert Lane, Snowmass Village, 970-923-3520, 800-837-4255; www.silvertreehotel.com

This year-round resort offers ski-in/ski-out access, two heated pools and a fitness center with a steam room and massage services as well as family-style suites. Rooms are simply furnished, but many have great views of the slopes.

260 rooms. Restaurant. Business center. Fitness center. Pool. Pets accepted. Ski in/ski out. $251-350

★★★SNOWMASS CLUB

0239 Snowmass Club Circle, Snowmass Village, 970-923-5600, 800-525-0710;
www.snowmassclub.com

This year-round resort is in the Elk Mountain range area and offers one-, two- and three-bedroom villas with daily maid service. All of the villas have full kitchens and most feature a fireplace, a deck with a grill and laundry. The 19,000-square-foot health club includes four pools, spa services and dozens of fitness classes. Sage Restaurant and Black Saddle Bar & Grille serve everything from barbecue to New York-style cuisine.

55 rooms. Restaurant. Business center. Spa. Golf. Tennis. $351 and up

★★★VICEROY SNOWMASS

130 Wood Road, Snowmass Village, 970-923-8000;
www.viceroyhotelsandresorts.com

Nestled between the new Snowmass Base Village and the rolling hills of Brush Creek Valley, this gorgeous mountain resort is steps from the Elk Camp Gondola and the Village Express Chairlift, making it the ideal winter destination for skiers. Custom-designed interiors, wall coverings, carpets, and furnishings by designer Jean-Michel Gathy make for stunning, yet ecologically friendly rooms. Earth tones abound in the rooms, from the deep, chocolate brown headboards to the polished black granite countertops and black and white framed photographs. One, two, three, and four bedroom condominiums are offered and all rooms, even the standard studios, have full kitchens. If private ski lessons or games at the Kid's Club don't appeal to the little ones, they can always just hang out in the condo and hook up an X-Box or Wii, both of which are available through the concierge. Serving breakfast, lunch and dinner, the exquisite Eight K restaurant specializes in contemporary American cuisine. Viceroy's poolside café, The Nest, also serves breakfast, lunch and dinner, but specializes in sushi. During winter, Viceroy provides its guests with complimentary hot cocoa, s'mores and even lollipops for the kids every afternoon in the lobby. During summer, water, soda, and other light refreshments are served.

173 rooms. Restaurant, bar. Business center. Fitness center. Pool. Spa. Ski in/ski out. $351 and up

VAIL

★★★THE LODGE AT VAIL

174 E. Gore Creek Drive, Vail, 970-476-5011, 877-528-7625;
www.rockresorts.com

This lodge perfectly marries the charm of an alpine inn with the amenities of a world-class resort. The individually decorated rooms are the ideal blend of Western style and European elegance. Located at the base of Vail Mountain, the lift—as well as boutiques and shops of Vail Village—are just steps away. Mickey's Piano Bar is a great spot for a drink.

165 rooms. Restaurant, bar. Pool. Ski in/ski out. $251-350

★★★MARRIOTT VAIL MOUNTAIN RESORT

715 W. Lionshead Circle, Vail, 970-476-4444, 800-648-0720; www.marriott.com

This hotel is in a great spot at the base of Vail Mountain near the lift and many boutiques and restaurants. The rustic guest rooms contain wood furnishings and marble and granite baths. Privately owned condos are also available. The

Golden Leaf Spa offers body wraps and massages. The full-service retail shop has rental equipment.

344 rooms. Restaurant, bar. Fitness center. Pool. Spa. $151-250

★★★SONNENALP RESORT OF VAIL

20 Vail Road, Vail, 970-476-5656, 800-654-8312;
www.sonnenalp.com

This charming family-owned and -operated resort recalls the Bavarian coun-tryside. Located in Vail Village, within walking distance of the ski lift, it's a natural choice for winter sports lovers while the 18-hole championship golf course and European style makes it a treasure any time of the year. A variety of dishes—from contemporary American fare at Ludwig's to ski favorites such as fondue at the Swiss Chalet—promise to keep your stomach happy. The King's Club fireside lounge is perfect for live entertainment and après-ski, serving everything from burgers to caviar.

127 rooms. Restaurant, bar. Spa. $251-350

★★★VAIL CASCADE RESORT & SPA

1300 Westhaven Drive, Vail, 970-476-7111, 800-282-4183;
www.vailcascade.com

Located on Gore Creek at the base of Vail Mountain, this European-style alpine village contains a combination of standard guest rooms, condominiums and private residences. This huge property boasts the largest athletic facility in the Vail Valley, a shopping arcade, two movie theaters, a beauty shop, two outdoor pools and five whirlpools. Camp Cascade keeps kids entertained throughout the day.

292 rooms. Restaurant, bar. Spa. Pool. Ski in/ski out. Fitness center. $151-250

WHERE TO EAT

ASPEN
★★★CACHE CACHE BISTRO

205 S. Mill St., Aspen, 970-925-3835; www.cachecache.com

This eatery has become something of an Aspen institution in the last two decades. Expect the highest-quality food, wine and service from the charming owner Jodi Larner herself, but don't anticipate getting a bargain or a quick seat après-ski. That said, if you're not married to the white-tablecloth experience and don't mind moseying up to the bar, you can relieve your tired legs and eat Alaskan king crab and foie gras terrine starters.

French. Dinner. Outdoor seating. Bar. $16-35

★★★JIMMY'S AN AMERICAN RESTAURANT & BAR

205 S. Mill St., Aspen, 970-925-6020;
www.jimmysaspen.com

This cozy restaurant is known for both the lively bar and seriously good food, such as the dry-aged rib-eye on the bone, Chesapeake Bay crab cakes and center-cut ahi tuna with herbed rice. The chocolate volcano cake is also a favorite.

American. Dinner. Outdoor seating. Children's menu. Bar. $36-85

★★★MATSUHISA ASPEN

303 E. Main St., Aspen, 970-544-6628;
www.matsuhisaaspen.com

Renowned chef Nobu Matsuhisa, who has built a mini-empire of restaurants from New York to L.A., gives Aspen a taste of his outstanding, heartfelt Japanese cuisine in this sleek restaurant located 9,000 feet above sea level. The service is polished and prompt, making for a superb experience.

Japanese. Dinner. Bar. $86 and up

★★★★MONTAGNA

The Little Nell, 675 E. Durant Ave., Aspen, 970-920-4600; www.thelittlenell.com

Located in the Little Nell hotel, Montagna is one of the top dining spots in Aspen. With its buttery walls, iron chandeliers and deep picture windows, the restaurant has the feel of a chic Swiss chalet. The menu, from the pasta with housemade lamb sausage to the crispy chicken, is outstanding, and the sommelier oversees a 20,000-bottle wine cellar.

American. Breakfast, lunch, dinner, Sunday brunch. Outdoor seating. Children's menu. Bar. $86 and up

★★★THE RESTAURANT

St. Regis Aspen, 315 E. Dean St., Aspen, 970-920-3300; www.stregisaspen.com

The Restaurant, located in the St. Regis Aspen, delivers American cuisine with strong Mediterranean influences. The seasonal menu contains dishes that incorporate local ingredients, such as braised Meyer ranch short ribs, Summit Creek farms brick-oven-roasted rack of lamb and wild Pacific Northwest sturgeon. The warm dining room with pinewood floors and antique furniture and the Tuscan-inspired exhibition kitchen strike just the right tone.

Mediterranean. Lunch, dinner. Children's menu. $36-85

★★★PINE CREEK COOKHOUSE

314 S. Second St., Aspen, 970-925-1044; www.pinecreekcookhouse.com

Dine on grilled quail salad and seared elk tenderloin in this cozy cabin set in a scenic valley in the Elk Mountains. Locals like to cycle up to the rustic restaurant for hearty lunches like vegetable panini.

American. Lunch, dinner. Bar. Outdoor seating. $36-85

★★★PIÑONS

105 S. Mill St., Aspen, 970-920-2021; www.pinons.net

A reservation here is one of the most sought-after in town. Hidden away on the second floor of a shop in downtown Aspen, the contemporary restaurant is decorated with a modern mountain style. It offers vistas of Aspen Mountain and the atmosphere is upbeat and festive. The service is warm and the innovative seasonal menu delights diners. There's lots of meat on the menu, including sautéed veal loin with panko breading, tomato fondue, buffalo mozzarella served with white truffle risotto and sesame-crusted sea bass with braised baby bok choy, coconut rice and basil-lemongrass sauce.

American. Dinner. Bar. $36-85

COLORADO

HIGHLIGHTS

WHAT ARE SOME OF THE BEST RESTAURANTS?

CACHE CACHE BISTRO
An Aspen Institution, Cache Cache Bistro serves the highest-quality food. You'll taste it in dishes like the filet mignon with Dijon-peppercorn sauce, whipped potatoes and haricots verts.

MIRABELLE AT BEAVER CREEK
This little cottage in the mountains serves up big flavors in its contemporary French dishes, like Colorado lamb chops and roasted elk medallions with fruit compote. Don't miss the delicious housemade ice cream.

MONTAGNA
This Swiss-chalet style restaurant inside the Little Nell hotel is one of the best in Aspen. The American menu features entrées like Colorado lamb loin with preserved lemon, radish, mint and pea spaetzle.

PIÑONS
It's hard to snag a reservation at this Aspen restaurant, a favorite among the locals. But it's worth it to dine on seasonal American fare such as grilled filet of beef with Hudson Valley foie gras with black truffle sauce.

SWEET BASIL
This Vail restaurant is popular for its innovative dishes, like the Colorado striped bass a la plancha with sweet corn and truffle purée, chorizo, hen-of-the-woods mushrooms, shaved sweet corn and Citron vinegar.

AVON
★★★GROUSE MOUNTAIN GRILL
The Pines Lodge, 141 Scott Hill Road, Avon, 970-949-0600; www.grousemountaingrill.com
Located in the Pines Lodge, this elegant, European-style restaurant is a good choice for breakfast, lunch or a quiet dinner. The dark wood furnishings, nightly piano music and tables topped with crisp white linens create a warm and cozy atmosphere. The dinner menu focuses on rustic American dishes such as Meyer ranch natural beef hanger steak with horseradish potato cake, spring bean and tomato relish, or pretzel-crusted pork chops with housemade chorizo and orange mustard sauce. The warm apple bread pudding is a perfect finish.
American. Breakfast, lunch, dinner. Outdoor seating. Children's menu. Bar. $36-85

BEAVER CREEK

★★★BEANO'S CABIN

Beaver Creek, 970-754-3463

This log cabin restaurant is amid the aspen trees on Beaver Creek Mountain. There are a few ways to get here: sleigh, horse-drawn wagon, van or horseback. Regardless of your mode of transport, Beano's is worth the trip. Listen to live music, sit by the crackling fire and enjoy a five-course meal, such as roasted Colorado beef tenderloin with blue cheese scalloped potatoes, asparagus salad and brandy sauce or gingerbread-crusted Colorado rack of lamb.

American. Dinner. Closed early April-late June, late September-mid-December. Bar. Children's menu. Reservations recommended. $86 and up

★★★★MIRABELLE AT BEAVER CREEK

55 Village Road, Beaver Creek, 970-949-7728; www.mirabelle1.com

Love is in the air at this charming 19th-century cottage in the mountains. Each of the spacious, bright rooms is cozy and warm, while the outdoor porch, lined with colorful potted flowers, is the perfect spot for alfresco dining. The food is just as magical. The kitchen offers sophisticated French fare prepared with a modern sensibility. Signature dishes include Colorado lamb chops and roasted elk medallions with fruit compote. The housemade ice cream is the best way to end the meal, even in the winter.

French. Dinner. Closed Sunday; also May, November. Outdoor seating. Children's menu. Bar. $36-85

★★★SPLENDIDO AT THE CHATEAU

17 Chateau Lane, Beaver Creek, 970-845-8808; www.splendidobeavercreek.com

Locals come to this picturesque, chalet-style dining room tucked into the hills of Beaver Creek to celebrate special occasions and enjoy the wonderful piano music offered nightly. The food is splendid, too. The menu changes each evening, but seasonal signatures have included dishes like sesame-crusted Atlantic salmon with coconut basmati rice and cilantro-lemongrass sauce, and grilled elk loin with braised elk osso bucco.

American. Dinner. Closed mid-April-mid-June, mid-October-mid-November. Reservations recommended. Children's menu. Bar. $36-85

EDWARDS

★★★MIRADOR

The Lodge & Spa at Cordillera, 2205 Cordillera Way, Edwards, 970-926-2200; www.cordilleralodge.com

Inside the luxurious Lodge & Spa at Cordillera, Mirador features breathtaking views of the Rocky Mountains and an elegant atmosphere. Its innovative menu of regional Colorado fare has won critical acclaim. It's complemented by an impressive wine list. If you and your group of VIPs want some privacy, reserve the 24-seat private dining area or the 12-seat family table in the wine cellar.

French. Dinner. Outdoor seating. Bar. $36-85

GRAND LAKE
★★CAROLINE'S CUISINE
9921 Highway 34, Grand Lake, 970-627-8125, 800-627-9636; www.sodaspringsranch.com

Dine at this cozy restaurant, and large windows will offer vistas of either the mountain or the hills. Admire the scenery as you nibble on bistro-style dishes, such as steak frites and roasted duck, or classic American fare such as grilled steaks and roasted chicken.

French, American. Dinner. Outdoor seating. Children's menu. Bar. $16-35

KEYSTONE
★★SKI TIP LODGE
764 Montezuma Road, Keystone, 800-354-4386; www.skitiplodge.com

This charming bed and breakfast, a former stagecoach stop, has been serving American regional cuisine for more than 50 years. The rotating four-course menu offers selections like house-smoked Icelandic Arctic char and an open-faced pork belly BLT. Check out desserts like the rich apple cobbler, with walnut streusel, mascarpone and cinnamon ice cream.

American. Dinner. Children's menu. Bar. $36-85

STEAMBOAT SPRINGS
★★HARWIGS-L'APOGEE
911 Lincoln Ave., Steamboat Springs, 970-879-1919; www.lapogee.com

Housed in a former saddlery store, L'Apogee has become local favorite. The interesting American menu features favorites like black Angus filet and lamb chops, as well as less traditional dishes such as venison. The large wine cellar is filled with many reasonably priced choices from around the world.

American, Thai. Dinner. Outdoor seating. Children's menu. Bar. $36-85

SNOWMASS VILLAGE
★★KRABLOONIK
4250 Divide Road, Snowmass Village, 970-923-3953; www.krabloonik.com

Celebrate the dog days of winter at this log restaurant with ski-in access and large picture windows framing the mountain views. More than 200 sled dogs live in the kennel next door—take a sled ride after a lunch of wild mushroom soup, fresh baked bread and smoked meat from the onsite smokehouse. (No lunch during summer.) At night, the sunken fire pit keeps everyone warm and toasty.

American, seafood. Lunch, dinner. Closed mid-April-mid-June, October-Thanksgiving. Reservations recommended. Children's menu. $36-85

★★SAGE
Snowmass Club, 239 Snowmass Circle, Snowmass Village, 970-923-0923; www.snowmassclub.com

Located in the Snowmass Club, this restaurant offers simple classics with fresh ingredients, like seared sea scallops with apple and house bacon relish and local arugula. In the summer, the patio is a lovely spot for lunch, thanks to unob-structed views of Mount Daly.

American. Breakfast, lunch, dinner. Outdoor seating. Children's menu. Bar. $36-85

VAIL

★★★LEFT BANK

183 Gore Creek Drive, Vail, 970-476-3696; www.leftbankvail.com

As the name suggests, this restaurant serves classic French cuisine in a friendly, casual atmosphere in the heart of the Village. The restaurant serves all the classics from escargot to steak au poivre. Start off with a Kir Royale.

French, Mediterranean. Dinner. Closed Sunday. Reservations recommended. Bar. $36-85

★★★RESTAURANT KELLY LIKEN

12 Vail Road, Vail, 970-479-0175; www.kellyliken.com

The warm burgundy and champagne colors, custom-made furniture, slate and glass tile floors and hand-blown glass chandelier create an elegant and romantic atmosphere. Chef Kelly Liken, from season seven's *Top Chef*, uses mostly locally produced and cultivated products for the seasonal American menu, including elk carpaccio, potato-crusted trout and Colorado lamb.

American. Dinner. Reservations recommended. Children's menu. Bar. $36-85

★★★SWEET BASIL

193 E. Gore Creek Drive, Vail, 970-476-0125; www.sweetbasil-vail.com

This contemporary American restaurant has been a local favorite since it opened in 1977. Understated modern décor with cherry wood accents and colorful artwork provides a comfortable setting in which to enjoy the inventive menu. The culinary adventure begins with starters like Dungeness crab salad and Spanish almond gazpacho with olive oil sorbet, flashed grapes and aged sherry vinegar. Entrées might include sea scallops with wild arugula, Spanish chorizo, warm artichoke salad, sunchoke purée and romesco sauce; or dry-aged Heritage pork chops with grilled Colorado peaches, fried green tomatoes, frisée and whiskey bacon jus. An award-winning wine list complements the full menu, and desserts can provide a nice capper to the meal.

Contemporary American. Lunch, dinner, Saturday-Sunday brunch. Reservations recommended. Outdoor seating. Bar. $86 and up

★★★THE WILDFLOWER

The Lodge at Vail, 174 Gore Creek Drive, Vail, 877-528-7625; www.lodgeatvail.rockresorts.com

If you're searching for a memorable dining experience, head to the Wildflower, a beautiful restaurant inside the Lodge at Vail. Filled with baskets of wildflowers and massive floral arrangements, the room boasts wonderful views and tables lined with country-style floral linens. The restaurant features a delicious and innovative selection of seafood, game and poultry (such as ostrich), accented with global flavors like lemongrass, curry and chilies, and local fruits and vegetables, including herbs grown in the Wildflower's garden. An extensive and reasonably priced wine list concentrates on Italy and matches the distinctive menu.

American. Lunch, dinner. Closed Monday. Reservations recommended. Outdoor seating. Bar. $86 and up

WINTER PARK

★★★THE LODGE AT SUNSPOT

239 Winter Park Drive, Winter Park, 970-726-1564; www.skiwinterpark.com

This dining room at the Winter Park Ski Resort can be reached only by chairlift—and it's worth the trip. The restaurant has the feel of a mountain lodge, built with logs from Grand County. The windows are eight feet high, so you have magnificent views of the Continental Divide. It is a glorious setting to enjoy the satisfying American menu.

American. Lunch, dinner. Reservations recommended. Children's menu. Bar. $36-85

SPAS

AVON

★★★★ALLEGRIA SPA AT PARK HYATT BEAVER CREEK

Park Hyatt Beaver Creek, 100 E. Thomas Place, Avon, 970-748-7500, 888-591-1234; www.allegriaspa.com

Aged copper fountains and a crackling fireplace set the mood at this spa inside the Park Hyatt Beaver Creek, which offers a blend of locally and Eastern-inspired therapies. The hydration facial is a lifesaver for parched, wind-burned skin. Body treatments incorporate gentle exfoliation, a nourishing body wrap and a rewarding massage into one blissful experience. The body scrubs take their cues from the garden. The warm milk and honey sugar scrub, sweet orange and citrus salt scrub, and cranberry orange scrub render skin supple. The lavender and rose and balancing hot-oil wraps are luxurious ways to hydrate skin. After a day on the slopes, treat your toes to the Allegria deluxe pedicure.

★★★★THE BACHELOR GULCH SPA AT THE RITZ-CARLTON

The Ritz-Carlton, Bachelor Gulch, 130 Daybreak Ridge, Avon, 970-748-6200, 800-576-5582; www.ritzcarlton.com

The Bachelor Gulch Spa captures the essence of its alpine surroundings with polished rock, stout wood and flowing water in its interiors. The rock grotto with a lazy-river hot tub is a defining feature, and the fitness rooms have majestic mountain views. The beauty of the outdoors also extends to treatments, which utilize ingredients indigenous to the region. Alpine berries, Douglas fir and blue spruce sap are just some of the natural components of the exceptional signature treatments. After a rigorous day of skiing, there are also plenty of massage options, from the Roaring Rapids, which uses hydrotherapy, to the Four-Hands, where two therapists work out knots.

NORTH CENTRAL COLORADO

This region may be most known for the beautiful Rocky Mountain National Park, 415 square miles of forests, meadows and tundra. But there are great spots to visit in North Central Colorado. Estes Park occupies an enviable swath of land at the eastern edge of the Rockies. Many claim that Estes Park offers the quintessential Colorado experience. The area has been a vacation destination for thousands of years. Archaeological evidence indicates that Native Americans were drawn here to escape the summer heat. Situated 7,500 feet above sea level, the town's elevation manages to keep summertime temperatures comfortably cool—and also brings an average of 63 inches of snow during the winter months. The snowfall draws hordes of skiers and snowboarders to the area, with a season that typically lasts from November until April. During the warmer months, Estes Park becomes even more crowded. The city's downtown area features an array of shops, restaurants and accommodations.

The city that perhaps best captures the spirit of the region is Boulder. Dubbed "the city between the mountains and reality," Boulder benefits from a combination of great beauty and great weather that makes the area ideal for outdoor activity. Its location between the base of the Rocky Mountains and the head of a rich agricultural valley provides an ideal year-round climate, with 300 sunny days annually. More than 30,000 acres of open, unspoiled land and 200 miles of hiking and biking paths make the city an outdoor-lover's paradise. Boulder is also sophisticated and artsy, offering a wealth of cultural activities from music to dance, art and one-of-a-kind shops. The mix of gorgeous scenery and cultural offerings showcases the best North Central Colorado has to offer.

WHAT TO SEE

BOULDER
BOULDER CREEK PATH
Boulder, from 55th St. and Pearl Parkway to Boulder Canyon, 303-413-7200; www.boulderparks-rec.org

This nature and exercise trail runs some 16 miles through the city and into the adjacent mountains, leading past a sculpture garden, a restored steam locomotive and several parks.
Daily.

BOULDER MUSEUM OF CONTEMPORARY ART
1750 13th St., Boulder, 303-443-2122; www.bmoca.org

View exhibits of contemporary and regional painting, sculpture and other media, along with changing exhibits featuring local, domestic and international artists. Check out the experimental performance series on Thursdays as well as the many lectures, workshops and special events.
Admission: adults $5, seniors and students $4, children free. Tuesday, Thursday, Friday 11 a.m.-5 p.m., Wednesday 11 a.m.-8 p.m., Saturday 9 a.m.-4 p.m., Sunday noon-3 p.m.

CELESTIAL SEASONINGS FACTORY TOUR
4600 Sleepytime Drive, Boulder, 303-581-1202, 303-530-5300; www.celestialseasonings.com

This 45-minute tour takes visitors through the beautiful gardens that produce

HIGHLIGHTS

WHAT ARE THE AREA'S TOP FACTORY TOURS?

ANHEUSER-BUSCH BREWERY TOUR
This Fort Collins brewery makes one of the most popular U.S. beer brands, Budweiser. Learn about the history of the company and go on a free tour of the brewery. End the tour with some suds samples.

CELESTIAL SEASONINGS FACTORY TOUR
If you prefer less potent drinks, visit the Celestial Seasonings Factory. You'll get a free tour of the gardens that grow the herbs for the company's delicious, aromatic teas. During the tour, you will get a chance to sip the newest tea blends.

COORS BREWERY TOUR
Coors is the country's third-largest brewer, so of course this brewery is going to have a free factory tour. Learn about the malting and brewing process, and taste the brews of the company's labors in the hospitality room.

the herbs and botanicals used in the company's teas, with stops in the sinus-clearing Mint Room and the production area, where 8 million tea bags are made every day. You can also check out the company's art gallery of original paintings, which decorate their tea boxes, and be among the first to sample some of the company's newest blends. Children must be older than five to enter the factory. Tours run hourly.

Tours: free. Monday-Friday 10 a.m.-4 p.m., Saturday 10 a.m.-3 p.m., Sunday 11 a.m.-3 p.m.

LEANIN' TREE MUSEUM OF WESTERN ART
6055 Longbow Drive, Boulder, 303-530-1442, 800-777-8716; www.leanintreemuseum.com
Check out the original works of art used in many of the greeting cards produced by Leanin' Tree, a major publisher. The museum also features the private collection of paintings and sculptures amassed by Edward P. Trumble, the chairman and founder of Leanin' Tree Inc.

Admission: free. Monday-Friday 8 a.m.-5 p.m., Saturday-Sunday 10 a.m.-5 p.m.; closed Thanksgiving Day, Christmas Day and New Year's Day.

MACKY AUDITORIUM CONCERT HALL
Pleasant Street and Macky Drive, Boulder, 303-492-8423; www.colorado.edu
This 2,047-seat auditorium hosts the Boulder Philharmonic Orchestra. Concerts are given during the academic year.

NATIONAL CENTER FOR ATMOSPHERIC RESEARCH
1850 Table Mesa Drive, Boulder, 303-497-1000; www.ncar.ucar.edu

Designed by noted architect I. M. Pei, the center includes exhibits on global warming, weather, the sun, aviation hazards and supercomputing. There's also a 400-acre nature preserve onsite. Guided tours are offered.

Admission: free. Visitor center: Monday-Friday 8 a.m.-5 p.m., Saturday-Sunday 9 a.m.-4 p.m.

ENGLEWOOD
COMFORT DENTAL AMPHITHEATRE
6350 Greenwood Plaza Blvd., Greenwood Village, 303-220-7000; www.livenation.com

Comfort Dental Amphitheatre, formerly Fiddler's Green Amphitheatre, is located 15 minutes south of downtown Denver. The park-like setting is an inviting venue for a wide variety of musical performances during the summer months, from marquee names to classical orchestras. Come early to enjoy the mountain sunset. Bring a blanket or tarp (no lawn chairs are allowed) and a picnic, or reserve an indoor seat, purchase dinner from one of the many vendors and watch the acts up close.

June-August.

THE MUSEUM OF OUTDOOR ARTS
1000 Englewood Parkway, Englewood, 303-806-0444; www.moaonline.org

This outdoor sculpture garden spans 400 acres. The museum, which counts more than 200 pieces in its collection, combines art, architecture and landscape into public spaces. Guided tours are available.

Admission: free. Monday-Thursday 9 a.m.-5 p.m., Friday 9 a.m.-4 p.m.

ESTES PARK
AERIAL TRAMWAY
420 Riverside Drive, Estes Park, 970-586-3675

Two cabins suspended from steel cables move up or down Prospect Mountain at 1,400 feet per minute. You get a superb view of the Continental Divide during the trip. Pack lunch; picnic facilities are available at the 8,896-foot summit. There's also a panoramic dome shelter and a snack bar.

Mid-May-mid-September, daily.

BIG THOMPSON CANYON
Estes Park, east on Highway 34

Big Thompson is one of the most beautiful canyon drives in the state.

ESTES PARK AREA HISTORICAL MUSEUM
200 Fourth St., Estes Park, 970-586-6256; www.estesnet.com

Three facilities include a building that served as the headquarters of Rocky Mountain National Park from 1915 to 1923. See exhibits on the history of the park and surrounding area.

Admission: free. Gallery: May-October, Monday-Saturday 10 a.m.-5 p.m., Sunday 1-5 p.m.; November-April, Friday-Saturday 10 a.m.-5 p.m., Sunday 1-5 p.m.

FORT COLLINS

ANHEUSER-BUSCH BREWERY TOUR

2351 Busch Drive, Fort Collins, 970-490-4691; www.budweisertours.com

The Anheuser-Busch Brewery in Fort Collins produces 2.6 million cans of beer a day. The tour includes an overview of the company's history (which dates back to the mid-1800s), a walking tour of the brewing and control rooms and a visit with the famous Budweiser Clydesdales, housed with their Dalmatian companions in picturesque stables on the beautiful Busch estate. The best part is the complimentary beer tasting at the end of the tour.

Admission: free. January-May, Thursday-Monday 10 a.m.-4 p.m.; June-August, daily 9:30 a.m.-4.30 p.m.; September, daily 10 a.m.-4 p.m.; October-December, Thursday-Monday 10 a.m.-4 p.m.

FORT COLLINS MUSEUM & DISCOVERY SCIENCE CENTER

Library Park, 200 Mathews St., Fort Collins, 970-221-6738; www.fcmdsc.org

This hands-on science and technology museum features more than 100 educational exhibits, like "Bright Ideas," which looks at the history of electricity. You can experiment with the electrical conductivity of the human body and learn how electricity revolutionized everything from hair curling to transportation.

Admission: adults $4, seniors and children 3-12 $3, children under 2 free. Tuesday-Saturday 10 a.m.-5 p.m., Sunday noon-5 p.m.

LINCOLN CENTER

417 W. Magnolia, Fort Collins, 970-221-6735; www.ci.fort-collins.co.us

Lincoln Center includes a theater for the performing arts, a concert hall, a sculpture garden, an art gallery and display areas with changing exhibits.

Daily.

ROOSEVELT NATIONAL FOREST

240 W. Prospect Road, Fort Collins, 970-498-1100; www.fs.fed.us

On the reserve's more than 780,000 acres of icy streams, mountains and beautiful scenery, you can enjoy trout fishing, hiking trails, a winter sports area, picnicking and camping. The Cache la Poudre River, five wilderness areas and the Peak-to-Peak Scenic Byway are all nearby.

GOLDEN

BUFFALO BILL MUSEUM & GRAVE

987 Lookout Mountain Road, Golden, 303-526-0744; www.buffalobill.org

Lookout Mountain is the final resting place of the man who virtually defined the spirit of the Wild West: William F. "Buffalo Bill" Cody, whose life included stints as a cattle driver, fur trapper, gold miner, Pony Express rider and scout for the U.S. Cavalry. He became world famous with his traveling Buffalo Bill's Wild West Show. At the Buffalo Bill Museum & Grave, Cody still draws crowds who come to see the museum's Western artifacts collection, take advantage of the beautiful hilltop vistas and pay homage to this legendary Western hero.

Admission: adults $5, seniors $4, children 6-15 $1, children 5 and under free. May-October: daily 9 a.m.-5 p.m.; November-April: Tuesday-Sunday 9 a.m.-4 p.m.

WHICH IS THE MOST ICONIC HOTEL IN NORTH CENTRAL COLORADO?

Stanley Hotel:
Built in 1909, the Stanley Hotel is listed on the National Register of Historic Places, but it's more famous for being the inspiration behind the eerie hotel-set flick *The Shining*. Writer Stephen King stayed in room 217, and the experience gave rise to the classic horror book and film.

COORS BREWERY TOUR

13th and Ford streets, Golden, 303-277-2337, 866-812-2337; www.coors.com

For a fun, free factory tour, visit Coors Brewing Company—the nation's third-largest brewer—to see how beer is made. The 40-minute walking tour reviews the malting, brewing and packaging processes and ends with a free sampling in the hospitality room (proper ID required). Visitors under 18 must be accompanied by an adult.

Admission: free. Monday-Saturday 10 a.m.-4 p.m.

GOLDEN GATE CANYON STATE PARK

Crawford Gulch Road, Golden, 303-582-3707; www.parks.state.co.us

On 12,000 acres, this park features nature and hiking trails, cross-country skiing, snowshoeing, biking, horseback riding, ice skating, picnicking and camping. Panorama Point Overlook provides a 100-mile view of the Continental Divide.

Daily.

HERITAGE SQUARE

18301 W. Colfax Ave., Golden, 303-279-2789; www.heritagesquare.info

Heritage Square family entertainment park is reminiscent of an 1870s Colorado mining town with its Old West streetscapes and Victorian façades. In addition to specialty shops, restaurants, museums and a theater, there are amusement rides, a waterslide, a 70-foot bungee tower, go-karts and a miniature golf course. Heritage Square is also home to Colorado's longest Alpine slide.

Admission: free. Winter: Monday-Saturday 10 a.m.-5 p.m., Sunday noon-5 p.m.; summer: Monday-Saturday 10 a.m.-8 p.m., Sunday noon-8 p.m.

MORRISON

RED ROCKS PARK AND AMPHITHEATER

18300 W. Alameda Parkway, Morrison, 720-865-2494; www.redrocksonline.com

Red Rocks Amphitheater is in the majestic 816-acre Red Rocks Park, 15 miles west of Denver. Two 300-foot sandstone monoliths serve as stadium walls for this open-air arena. During the summer, the 8,000-seat amphitheater, with its perfect acoustical conditions, awe-inspiring beauty and panoramic view of Denver, serves as a stunning stage for performers ranging from chart-topping rock bands to world-renowned symphony orchestras.

WHERE TO STAY

BOULDER

★★★HOTEL BOULDERADO

2115 13th St., Boulder, 303-442-4344, 800-433-4344; www.boulderado.com

Boulder was a sleepy little town of 11,000 back in 1905, when the city fathers decided they could move things along by providing the comfort of a first-class hotel. Back then, men worked 24 hours a day stoking the huge coal furnace to keep the hotel evenly heated, and rooms went for $1 per night. The hotel has since been restored to its original grandeur. You'll feel like you've stepped back in time when you enter the lobby with its stained-glass ceiling, cherry staircase, plush velvet furniture and swirling ceiling fans. The rooms are individually decorated, but they all have a Victorian theme, with floral patterns and period furnishings.

160 rooms. Restaurant, bar. Business center. $151-250

★★★MARRIOTT BOULDER

2660 Canyon Blvd., Boulder, 303-440-8877, 888-238-2178; www.marriott.com

This hotel sits at the base of the Flatiron Mountains in downtown Boulder, which means many rooms have a nice view of the Flatirons. Rooms also have free Internet and fitness kits. Opting for the Concierge level will get you access to two private rooftop terraces, complimentary continental breakfast and evening appetizers. Take a dip in the outdoor pool or hit the spa. If you feel like getting out, the hotel is within walking distance of downtown's galleries, shops and restaurants.

157 rooms. Restaurant, bar. Pool. Spa. $151-250

★★★ST. JULIEN HOTEL & SPA

900 Walnut St., Boulder, 720-406-9696, 877-303-0900; www.stjulien.com

Relax at this luxurious yet casual hotel with a 10,000-square-foot spa and fitness center, two-lane infinity pool and outdoor terrace. The elegant rooms feature custom pillow-top beds with fluffy duvets and oversized slate bathrooms with separate showers. They also include complimentary high-speed Internet access and organic coffee. The martini bar, T-Zero, is an intimate spot for a drink. Or go shopping at Pearl Street Mall, which is only a block away from the hotel.

201 rooms. Restaurant, bar. Business center. Fitness center. Pool. Spa. $151-250

BROOMFIELD

★★★OMNI INTERLOCKEN RESORT

500 Interlocken Blvd., Broomfield, 303-438-6600, 888-444-6664; www.omnihotels.com

Set against the backdrop of the Rocky Mountains, this 300-acre resort has something for everyone. Golfers needing to brush up on their game head for the L.A.W.S. Academy of Golf for its celebrated clinics and courses before hitting the resort's three nine-hole courses. There's a well-equipped fitness center and pool and a full-service spa that offers a variety of treatments. The guest rooms are comfortable and elegant and include amenities like WebTV and high-speed Internet. Three restaurants run the gamut from traditional to pub style.

390 rooms. Restaurant, bar. Fitness center. Pool. Spa. Pets accepted. Golf. $251-350

ENGLEWOOD

★★★THE INVERNESS HOTEL AND CONFERENCE CENTER

200 Inverness Drive W., Englewood, 303-799-5800, 800-832-9053; www.invernesshotel.com

This hotel and conference center, with 60,000 square feet of function space, is the perfect choice for corporate retreats, thanks to naturally lit boardrooms, "fatigue-free" chairs, built-in audiovisual equipment and more. All rooms feature views of the golf course or the Rocky Mountains and suites on the Club Floor have sunken living rooms. The spa offers a variety of treatments.

302 rooms. Restaurant, bar. Business center. Fitness center. Pool. Spa. Golf. Tennis. $151-250

★★★SHERATON DENVER TECH CENTER HOTEL

7007 S. Clinton St., Greenwood Village, 303-799-6200, 800-325-3535; www.starwoodhotels.com

The spacious guest rooms at this hotel will appeal to both business and leisure travelers. Nearby attractions include the Denver Museum of Natural History, the Denver Zoo and the Coors Brewery. You can get to the attractions via the complimentary shuttle service provided within a five-mile radius.

262 rooms. Restaurant, bar. Pool. Pets accepted. $61-150

ESTES PARK

★★★THE STANLEY HOTEL

333 Wonderview Ave., Estes Park, 970-577-4000, 800-976-1377; www.stanleyhotel.com

The inspiration behind *The Shining*, the Stanley Hotel was built in 1909 by automaker F. Stanley and is only six miles from Rocky Mountain National Park. You can tour the room that inspired Stephen King to write the story, as well as the hotel's underground tunnels, on a ghost tour of the property. Multimillion-dollar renovations have restored the gorgeous white hotel, which occupies 35 acres surrounded by the Rocky Mountains, to its original grandeur. The cozy rooms are classically styled and feature pillow-top mattresses and free wireless Internet.

138 rooms. Restaurant, bar. Pool. Spa. Tennis. $61-150

FORT COLLINS

★★★MARRIOTT FORT COLLINS

350 E. Horsetooth Road, Fort Collins, 970-226-5200, 800-342-4398; www.marriott.com

Located just three miles from Colorado State University, this hotel is a great place to stay during CSU parents' weekend. Rooms feature luxury bedding with down comforters and fluffy pillows. Take a swim in the indoor or outdoor pool and hit the gym for a workout.

229 rooms. Restaurant, bar. Business center. Pool. $61-150

GOLDEN

★★★MARRIOTT DENVER WEST

1717 Denver West Blvd., Golden, 303-279-9100, 888-238-1803; www.marriott.com

Rooms at this hotel come with Revive bedding. The renovated health club is stocked with cutting-edge equipment, while the sports bar has 37 flat-screen high-definition TVs.

305 rooms. Restaurant, bar. Fitness center. Pool. $61-150

LAKEWOOD
★★★SHERATON DENVER WEST HOTEL
360 Union Blvd., Lakewood, 303-987-2000, 800-325-3535; www.sheraton.com

Adjacent to the Denver Federal Center, this hotel is a perfect launching pad to explore nearby attractions, including Coors Brewery and Red Rocks Concert Amphitheater. To unwind back at the hotel, the 10,000-square-foot health club includes a heated indoor lap pool and the spa offers a variety of relaxing treatments. Even dogs can take a load off in the Sheraton Sweet Sleeper beds. The rooms are warm and cozy in deep maroons with traditional décor.

242 rooms. Restaurant, bar. Business center. Pool. Spa. Fitness center. $151-250

WHERE TO EAT

BOULDER
★★★★FLAGSTAFF HOUSE RESTAURANT
1138 Flagstaff Road, Boulder, 303-442-4640; www.flagstaffhouse.com

From its perch on Flagstaff Mountain, this restaurant is easily one of the most amazing spots to watch the sunset. The upscale and inspired menu changes daily, with plates like beef Wellington dressed up with black truffle sauce and Hawaiian ono with ginger, scallions and soft-shell crabs. The wine list is massive—the restaurant has a 20,000-bottle wine cellar—so enlist the assistance of the attentive sommelier for guidance. The restaurant is owned by the Monette family, which means that you'll be treated to refined service and homegrown hospitality, making dining here a delight from start to finish. If you can, arrive early and sit at the mahogany bar for an enjoyable pre-dinner cocktail.

American. Dinner. Reservations recommended. Outdoor seating. Bar. $86 and up

★★★THE GREENBRIAR INN
8735 N. Foothills Highway, Boulder, 303-440-7979, 800-253-1474; www.greenbriarinn.com

Originally built in 1893, this Boulder landmark sits on 20 acres at the mouth of Left Hand Canyon. The atrium room has French doors that open up to the south garden and lawn. The mouthwatering food includes blue-crab-crusted beef tournedos and maple-cured duck breasts. A champagne brunch is served on Saturday and Sunday.

American. Dinner, Saturday-Sunday brunch. Closed Monday. Outdoor seating. Bar. $36-85

★★★JOHN'S RESTAURANT
2328 Pearl St., Boulder, 303-444-5232; www.johnsrestaurantboulder.com

You'll feel like you're stepping into someone's home when you enter this century-old cottage with lace curtains and white tablecloths. In the spring and summer, windows open to courtyards filled with bright flowers. On the menu, you'll find contemporary European dishes with specialties like smoked Scottish salmon, filet mignon with Stilton cheese and ale sauce, and gelato.

International. Dinner. Closed Sunday-Monday. $36-85

★★★Q'S
Hotel Boulderado, 2115 13th St., Boulder, 303-442-4880; www.qsboulder.com

This welcoming, bistro-style restaurant in the Hotel Boulderado offers a superb selection of seafood, meat and game. Go for the seared scallops with lemon and crab risotto, grilled leeks, and a spinach and parsley purée, or a grilled New York strip steak with béarnaise relish and a smoked-tomato jus. The international wine collection is eclectic and includes small-barrel and boutique selections as well as a proprietor's reserve list. The service is friendly and efficient.

American. Breakfast, lunch (Monday-Friday), dinner (Monday-Friday), Saturday-Sunday brunch. Children's menu. Bar. $36-85

LAKEWOOD
★★★240 UNION
240 Union Blvd., Lakewood, 303-989-3562; www.240union.com

This contemporary American grill with a large open kitchen is known for having some of the best seafood in the Denver area. Other favorites include wood-fired oven pizzas, Colorado lamb sirloin with Camembert potatoes and beef tenderloin with black garlic butter, asparagus and three-onion mashed potatoes. The wine list features a number of good selections, and desserts include classics like key lime pie and chocolate mousse cake.

American. Lunch, dinner. Reservations recommended. Bar. $16-35

LYONS
★★★BLACK BEAR INN
42 E. Main St., Lyons, 303-823-6812; www.blackbearinn.com

Since 1977, owners Hans and Annalies Wyppler have welcomed guests to their cozy Alpine-style restaurant. The menu features hearty dishes such as roasted duck and pork schnitzel. The fried Camembert cheese with housemade spaetzle is meant for vegetarians, but even meat eaters will be tempted to order the tasty dish.

American. Lunch, dinner. Closed Monday-Thursday. Outdoor seating. Bar. $36-85

★★★LA CHAUMIÈRE
Highway 36, Lyons, 303-823-6521; www.lachaumiere-restaurant.com

This charming fine dining restaurant offers friendly service and a simple but delicious menu of French cuisine. The menu changes with the seasons, but you might see filet mignon with red wine sauce, stuffed quail with wild mushrooms and a port wine demi-glaze. One mainstay is the chef's award-winning Maryland crab soup. The mountain setting adds to the relaxing atmosphere.

French. Dinner. Closed Monday. Children's menu. $16-35

MORRISON
★★★THE FORT
19192 Highway 8, Morrison, 303-697-4771; www.thefort.com

Sam Arnold's popular, kitschy restaurant has been serving buffalo steaks for 30 years. The menu also features other game, such as elk chops, as well as beef and seafood. The adobe re-creation of the historic Bent's Fort is reason enough to come here.

American. Dinner. Outdoor seating. Children's menu. Bar. $86 and up

WHERE TO SHOP

BROOMFIELD
FLATIRON CROSSING
1 W. FlatIron Circle, Broomfield, 720-887-7467, 866-352-8476; www.flatironcrossing.com

This architecturally innovative 1.5 million-square-foot retail and entertainment complex between Denver and Boulder was designed to reflect the natural Flatirons (rock formations), canyons and prairies of its surroundings. The result is a one-of-a-kind visual and shopping experience, with more than 200 stores—like Aveda, Macy's and the Gap—and numerous restaurants for indoor and outdoor dining. *Daily.*

BOULDER
PEARL STREET MALL
900-1500 Pearl St., Boulder, 303-449-3774; www.boulderdowntown.com

Open year-round, this retail and restaurant district is particularly appealing in the summer with its brick walkways, Victorian storefronts, lush landscaping and parade of colorful personalities. You'll find stores ranging from American Apparel to the Rocky Mountain Chocolate Factory. Offering four blocks of mostly upscale restaurants, galleries, bars and boutiques, the mall invites visitors to conclude a day of shopping with a meal at one of its many European-style cafés while taking in the impromptu performances of street musicians, jugglers, artists and mimes. *Hours vary.*

LAKEWOOD
COLORADO MILLS
14500 W. Colfax Ave., Lakewood, 303-384-3000; www.coloradomills.com

This new 1.2-million-square-foot state-of-the-art retail and entertainment complex is just 10 minutes from downtown Denver, and brings a vast array of value-oriented stores, restaurants and entertainment venues together. Stores include a Super Target, Gap Outlet, Guess Factory Store, Nike Factory Store and much more. Movie theaters, shops, restaurants, an interactive play area for kids and a 40,000-square-foot ESPN X Games Skatepark for older kids form the core of the entertainment center. *Monday-Saturday 10 a.m.-9 p.m., Sunday 11 a.m.-6 p.m.*

WHICH NORTH CENTRAL COLORADO RESTAURANTS HAVE THE BEST AMERICAN FOOD?

240 Union:
Amazing seafood takes the spotlight at this Lakewood restaurant. Taste treasures from the sea like cioppino, a seafood stew, or the chicken-fried lobster tail with tarragon cream.

Flagstaff House Restaurant:
The restaurant's menu changes nightly, but the kitchen consistently turns out excellent fare. You can expect dishes like Copper River king salmon with Hawaiian blue prawns, or butter-poached Maine day boat lobster.

Q's:
You'll find succulent seafood and meat at this bistro inside the Hotel Boulderado. Fill up on the seared scallops with lemon and crab risotto, or the roasted rack of Colorado lamb.

DENVER

The capital of Colorado, nicknamed the "Mile High City" because its official elevation is exactly one mile above sea level, began as a settlement of gold seekers, many of them unsuccessful. In its early years, Denver almost lost out to several booming mountain mining centers in the race to become the state's major city.

Today Denver has won that race. With the Great Plains sweeping away to the east, the foothills of the Rocky Mountains immediately to the west, and a dry, mild climate (where you'll find 300 days of sunshine), Denver is a growing city with 2.5 million people in the metropolitan area. A building boom in the 1990s resulted in a new airport; a downtown baseball park surrounded by a lively nightlife district dubbed LoDo (lower downtown); new football, basketball and hockey stadiums; and a redeveloped river valley just west of downtown with an aquarium, an amusement park and a shopping district.

Once economically tied to Colorado's natural resources, Denver now boasts one of the most diverse economies in the United States and is a hub for the cable and telecom industries. Parks have long been a point of civic pride in the city. The Denver Mountain Park System covers 13,448 acres, scattered over 380 square miles. The chain begins 15 miles west of the city at Red Rocks Park, the site of a renowned musical venue, and extends 60 miles to the west to Summit Lake perched 12,740 feet above sea level.

WHAT TO SEE

16TH STREET MALL
16th Street between Civic Center and Denver Union Station, Denver, 303-534-6161; www.downtowndenver.com

This tree-lined pedestrian promenade of red and gray granite runs through the center of Denver's downtown shopping district—outdoor cafés, shops, restaurants, hotels, fountains and plazas line its mile-long walk. European-built shuttle buses offer transportation from either end of the promenade. Along the mall you'll find Larimer Square. This restoration of the first street in Denver includes a collection of shops, galleries, nightclubs and restaurants set among Victorian courtyards, gaslights, arcades and buildings. You can take a carriage ride around the square.

ANTIQUE ROW
From 300 to 2100 South Broadway, Denver; www.antique-row.com

More than 400 shops along a 14-block stretch of South Broadway sell everything from books to music to vintage Western wear to museum-quality furniture. Take the light rail to Broadway and Interstate 25 (I-25) to begin your tour. Most dealers are between the 400 and 2000 blocks of South Broadway and the 25 and 27 blocks of East Dakota Avenue.

ARVADA CENTER FOR THE ARTS & HUMANITIES
6901 Wadsworth Blvd., Arvada, 720-898-7200; www.arvadacenter.org

This performing arts center hosts concerts, plays, classes, demonstrations, art galleries and a banquet hall. The amphitheater seats 1,200 (June-early September). There's also a historical museum with an old cabin and pioneer artifacts.

Museum and gallery: Monday-Friday 9 a.m.-6 p.m., Saturday 9 a.m.-5 p.m., Sunday 1-5 p.m.

HIGHLIGHTS

WHAT ARE SOME OF THE BEST PLACES IN DENVER FOR OUTDOOR FUN?

DENVER BOTANIC GARDENS
Entering these gardens is like stepping into a tropical paradise. Roam the 23 acres of more than 15,000 plants. Stop by the Cloud Forest Tree, which is blanketed in orchids and other rare plants.

DENVER ZOO
The beautiful grounds of this zoo host more than 4,000 animals. Visit the unusual monkeys and apes in the Primate Panorama and the polar bears and sea lions in the Northern Shores Arctic.

HYLAND HILLS WATER WORLD
Water World is one of the largest water parks in the country. Adults can cool off in the football-sized wave pool, the 16 water slides and more. Then bring the little ones to Wally World, a miniature water park specifically for the short set.

BOETTCHER CONCERT HALL
1245 Champa St., Denver, 720-865-4220; www.artscomplex.com
Boettcher is the first fully in-the-round symphonic hall in the U.S.—all of its 2,630 seats are within 75 feet of the stage. It's home to the Colorado Symphony Orchestra (September-early June) and Opera Colorado with performances in the round (May).

BYERS-EVANS HOUSE MUSEUM
1310 Bannock St., Denver, 303-620-4933; www.coloradohistory.org
This restored Victorian house features the history of two noted Colorado pioneer families. Guided tours are available.
Admission: adults $6, seniors $5, children 6-12 $4, children 5 and under free. Tuesday-Sunday 11 a.m.-3 p.m.

CHEESMAN PARK
East Eighth Avenue and Franklin Street, Denver
This park has excellent views of nearby mountain peaks, marked off by dial and pointers. The Congress Park swimming pool is next to it and the Denver Botanical Gardens are also nearby.

THE CHILDREN'S MUSEUM OF DENVER

2121 Children's Museum Drive, Denver, 303-433-7444; www.cmdenver.org

This 24,000-square-foot, two-story hands-on museum allows children to learn and explore the world around them. Exhibits include a bubbles station where kids can create six-foot-long soapsuds or encase themselves in one humongous bubble. Mini-firefighters can practice their skills in the "CMD Fire Station No. 1" exhibit, where they can don fire gear, play with a hose and explore an authentic firetruck.

Admission: adults and children $8, seniors $6, children under 1 free. Monday-Friday 9 a.m.-4 p.m., Wednesday until 7:30 p.m., Saturday-Sunday 10 a.m.-5 p.m.

COLORADO AVALANCHE (NHL)

Pepsi Center, 1000 Chopper Circle, Denver, 303-405-1100; www.coloradoavalanche.com

The two-time Stanley Cap champions the Avalanche, Colorado's professional hockey team, call the Pepsi Center home.

COLORADO RAPIDS (MLS)

Dick's Sporting Goods Park, 6000 Victory Way, Commerce City, 303-727-3500; www.coloradorapids.com

Colorado's professional soccer team, the Rapids, play here. Tours of the park are available.

Thursday-Saturday 10 a.m.-3 p.m., every 30 minutes.

COLORADO ROCKIES (MLB)

Coors Field, 2001 Blake St., Denver, 303-762-5437, 800-388-7625; www.coloradorockies.com

Coors Field is the official ballpark of the Rockies, Colorado's pro baseball team. Tours of Coors Field are available; call for fees and schedule.

DOWNTOWN AQUARIUM — DENVER

700 Water St., Denver, 303-561-4450, 888-561-4450; www.aquariumrestaurants.com

This world-class 106,500-square-foot aquarium brings visitors face-to-face with more than 300 species of fish, birds, mammals and invertebrates from around the world. Check out the pool stocked with stingrays.

Admission: adults $15.99, seniors $14.99, children 3-11 $9.99, children 2 and under free. Sunday-Thursday 10 a.m.-9 p.m., Friday-Saturday 10 a.m.-9:30 p.m.

DENVER ART MUSEUM

100 W. 14th Ave. Parkway, Denver, 720-865-5000; www.denverartmuseum.org

The DAM houses a collection of art objects representing almost every culture and period, with more than 68,000 works. A standout is the fine collection of Native American art.

Admission: Tuesday-Thursday: adults $25, seniors and students $23, children 6-17 $16.50, children 5 and under free; Friday-Sunday: adults, seniors and students $30, children 6-17 $16.50, children 5 and under free. Tuesday-Saturday 10 a.m.-5 p.m., Sunday noon-5 p.m.

DENVER BOTANIC GARDENS

1005 York St., Denver, 720-865-3500; www.botanicgardens.org

This tropical paradise, which occupies 23 acres about 10 minutes east of downtown, is home to more than 15,000 plant species from around the world. The Conservatory, which holds more than 850 tropical and subtropical plants in an enclosed rainforest setting, is a soothing retreat for midwinter guests. Check out the Cloud Forest Tree, which is covered with hundreds of orchids and rare tropical plants. There are also alpine, herb, Japanese and wildflower gardens. Children particularly enjoy navigating the mazes in the Secret Path garden and climbing the resident banyan tree.

Admission: adults $12.50, seniors $9.50, children 4-15 $9, children 3 and under free. Mid-September-April, daily 9 a.m.-5 p.m.; May-mid-September, Saturday-Tuesday 9 a.m.-8 p.m., Wednesday-Friday 9 a.m.-5 p.m.

DENVER BRONCOS (NFL)

Invesco Field at Mile High, 1701 Bryant St., Denver, 720-258-3333; www.denverbroncos.com

Invesco Field is the home field of the Broncos, Denver's professional football team. Tours are available; call for fees and schedule.

DENVER MUSEUM OF NATURE AND SCIENCE

City Park, 2001 Colorado Blvd., Denver, 303-322-7009, 800-925-2250; www.dmns.org

Ninety habitat exhibits from four continents are displayed against natural backgrounds. The Prehistoric Journey exhibit displays dinosaurs in re-created environments. There's also an earth sciences lab, gems and minerals, and a Native American collection. The museum includes the Charles C. Gates Planetarium, where a variety of star and laser light shows are shown daily, and the Phipps IMAX Theater, which has an immense motion picture system projecting images on a screen 4½ stories tall and 6½ stories wide.

Admission: adults $11, seniors and children 3-18 $6. Daily 9 a.m.-5 p.m.

DENVER NUGGETS (NBA)

Pepsi Center, 1000 Chopper Circle, Denver, 803-405-1100; www.nba.com

The Nuggets, Denver's professional basketball team, plays ball at the Pepsi Center. Tours of the arena are available.

DENVER PERFORMING ARTS COMPLEX

Speer Boulevard and Arapahoe Street, Denver, 720-865-4220; www.artscomplex.com

This is one of the most innovative and comprehensive performing arts centers in the county. The addition of the Temple Hoyne Buell Theatre makes it one of the largest performing arts centers under one roof. The complex also contains shops and restaurants.

DENVER ZOO

City Park, 2300 Steele St., Denver, 303-376-4800; www.denverzoo.org

Located in City Park just east of downtown, this 80-acre zoological wonderland is home to more than 4,000 animals representing 700 species. Founded in 1896, the zoo has evolved into one of the nation's premier animal exhibits, noted for its beautiful grounds, innovative combination of outdoor and enclosed habitats and world-class conservation and breeding programs. Don't miss the Primate Panorama, a 7-acre showcase of rare monkeys and apes. Visit the 22,000-square-foot, glass-enclosed Tropical Discovery and feel what its like to walk into a tropical rain forest complete with caves, cliffs, waterfalls and some of the zoo's most exotic and dangerous creatures. The Northern Shores Arctic wildlife habitat provides a nose-to-nose underwater look at swimming polar bears and sea lions. Be sure to check out the feeding schedule posted just inside the zoo's entrance. During evenings throughout December, holiday music and millions of sparkling lights transform the zoo as part of the traditional Wonderlights festival.

Admission: March 1-November 1: adults $13, seniors $10, children 3-11 $8, children 2 and under free; November 2-February 28: adults $10, seniors $8, children 3-11 $6, children 2 and under free. April-September, daily 9 a.m.-6 p.m.; October-March, daily 10 a.m.-5 p.m.

ELITCH GARDENS

2000 Elitch Circle, Denver, 303-595-4386; www.elitchgardens.com

Located in downtown Denver, this park is best known for its extreme roller coaster rides. Other favorites include a 22-story freefall in the Tower of Doom, white-water rafting and the Flying Coaster, which simulates the experience of flying. The grounds have a kid park, the popular Island Kingdom water park and live entertainment nightly.

Admission: varies. June-August 10 a.m.-10 p.m.; limited hours May and September.

FORNEY MUSEUM OF TRANSPORTATION

4303 Brighton Blvd., Denver, 303-297-1113; www.forneymuseum.com

This museum houses more than 300 antique cars, carriages, cycles, sleighs, steam locomotives and coaches. One of the most notable permanent exhibits is that of Union Pacific "Big Boy" locomotive X4005, which was involved in a horrific crash in 1953, but has been restored and sits on the museum's grounds. You can also see the "Gold Bug" Kissel automobile once owned by Amelia Earhart and the Rolls-Royce that belonged to Crown Prince Aly Khan.

Admission: adults $8, seniors $6, children 3-15 $4, children 2 and under free. Monday-Saturday 10 a.m.-4 p.m.

FOUR MILE HISTORIC PARK

715 S. Forest St., Denver, 720-865-0800; www.fourmilehistoricpark.org

Once a stage stop, this 14-acre living history museum encompasses the oldest house still standing in Denver (circa 1859), plus other outbuildings and farm equipment from the late 1800s. Guides in period costume reenact life on a farmstead. And it's a great place for a picnic.

Admission: adults $5, seniors $4, children 7-17 $3, children 6 and under free. April-September, Wednesday-Friday noon-4 p.m., Saturday-Sunday 10 a.m.-4 p.m.; October-March, Wednesday-Sunday noon-4 p.m.

THE HELEN BONFILS THEATRE COMPLEX

Denver, 303-572-4466; www.artscomplex.org

This theater complex is the home of the Denver Center Theatre Company. It contains three theaters: the Stage, seating 547 in a circle around a thrust platform; the Space, a theater-in-the-round seating 450; and the Source, a small theater presenting plays by American playwrights. The complex also houses the Frank Ricketson Theatre, a 195-seat theater available for rental for community activities, classes and festivals.

MOLLY BROWN HOUSE MUSEUM

1340 Pennsylvania St., Denver, 303-832-4092; www.mollybrown.org

This museum stands as an enduring tribute to Margaret Molly Brown, the "unsinkable survivor" of the *Titanic*. A spectacular example of Colorado Victorian design, the fully restored 1880s sandstone and lava stone mansion—designed by one of Denver's most famous architects, William Lang—is filled with many of the Brown's lavish furnishings and personal possessions.

Admission: adults $8, seniors $6, children $4. September-May, Monday-Saturday 10 a.m.-3:30 p.m., Sunday noon-3:30 p.m.; June-August, Monday-Saturday 9 a.m.-4 p.m., Sunday noon-4 p.m.

SAKURA SQUARE

Larimer Street between 19th and 20th streets, Denver

Denver's Japanese Cultural and Trade Center features Asian restaurants, shops, businesses and authentic Japanese gardens. It's also the site of a famed Buddhist Temple.

SKI TRAIN

Union Station, 555 Seventh St., Denver, 303-296-4754; www.skitrain.com

A ride on the Ski Train from downtown Denver to Winter Mountain Ski Resort in Winter Park has been a favorite day trip for skiers, hikers, bikers and family vacationers since 1940. Operating on weekends year-round, the 14-car train takes you on a spectacular 60-mile wilderness ride through the Rockies and across the Continental Divide, climbing 4,000 feet and passing through 28 tunnels before dropping you off at the front entrance of the beautiful Winter Park Resort. Tickets are for round-trip, same-day rides only, and reservations are highly recommended.

Winter: Saturday-Sunday; June-August: Saturday.

STATE CAPITOL

200 E. Colfax Ave., Denver, 303-866-2604; www.milehighcity.com

This magnificent edifice overlooking Civic Center Park is a glorious reminder of Denver's opulent past. Designed by architect Elijah Myers in the classical Corinthian style, it was 18 years in the making before its official dedication in 1908. The building is renowned for its exquisite interior details and use of native materials such as gray granite, white marble, pink Colorado onyx and of course, the gold that covers its dome. Tours include a climb to the dome, 272 feet up, for a spectacular view of the surrounding mountains. Look for the special marker on the steps outside noting that you are, indeed, a mile high.

Monday-Friday 7 a.m.-5:30 p.m.

TEMPLE HOYNE BUELL THEATER

1050 13th St., Denver, 303-893-4100; www.denvercenter.org

This 1908 theater—which has hosted operas, political conventions, revivalist meetings and more—is now the stage for Broadway productions and the Colorado Ballet. It's also the home of Colorado Contemporary Dance.

WASHINGTON PARK

Downing Street between East Virginia and East Louisiana avenues, Denver, 303-698-4962

This 165-acre park features a large recreation center with an indoor pool and floral displays as well as a replica of George Washington's gardens at Mount Vernon.

WATER WORLD

1800 W. 89th Ave., Federal Heights, 303-427-7873; www.waterworldcolorado.com

Ranked among the nation's largest water parks, this 64-acre aquatic extravaganza is a great time for all ages. Water World's beautifully landscaped grounds include a wave pool the size of a football field, 16 water slides, nine inner-tube rides and a splash pool for tots. Hours vary according to season and weather, so be sure to call ahead.

Admission: varies. Late May-early September, daily 10 a.m.-6 p.m.

WHERE TO STAY

★★★★THE BROWN PALACE HOTEL

321 17th St., Denver, 303-297-3111, 800-321-2599; www.brownpalace.com

Denver's most celebrated and historic hotel, the Brown Palace has hosted presidents, royalty and celebrities since 1892. The elegant lobby features a magnificent stained-glass ceiling that tops off six levels of cast-iron balconies. The luxurious guest rooms have two styles—Victorian or Art Deco. The award-winning Palace Arms restaurant features signature favorites like rack of lamb and pan-roasted veal. Cigar aficionados take to the library-like ambience of the Churchill Bar. Those who prefer an Earl Grey over a Scotch can try the afternoon tea, which is accompanied by live harp music. And Ellygnton's Sunday brunch is legendary. After a busy day of exploring nearby attractions like the 16th Street Mall and the Museum of Natural History, the full-service spa is the perfect place to unwind with a deep massage, body treatment or facial.

241 rooms. Restaurant, bar. Business center. Fitness center. Pool. Spa. Pets accepted. $251-350

★★★GRAND HYATT

1750 Welton St., Denver, 303-295-1234, 888-591-1234; www.grandhyattdenver.com

The beautiful lobby of this centrally located hotel has a 20-foot sandstone fireplace and cozy seating areas with touches of mahogany, granite and wrought iron. The contemporary rooms feature soothing brown and cream tones and bathrooms with granite and marble tubs and massaging showerheads. Stay fit with the rooftop tennis courts surrounded by a jogging track, indoor pool and health club. The hotel's restaurant 1876, which is the year Colorado became a state, is a nice spot for dinner.

513 rooms. Restaurant, bar. Complimentary breakfast. Business center. Fitness center. Pool. $251-350

★★★HOTEL MONACO DENVER

1717 Champa St., Denver, 303-296-1717, 800-990-1303; www.monaco-denver.com

The lobby feels like an elegant, somewhat exotic living room with cushy couches, recessed bookshelves and potted palms. But the scene-stealer at this hotel is the domed ceiling, described as a Russian Circus Tent, with diamond shapes in blue, green and gold. The punchy décor carries through to the hallways and guest rooms, with bold, colorful stripes on the walls and glam black and white ottomans. The rooms also include plush duvet covers, bathroom phones and terry-cloth shower curtains.

189 rooms. Restaurant. Business center. Fitness center. Spa. Pets accepted. $251-350

★★★HOTEL TEATRO

1100 14th St., Denver, 303-228-1100, 888-727-1200; www.hotelteatro.com

Located across from the Denver Center for the Performing Arts, the Hotel Teatro inspires its guests with creative design and contemporary flair. Down comforters, Frette linens, Aveda bath products and Starbucks coffee keep you feeling relaxed, while the staff attends to your every whim. Want someone to draw you an aromatherapy bath? This is the place. Even pets get the VIP treatment, with a doggie dish with his name on it and Fiji water. Chef Kevin Taylor, who oversees two restaurants here, is something of a local sensation.

110 rooms. Restaurant, bar. Business center. Fitness center. Pets accepted. $251-350

★★★JET HOTEL

1612 Wazee St., Denver, 303-572-3300, 877-418-2462; www.thejethotel.com

The dimly lit lobby gives you an idea of what you can expect from this ultra-modern boutique hotel. To the right is the open counter of Velocity, where you can get crêpes and organic coffee each morning. To the left, stretching almost the entire length of the lobby, is the futuristic Flow Bar, backlit in soft colors that change every few minutes. Step around a handful of tall, round cocktail tables to get to the inconspicuous reception desk. There are just 19 rooms, in which standard amenities are anything but. No coffeemakers—just French plunge pots. No ice buckets—only funky insulated pitchers. No clock radios, either. Instead, there's a CD alarm clock with a library of CDs.

19 rooms. Restaurant, bar. Complimentary breakfast. $251-350

WHICH DENVER HOTELS HAVE THE BEST ROOM AMENITIES?

Jet Hotel:
The Jet Hotel puts a fun and modern spin on traditional in-room amenities. Rooms come with French presses for your morning caffeine fix, insulated pitchers to tote around ice and a CD alarm clock with a library of discs.

Loews Denver Hotel:
Families will find the amenities at this hotel a godsend. Parents won't have to lug around baby equipment, since the hotel provides tubs, bottle warmers and outlet plugs. Older kids will stay busy with kits that include games.

Oxford Hotel:
The Oxford is one of Denver's oldest hotels, but it provides some of its most modern conveniences. Rooms have free WiFi, Bose stereo systems and plasma TVs. Plus, a bath butler will come in and draw an aromatic bath whenever you request it.

★★★JW MARRIOTT DENVER AT CHERRY CREEK

150 Clayton Lane, Denver, 303-316-2700; www.jwmarriottdenver.com

There is plenty to do right outside the doors of this property just a few miles east of downtown in Cherry Creek. The area is filled with high-end boutiques, art galleries and trendy restaurants. This luxury boutique hotel has modern décor and features comfortable guest rooms with 32-inch flat-screen TVs and minibars—though you may wind up hanging out in the lobby, which has a waterfall, fireplace and live jazz. Pets are welcomed with sheepskin beds, their own dining menus and designer bowls.

196 rooms. Restaurant, bar. Business center. Spa. $251-350

★★★LOEWS DENVER HOTEL

4150 E. Mississippi Ave., Denver, 303-782-9300, 800-345-9172; www.loewshotels.com

Saying this hotel caters to the entire family is an understatement. Kids get Frisbees, backpacks and games. The hotel also offers a variety of amenities for babies, including tubs, electric bottle warmers and invisible outlet plugs. For parents, there's a menu of comfort items like chenille throws, a pillow menu and CDs. Everyone will appreciate the Italian restaurant Tuscany.

183 rooms. Restaurant, bar. Fitness center. Business center. $151-250

★★★THE MAGNOLIA HOTEL

818 17th St., Denver, 303-607-9000, 888-915-1110; www.magnoliahoteldenver.com

Many visitors to Denver make the Magnolia their home for extended stays. It's easy to see why. Set back from busy 17th Street, the Magnolia says cozy, from the wingback chairs and fireplace in its lobby to the full-size kitchens in its suites. Access to a snazzy health club is included with your stay. Upgrading to the Magnolia Club gets you wireless Internet access, nightly cocktail reception, a continental breakfast and late-night milk and cookies. Pets are welcome and receive a goodie bag at check-in.

246 rooms. Restaurant, bar. Complimentary breakfast. $251-350

★★★MARRIOTT DENVER CITY CENTER

1701 California St., Denver, 303-297-1300, 800-228-9290; www.denvermarriott.com

You'd be hard-pressed to find a better health club in an urban hotel than this one. There is a wide variety of equipment, personal trainers, massage therapy, body treatments and a pool and whirlpool—all of which will come in handy if you're here on business. Located on the first 20 floors of an office building in downtown Denver, this property is within walking distance of Coors Field, as well as several restaurants and shops.

627 rooms. Restaurant, bar. Business center. Fitness center. Pool. $251-350

★★★OXFORD HOTEL

1600 17th St., Denver, 303-628-5400, 800-228-5838; www.theoxfordhotel.com

Built in 1891, this restored hotel is touted as the city's "oldest grand hotel." The luxurious property is filled with antiques, marble floors, stained glass and beautiful paintings. The rooms have a blend of Victorian and early-20th-century décor, as well as modern-day amenities like complimentary wireless Internet access, Bose stereo systems and bath butlers, who will come to your room and draw you a bath for your soaking pleasure. The hotel's near many attractions, including Coors Field, the 16th Street Mall, Larimer Square and many shops and galleries. If you don't feel like going out on the town, spend the day getting pampered at the hotel's full-service spa.

80 rooms. Restaurant, bar. Business center. Fitness center. Spa. Pets accepted. $251-350

★★★RENAISSANCE DENVER HOTEL
3801 Quebec St., Denver, 303-399-7500; www.denverrenaissance.com

This atrium hotel has Rocky Mountain views and large rooms with mini-refrigerators, free laundry and porches, making it a good choice for families looking for a full-service hotel while trying to stay within a budget, or business travelers who prefer to stay near the airport. Downtown Denver is about a 10-minute drive. There's also a pool and an exercise facility.

400 rooms. Restaurant, bar. Complimentary breakfast. Business center. Fitness center. Pool. Spa. $151-250

★★★THE RITZ-CARLTON, DENVER
1881 Curtis St., Denver, 303-312-3800; www.ritzcarlton.com

It's the numbers that speak for this Ritz-Carlton's luxury: 400 thread-count Frette linens, 550 square-foot and larger guest rooms, and 24-hour room service. Rooms hold a number of other treats, including featherbeds, plush Frette terry robes, flat-panel HD TVs, cappuccino makers, iPod alarm clocks, rain showerheads and Bulgari bath amenities. This outpost of the brand was designed with a focus on the state's natural beauty, with red rocks, stones and water features incorporated into the construction.

202 rooms. Restaurant, bar. Business center. Fitness center. Pool. Spa. Pets accepted. Tennis. $251-350

★★★THE WESTIN TABOR CENTER, DENVER
1672 Lawrence St., Denver, 303-572-9100, 800-937-8461; www.starwoodhotels.com

Located in downtown Denver, adjacent to the 16th Street Mall, this hotel boasts some of the largest guest rooms in the city, many with panoramic views of the Rocky Mountains. The signature Heavenly beds and baths and nightly wine service ensure a relaxing stay. Get a massage, hit the rooftop pool or whirlpool, work out in the outstanding fitness center (with a personal flat-screen TV on each piece of cardio equipment) or get in a game at the indoor half-basketball court. Afterward, relax in the lobby with Starbucks coffee.

430 rooms. Restaurant, bar. Business center. Fitness center. Pool. Spa. Pets accepted. $251-350

WHERE TO EAT

★★★BAROLO GRILL
3030 E. Sixth Ave., Denver, 303-393-1040; www.barologrilldenver.com

This upscale Italian farmhouse, named after the famous wine, serves authentic Northern Italian food. The interior is rustic and romantic, with grapevines covering one corner and hand-painted porcelain on display throughout, and the fireplace casts a warm glow. Be sure to ask about the daily tasting menu. And yes, the extensive wine list includes more than Barolo, but why bother?

Italian. Dinner. Closed Sunday-Monday. Reservations recommended. Bar. $36-85

WHAT ARE THE BEST STEAK HOUSES IN DENVER?

The Broker Restaurant:
This restaurant is housed in a former bank, and the dining room sits in what used to be the vault. A good investment is the roasted prime rib, which comes with creamed horseradish and steak fries.

Elway's:
A guy like John Elway didn't get to be quarterback for the Broncos by eating light. So you can be sure that his steak house, Elway's, only serves up hearty fare. Try the bone-in rib-eye for a meal befitting a Bronco.

★★★THE BROKER RESTAURANT

821 17th St., Denver, 303-292-5065; www.thebrokerrestaurant.com

Located in downtown Denver in what was once the Denver National Bank, the Broker is a fun place to dine. Private parties can take over one of the old boardrooms. The restaurant's centerpiece is a huge bank vault, now a dining room. Go down some stairs and through what seems like it might have been a secret passageway, and you find yourself in the restaurant's massive wine cellar, which has a dining table that can seat up to 20—or just two, if you're feeling romantic. The steakhouse features dishes like roasted prime rib with creamed horseradish and steak Diane with a Courvoisier cream sauce. But one of the highlights precedes the main course: a complimentary bowl of chilled shrimp.

Steak. Lunch (Monday-Friday), dinner. Reservations recommended. Children's menu. Bar. $36-85

★★★ELWAY'S

The Ritz-Carlton, Denver, 1881 Curtis St., Denver, 303-312-3107; www.elways.com

Because it wouldn't be a Colorado vacation without a hearty steak dinner, and Denver wouldn't be Denver without Bronco Hall-of-Famer John Elway, add Elway's to your must-do list. This steakhouse is a touchdown all around. The smart décor features a floor-to-ceiling wine wall holding thousands of bottles. The lamb fondue appetizer, Elway's salmon, and the bone-in rib-eye are sure bets. Try the Bison burger or sliced prime rib sandwich.

Steak. Breakfast, lunch, dinner. Reservations recommended. Bar. $16-35

★★★HIGHLANDS GARDEN CAFÉ

3927 W. 32nd Ave., Denver, 303-458-5920; www.highlandsgardencafe.com

This unique Denver mainstay is actually two converted Victorian houses from about 1890. The main dining room has exposed brick, polished hardwood floors and crisp white tablecloths, but other rooms have a different feel. The country room is painted white and has French doors leading out to the gardens. The eclectic American menu takes advantage of seasonal ingredients in dishes like pan-seared salmon with bourbon honey glaze and fresh berries or scallops with passion fruit glaze and grilled pineapple.

American. Lunch, dinner, Sunday brunch. Closed Monday. Outdoor seating. $36-85

★★★IMPERIAL CHINESE
431 S. Broadway, Denver, 303-698-2800; www.imperialchinese.com

From the giant fish tank at the entrance to the inventive Szechuan, Cantonese and Mandarin menu, this restaurant dazzles. The large dining room is segmented with partitions that provide a sense of privacy. The service is unobtrusive, and the dishes are as eye-catching as they are delicious. Go for the restaurant's signatures, which include lightly battered sesame chicken, Chilean sea bass with black bean sauce and whole roasted Peking duck with pancakes.

Chinese. Lunch, dinner. Reservations recommended. Bar. $16-35

★★★MORTON'S, THE STEAKHOUSE
1710 Wynkoop St., Denver, 303-825-3353; www.mortons.com

This national chain fits right into the upscale Denver meat-and-potatoes scene. It's very simple here: Order a martini, listen to the server recite the menu, choose either the double-cut filet mignon or the porterhouse, dig in. And go home stuffed.

Steak. Dinner. Bar. $36-85

★★★PALACE ARMS
The Brown Palace Hotel, 321 17th St., Denver, 303-297-3111, 800-321-2599; www.brownpalace.com

The Palace Arms opened its doors in 1892—and has carried on a tradition of culinary excellence ever since. Located on the ground level of the Brown Palace Hotel, the majestic Palace Arms' dining room has a unique Western charisma, with rich wood, brocade-upholstered seating, wood shutters and antiques. The delicious international cuisine is prepared with regional accents, like Colorado bison Rossini with foie gras, brioche and Swiss chard. Taste some of the oldest-known blended cognac, which dates back to Napoleonic times.

International. Dinner. Reservations recommended. Children's menu. Bar. $36-85

★★★★RESTAURANT KEVIN TAYLOR
Hotel Teatro, 1106 14th St., Denver, 303-820-2600; www.ktrg.net

Located inside the stylish Hotel Teatro and across from the Denver Center for Performing Arts, this 70-seat restaurant brings French style to downtown Denver. Vaulted ceilings are offset with Versailles mirrors and alabaster chandeliers. Chairs are covered in green-and-yellow-striped silk fabric, and tables are topped with yellow Frette linens, Bernardaud china and Christofle silver. Chef Kevin Taylor earns applause for his unpretentious contemporary cuisine. Start with seared Grade A French foie gras, and then try one of the signature dishes, such as butter-poached Maine lobster, Serrano ham, roasted Berkshire pork tenderloin and Colorado lamb sirloin. Top it off with a killer dessert like the German chocolate ice cream sandwich. The restaurant features seasonal menus that change every two months; four-, five- and seven-course tasting menus; and a prix fixe pre-theater menu. There are also 900 vintages here; oenophiles should ask for a private table in the wine cellar.

American, French. Dinner. Closed Sunday. Reservations recommended. Bar. $36-85

★★★STRINGS

1700 Humboldt St., Denver, 303-831-7310; www.stringsrestaurant.com

Strings is like no other restaurant in Denver. The locals know it—and so do the scores of celebrities and politicians who have dined here, many of whom have left autographed pictures on the walls. Some love it for the unusual, eclectic cuisine, like housemade pappardelle with chunks of Maine lobster, sweet corn, haricots verts and pancetta, served in the light and airy dining room with an open kitchen. Others are admirers of owner Noel Cunningham, a well-known humanitarian who constantly holds fund-raisers at the restaurant to help fight illiteracy and hunger.

International. Lunch, dinner. Reservations recommended. Outdoor seating. Bar. $36-85

★★★TUSCANY

Loews Denver Hotel, 4150 E. Mississippi Ave., Denver, 303-639-1600; www.loewshotels.com

Located in the Loews Denver Hotel, Tuscany is decorated in creamy earth tones and luxurious fabrics with soft lighting. Pen-and-ink drawings and paintings of the Tuscan countryside dot the walls, and a marble fireplace serves to divide the room. The feeling is contemporary and comfortable, and the restaurant uses only the freshest ingredients to create its outstanding fare—like cheese tortellini with salmon, squid, shrimp, roasted red peppers, spinach and zucchini in an Alfredo sauce, or roasted half chicken with Southern barbecue sauce—paired with wines from the exceptional list.

Italian. Breakfast, lunch, dinner. Reservations recommended. Children's menu. Bar. $36-85

★★★WELLSHIRE INN

3333 S. Colorado Blvd., Denver, 303-759-3333; www.wellshireinn.com

The tables at this restaurant are topped with crisp white linens and beautiful china that was created exclusively for the Wellshire and based on the Tudor period, a theme that is richly executed here. Built in 1926 as a clubhouse for the exclusive Wellshire Country Club, the castle-like building fell into disrepair. Today, it has been restored with four intimate dining rooms. Classics like shrimp cocktail and Maryland crab cakes are featured as appetizers, while entrées include steak Oscar, pan-roasted Cornish game hen and grilled North Atlantic salmon.

American. Lunch, dinner, Sunday brunch. Reservations recommended. Outdoor seating. Children's menu. Bar. $36-85

SPAS

★★★★THE RITZ-CARLTON SPA, DENVER

The Ritz-Carlton, Denver, 1881 Curtis St., Denver, 303-312-3830; www.ritzcarlton.com

Spending the day in the mountains and heading back to the city to rest? Then wind down at this elegant spa. With eight treatment rooms, including a VIP Suite, this is Denver's largest full-service luxury spa. Choose from all manner of treatments, including massage therapies, body treatments, skin care, nail services and makeup application; or skip the slopes and spend the whole day in the spa, indulging in the only-in-Denver hops n' honey ultimate pedicure, which pays homage to the city's brewery roots; it'll leave your skin fragrant with notes of amber, caramel, oats and honey. And your pampering comes with tastings of three local microbrews (or herbal teas, but c'mon, you're in Denver—drink the beer), just another Rocky Mountain twist.

★★★★THE SPA AT THE BROWN PALACE

The Brown Palace Hotel, 321 17th St., Denver, 303-312-8940, 800-321-2599; www.brownpalace.com

An artesian well has supplied the Brown Palace Hotel since it opened in 1892. The soothing natural rock waterfall at its spa's entrance speaks to this history. The Spa at the Brown Palace's six massage, facial and water treatment rooms; separate men's and women's lounges; and private couples' suite are spread over two floors. The facility also has a full-service hair and nail salon. This commitment to guest pampering isn't new—the spa occupies the same space as a spa that opened with the hotel more than a century ago. The treatment menu offers five distinct soaks, and the relaxing artesian plunge is 20 minutes of tub time followed by a sea algae mask.

SOUTHERN COLORADO

While you can find gorgeous scenery all over Colorado, the setting of Southern Colorado is particularly awe-inspiring with Mesa Verde National Park and the San Juan Mountains looming above. Lying at the eastern edge of the Collegiate Range and the central Colorado mountain region, Buena Vista draws in thrill-seekers with its rapids, which are ideal for whitewater rafting. Within 20 miles you'll find four rivers, 12 peaks with elevations above 14,000 feet and more than 500 mountain lakes and streams. For less strenuous water fun, travelers head to Pagosa Springs for its remarkable mineral springs. The town is surrounded by the San Juan National Forest, and deer and elk hunting are popular activities.

If you prefer to stay dry, Ouray's location in a natural basin surrounded by the majestic 12,000 to 14,000-foot peaks of the San Juan Mountains has made it a nice spot for visitors. Ouray, named for a Ute chief, is reached by the magnificent Million Dollar Highway section of the San Juan Skyway, which was blasted from cliff walls high above the Uncompahgre River. Telluride has a similarly impressive craggy landscape. Gray granite and red sandstone mountains surround this mining town, named for the tellurium ore containing precious metals found in the area. Telluride, proud of its bonanza past, has not changed its façade. Because of its remoteness and small size, Telluride is a favorite getaway spot for celebrities. Summer activities include fly-fishing, mountain biking, river rafting, hiking, Jeep trips, horseback riding and camping, as well as many annual events and festivals from May to October. Not to be outdone, Colorado Springs is surrounded by fantastic rock formations at the foot of Pikes Peak. The headquarters of Pike National Forest is in Colorado Springs, which got its name from the many mineral springs in the city.

Nestled at the foot of Pikes Peak, only seven miles west of downtown Colorado Springs, Manitou Springs is one of the state's definitive—and most accessible—mountain communities. The natives, attributing supernatural powers to the waters (Manitou is a Native American word for "Great Spirit"), once marked off the surrounding area as a sanctuary. Today, the town is a National Historic District and a popular tourist resort area filled with many artists' studios, restaurants and boutiques.

HIGHLIGHTS

WHAT ARE THE TOP OUTDOOR ACTIVITIES IN SOUTHERN COLORADO?

SEE THE OTHERWORLDLY GARDEN OF THE GODS

Visit this 1,350-acre park at the base of Pikes Peak at either sunrise or sunset, when the red sandstone formations glow so fiercely they look like they are going to erupt in flames.

TACKLE PIKES PEAK

Pikes Peak is the second-most-visited mountain in the world, only trailing behind Mt. Fuji. So unless you plan on going to Japan sometime soon, this mountain is the next best thing.

EXPLORE THE RUINS AT UTE MOUNTAIN TRIBAL PARK

Explore the roots of this area's native people at this 125,000-acre park. Learn about the Ute Mountain Tribe and tour the 800-year-old Anasazi ruins with a Ute guide.

CHECK OUT THE SAN JUAN NATIONAL FOREST

This is one sprawling forest. Its almost 2 million acres contain the state's largest wilderness area, peaks that reach 14,000 feet and the starting point of the Colorado Trail.

TAKE A DRIVE ON WOLF CREEK PASS

Go for a scenic jaunt across the Continental Divide. Try to schedule the drive for September; it's the best time to witness the changing fall colors of the lovely aspen trees.

VIEW BRIDAL VEIL FALLS

Telluride offers lots of picturesque places, but it will be worth your while to stop at these cascading waters. At four miles long from the top of the waters, Bridal Veil Falls is the highest in the state.

WHAT TO SEE

BUENA VISTA

ARKANSAS RIVER TOURS

126 S. Main St., Buena, Vista, 719-942-4362, 800-321-4352; www.arkansasrivertours.com

The upper Arkansas River in South Central Colorado offers some of the most beautiful and challenging rafting experiences in the region. With its long, placid stretches of scenic wilderness punctuated by plunges through dramatic white-water canyons, the river accommodates all levels of river-rafting thrill-seekers. Experienced rafters won't want to miss an adrenaline-pumping ride through the magnificent Royal George Canyon. Families will love a scenic float

through the gently rolling Cottonwood Rapid. Arkansas River Tours is one of several rafting outfitters along Highway 50 offering a variety of outings, from quarter-day trips to multiple-day high-adventure expeditions.
Admission: varies. Daily; weather permitting.

NOAH'S ARK WHITEWATER RAFTING COMPANY
23910 Highway 285 S, Buena Vista, 719-395-2158; www.noahsark.com
Want to tackle the Arkansas River? This company will help you out with everything from half-day to three-day trips.
Admission: varies. Mid-May-late August.

WILDERNESS AWARE
12600 Highway 24/285, Buena Vista, 719-395-2112, 800-462-7238; www.inaraft.com
This company offers half-day to 10-day river rafting trips on the Arkansas, Colorado, Dolores, North Platte and Gunnison rivers.
Admission: varies. May-September.

CAÑON CITY

BUCKSKIN JOE FRONTIER TOWN & RAILWAY
1193 Fremont County Road, Cañon City, 719-275-5149; www.buckskinjoes.com
This Old West theme park includes a Western town with 30 authentic buildings. Check out daily gunfights, take a horse-drawn trolley ride, or see the magic shows and other entertainment. The park also offers a chance to take a 30-minute train ride to the rim of Royal Gorge Railway.
Admission (park and scenic railway): adults $20, children $18. Park: March-September, daily. Scenic railway: March-October, daily; November-December, Saturday-Sunday only.

DINOSAUR DEPOT MUSEUM
330 Royal Gorge Blvd., Cañon City, 719-269-7150, 800-987-6379; www.dinosaurdepot.com
See an entire Stegosaurus skeleton that was discovered less than 10 miles away.
Admission: adults $4, children $2, children age under 3 free. Daily 10 a.m.-4 p.m.; winter, Wednesday-Sunday only, 10 a.m.-4 p.m.

GARDEN PARK FOSSIL AREA
3170 E. Main St., Cañon City, 719-269-7150; www.dinosaurdepot.com
Fossils of well-known species of large dinosaurs have been discovered at this site over the last 120 years. Many of them are on exhibit at museums around the country, including the Smithsonian. In addition, fossils of dinosaurs, dinosaur eggs and dinosaur tracks have been discovered in the Garden Park Fossil Area, along with fossils of rare plants.
Admission: free. Daily.

ROYAL GORGE BRIDGE AND PARK
4218 County Road, Cañon City, 719-275-7507, 888-333-5597; www.royalgorgebridge.com
This magnificent canyon has cliffs rising more than 1,000 feet above the Arkansas River. The Royal Gorge Suspension Bridge, 1,053 feet above the river, is the highest in the world. The Royal Gorge Incline Railway, the world's steepest, takes passengers 1,550 feet down to the bottom of the canyon. A 2,200-foot aerial tramway glides across the spectacular canyon.
Daily 10 a.m.-4:30 p.m.

COLORADO SPRINGS

BROADMOOR-CHEYENNE MOUNTAIN AREA

1 Lake Ave., Colorado Springs

Broadmoor-Cheyenne Mountain Highway zigzags up the east face of Cheyenne Mountain with a view of plains to the east. The Will Rogers Shrine of the Sun is nearby.

Daily.

CHEYENNE MOUNTAIN ZOOLOGICAL PARK

4250 Cheyenne Mountain Zoo Road, Colorado Springs, 719-633-9925; www.cmzoo.org

This little gem on the side of the Cheyenne Mountains in Colorado Springs is known for its beautiful setting and for the diversity of its animal collection. There are more than 650 creatures here, including many endangered species. You can feed the giraffes and check out the monkeys. Admission includes access to the Will Rogers Shrine of the Sun.

Admission: adults $14.25, children $7.25, children under 2 free. Memorial Day-Labor Day, daily 9 a.m.-6 p.m.; Labor Day-Memorial Day, daily 9 a.m.-5 p.m.

COLORADO SPRINGS FINE ARTS CENTER

30 W. Dale St., Colorado Springs, 719-634-5581; www.csfineartscenter.org

This fine arts center's permanent collections include Native American and Hispanic art, Guatemalan textiles, 19th- and 20th-century American Western paintings, graphics and sculpture by Charles M. Russell and other American artists.

Admission: adults $10, children, students $8.50 children under 4 free. Tuesday-Friday 10 a.m.-5 p.m., Saturday 10 a.m.-8 p.m., Sunday 10 a.m.-5 p.m.

EL POMAR CARRIAGE MUSEUM

10 Lake Circle, Colorado Springs, 719-577-7000; www.elpomar.org

The museum features an extensive collection of fine carriages, vehicles and Western articles of the 1890s. It's located next to Broadmoor Hall.

Admission: free. Monday-Saturday 9 a.m.-5 p.m., Sunday 1-5 p.m.

FLYING W RANCH

3330 Chuckwagon Road, Colorado Springs, 719-598-4000, 800-232-3599; www.flyingw.com

This working cattle and horse ranch offers a Western spin on dinner and a show; you'll enjoy a chuckwagon supper and a country-music performance. The grounds have more than 12 restored buildings with period furniture. Reservations are required.

Admission: adults $22, children 6-12 $12, children 3-5 $5. Mid-May-September, daily; rest of year, Friday-Saturday; closed December 25-February.

GARDEN OF THE GODS

1805 N. 30th St., Colorado Springs, 719-634-6666; www.gardenofgods.com

This 1,350-acre park at the base of Pikes Peak is a showcase of geological wonders. It's best known for its outstanding red sandstone formations, including the famous Balanced Rock and Kissing Camels. The park offers eight miles of well-groomed trails to view the geological treasures, plants and wildlife. Take a free guided walking tour or hop on a bus to tour the garden. Other activities include horseback riding (*Academy Riding Stables, 719-633-5667*) and rock climbing (by permit only). Plan a visit at sunrise or sunset, when you'll get a true understanding of where the area gets its name.

Memorial Day-Labor Day, daily 8 a.m.-8 p.m.; rest of year, daily 9 a.m.-5 p.m.

GHOST TOWN WILD WEST MUSEUM

400 S. 21st St., Colorado Springs, 719-634-0696; www.ghosttownmuseum.com

This authentic Old West town is housed in an 1899 railroad building and includes a general store, a jail, a saloon, a re-created Victorian home, horseless carriages and buggies and a 1903 Cadillac. You'll also have fun with old-time nickelodeons, player pianos, arcade "movies" and a shooting gallery.

Admission: adults $6.50, children $4. June-August, Monday-Saturday 9 a.m.-6 p.m., Sunday 11 a.m.-6 p.m.; September-May, Monday-Saturday 10 a.m.-5 p.m., Sunday 11 a.m.-5 p.m.

MAY NATURAL HISTORY MUSEUM

710 Rock Creek Canyon Road, Colorado Springs, 719-576-0450, 800-666-3841; www.maymuseum-camp-rvpark.com

See a collection of more than 8,000 invertebrates from the tropics at this natural history museum. Then, check out the Museum of Space Exploration, which includes NASA space photos and movies.

Admission: adults $6, children $3. May-October, daily; and by appointment.

MUSEUM OF THE AMERICAN NUMISMATIC ASSOCIATION

818 N. Cascade Ave., Colorado Springs, 719-632-2646, 800-367-9723; www.money.org

Learn all about the study of currency through the collections of coins, tokens, medals and paper money here. The museum has changing exhibits and a library.

Admission: free. Tuesday-Friday 9 a.m.-5 p.m., Saturday 10 a.m.-5 p.m., Sunday noon-5 p.m.

OLD COLORADO CITY

West Colorado Avenue, between 24th to 28th streets, Colorado Springs, 719-577-4112; www.shopoldcoloradocity.com

This renovated historic district features more than 100 quaint shops, art galleries and restaurants.

PALMER PARK

3650 Maizeland Road, Colorado Springs, 719-578-6640

Occupying 710 acres on the Austin Bluffs, this park boasts magnificent views from its scenic roads and trails. There are also plenty of lovely spots for a picnic.

PETERSON AIR & SPACE MUSEUM

150 E. Ent Ave., Peterson Air Force Base, 719-556-4915; www.petemuseum.org

This air and space museum displays 17 historic aircraft from World War I to the present, plus exhibits on the history of the Air Force base. The museum is open on a restricted basis; call for times.

Admission: free. Tuesday-Saturday 9 a.m.-4 p.m.

PIKE NATIONAL FOREST
1920 Valley Drive, Pueblo, 719-545-8737; www.fs.fed.us

The massive 1.1 million acres of national land includes the world-famous Pikes Peak. Wilkerson Pass (9,507 feet) is 45 miles west on Highway 24, with an information center.

Memorial Day-Labor Day.

PIKES PEAK
Pikes Peak Highway, Cascade, 719-385-7325, 800-318-9505; www.pikespeakcolorado.com

Soaring 14,110 feet, Pikes Peak is the second-most-visited mountain in the world behind Mt. Fuji. To reach the peak, you can undertake an eight-hour hike or drive an hour up the 19-mile road, the last half of which is unpaved, has no guardrails and contains steep drops (a four-by-four vehicle isn't necessary, but weather causes road closures even in the summer).

Daily; weather permitting. Closed during annual Hill Climb in July.

PIKES PEAK MOUNTAIN BIKE TOURS
302 S. 25th St., Colorado Springs, 888-593-3062; www.bikepikespeak.com

These mountain bike tours vary in length and endurance level, and professional guides provide all the necessary equipment to make your ride safe and comfortable.

Admission: varies. Tour schedules vary.

PRORODEO HALL OF FAME AND MUSEUM OF THE AMERICAN COWBOY
101 ProRodeo Drive, Colorado Springs, 719-528-4764; www.prorodeohalloffame.com

The Hall of Fame pays tribute to giants like nine-time world champion Casey Tibbs, while the museum will help you appreciate the life of a cowboy—try roping one of the dummy steers. Outdoor exhibits include live rodeo animals and a replica rodeo arena.

Admission: adults $6, seniors $5, youth $3, children under 6 free. Daily 9 a.m.-5 p.m.

ROCK LEDGE RANCH HISTORIC SITE
1401 Recreation Way, Colorado Springs, 719-578-6777; www.rockledgeranch.com

This living history program and working ranch demonstrates everyday life in the region. There's also a Braille nature trail.

June-Labor Day, Wednesday-Sunday 10 a.m.-5 p.m.; Labor Day-December, Saturday 10 a.m.-4 p.m., Sunday noon-4 p.m.

SEVEN FALLS
2850 S. Cheyenne Canyon Road, Colorado Springs, 719-632-0765; www.sevenfalls.com

This is the only completely lighted canyon and waterfall in the world. It's best seen from Eagle's Nest, reached by a mountain elevator. Native American dance interpretations occur daily in the summer.

Admission: day: adults $9.25, children 6-15 $5.75, children 5 and under free; night: adults $10.75, children 6-15 $6.75, children 5 and under free. Daily 9 a.m.-4:15 p.m.

SHRINE OF THE SUN
4250 Cheyenne Mountain Zoo Road, Colorado Springs, 719-577-7000

This memorial to Will Rogers, who was killed in a plane crash in 1935, is built of Colorado gray-pink granite and steel. It contains memorabilia inside of it. The fee for the visit is included in the admission price to the Cheyenne Mountain Zoo.

Memorial Day-Labor Day, daily 9 a.m.-5 p.m.; Labor Day-Memorial Day, daily 9 a.m.-4 p.m.

U.S. OLYMPIC TRAINING CENTER

1 Olympic Plaza, Colorado Springs, 719-632-5551, 888-659-8687; www.usoc.org

Tours of this center offer an insider's view of how Olympic-level athletes train. For most of us, the closest we'll get to a medal are the replicas available in the gift shop.

Monday-Saturday 9 a.m.-5 p.m., last tour at 4 p.m., Sunday 11 a.m.-6 p.m.

WORLD FIGURE SKATING HALL OF FAME AND MUSEUM

20 First St., Colorado Springs, 719-635-5200; www.usfsa.org

This museum features exhibits on the history of figure skating, including a video collection. The skate gallery features artists like Andy Warhol, who offer their interpretations of the sport on canvas, and there's even a work by skaters using their skate blades as brushes.

Admission: adults $5, seniors and children 6-12 $3, children 5 and under free. Monday-Friday 10 a.m.-4 p.m.; November-April: Saturday 10 a.m.-4 p.m.; May-October: Saturday 10 a.m.-5 p.m.

CORTEZ

ANASAZI HERITAGE CENTER AND ESCALANTE

27501 Highway 184, Dolores, 970-882-5600; www.co.blm.gov

This museum showcases the Anasazi and other Native American cultures. See exhibits on archaeology and local history. The Escalante site, discovered by a Franciscan friar in 1776, is within a half-mile of the center. This is also the starting point for the Canyons of the Ancients National Monument.

Admission: March-October: adults $3, children free; November-February: adults and children free. March-October, daily 9 a.m.-5 p.m.; November-February, daily 9 a.m.-4 p.m.

HOVENWEEP NATIONAL MONUMENT

McElmo Route, Cortez, 970-562-4282; www.nps.gov

This monument consists of six units of prehistoric ruins—the best-preserved site is at Square Tower, which includes the remains of pueblos and towers.

Admission: $3. Self-guided trail (park ranger on duty); visitor area. Daily 8 a.m.-5 p.m.

LOWRY PUEBLO

27501 Highway 184, Cortez, 970-882-5600; www.blm.gov

Part of the Canyons of the Ancients National Monument, the Lowry Pueblo was constructed by the Anasazi (circa 1075) and has 40 excavated rooms.

Daily, weather and road conditions permitting.

UTE MOUNTAIN TRIBAL PARK

Highway Junction 160/491 near Cortez, 970-749-1452; www.utemountainute.com

The Ute Mountain Tribe developed this 125,000-acre park on its tribal lands, opening hundreds of largely unexplored 800-year-old Anasazi ruins to the public. Tours begin at the Ute Mountain Visitor center/Museum, 19 miles south of Cortez via Highway 666 (daily); reservations are required. Primitive camping is available.

DURANGO

DURANGO & SILVERTON NARROW GAUGE RAILROAD

479 Main Ave., Durango, 970-247-2733, 877-872-4607; www.durangotrain.com

This historic Narrow Gauge Railroad, in operation since 1881, links Durango in southwest Colorado with the Victorian-era mining town of Silverton, 45 miles away. A journey on this coal-fired, steam-powered locomotive up the Animas River and through the mountainous wilderness of the San Juan National Forest gives you the chance to relive history while taking in some of the most breathtaking scenery Colorado has to offer. Round-trip travel takes approximately nine hours. Same-day travelers may opt to return by bus; others can stay overnight in historic Silverton with a return train ride the next day. During the winter season, the train makes a shorter round-trip journey to and from Cascade Canyon.

Admission: varies. May-October; shorter routes during the winter months.

DURANGO MOUNTAIN RESORT (ALSO KNOWN AS PURGATORY LODGE)

1 Skier Place, Durango, 970-247-9000, 800-982-6103; www.ski-purg.com

Durango Mountain Resort has one quad, four triple and three double chair-lifts, a patrol, a school, rentals, five restaurants, five bars, a nursery, a lodge and specialty stores. The property boasts 85 runs, the longest of which is two miles with a vertical drop 2,029 feet. Multiday and half-day rates are offered.

Late November-early April. Cross-country skiing. Chairlift and alpine slide also operate mid-June-Labor Day.

SAN JUAN NATIONAL FOREST

15 Burnett Court, Durango, 970-247-4874; www.fs.fed.us

This forest consists of nearly 2 million acres and includes the Weminuche Wilderness, Colorado's largest designated wilderness area, with several peaks topping 14,000 feet. The Colorado Trail begins in Durango and traverses the backcountry all the way to Denver. Recreation includes fishing in high mountain lakes and streams, boating, white-water rafting, hiking, biking and camping. The San Juan Skyway is a 232-mile auto loop through many of these scenic areas.

Daily.

MANITOU SPRINGS

CAVE OF THE WINDS

Cave of the Winds Road, Manitou Springs, 719-685-5444; www.caveofthewinds.com

This fascinating 45-minute guided tour—which goes through underground passageways filled with beautiful stalactites, stalagmites and flowstone formations created millions of years ago—leaves every 15 minutes and includes a laser-light show.

Admission: varies. Summer, 9 a.m.-9 p.m.; winter, 10 a.m.-5 p.m.

MANITOU CLIFF DWELLINGS MUSEUM

Highway 24 W., Manitou Springs, 719-685-5242, 800-354-9971; www.cliffdwellingsmuseum.com

See the architecture of the cliff-dwelling natives, circa 1100 to 1300. Native American dancing is performed June through August.

Admission: adults $9.50, children 7-11 $7.50, children 6 and under free. March-November, daily.

MIRAMONT CASTLE MUSEUM
9 Capitol Hill Ave., Manitou Springs, 719-685-1011; www.miramontcastle.org

The museum is housed in a 46-room, four-story Victorian house (circa 1895) featuring nine styles of architecture, a miniatures and doll collection, a tea room, a soda fountain and gardens.

Admission: adults $6, seniors $5.50, children $2, children under 6 free. Tuesday-Sunday.

OURAY

BACHELOR-SYRACUSE MINE TOUR
1222 County Road 14, Ouray, 970-325-0220, 888-227-4585; www.bachelorsyracusemine.com

This mine has been in continuous operation since 1884. Guided tours are aboard a mine train that advances 3,350 feet horizontally into Gold Hill (mine temperature 47 F), where you can see mining equipment, visit work areas and learn how explosives are used. You'll even get a chance to strike it rich by doing some gold panning.

Admission: Late May-September, daily.

BEAR CREEK FALLS
1230 Main, Ouray, 970-325-4746; www.ouraycolorado.com

A scenic observational point lets you take in the 227-foot falls.

BOX CANON FALLS PARK
Highway 550, Ouray, 970-325-7080; www.ouraycolorado.com

Canyon Creek has cut a natural canyon 20 feet wide and 400 feet deep. Take the stairs and a suspended bridge to the floor of the canyon, where you can see the thundering falls.

Daily.

HOT SPRINGS POOL
Ouray City Park, 1220 Highway 50, Ouray, 970-325-7073; www.cityofouray.com

Forget cold lakes and oceans, soak in this outdoor million-gallon pool fed by natural mineral hot springs (sulphur-free). There's also a bathhouse and spa on the premises.

Daily.

PAGOSA SPRINGS

CHIMNEY ROCK ARCHAEOLOGICAL AREA
180 N. Pagosa Blvd., Pagosa Springs, 970-883-5359; www.chimneyrockco.org

This area features twin pinnacles that are held sacred by the Anasazi. The Fire Tower offers a spectacular view of nearby ruins. Four guided scheduled tours are given daily.

FRED HARMAN ART MUSEUM
85 Harman Park Drive, Pagosa Springs, 970-731-5785; www.harmanartmuseum.com

See original paintings of the American West by Fred Harman—best known for his famous *Red Ryder and Little Beaver* comic strip. Rodeo, movie and Western memorabilia is found here.

Admission: adults $4, children under 6 $.50. Monday-Saturday 10:30 a.m.-5 p.m., Sunday noon-4 p.m.; winter, Monday-Friday 10:30 a.m.-5 p.m.

ROCKY MOUNTAIN WILDLIFE PARK

4821 Highway 84, Pagosa Springs, 970-264-5546;
www.alldurango.com

This park features animals indigenous to the area along with a wildlife museum and photography displays.

Summer, daily 9 a.m.-6 p.m.; winter, daily noon-4 p.m.

TREASURE MOUNTAIN

Pagosa Springs

Begin at the Wolf Creek Pass, just east of the summit marked where the Continental Divide Trail winds southward and connects with the Treasure Mountain Trail. Legend states that in 1790, 300 men mined $5 million in gold and melted it into bars but were forced to leave it behind. The gold has never been found.

WOLF CREEK PASS

Pagosa Springs, 20 miles northeast on Highways 160 and 84

Take a scenic drive across the Continental Divide. The eastern approach is through the Rio Grande National Forest; the western approach through the San Juan National Forest. The best time to drive through is September, when you'll see gorgeous views of the aspens changing color. The drive takes approximately one hour.

WOLF CREEK SKI AREA

Pagosa Springs, 20 miles northeast of Highways 160 and 84, 970-264-5639; www.wolfcreekski.com

Wolf Creek has two triple and two double chairlifts, a Poma lift, a patrol, a school, rentals, a cafeteria, a restaurant, a bar and a day lodge. Among the 50 runs, the longest is two miles with a vertical drop 1,604 feet. Shuttle bus service is available.

Early November-April, daily.

PUEBLO

EL PUEBLO MUSEUM

301 N. Union, Pueblo, 719-583-0453; www.coloradohistory.org

Check out this full-size replica of Old Fort Pueblo, which served as a base for fur traders and other settlers from 1842-1855.

Admission: adults $4, seniors and children 6-12 $3, children 5 and under free. Tuesday-Saturday 10 a.m.-4 p.m.

PUEBLO WEISBROD AIRCRAFT MUSEUM

Pueblo Memorial Airport, 31001 Magnuson Ave., Pueblo, 719-948-9219; www.pwam.org

This outdoor museum features static aircraft displays. Adjacent is the B-24 Aircraft Memorial Museum, with displays of the history of the B-24 bomber.

Admission: $7. Monday-Saturday 10 a.m.-4 p.m., Sunday 1-4 p.m.

SAN ISABEL NATIONAL FOREST

2840 Kachina Drive, Pueblo, 719-553-1400

This forest, spread over more than 1 million acres, offers camping and two winter sports areas, Monarch and Ski Cooper. In the southern part of the forest is the Spanish Peaks National Natural Landmark. Collegiate Peaks, Mount Massive and Holy Cross Wilderness areas are also within the forest.

Colorado's highest peak, Mount Elbert (14,433 feet), is within the forest south of Leadville.

SANGRE DE CRISTO ARTS AND CONFERENCE CENTER

210 N. Santa Fe Ave., Pueblo, 719-295-7200; www.sdc-arts.org

The four art galleries here include the Francis King Collection of Western Art, which is on permanent display. There's also a children's museum, dance studios and a theater.

Admission: adults $4, children $3. Monday-Saturday.

SALIDA

ARKANSAS HEADWATERS STATE RECREATION AREA

307 W. Sackett Ave., Salida, 719-539-7289

This outstanding waterway cuts its way through rugged canyons for 148 miles, from Leadville to Pueblo, making it one of the world's premier places for kayaking and white-water rafting. Or opt to do some fishing, boating, hiking, horseback riding, picnicking and camping.

MONARCH SCENIC TRAM

Chamber of Commerce, 406 W. Rainbow Blvd., Salida, 719-539-4789, 888-996-7669

This trip to an observatory at 12,000 feet offers panoramic views of the beautiful Rocky Mountains.

May-September, daily.

MONARCH SKI & SNOWBOARD AREA

1 Powder Place, Monarch, 719-539-3573, 888-996-7669; www.skimoarch.com

Monarch has four double chairlifts, a patrol, a school and rentals. Of its 63 runs, the longest is one mile with a vertical drop 1,170 feet. Cross-country skiing is also available.

Mid-November-mid-April, daily.

MOUNTAIN SPIRIT WINERY

16150 County Road 220, Salida, 719-539-1175, 888-679-4637; www.mountainspiritwinery.com

This family-operated boutique winery is on 5 acres with an apple orchard, a homestead, tours and tastings. Sample the blackberry cabernet franc or the fruity Angel Bush, which has notes of apple, pear and raspberry.

Memorial Day-Labor Day, Monday-Saturday 10 a.m.-5 p.m.

SILVERTON

CIRCLE JEEP TOUR

414 Greene St., Silverton, 970-387-5654, 800-752-4494; www.silvertoncolorado.com

Take in the history of the area, including information on mines and ghost towns, on a Jeep tour.

OLD HUNDRED GOLD MINE TOUR

721 County Road 4 A, Silverton, 970-387-5444, 800-872-3009; www.minetour.com

Learn all about the methods of hard rock mining. This guided one-hour tour of an underground mine offers views of the equipment and crystal pockets.

Memorial Day-September, daily.

RED MOUNTAIN PASS
Silverton, Highway 550 between Ouray and Silverton

Stretching through the towering San Juan Mountains, the 23-mile tract of Highway 550 between Ouray and Silverton passes through some of Colorado's wildest country. The road rises to 11,075 feet to cross the Red Mountain Pass, a favorite spot for hikers, rock climbers, mountain bikers and backcountry ski enthusiasts. Along the way you'll see numerous gorges and falls, as well as abandoned log cabins and mining equipment.

TELLURIDE
BEAR CREEK TRAIL
South end of Pine Street, Telluride

This two-mile canyon walk features a view of a tiered waterfall.
May-October.

BRIDAL VEIL FALLS
Telluride, 2½ miles east on Highway 145

These falls are the highest in Colorado. They measure four miles long to the top of the cascading waters.

TELLURIDE GONDOLA
Aspen and San Juan, Telluride

Passengers can hop on this gondola to be transported from downtown Telluride to Mount Village.
Early June-early October and late November-mid-April, daily.

TELLURIDE HISTORICAL MUSEUM
201 W. Gregory Ave., Telluride, 970-728-3344; www.telluridemuseum.org

Built in 1893 as the community hospital, this historic building houses artifacts, historic photos and exhibits that show what Telluride was like in its Wild West days.
Admission: adults $5, seniors and children 6-17 $3, children 5 and under free.
Tuesday-Saturday 11 a.m.-5 p.m., Sunday 1-5 p.m.

TELLURIDE SKI RESORT
565 Mountain Village Blvd., Telluride, 800-778-8581; www.tellurideskiresort.com

Telluride Ski Resort offers a three-stage gondola, seven quads, two triple and two double chairlifts, a patrol, a school, rentals, restaurants and a nursery. It has 92 runs; the longest is 4½ miles with a vertical drop of 3,530 feet.
Thanksgiving-early April, daily.

WHERE TO STAY

COLORADO SPRINGS
★★★★★THE BROADMOOR
1 Lake Ave., Colorado Springs, 719-634-7711; www.broadmoor.com

Located at the foot of the Rocky Mountains and surrounded by beautiful Cheyenne Lake, the Broadmoor has been one of America's favorite resorts since 1918. This all-season paradise is in Colorado Springs, yet feels a million miles away. The opulent rooms offer views of the mountains or lake, feather-beds, goose-down pillows, DVD players and upscale Molton Brown toiletries.

If the outdoors beckon, hit the tennis club, three championship golf courses or the lake for paddle boating. You also can do some horseback riding. Kids will love the "mountain" waterslide and the pools. You won't have to search far for a good meal; the resort has 18 restaurants, cafés and lounges. When you need some down time, visit the world-class spa, which incorporates indigenous botanicals and pure spring water into its treatments.

744 rooms. Restaurant, bar. Business center. Fitness center. Pool. Spa. Pets accepted. Golf. Tennis. $251-350

CRIPPLE CREEK

★★★CARR MANOR

350 E. Carr Ave., Cripple Creek, 719-689-3709; www.carrmanor.com

School's back in session at Carr Manor, a former 1890's schoolhouse. You can see the building's schoolhouse roots in some of the rooms, which feature the original chalkboards. A night at this boutique hotel includes a full breakfast served in the original high school cafeteria. There's also a small fitness spa.

13 rooms. Complimentary breakfast. No children under 12 years. Closed January-February; also weekdays March-April. $61-150

DURANGO

★★★APPLE ORCHARD INN

7758 County Road 203, Durango, 970-247-0751, 800-426-0751; www.appleorchardinn.com

This lovely inn is just 15 minutes from town and a 20-minute drive to Durango Mountain Resort. The property includes beautiful gardens, trout ponds, waterfalls and streams. All rooms are uniquely decorated and feature featherbeds. Homemade baked goods and jam at breakfast—as well as fresh chocolate chip cookies anytime—make visits extra sweet. Gourmet dinners are also available with a reservation.

10 rooms. Complimentary breakfast. $151-250

★★★LIGHTNER CREEK INN

999 County Road 207, Durango, 970-259-1226, 800-268-9804; www.lightnercreekinn.com

This inn, built in 1903, resembles a French country manor and offers finely decorated rooms, some of which have coffeemakers, coffee bean grinders, microwaves and refrigerators. The mountain getaway feels very secluded but is only five minutes from downtown. Guests are encouraged to make themselves at home here—grab a drink from the kitchen and watch a movie in the living room.

9 rooms. $151-250

★★★THE ROCHESTER HOTEL

721 E. Second Ave., Durango, 970-385-1920, 800-664-1920; www.rochesterhotel.com

Built in 1892, this Victorian hotel has been authentically restored and evokes the Old West, and it's only one block from downtown Durango. It bills itself as a "green" hotel—Electra Cruiser bikes are available for guests to get around and all-natural Aveda products are provided. The rooms' décor is inspired by Old West flicks that were shot in the Durango area.

15 rooms. Complimentary breakfast. Pets accepted. $151-250

★★★THE LODGE AT TAMARRON

40292 Highway 550 N., Durango, 970-259-2000, 800-982-6103

Pine trees surround this scenic resort, located on a 750-acre site in the San Juan Mountains. The property is just a short drive or shuttle from Durango and Purgatory Village and the chairlifts. Accommodations range from studios and lofts to suites, and amenities include tennis and indoor/outdoor pools.

210 rooms. Restaurant, bar. Fitness center. Pool. Spa. Pets accepted. $61-150

MANITOU SPRINGS

★★★THE CLIFF HOUSE AT PIKES PEAK

306 Canon Ave., Manitou Springs, 719-685-3000, 888-212-7000; www.thecliffhouse.com

Built in 1873—before Colorado was even a state—this hotel has retained every charming detail of the Victorian age while adding modern touches. Each room is different and may include a gas fireplace, a steam shower and towel warmers. Galleries, shops, restaurants and museums surround the hotel, and bicycles are available for rent. The dining room and wine cellar repeatedly win awards.

55 rooms. Restaurant. Complimentary breakfast. $251-350

★★★RED CRAGS BED & BREAKFAST COUNTRY INN

302 El Paso Blvd., Manitou Springs, 719-685-1920, 800-721-2248; www.redcrags.com

Housed in an 1884 mansion that was originally built as a clinic, this charming and elegant inn, surrounded by the Rocky Mountains, has high ceilings, hardwood floors and beautiful antiques. In-room fireplaces provide a romantic atmosphere. All rooms also have plasma TVs.

8 rooms. Complimentary breakfast. No children under 10 years. $151-250

★★★ROCKLEDGE COUNTRY INN

328 El Paso Blvd., Manitou Springs, 719-685-4515, 888-685-4515; www.rockledgeinn.com

Situated atop a hill and surrounded by lush juniper and pine trees, the Rockledge Country Inn is at the foot of Pikes Peak and has a beautiful view of the Rocky Mountains. Instead of having the gratis breakfast in your room, take it on the terrace overlooking the peak. This 1912 inn is built in an Arts and Crafts style. The living room has leather couches, a marble fireplace and a grand piano. And there's plenty to do here, from bike rentals to private hiking trails to croquet. Or stay cozy in front of a gas fireplace, available in most rooms, with reading material from the in-house library.

7 rooms. Complimentary breakfast. $151-250

OURAY

★★★ST. ELMO HOTEL

426 Main St., Ouray, 970-325-4951; www.stelmohotel.com

The guest rooms at this restored 1898 hotel are individually decorated in Victorian style, with rich woods and lots of floral-patterned items, and feature period antiques. Enjoy a wine and cheese social hour every afternoon in the parlor and a full breakfast every morning in the sun room.

9 rooms. Restaurant. Complimentary breakfast. $61-150

PUEBLO
★★★MARRIOTT PUEBLO CONVENTION CENTER
110 W. First St., Pueblo, 719-542-3200, 800-228-9290;
www.marriott.com

Business travelers will find this hotel a convenient choice, since it is connected to the convention center downtown. Travelers of all stripes will like that the hotel is on the River Walk and surrounded by beautiful landscaping. Guest rooms feature modern furnishings and include microwaves and writing desks with ergonomic desk chairs.

164 rooms. Restaurant, bar. Business center. Fitness center. Pool. Pets accepted. $151-250

TELLURIDE
★★★CAPELLA TELLURIDE
568 Mountain Village Blvd., Telluride, 970-369-8963;
www.capellatelluride.com

Located in the heart of Telluride's Mountain Village, a quaint ski area that boasts breathtaking views of the San Juan Mountain Range, this elegant hotel is the perfect place from which to take in the beauty of the area. The hotel's living room is a cozy space with a stone fireplace, leather couches, bookshelves with plenty of reading material and games, and a common area where coffee, tea, pastries, snacks, soda and juice are served daily. Rooms feature European alpine décor and crisp, cool color schemes with suede ottomans, leather chairs and headboards. Capella's King-sized beds have custom pillowtop mattresses, 450-thread count Pratesi linens and hypoallergenic down feather pillows. The spa at Capella is peaceful and serene, and the restaurant, Onyx, is worth a stop for dinner or a drink.

106 rooms. Restaurant, bar. Business center. Fitness center. Pool. Spa. $351 and up

★★★HOTEL COLUMBIA, TELLURIDE
300 W. San Juan Ave., Telluride, 970-728-0660, 800-201-9505;
www.columbiatelluride.com

Situated on the San Miguel River at the base of the Telluride Ski Resort, this hotel feels more like a small inn, with only 21 Victorian-style rooms, each with a gas fireplace. The hotel got its moniker from the town's early beginnings; Columbia was Telluride's original name. Spring for the penthouse—it has a steam shower and two-person jetted tub surrounded by windows overlooking the mountains and river.

21 rooms. Restaurant, bar. Fitness center. Pets accepted. Spa. $151-250

WHAT ARE THE MOST LUXURIOUS HOTELS IN SOUTHERN COLORADO?

The Broadmoor:
The grounds at this lavish hotel cater to every whim: There are 18 restaurants, a first-run movie theater, a spa, three championship golf courses, seven tennis courts, three pools and several waterslides on the premises.

The Peaks Resort & Golden Door Spa:
Skiers not only have the luxury of easy ski-in/ski-out access at this hotel, but a dedicated ski valet who will take care of their equipment. Whether you ski or not, this hotel is a must just for its world-class Golden Door Spa.

WHAT ARE THE MOST SCENIC DINING SPOTS IN SOUTHERN COLORADO?

Charles Court:
This restaurant is tucked inside the Broadmoor hotel, but when the weather's fine, take advantage of the alfresco dining. You can enjoy the American cuisine near the pretty lake.

Penrose Room:
Also a part of the Broadmoor hotel, the Penrose Room is known for its excellent contemporary French fare and tremendous views of the Colorado Springs and Cheyenne Mountain.

Tennessee Pass Cookhouse:
This restaurant isn't easy to visit; you have to trek a mile either on foot, bike or off-road vehicle to reach it. But the breathtaking panoramas from this mountaintop restaurant will be worth it.

★★★THE PEAKS RESORT & GOLDEN DOOR SPA

136 Country Club Drive, Telluride, 866-282-4557, 800-789-2220; www.thepeaksresort.com

This is the perfect home for outdoor enthusiasts who like to rough it a bit outdoors—and live it up indoors. Situated on top of the mountain, Peaks Resort is a skier's heaven with ski-in/ski-out access and a ski valet who will warm and tune your equipment. The guest rooms and suites are cocoons of luxury, with huge picture windows with plantation shutters, fluffy duvets and glass-enclosed showers with separate tubs. Suites boast leather furniture and stone fireplaces. The centerpiece of this first-class resort is the Golden Door Spa, an outpost of the legendary California destination spa featuring a variety of restorative treatments. If you're here in summer, challenge yourself on one of the country's highest golf courses.

175 rooms. Restaurant, bar. Fitness center. Pool. Spa. Pets accepted. Ski in/ski out. Tennis. Closed mid-April-mid-May, mid-October-mid-November. $251-350

★★★NEW SHERIDAN HOTEL

231 W. Colorado Ave., Telluride, 970-728-4351, 800-200-1891; www.newsheridan.com

Built in 1891, this hotel is in the heart of Telluride. Many of the elegant guest rooms feature mountain views, LCD flat-screen televisions and separate sitting rooms. Warm up with a hearty gourmet breakfast and then relax in the afternoon with a complimentary glass of Pine Ridge wine at the New Sheridan Bar. Or unwind in one of the two rooftop hot tubs.

26 rooms. Restaurant. Complimentary breakfast. Closed mid-April-mid-May. $151-250

WHERE TO EAT

COLORADO SPRINGS
★★★CHARLES COURT

The Broadmoor, 1 Lake Ave., Colorado Springs, 719-577-5733, 806-634-7711; www.broadmoor.com

One of the many restaurants at the luxurious Broadmoor hotel, Charles Court offers progressive American fare in a relaxed and contemporary setting. In warm weather, you can dine outdoors with lakeside views. The menu features regional Rocky Mountain fare such as Colorado rack of lamb and the signature Charles Court Game Grill. The wine list boasts more than 600 selections from all around the world. For special occasions, opt for the chef's table in the kitchen (four guests minimum).

American. Breakfast, dinner (Thursday-Monday), Sunday brunch. Reservations recommended. Outdoor seating. Bar. $36-85

★★★★★PENROSE ROOM
The Broadmoor, 1 Lake Ave., Colorado Springs, 719-577-5733, 866-381-8432; www.broadmoor.com

Located within the Broadmoor, the sophisticated Penrose Room offers a spectacular dining experience set against magnificent views of Colorado Springs and Cheyenne Mountain. Chef Bertrand Bouquin serves up contemporary continental cuisine influenced by the food of Italy, Spain, Africa and France. The menu changes often and offers prix fixe meals of three, four and seven courses. Favorite appetizers include pistachio-laden warm goat cheese salad, five herbs ravioli and chilled peekytoe crab with cherry relish salad. Entrées include roasted loin of Colorado lamb with purple mustard and slowly cooked halibut in black olive oil. After dinner, enjoy live music and dancing.

French. Dinner. Closed Sunday. Reservations recommended. Jacket required. Children's menu. Bar. $86 and up

★★★SUMMIT
The Broadmoor, 1 Lake Ave., Colorado Springs, 719-577-5777, 800-634-7711; www.broadmoor.com

At one of the country's premier resorts, Summit fills every bill—from gracious service to memorable meals to the inventive interior. Chef Bertrand Bouquin was privileged enough to spend time under the tutelage of world-class chefs, including Alain Ducasse, Daniel Boulud and Jean-Pierre Bruneau, before coming to Summit to create excellent dishes such as braised beef short ribs with rioja, baby carrots and roasted garlic mashed potatoes. The food is accented by the edgy design, which centers on a turning glass turret of wine bottles—the ultimate wine rack, if you will.

American. Dinner. Closed Monday. Reservations recommended. Children's menu. Bar. $36-85

LEADVILLE
★★★TENNESSEE PASS COOKHOUSE
1892 Highway 25, Leadville, 719-486-8114; www.tennesseepass.com

This ski-oriented dining room serves one prix fixe meal nightly with entrées ordered 24 hours in advance. Expect dishes such as baked brie with caramelized apples and croissants, and main courses like grilled elk tenderloin with blueberry and sage port reduction and Yukon Gold sweet potatoes. You'll have to work for your food; the secluded mountain-top restaurant can only be reached by a one-mile hike, bike or off-road vehicle ride through the woods.

American. Dinner. Reservations recommended. $36-85

MANITOU SPRINGS
★★★BRIARHURST MANOR ESTATE
404 Manitou Ave., Manitou Springs, 719-685-1864, 877-685-1448; www.briarhurst.com

Located in a pink sandstone Tudor manor house built in 1876 by the founder of Manitou Springs, this elegant fine-dining restaurant's kitchen is headed up by executive chef Tyler Peoples, who uses homegrown vegetables and herbs in his recipes. Menu items include artisan cheeses, trout amandine, salmon filet, calamari steak piccata and bison short ribs. The dessert sampler is the perfect ending to a delicious meal. You can choose three sweets from the dessert menu, including the Oaxacan flourless dark chocolate torte with cinnamon, clove and chili spice over espresso reduction.

American. Dinner. Outdoor seating. Children's menu. Bar. $36-85

★★★THE CLIFF HOUSE DINING ROOM

Cliff House, 306 Canon Ave., Manitou Springs, 719-685-3000, 888-212-7000; www.thecliffhouse.com

Located in the historic Cliff House hotel, this elegant dining room serves up contemporary American cooking presented with flair. Look for dishes like Colorado lamb loin with Fuji apples, apricots and spinach in phyllo dough, rosemary rissolé potato and balsamic reduction. The ingredients in each dish are fresh and local, and there are more than 700 bottles of wine to accompany them.

American. Breakfast, lunch, dinner. $16-35

★★★CRAFTWOOD INN

404 El Paso Blvd., Manitou Springs, 719-685-9000; www.craftwood.com

This romantic restaurant located in a 1912 Tudor manor house serves Southwestern-influenced cuisine. The focus is on steaks, elk, pheasant, venison, quail and seafood. When in season, the kitchen also uses Colorado vegetables and produce. Dining here is an adventure, with wild game dishes including Colorado elk steak, grilled blue Russian wild boar and aged buffalo rib-eye.

American. Dinner. Outdoor seating. Bar. $36-85

PUEBLO

★★★LA RENAISSANCE

217 E. Routt Ave., Pueblo, 719-543-6367; www.larenaissancerestaurant.com

This restaurant was originally built in 1886 as a Presbyterian church and still includes the pews and stained-glass windows. It's an interesting atmosphere, and the food is superb, from lobster tail to prime rib.

American. Dinner. Closed Sunday. Reservations recommended. Bar. $16-35

TELLURIDE

★★★ALLRED'S

2 Coonskin Ridge, Telluride, 970-728-7474; www.allredsrestaurant.com

At more than 10,000 feet above sea level, Allred's offers mountain views to complement its delicious culinary creations. The menu is made up of regional Colorado cuisine with international accents such as free-range chicken breast with creamy polenta, Manchego, spinach and roasted peppers and elk short loin with summer squash and braised figs. If you're looking for a special treat, reserve the chef's table (for four to six guests), where you'll be treated to a five-course, chef-prepared menu with the option to pair wines with each course.

American. Dinner. Closed mid-April-mid-June, late September-mid-December. Reservations recommended. Children's menu. Bar. $36-85

★★★COSMOPOLITAN

Hotel Columbia, 300 W. San Juan Ave., Telluride, 970-728-1292; www.cosmotelluride.com

Housed in the luxurious Hotel Columbia, Cosmopolitan is an elegant restaurant where fresh ingredients and flavors from around the world blend together to create an innovative contemporary American menu. Dishes, which change on a weekly basis, have included creations such as crab-stuffed roasted chicken breast with risotto, mushrooms, Gruyère cheese, asparagus, truffle oil and chicken jus as well as barbecued wild king salmon with fried sweet potatoes, sweet corn broth and bacon-braised Swiss chard.

French, American. Dinner. Closed mid-April-mid-May and the last week in October. Reservations recommended. Children's menu. Bar. $16-35

SPAS

COLORADO SPRINGS

★★★★★THE SPA AT THE BROADMOOR

The Broadmoor, 1 Lake Ave., Colorado Springs, 719-577-5770, 866-686-3965; www.broadmoor.com

With the beautiful scenery of the Rocky Mountains as a backdrop, the Spa at the Broadmoor already has an advantage over other luxury spas. Even without these surroundings, an experience at this two-level lakefront spa is pure bliss. With Venetian chandeliers, earth tones and an overall feeling of serenity, the treatment rooms perfectly set the scene for the spa's heavenly massage therapies and skin treatments. If your Rocky Mountain adventures have left you with aching muscles, the spa's variety of massage therapies will make you feel like new again, while facials such as the luxe facial will get your skin glowing. The Junior Ice Cream manicure and pedicure are reserved for those guests ages 11 and under.

WELCOME TO NEVADA

THERE'S MORE TO NEVADA THAN LAS VEGAS AND GAMBLING.

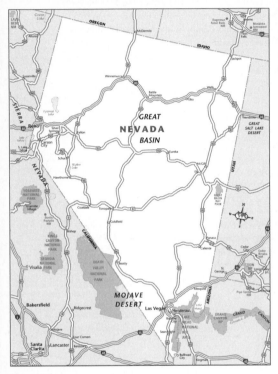

Nevada also has a rich history, magnificent scenery and some of the wildest desert country on the continent. You'll find large mountain peaks and beautiful lakes, including Lake Tahoe. Ghost towns hint at earlier days filled with fabulous gold and silver streaks that made men millionaires overnight.

Nevada became part of U.S. territory after the Mexican-American War in 1846. It became a state in 1864 (for a while, it was part of Utah). Gold was found along the Carson River in Dayton Valley in May of 1850. A decade later, the impressive Comstock Lode (silver and gold ore) was discovered. The gold rush was on, and Virginia City mushroomed into a town of 20,000.

Unregulated gambling was common in these early mining towns but was outlawed in 1909. It was legalized in 1931, when construction on the Hoover Dam began and there was a population boom. This was also the same year residency requirements for obtaining a divorce were relaxed. Soon, Las Vegas transformed from a sleepy desert town to become the world's top gaming and entertainment destination. And Las Vegas keeps reinventing itself. These days, it's known for being home to some of the best dining in the country as much as it is for gambling. You'll also find some of the best hotels, spas and shopping.

NORTHWESTERN NEVADA

You may be in the desert, but there's plenty to see in Nevada, especially the Northwestern region. Carson City, the state capital, rests near the edge of the forested eastern slope of the beautiful Sierra Nevada in Eagle Valley. Swanky and affluent, Incline Village sits on the north rim of scenic Lake Tahoe. And between the steep slopes of the Sierra and the low eastern hills, Reno, "the biggest little city in the world," spills across the Truckee Meadows. The neon lights of the night-clubs, gambling casinos and bars give it a glitter that belies its many quiet acres of fine houses, churches and schools. The surrounding area is popular for sailing, boating, horseback riding and deer and duck hunting. The downtown Riverwalk along the Truckee's banks is loaded with coffee shops, art galleries, chic eateries, eclectic boutiques, antique stores, salons and theaters, in case you want to do something other than admire the view.

WHAT TO SEE

CARSON CITY

CHILDREN'S MUSEUM OF NORTHERN NEVADA
813 N. Carson St., Carson City, 775-884-2226; www.cmnn.org

This excellent kids' museum provides 8,000 square feet of education and playground-style fun. A grocery store, an arts and crafts station and a walk-in kaleidoscope are among the permanent exhibits.

Admission: adults $5, seniors $4, children $3, children 1 and under free. Daily 10 a.m.-4:30 p.m.

NEVADA STATE MUSEUM
600 N. Carson St., Carson City, 775-687-4810; www.nevadaculture.org

The former site of the U.S. Mint contains varied exhibits showcasing Nevada's natural history and anthropology, including life-size displays of a Nevada ghost town and a Native American camp. A 300-foot mine tunnel with displays runs beneath the building.

Admission: adults $8, children free. Daily 8:30 a.m.-4:30 p.m.

NEVADA STATE RAILROAD MUSEUM
2180 S. Carson St., Carson City, 775-687-6953; www.nsrm-friends.org

All aboard at this museum, which houses more than 600 pieces of railroad equipment. It exhibits 50 freight and passenger cars, as well as five steam locomotives that once belonged to the Virginia and Truckee railroad, and also contains a pictorial history gallery and artifacts of the famed Bonanza Road.

Admission: adults $5, children free. Daily 8:30 a.m.-4:30 p.m.

STATE CAPITOL
101 N. Carson St., Carson City, 775-684-5700; www.nv.gov

The capitol building is a large Classical Revival structure with Doric columns and a silver dome. It features portraits of past Nevada governors. Self-guided tours are available.

Daily 8 a.m.-5 p.m.

HIGHLIGHTS

WHAT ARE NORTHWESTERN NEVADA'S BEST MUSEUMS?

DRIVE OVER TO THE NATIONAL AUTOMOBILE MUSEUM

More than 200 cars are on display at this automotive-history museum. Check out the classic rides driven by celebrities like James Dean, Frank Sinatra, Elvis Presley and John Wayne.

REVISIT THE PAST AT THE NEVADA HISTORICAL SOCIETY MUSEUM

Nevada's oldest museum is also one of its best. Learn all about the Silver State's history, including the Native Americans of the region, the mining upswing and, of course, its glitzy gaming roots.

GET ARTSY AT THE NEVADA MUSEUM OF ART

You won't miss this museum—the curved, uneven-seamed black building looks like the Black Rock from the desert. After gawking at the façade, duck inside to see the excellent collection of landscape photography.

INCLINE VILLAGE

DIAMOND PEAK SKI RESORT

1210 Ski Way, Incline Village, 775-832-1177; www.diamondpeak.com

Diamond Peak has three quads, three double chairlifts, a patrol, a school, rentals and snowmaking. There are 30 runs, the longest of which is approximately two miles with a vertical drop of 1,840 feet.

Mid-December-mid-April, daily.

LAKE TAHOE NEVADA STATE PARK

2005 Highway 28, Incline Village, 775-831-0494; www.parks.nv.gov

Wander the approximately 14,200 acres on the eastern shore of beautiful Lake Tahoe. There's a gently sloping sandy beach where you can do some swimming, fishing and boating (ramp). Or stay on land and go hiking, mountain biking or cross-country skiing.

RENO

FLEISCHMANN PLANETARIUM AND SCIENCE CENTER

1650 N. Virginia St., Reno, 775-784-4811; www.planetarium.unr.edu

This facility projects public shows on the inside of its 30-foot dome. The museum here also houses all four of the meteorites that have landed in Nevada—including a massive specimen that weighs more than a ton—and scales rigged to reflect the gravity on Jupiter or a neutron star. On cloudless Friday nights, you can peer through telescopes with members of the Astronomical Society of Nevada.

Admission: free. Daily.

GREAT BASIN ADVENTURE

Rancho San Rafael Regional Park, 1595 N. Sierra St., Reno, 775-785-4064; www.maycenter.com

Part of the Wilbur D. May Center in Rancho San Rafael Regional Park, Great Basin Adventure consists of several attractions designed to educate and entertain kids. At Wilbur's Farm, pint-sized visitors can take a pony ride or explore the 1-acre petting zoo. Guests can pan for gold at a replica mine building, with faux mine shafts that double as slides and displays on minerals and the area's mining history.

Admission: varies for exhibit; call for information. Tuesday-Saturday 10 a.m.-5 p.m., Sunday noon-5 p.m.

HUMBOLDT-TOIYABE NATIONAL FOREST

1200 Franklin Way, Sparks, 775-331-6444; www.fs.fed.us

At 6.3 million acres, this is the largest national forest in the lower 48 states. It extends across Nevada from the California border in a scattershot pattern, comprising 10 ranger districts that encompass meadows, mountains, deserts and canyons. Just northwest of the Reno city limits, Peavine Mountain is crisscrossed by a number of old mining roads now reserved for hikers and mountain bikers. Other Humboldt-Toiyabe highlights include scenic Lamoille Canyon and the Ruby Mountains, southeast of Elko; the rugged, isolated Toiyabe Range, near the geographic center of Nevada; and Boundary Peak, the state's highest point at 13,143 feet, southeast of Reno on the California-Nevada border.

Monday-Friday.

MOUNT ROSE SKI AREA

22222 Mt. Rose Highway, Reno, 775-849-0704, 800-754-7673; www.mtrose.com

Of all the ski resorts in the Reno-Tahoe area, Mount Rose has the highest base elevation (a precipitous 7,900 feet above sea level), making it the best bet for late-season skiing. Eight lifts, including two six-person, high-speed chairlifts, take skiers and snowboarders to the 9,700-foot summit to 1,200 acres of terrain nearly evenly split among skill levels (20 percent beginner, 30 percent intermediate and 40 percent advanced) and a pair of snowboarding parks. Located northwest of Lake Tahoe, Mount Rose is also known for its excellent beginners' program. There are no on-mountain accommodations.

Mid-November-mid-April, daily.

NATIONAL AUTOMOBILE MUSEUM (THE HARRAH COLLECTION)
10 Lake St. S., Reno, 775-333-9300; www.automuseum.org

The brainchild of car collector and gaming titan Bill Harrah, this excellent facility covers more than a century of automotive history. Four galleries house the museum's collection of more than 200 cars: The first gallery details the late 19th and early 20th centuries, complete with a blacksmith's shop, the garage of the day; the second covers 1914 to 1931; the third, 1932 to 1954; and the fourth, 1954 to modern day. The Masterpiece Circle Gallery in the fourth gallery also accommodates temporary themed exhibits on subjects ranging from Porsches to pickup trucks. The oldest car in the museum dates from 1892, and there are a number of collector's trophies, such as the sweet 1949 Mercury Coupe driven by James Dean in *Rebel Without a Cause*, and one-of-a-kind oddities, like the steam-powered 1977 Steamin' Demon.

Admission: adults $10, seniors $8, children 6-18 $4, children 5 and under free. Monday-Saturday 9:30 a.m.-5:30 p.m., Sunday 10 a.m.-4 p.m.

NEVADA HISTORICAL SOCIETY MUSEUM
1650 N. Virginia St., Reno, 775-688-1190; www.nevadaculture.org

Founded in 1904, this is both Nevada's oldest museum and one of its best. On permanent display is "Nevada: Prisms and Perspectives," which examines the Silver State's five biggest historical stories: the Native American perspective, the mining boom, the neon-lit story of gaming, transportation and the "Federal Presence," since the federal government owns 87 percent of the land.

Admission: adults $4, children free. Wednesday-Saturday 10 a.m.-5 p.m.

NEVADA MUSEUM OF ART
160 W. Liberty St., Reno, 775-329-3333; www.nevadaart.org

The only nationally accredited art museum in the entire state, the Nevada Museum of Art would be a top-notch facility no matter where it was located. Perhaps the most distinctive architectural specimen in all of artsy Reno, the curved, sweeping structure is a work of art in and of itself: modern (it opened in 2003) and monolithic (60,000 square feet), evoking the image of the legendary Black Rock of the Nevada desert. The collection housed within is equally impressive, broken into five different themes: contemporary art, contemporary landscape photography—one of the best of its kind anywhere—regional art, American art from 1900 to 1945, and the E. L. Weigand Collection, American art with a work-ethic theme.

Admission: adults $10, seniors and students $8, children 6-12 $1, children 5 and under free. Tuesday-Wednesday, Friday-Sunday 10 a.m.-5 p.m., Thursday 10 a.m.-8 p.m.

RENO ARCH
Virginia Street, Downtown Reno

In 1926, Reno commemorated the completion of the first transcontinental highway in North America, which ran through the city en route to San Francisco, with an arch that traverses Virginia Street downtown. Three years later, locals adopted the tagline "the biggest little city in the world" and added it to the now-iconic landmark. The arch has since been replaced twice, in 1964 and in 1987.

RENO-SPARKS THEATER COALITION

528 W. First St., Reno, 775-786-2278; www.theatercoalition.org

Consisting of more than 20 separate companies in the Reno-Sparks area, this organization is a cooperative effort to market a varied slate of theater, dance and other performing arts. Member troupes range from the avant-garde to the kid-friendly, and the Coalition puts together an events schedule for all of them.

SIERRA SAFARI ZOO

10200 N. Virginia St., Reno, 775-677-1101; www.sierrasafarizoo.org

The largest zoo in Nevada, Sierra Safari is home to 150 animals representing more than 40 species. The majority of the animals were selected for the rugged Reno climate, including a Siberian tiger and a number of other felines, but there are also tropical birds, a few reptiles and a number of primates. A petting zoo and a picnic area are onsite.

Admission: adults $7, seniors and children 3-12 $6, children 2 and under free. April-October, daily 10 a.m.-5 p.m.

W. M. KECK EARTH SCIENCES AND ENGINEERING MUSEUM

Mackay School of Mines Building, 1664 N. Virginia St., Reno, 775-784-4528; www.mines.unr.edu

Located in the Mackay School of Mines Building, the Keck Museum focuses on the state's mining history. The collection of specimens originated from Nevada's most renowned mining districts—the Comstock Lode, Tonopah and Goldfield—but exotic minerals from all over the world share the space. There are also displays of fossils, vintage mining equipment and a collection of fine silver donated by the family of mining tycoon John Mackay.

Admission: free. Monday-Friday 9 a.m.-4 p.m.

SPARKS

WILD ISLAND FAMILY ADVENTURE PARK

250 Wild Island Court, Sparks, 775-359-2927; www.wildisland.com

Primarily known as a summer water park, Wild Island is now a year-round facility with the 2003 addition of Coconut Bowl, a state-of-the-art 20-lane bowling alley, and the surprisingly chic Smokin' Marlin Grill. The water park is huge, with a wave pool, tubing river and myriad slides.

Hours vary by attraction and season.

WHERE TO STAY

INCLINE VILLAGE

★★★HYATT REGENCY LAKE TAHOE RESORT, SPA & CASINO

1111 Country Club Drive, Incline Village, 775-832-1234; www.hyatt.com

This resort is a top pick for rustic, upscale accommodations on the North Shore of Lake Tahoe. It's not on a mountain, but the resort will shuttle you to the slopes. Spa services are offered through the fitness center. The hotel also houses a small but charming old-style casino, a private hotel beach and a destination restaurant with arguably one of the best dining views of the lake.

422 rooms. Restaurant, bar. Business center. Fitness center. Pool. Spa. Beach. Casino. $151-250

RENO

★★★ATLANTIS CASINO RESORT SPA

3800 S. Virginia St., Reno, 775-825-4700, 800-723-6500; www.atlantiscasino.com

Located about three miles south of downtown, Atlantis is among Reno's top resorts, with several smoke-free gaming areas in the casinos, a top-notch business center and an array of rooms. Reserve one of the concierge tower rooms, which are 450 square feet—20 percent larger than the rest—and give you a view of the Sierra Nevada mountains. Plus, concierge rooms get you access to a special lounge stocked with a full-service no-host bar, complimentary continental breakfasts and afternoon hors d'oeuvres. A hotel highlight is the spa, which offers a variety of treatments using Ahava and Dermalogica products.

973 rooms. Restaurant, bar. Spa. Casino. Pets accepted. $61-150

★★★ELDORADO HOTEL AND CASINO

345 N. Virginia St., Reno, 800-879-8879; www.eldoradoreno.com

Of the casinos in downtown Reno, Eldorado attracts the youngest crowd, thanks to its myriad nightspots, which include a microbrewery with live rock and blues, a martini/piano bar and BuBinga, a popular dance club with DJs and live bands. If you plan to stay the night, go for a Euro-chic Studio Suite, with a memory foam mattress and a flat-screen TV, or the Player Spa Suite, which comes with a Jacuzzi.

17 rooms. Restaurant, bar. Business center. Pool. Casino. $61-150

★★★HARRAH'S HOTEL RENO

219 N. Center St., Reno, 775-786-3232; www.harrahsreno.com

Located downtown next to the Reno Arch, Harrah's Reno is one of the glitziest casinos in the city, a distinction it has held since opening in the early 1960s. The casino is immense and diverse, featuring more than 1,000 slot machines, table games of all kinds and a sports book. Sleek hotel accommodations range from standard rooms to skyline suites. There are seven restaurants, including the renowned Steak House at Harrah's Reno. Entertainers work the crowd onstage at Sammy's Showroom, named after Sammy Davis, Jr., who performed here 40 times.

928 rooms. Restaurant, bar. Pool. Spa. Pets accepted. Casino. $61-150

★★★PEPPERMILL HOTEL AND CASINO RENO

2707 S. Virginia St., Reno, 775-826-2121, 800-648-6992; www.peppermillreno.com

Consistently ranked one of the best casinos in the city, Peppermill's flagship resort is a fixture in the entertainment district near the airport, about two miles south of downtown. The property features 2,000 slot machines; the full spectrum of table gaming, poker and sports betting; plus nightly live entertainment in the swanky cabaret and the more intimate piano lounge. In addition to seven restaurants, the resort boasts a dozen nightspots, including Oceano, with large aquariums, and the domed-shaped Romanza Bar. There are a variety of rooms from which to choose, but they all have 42-inch high-definition TVs, triple sheets and plush double pillow-top mattresses, all of which will make it hard for you to get out of bed and hit up the casino.

1,635 rooms. Restaurant, bar. Business center. Fitness center. Pool. Spa. Casino. $61-150

★★★SIENA HOTEL SPA CASINO

1 S. Lake St., Reno, 775-327-4362, 877-743-6233; www.sienareno.com

Designed to resemble a Tuscan village, this comprehensive resort, located along the banks of the Truckee River, includes a 23,000-square-foot casino and a full-service spa with a variety of treatments. The bright and comfortable rooms include custom fabrics reflecting the sun-drenched palette of Tuscany and have views of the mountains or river. Among the three restaurants, Lexie's offers view of the water.

214 rooms. Restaurant, bars. Pool. Spa. Casino. $61-150

★★★SILVER LEGACY RESORT CASINO RENO

407 N. Virginia St., Reno, 775-325-7401, 800-687-7733; www.silverlegacyreno.com

This Victorian-themed resort has a steel-and-brass dome and a façade designed to resemble an 1890s storefront. Beyond the gaming—2,000 slots, table games, sports book and a keno lounge—there's a comedy club and a rum bar with dueling pianos. The showroom attracts big-name entertainers.

1,720 rooms. Restaurant, bar. Business center. Pool. Spa. $61-150

SPARKS

★★★JOHN ASCUAGA'S NUGGET

1100 Nugget Ave., Sparks, 775-356-3300, 800-648-1177; www.janugget.com

An anchor in downtown Sparks, the Nugget is right on the doorstep of Victorian Square, the site of numerous special events. The casino is loaded with all of the standards: slots, table games, a poker room and a sports book. The Celebrity Showroom is the place to go for entertainment; the 700-seat theater hosts everything from R&B flashback act Boyz II Men to a production of the musical *Funny Girl*. The hotel itself is a landmark, with a pair of 29-story towers flanking the casino, and a slate of amenities that includes everything from an arcade to a wedding chapel. Try to get a neutral-hued room in the east tower, which provides views of either the city or the mountains and 42-inch plasma televisions.

1,407 rooms. Restaurant, bar. Business center. Pool. Spa. Casino. $61-150

STATELINE

★★★HARRAH'S LAKE TAHOE

15 Highway 50, Stateline, 775-588-6611, 800-427-7247; www.harrahstahoe.com

This property offers 18,000 square feet of function space and plenty of recreation options for leisure visitors. Deluxe rooms are done up in browns and creams. Shop at the Galleria, swim in the glass-domed pool and, of course, hit the casino.

532 rooms. Restaurant, bar. Pool. Spa. Pets accepted. Casino. $61-150

★★★HARVEY'S LAKE TAHOE

Stateline Ave., Stateline, 775-588-2411, 800-427-8397; www.harveys.com

Most rooms at this resort, the first built in South Lake Tahoe, have a view of Lake Tahoe or the Sierra Nevada mountains. The resort offers a variety of ski packages in the winter and the outdoor arena draws top music guests, including Beyoncé and Diana Krall, in the summer.

740 rooms. Restaurant, bar. Casino. Pool. Fitness center. $61-150

WHERE TO EAT

STATELINE

★★★FRIDAY'S STATION STEAK & SEAFOOD GRILL
15 Highway 50, Stateline, 775-588-6611; www.harrahs.com

The view of the lake from this restaurant, located on the 18th floor of Harrah's Lake Tahoe, is memorable. Several steak and seafood combos are offered, such as filet mignon and Alaskan king crab or blackened shrimp.

Seafood, steak. Dinner. Reservations recommended. Bar. $36-85

★★★SAGE ROOM
Highway 50, Stateline, 775-588-2411; www.harrahs.com

Since 1947, the Sage Room Steak House has been world-renowned for its old Western ambience and fine cuisine. Dine among the works of Russell and Remington while enjoying traditional steakhouse dining highlighted by tableside flambé service. Top off your meal with the Sage Room's famous bananas Foster.

American. Dinner. Bar. $36-85

★★★THE SUMMIT
15 Highway 50, Stateline, 775-588-6611; www.harrahs.com

Located on the 16th and 17th floors of Harrah's, this restaurant has stunning views and sophisticated cuisine. Try the filet mignon with truffled parsnip purée or pistachio-encrusted rack of lamb.

American. Dinner. Bar. $86 and up

SOUTHERN NEVADA

Although glitzy cities like Las Vegas and Reno get the most attention in Nevada, there are some spots right outside the Strip that are worth a visit. A mere 20 miles from Sin City, Boulder City is also a world away from the bright lights. This quiet town is a haven for visitors seeking thrills outside the casinos. Its proximity to Lake Mead National Recreation Area makes it a perfect spot to rest after a day of fishing, swimming, hiking and sightseeing in one of the Southwest's most beautiful playgrounds. The fastest-growing city in Nevada, Henderson has become the third-largest city in the state, thanks to its proximity to Vegas. Many of the area's most luxurious resorts are in Henderson.

BOULDER CITY

HOOVER DAM
Highway 93, Boulder City, 702-494-2517, 866-730-9097; www.usbr.gov

It took 6.6 million tons of concrete—enough to pave a highway between New York and San Francisco—to stop the mighty Colorado River at Hoover Dam, which was completed in 1935 and is now a National Historic Landmark. Check out the visitor center, where you can watch a short film that tells the story of the dam's construction in Black Canyon. An elevator plunges 500 feet down the canyon wall, depositing passengers in a tunnel that leads to the power plant and its eight enormous generators. The observation deck takes in both sides of the dam, including Lake Mead and the Colorado River. Paddle wheelers take you on a 90-minute sightseeing cruise to the Hoover Dam (Lake Mead Cruises, Lake Mead Marina, 480 Lakeshore Road, Boulder City, 702-293-6180; www. lakemeadcruises.com).

LAKE MEAD NATIONAL RECREATION AREA

601 Nevada Highway, Boulder City, 702-293-8906; www.nps.gov

Lake Mead formed when Hoover Dam was completed in 1935. Located 30 miles from the Strip, visitors come here for boating and fishing. Several marinas around the lake and on neighboring Lake Mojave offer rentals, with everything from kayaks to houseboats that sleep up to 14 people (because of the great demand for the latter, call six months prior to your visit). Hikers can take in the desert basins, steep canyons, rainbow-hued rocks and wildlife, including bighorn sheep in the recreation area surrounding the lake.

Open 24 hours; visitors center 8:30 a.m.-4:30 p.m.

HENDERSON
REFLECTION BAY GOLF CLUB

1605 Lake Las Vegas Parkway, Henderson, 702-740-4653, 877-698-4653; www.lakelasvegas.com

Designed by golf great Jack Nicklaus, the public, par-72 resort course follows the rugged desert contours with the final holes along the shore of the 320-acre man-made Lake Las Vegas. Arroyo-meets-grass flora, maddening bunkers and interesting (and frustrating) water features make the course memorable. Afterward, kick back at the Mediterranean-style clubhouse with patio dining under a colonnade.

Winter 7 a.m.-dusk, summer 6:30 a.m.-dusk.

RIO SECCO GOLF CLUB

2851 Grand Hills Drive, Henderson, 702-777-2400; www.riosecco.net

Rio Secco is an expensive course, but its variety makes it well worth playing. The course is essentially divided into thirds, with six holes in small canyons, six on plateaus with views of the local skyline and six built to resemble the Nevada desert. The course is more than 7,300 yards long, so be prepared to swing for the fences. Number 9 is a long par-5 with bunkers surrounding the green. Make the turn facing the city and count yourself lucky if you've played 8 and 9 (back-to-back par-fives measuring 1,150 yards combined) at one or two over.

WHERE TO STAY

HENDERSON
★★★GREEN VALLEY RANCH RESORT, SPA AND CASINO

2300 Paseo Verde Parkway, Henderson, 702-617-7777, 866-782-9487;
www.greenvalleyranchresort.com

A Mediterranean-style oasis in the middle of the desert, the Green Valley Ranch Resort is situated in Henderson, between the Strip and the Lake Las Vegas resorts. The sprawling property feels more like an estate than a Vegas hotel, with personal touches like one-of-a-kind furnishings, plush sitting areas and textured accents. The casino does have a solid supply of dinging slot machines, but it's all done with a level of class that is rarely found on the Strip. Goose-down pillows, separate tubs and showers, twice daily housekeeping service, and plush, terry-cloth robes turn guest rooms into refuges. Whether you spend your day at The Beach (with actual sand) or The Pond, you'll be treated to pools that promote excess. Of course, the property would be lost without an equally luxuriant spa that includes tempting treatments and a private lap pool.

495 rooms. Restaurant, bar. Fitness center. Pool. Spa. Business center. $151-250

★★★LOEWS/LAKE LAS VEGAS RESORT

101 Montelago Blvd., Henderson, 702-567-6000; www.loewshotels.com

Golf, kayaking, fishing, hiking and spa treatments? Is this Vegas? Well technically it's Lake Las Vegas, a 320-acre man-made and privately owned lake that is closer to the town of Henderson than to Las Vegas proper (it is 17 miles from the Strip, for those who want to take in a show after all the outdoor recreation). The resort has a Moroccan theme and guest rooms offer amenities that include flat-screen TVs, plush terry robes, Lather bath products and twice-daily maid service. Entertainment in the area includes a concert series in the summer and a floating skating rink (yes, ice skating in the desert) in the nearby MonteLago Village during winter. Duffers will enjoy the Reflection Bay Golf Course and the Falls Golf Course. And, lest the kids and pets feel left out, Loews offers onsite specialty programs for both.

493 rooms. Restaurant, bar. Fitness center. Pool. Spa. Business center. Pets accepted. $151-250

LAUGHLIN

★★★AQUARIUS CASINO RESORT

1900 S. Casino Drive, Laughlin, 702-298-5111, 888-662-5825; www.aquariuscasinoresort.com

The largest resort on the Colorado River, this enormous property offers activities for every member of the family. Visitors will enjoy the 3,300-seat outdoor amphitheater and 60,000-square-foot casino as well as recently renovated hotel rooms.

1,907 rooms. Restaurant, bar. Business center. Fitness center. Pool. Spa. Casino. Tennis. $61-150

★★★GOLDEN NUGGET LAUGHLIN

2300 S. Casino Drive, Laughlin, 702-298-7111, 800-955-7278; www.goldennugget.com

This resort is like a tropical oasis in the desert. A jungle theme is carried from the rain-forest-inspired lobby to the tropical-inspired rooms. Tarzan's Night Club completes the illusion.

300 rooms. Restaurant, bar. Pool. Casino. $61-150

WHERE TO EAT

RECOMMENDED

SETTEBELLO

140 Green Valley Parkway, Henderson, 702-222-3556; www.settebello.net

It isn't easy finding good pizza in Las Vegas. Located in a strip mall, like most Vegas venues off the Strip, this Henderson eatery is a hit with locals for its honest-to-goodness Napoletana-style pizza. The brick oven, imported from

Italy, is what makes these thin crust beauties so tasty. It gets up to temperatures of 950 degrees Fahrenheit, which chars the bottom of the pizza, while keeping the top warm and gooey. Simple toppings like crushed tomatoes, luscious fresh mozzarella and fruity olive oil are all you need to satisfy your pizza craving.
Pizza. Lunch, dinner. $16-35

LAS VEGAS

The first thing you'll see as your plane touches down at McCarran International Airport is a skyline that's an amalgam of international whimsy, from the Eiffel Tower to the Luxor pyramid to Excalibur castle and everything in between. This fantasyland prides itself on being the ultimate escape—and encourages visitors to interpret it in any way they'd like. The goal of each casino resort is simple: To keep visitors happy and satisfied for as long as humanly possible, 24 hours a day. That translates, in part, into the over-the-top free attractions for which Las Vegas is known, from the erupting volcano at the Mirage to the dazzling water show at Bellagio. As the casinos see it, the less you invest in sightseeing, the more money you'll have for gaming.

If it's your first trip to the city, you'll likely spend most of your time on Las Vegas Boulevard, also known as the Strip. Though Las Vegas' reputation is first and foremost based on gambling, in recent years shopping, dining, spa-ing and clubbing have been vying to oust blackjack as the primary diversion. The constant reinvention of Las Vegas is a way of keeping the visitors streaming in.

Living large in Las Vegas is no tall order, especially since the city contains more over-the-top luxury hotels than anywhere else in the country. But Sin City isn't just a playground for the privileged. Last-minute hotel deals run rampant, allowing anyone to have a taste of the good life. You'll be hard-pressed to find a restaurant in Las Vegas that doesn't have a celebrity chef on its roster. The city has burst onto the culinary scene with a slew of elite dining experiences that would give any major metropolitan area a run for its money.

WHAT TO SEE

THE ADVENTUREDOME
Circus Circus, 2880 Las Vegas Blvd. S., Las Vegas, 866-456-8894; www.adventuredome.com

The Adventuredome is the largest indoor amusement park in the United States. The operative word is, of course, "indoor"; it offers rides and respite from the desert's brutal summer heat. With 25 rides and attractions, there are options for kids of all ages and heights. Canyon Blaster, the world's only indoor double-loop, double-corkscrew coaster, is one of the most popular thrill rides. Other options include Chaos, which whirls you into oblivion, and the Inverter, with its extreme G-force action. What the rides lack in white-knuckle-gripping terror, they make up for with variety and volume.

Admission: $4-$7 per ride. All-day passes adults $24.95, children 33˝-47˝ tall $14.95. Summer: 10 a.m.-midnight; school year: Monday-Thursday 11 a.m.-6 p.m., Friday-Saturday 10 a.m.-midnight, Sunday 10 a.m.-9 p.m.

HIGHLIGHTS

WHAT ARE THE TOP THINGS TO DO IN LAS VEGAS?

CATCH A FREE SHOW
See the Bellagio's aquatic ballet where water, music and light meld together.

SEE THE SHARKS
Mandalay Bay's stunning aquarium holds more than 2,000 animals, including a variety of sharks, giant sting rays, piranha, golden crocodiles and its newest addition, an 87-pound, 7-foot-long Komodo dragon.

HIT THE CASINOS
Whether it's the casino at Wynn Las Vegas, Hard Rock Hotel or MGM Grand, there are plenty of places to try and win big.

EXPLORE THE STRIP
A stroll down this legendary street will take you from Paris to New York without spending a dime. Ogle the massive resorts with their Strip-side pools, fountains and spectacles before stepping inside to dine, shop or try your luck at the casinos.

THE ATOMIC TESTING MUSEUM
755 E. Flamingo Road, Las Vegas, 702-794-5161; www.atomictestingmuseum.org

Few states have as explosive a history as Nevada does. The Atomic Testing Museum, in association with the Smithsonian Institute, educates you about the Nevada Test Site, which is a piece of land the size of Rhode Island that witnessed the bulk of American nuclear tests from 1951 to 1992, only 65 miles from Las Vegas. Get a better understanding of the nuclear world through simulations, artifacts, films and a glimpse into what it was like to work at the test site, as told by the former employees. Be sure to stop by the gift shop to see the assortment of nuclear-themed gifts—including an Albert Einstein action figure.

Admission: adults $12, seniors, military, students, Nevada residents and youth 7-17 $9, children 6 and under free. Monday-Saturday 10 a.m.-5 p.m., Sunday noon-5 p.m.

BELLAGIO CONSERVATORY & BOTANICAL GARDENS

Bellagio Las Vegas, 3600 Las Vegas Blvd. S., Las Vegas, 888-987-6667; www.bellagio.com

Picture an organic art museum, where the displays are made of flowers, shrubs, plants and trees, and change with the seasons. The Bellagio Conservatory and Botanical Gardens does just that, and it's even more beautiful than it sounds. The 13,500-square-foot palatial setting, located across from the resort's lobby, is home to five alternating displays throughout the year, with themes that include the holidays, Chinese New Year, spring, summer and fall. Each season manages to outdo the last. In winter, you might find reindeers made of whole pecans, giant greeting cards comprising thousands of flowers and a 21-foot wreath built from pinecones. Come spring, a whole new world awaits with a live butterfly garden, leaping fountains and butterfly-shaped topiaries. On average, each display consists of 40 trees, 1,500 shrubs and 10,000 blooming plants. Considering that the hotel spends $8 million annually on the Conservatory, this free attraction is a jackpot all around.

Daily 24 hours. Closed for five weeks a year, as the displays are changed.

THE BELLAGIO GALLERY OF FINE ART

3600 Las Vegas Blvd., Las Vegas, 702-957-9777; www.bellagio.com

If you think a casino is a strange bedfellow for a museum, you haven't been to Bellagio Gallery of Fine Art. Sure, critics harrumphed when they heard about a highbrow museum in "low-brow" Las Vegas, but they've since given BGFA an all-approving nod. Exhibits at this small space, located near the pool area, change throughout the year and display paintings, sculpture and other artistic mediums. Past exhibits have included American modernism, Claude Monet's masterworks, Faberge treasures, Picasso's ceramics and more. A recent installation, Figuratively Speaking: A Survey of the Human Form, featured the work of artists who helped define figurative art.

Admission: adults $15, seniors $12, students $10, children under 12 free. Sunday-Tuesday, Thursday 10 a.m.-6 p.m., Wednesday, Friday-Saturday 10 a.m.-7 p.m.

BODIES...THE EXHIBITION

Luxor, 3900 Las Vegas Blvd. S., Las Vegas, 800-288-1000; www.bodiestheexhibition.com

This show is something between art, science and just plain macabre. BODIES... The Exhibition is just what it sounds like: human cadavers displayed for all to see. The polymer-preserved bodies, each with its dermis removed, demonstrate everything from the muscular to the vascular systems of the body, so you can see just what you and your muscles look like from the inside when you're, say, playing baseball or throwing darts. Partial-body specimens show what a smoker's lung looks like compared to a healthy lung (try buying a pack of cigarettes after seeing that), and what kind of damage over-eating can do to your organs. The exhibition is educational, but it has raised some controversy since its inception because the bodies were acquired from the Chinese police (visit the website if you're curious).

Admission: adults $31, seniors $29, children 4-12 $23. Daily 10 a.m.-10 p.m.

BONANZA "THE WORLD'S LARGEST GIFT SHOP"

2440 Las Vegas Blvd. S., Las Vegas, 702-385-7359; www.worldslargestgiftshop.com

The self-proclaimed "world's largest gift shop" has far more than the typical tourist knickknacks you'd expect. You'll find fuzzy dice (just begging for a rearview mirror to call their own) and miniature, lighted "Welcome to Fabulous Las Vegas" signs, but there's also an impressive array of bachelor and bachelorette gag gifts, and even a sombrero-wearing dog that sings "La Bamba" when activated. Located at the corner of Las Vegas Boulevard and Sahara Avenue, this 40,000-square-foot space is a Sin City staple even locals frequent. It's the go-to spot for anyone in need of a new nunzilla wind-up doll or "Polly the Insulting Parrot."

Daily 8 a.m.-midnight.

THE EIFFEL TOWER EXPERIENCE

Paris Las Vegas, 3655 Las Vegas Blvd. S., Las Vegas, 877-603-4386; www.parislasvegas.com

Las Vegas is a city obsessed with replication—and we're not talking carbon copies and model airplanes. Though the Eiffel Tower at Paris Las Vegas is half the size of the original at 460 feet, the view from the top is equally stunning. A dizzying windowed elevator ride takes guests up nearly 50 floors to the open-air observation deck, which allows for 360-degree views of Las Vegas. It's intimate up here, and gets packed with tourists on the weekends. If you can get to the border of the deck facing west, you're in for perhaps the best view of the Fountains of Bellagio water show in town. Avoid tripping over men down on one knee. This is a popular spot for marriage proposals.

Admission daily from 9:30 a.m.-7:15 p.m.: adults $10, seniors and children $7, children under 5 free. Admission daily from 7:30 p.m.-12:30 a.m.: adults $15, seniors and children $10. Daily 9:30-12:30 a.m., weather permitting.

FOUNTAINS OF BELLAGIO

Bellagio Las Vegas, 3600 Las Vegas Blvd. S., Las Vegas, 888-987-6667; www.bellagio.com

Romance is anything but watered down at Lake Bellagio, as water, music and light meld together in an aquatic ballet. The water echoes human motion seen in dance, swaying while spraying more than 460 feet into the air. The jets' moves are perfectly choreographed to music, with scores from Broadway, the classics and more. If you can't snag a prime place along the Lake Bellagio railing, head to Paris, located across the street from Bellagio, for an equally stellar view. Or book a veranda table inside the Bellagio at Olives restaurant, have a glass of wine (and some delicious freshly made pasta), and enjoy multiple shows throughout your meal. It's one of the most mesmerizing sights in Vegas and, since it's free, you're saving up blackjack dollars every time you watch.

Performances take place every 30 minutes Monday-Friday 3-8 p.m., Saturday-Sunday noon-8 p.m. After 8 p.m. daily, performances are every 15 minutes until midnight.

FREMONT STREET EXPERIENCE

425 Fremont St., Las Vegas, 702-678-5777; www.vegasexperience.com

The Fremont Street Experience light canopy typifies vintage Las Vegas. Located downtown, the production spans five football fields and a whole host of historic casinos and neon signs. Despite the live music and street-fair atmosphere on the ground, the real action is in the sky. Six times nightly, the canopy springs into a vibrant show, as 12 million lights draw all eyes up. Music ranging from classic rock to classic Vegas blasts from surrounding speakers, and is choreographed to match the illumination. One of the best spots to watch is at Gold Diggers, the second-story nightclub at the Golden Nugget. Their patio is directly under the canopy, affording great views of the show, and the tourists swigging beer from football-shaped containers.

Show hours vary. See website for details.

GONDOLA RIDES

The Venetian Resort Hotel Casino, 3355 Las Vegas Blvd. S., Las Vegas, 877-883-6423; www.venetian.com

Who needs the murky waterways of Venice when you can take a gondola ride through the pristine, chlorinated canals of the Venetian Resort Hotel Casino? Choose the indoor canal or the outdoor one, and float in a gondola modeled after the real deal. Of course, rather than floating under historic bridges and sidewalk cafes, you'll be floating past stores like Banana Republic and Ann Taylor. Don't let that detract from the romantic lilt of your gondolier's serenades. The ride takes you through The Grand Canal Shoppes, which cover 500,000 feet of retail space and restaurants—not that you have much buying power from the confines of your romantic vessel.

Admission: adults and children $16, children 2 and under free. Sunday-Thursday 10 a.m.-11 p.m., Friday-Saturday 10 a.m.-midnight.

IMPERIAL PALACE AUTO COLLECTION

Imperial Palace, 3535 Las Vegas Blvd. S., Las Vegas, 702-794-3174; www.autocollections.com

We all know money and nice cars go hand-in-hand. So it makes sense that Imperial Palace houses one of the largest collections of classic cars in the world. The Auto Collection includes more than $100 million in inventory, and over 250 cars of all varieties—muscle, classic, historic and more. From Johnny Carson's 1939 Chrysler Royal Sedan to the 1957 Jaguar XKSS valued at more than $7 million, the vintage variety is endless. Buy, sell or just stroll through the 125,000-square-foot showroom at your leisure. It's certainly something to keep in mind as you double down or go all in.

Admission: adults $8.95, seniors and children under 12 $5, children under 3 free. Daily 10 a.m.-6 p.m.

JUBILEE! BACKSTAGE TOUR

Bally's, 3645 Las Vegas Blvd. S., Las Vegas, 800-237-7469; www.harrahs.com

There's a lot more to being a showgirl than having a knockout body. It takes stamina, style and an incredibly strong neck to hoist up those headdresses. Peek into the showgirl's world with the Donn Arden's Jubilee! backstage tour. A showgirl leads you across the stage, around the set and through the costume room, sharing fun facts about the current production. Did you know that the heaviest headdress weighs 35 pounds? Or, that there is a minimum of nine costume changes for each person throughout the show, and that five different kinds of feathers are used? As more and more traditional showgirl-themed shows are replaced by Cirque du Soleil and other large-scale productions, this is your chance to check out a Vegas icon, before it hits the road for good.

Admission: adults and children over 13 $15. Monday, Wednesday and Saturday 11 a.m.

LAKE OF DREAMS

Wynn Las Vegas, 3131 Las Vegas Blvd. S., Las Vegas, 877-321-9966; www.wynnlasvegas.com

No multi-star hotel on Las Vegas Boulevard is worth its weight without a manmade lake, and the one at Wynn is particularly special. Surrounded by a 120-foot-tall artificial mountain that shields it from Las Vegas Boulevard, the Lake of Dreams breathes an air of exclusivity, just like the rest of Wynn resort. But the lake's true purpose is to wow onlookers throughout the evening, as it plays host to a variety of surreal shows: statues of men and women arise from the water, light and music spring to life, and there's even a giant inflatable frog whose mouth moves in sync with Louis Armstrong's What a Wonderful World. For the best view of the show, make a reservation on the patio at SW Steakhouse or Daniel Boulud Brasserie, since everyone knows inflatable frogs are best seen on a full stomach, following a bottle of wine. The free shows begin after dark and occur approximately every half hour.

Daily 7 p.m.-12:30 a.m., times vary seasonally.

LAS VEGAS MOTOR SPEEDWAY

7000 Las Vegas Blvd. N., Las Vegas, 702-644-4444; www.lvms.com

You may not understand the appeal, but that shouldn't deter you from feeling the power, smelling the oil and reveling in the grit of NASCAR at the Las Vegas Motor Speedway. Every March the city's neck turns a touch redder, as more than 100,000 fans fire up their grills and head to NASCAR's Sprint Cup and Nationwide Series races. The $200 million track, which was built in 1995, extends 1,500 acres and includes the 1.5-mile super speedway, in addition to a 2.5-mile road course, a half-mile dirt oval and a drag strip. Technicalities aside, the people-watching here is priceless. So when your eyes tire of following the blurry left turns on the track, grab a hot dog and check out your neighbor's head-to-toe Jimmie Johnson-themed wardrobe.

Admission: adults $8, children under 12 and seniors $6. Daily. Race prices vary. Tours: Monday-Saturday 9 a.m.-4 p.m., Sunday 11-4 p.m.

LION HABITAT

MGM Grand Hotel & Casino, 3799 Las Vegas Blvd. S., Las Vegas, 877-880-0880; www.mgmgrand.com

Superstitious folks may choose to toss their chips at MGM Grand, and it's not because the dealers are better or the drinks are more potent. It's because of the lions. An Asian good-luck symbol, lions have made a home at MGM Grand for years, frolicking in their own expansive habitat, just a few feet from the slots. The multi-level dwelling hosts a handful of lions, and even a translucent tunnel that makes you feel as though you're in with the beasts. Before your inner animal advocate gets upset, know that the lions only spend "shifts" in the habitat. When they're not here, lying amid the waterfalls and foliage, they live on an 8.5-acre ranch nearby. Because they're in the habitat for such a limited time, trainers engage them in play or feed them, keeping them on their paws.

Daily 11 a.m.-7 p.m.

THE MIDWAY AT CIRCUS CIRCUS

Circus Circus, 2880 Las Vegas Blvd. S., Las Vegas, 800-634-3450; www.circuscircus.com

Located across the casino from the Adventuredome, the Midway and Arcade has games for kids, ranging from ski ball to frog toss and more. Clowns, jugglers, acrobats, trapeze artists and other performers put on impressive shows (considering they're free) on a stage by the Midway. If your head isn't spinning yet from the carnival games, hop into the Horse-A-Round bar. The revolving carousel-of-a-bar enamored Hunter S. Thompson in Fear and Loathing in Las Vegas, and judging from its surreal Midway backdrop, it's easy to see why. While Horse-A-Round keeps your body moving physically, the amount of mental spinning is up to you.

Daily 11 a.m.-midnight.

THE NEON MUSEUM

509 E. McWilliams Ave., Las Vegas, 702-387-6366; www.neonmuseum.org

It's referred to as the Boneyard for a reason. The Neon Museum holds the vestiges of vintage Vegas. This is where the history comes to rest—that which avoided implosion, that is. The signs and architecture date back to the 1940s, and include relics such as The Golden Nugget sign. The most recent addition is La Concha, a shell-shaped building designed by Paul Revere Williams that was saved from demolition and painstakingly moved here. While restoration of the historic mid-century modern building continues, tours of the museum are by appointment only and must be made at least one day in advance.

Admission: $15 minimum donation. Tours: by appointment.

PENSKE-WYNN FERRARI/MASERATI LAS VEGAS

Wynn Las Vegas, 3131 Las Vegas Blvd. S., Las Vegas, 702-770-2000; www.penskewynn.com

Before you go all in with your latest jackpot, swing by Wynn to consider taking home a Ferrari from the only factory-authorized dealership in Nevada. It's actually a wise investment—these are some of the few cars that actually increase in value. That is, if you're patient enough to weather the three- to five-year waiting list. There's a $10 fee to enter and nab a look at the vehicles, which can cost more than $400,000 each. The 10,000 square-foot showroom carries an average of 35 new and used luxury vehicles. And for those who can't afford the wheels, there are plenty of auto-branded trinkets to bring home.

Admission: $10. Monday-Saturday 9 a.m.-6 p.m.

PINBALL HALL OF FAME

1610 E. Tropicana Ave., Las Vegas; www.pinballmuseum.org

Sin City's "most unique" museum award goes to the Pinball Hall of Fame, a 10,000-square-foot warehouse packed with loads of bleeping, beeping, pinging interaction. The museum holds the world's largest collection of pinball machines dating as far back as the 1950s. Test your reflexes on machines from the Bride of Pinbot to The Family Guy—some even have antique wood rails. Most games only cost a quarter or two, and all proceeds are donated to the Salvation Army. The more you play, the more pinball pays—as if you needed a reason to go another round.

Sunday-Thursday 11 a.m.-11 p.m., Friday-Saturday 11 a.m.-midnight.

RED ROCK CANYON NATIONAL CONSERVATION AREA

SR 159, 702-515-5350, Summerlin; www.redrockcanyonlv.org

Grab that karabiner and head to Red Rock Canyon National Conservation Area. Located just 17 miles from the Las Vegas Strip, Red Rock Canyon is a popular spot for rock climbing, but it's also a naturalist's heaven with nearly 200,000 acres, and miles and miles of hiking and biking trails complemented by waterfalls, springs, wild burros, creosote bushes, pinion pine trees and more. The canyon is one of the world's largest wind-deposited formations, and is part of the Navajo Formation, created nearly 200 million years ago. A 13-mile paved scenic road circles through Red Rock, with stops and lookout points marked along the way, so even the car-dependent can feel at one with nature.

Admission: $7 per car, $3 per motorcycle. Park: Daily 6 a.m.-7 p.m. Hours vary seasonally; call for details. Visitor center: Daily 8 a.m.-4:30 p.m.

THE ROLLER COASTER

New York-New York, 3790 Las Vegas Blvd. S., Las Vegas, 800-689-1797; www.nynyhotelcasino.com

If you're going to ride one coaster in Las Vegas, it should be the roller coaster at New York-New York. Zip through the faux New York skyline, past the Statue of Liberty, while admiring the view of Las Vegas Boulevard from 200 feet up. With barrel rolls, a loop and multiple heart-wrenching drops at speeds nearing 70 miles per hour, this coaster is good old nail-biting fun. For those who are afraid of heights (and speed), New York-New York's Coney Island Emporium allows you to keep your feet on the ground and still relish in the flavor of the Big Apple with 12,000 square feet of games and carnival-style entertainment.

Admission: $14. Sunday-Thursday 11 a.m.-11 p.m., Friday-Saturday 10:30 a.m.-midnight; Coney Island Emporium: Sunday-Thursday 8 a.m.-midnight, Friday-Saturday 8 a.m.-2 a.m.

SECRET GARDEN AND DOLPHIN HABITAT

The Mirage, 3400 Las Vegas Blvd. S., Las Vegas, 800-374-9000; www.miragehabitat.com

The cats here hold magical secrets behind their eerie blue eyes—literally. These are the white tigers that once performed in Siegfried and Roy's magic show, prior to the incident in which their brother, Montecore, nearly killed magician and trainer Roy Horn in 2003. Though they're no longer disappearing and reappearing on stage, the cats lead a pretty luxurious life, surrounded by exotic plants and waterfalls and other felines, such as snow leopards, lions, golden tigers and black panthers. Following the cats, make your way over to the nearby Dolphin Habitat. It's home to six Atlantic bottlenose dolphins, whom you'll spot leaping, "walking" on water, swimming and doing whatever it is that dolphins do. Because it's primarily a research facility, the Dolphin Habitat doesn't host regular "shows," but the trainers interact with the creatures throughout the day for the public to see. To get even more up-close, inquire about the Trainer for a Day program. Visitors can suit up and rub dorsal fins with some of the earth's smartest creatures.

Admission: adults $15, children 4-12 $10, children 3 and under free. Monday-Friday 11 a.m.-6:30 p.m., Saturday-Sunday 10 a.m.-6:30 p.m.

SHARK REEF AQUARIUM

Mandalay Bay, 3950 Las Vegas Blvd. S., Las Vegas, 877-632-7800; www.sharkreef.com

Pardon the pun, but this attraction carries a serious bite. Mandalay Bay's stunning aquarium holds more than 2,000 animals, including a variety of sharks, giant sting rays, piranha, golden crocodiles and its newest addition, an 87-pound, 7-foot-long Komodo dragon. With 1.6 million gallons of water, the cool, cavernous shark reef is a quiet yet thrilling escape from the buzzing of the slots. Be sure to swing by the sting ray petting pool before settling in for an underwater aquatic ballet, as floor-to-ceiling glass walls show sea turtles, sharks and a variety of fish frolicking about in their impressive Vegas digs. Part of the floor is glass, too, allowing an eerie view of the sharks as they swim below.

Admission: adults $16.95, children under 12 $10.95, children 4 and under free. Sunday-Thursday 10 a.m.-8 p.m., Friday-Saturday 10 a.m.-10 p.m.

SHOWCASE MALL

3785 Las Vegas Blvd. S., Las Vegas

The words "Showcase Mall" should be code for sugar kingdom. Kids love the place as it boasts a slew of family-friendly activities. (There are a few shops, too, but "Mall" is a bit of an exaggeration.) At M&M's World (702-736-7611) you'll find every color of M&M imaginable—purple, gray, black, pink, turquoise. Head to World of Coca-Cola (702-270-5952) for a refreshing fizzy drink made by an old-fashioned soda jerk as you browse the Coca-Cola memorabilia. Once the kids are fully buzzed on sugar, head upstairs to GameWorks (702-432-4263) and let them play video games to their hearts' content. When they start crashing, the United Artists movie theater (702-225-4828) provides the perfect respite (and relief from the desert sun thanks to constantly cranked air conditioning).

Store hours vary. M&M's World: Sunday-Thursday 9 a.m.-11 p.m., Friday-Saturday 9 a.m.-midnight. World of Coca-Cola: Daily 10 a.m.-11 p.m. GameWorks: Sunday-Thursday 10 a.m.-midnight, Friday-Saturday 10 a.m.-1 a.m.

SIRENS OF TI

Treasure Island, 3300 Las Vegas Blvd. South, Las Vegas, 702-894-7111, 800-288-7206; www.treasureisland.com

Stand your ground early for the Sirens of TI show, because it fills up quickly. This battle between buff young pirates and barely clad sirens takes place in the lake in front of TI (formerly called Treasure Island, and once with a family-friendly pirate show), on Las Vegas Boulevard. There are powerful pyrotechnics, amazing acrobatics and nearly 12 minutes of dialogue. Back in the days of Odysseus, Sirens were best seen, not heard, and that adage hasn't changed, but the visual charade is entertaining nevertheless. Spoiler alert: The sinking of the ship at the end of the melee makes it worth the wait (and maybe even the banter).

Daily 7 p.m., 8:30 p.m. and 10 p.m.

SPRINGS PRESERVE

333 S. Valley View Blvd., Las Vegas, 702-822-7700; www.springspreserve.org

The Mojave Desert isn't all browns and grays. At the Springs Preserve, it's actually green—in more ways than one. This 180-acre historic preservation project is located just a couple of miles from the Strip, and embraces the concept of sustainability—a positive step in a city known for its frequent building implosions. Without these historic springs, Las Vegas wouldn't be what it is today. Originally, this central spot in the valley was the water source for residents and travelers. The springs dried up in 1962, but the Las Vegas Valley Water District has re-created them. The $250 million project hosts a variety of LEED-certified buildings that includes museums, galleries and interactive displays such as a flash flood, an actual fossil digging area, animal exhibits and more. With eight acres of gardens, miles of walking paths, a play area for kids, an amphitheater and even a Wolfgang Puck restaurant (and you thought all the good grub was on the Strip), the Springs Preserve celebrates the history and culture of Southern Nevada, while also keeping its sights on the future.

Special exhibits: adults $18.95, student and seniors $17.05, children $10.95, children under 5 free. Daily 10 a.m.-6 p.m.

STRATOSPHERE RIDES

The Stratosphere, 2000 Las Vegas Blvd. S., Las Vegas, 800-998-6937; www.stratospherehotel.com

The screams carry for miles from the top of the Stratosphere, as riders dangle, shoot and blast over Las Vegas Boulevard, nearly 900 feet up. The Big Shot propels passengers up at 45 miles per hour, losing their stomachs and then catching them as they fall back down. X-Scream is like a giant teeter-totter that shoots passengers off the edge of the Stratosphere. And Insanity, the Ride is a giant arm that twirls riders off the edge of the tower, spinning at three Gs. For those who are less inclined to heighten their heart rates, an enclosed 109th-floor observation deck gives a tremendous view of the Las Vegas Valley—and the horrified faces of riders as they're hurled over the edge.

Tower tickets: adults $15.95, seniors and hotel guests $12, children $10. Rides are $12-$13. Tower/ride packages are available. Sunday-Thursday 10-1 a.m., Friday-Saturday and holidays 10-2 a.m.

THE TANK

The Golden Nugget, 129 E. Fremont St., Downtown, 800-634-3454; www.goldennugget.com

This should be as close as you'll ever come to swimming with the fishes. The $30 million tank at the Golden Nugget is a 200,000-gallon aquarium full of sharks, sting rays and fish—and a three-story, translucent waterslide goes right through the center of it. The Tank is located smack-dab in the middle of the hotel's swimming pool, so even non-sliders can go head-to-head with the sharks, swimming loops around the Tank and making faces at the toothsome fin-flappers. Those who get their fill of sharks from Discovery Channel's *Shark Week* can lounge in the partially submerged chaises that line the pool.

Admission: adults $20, children under 11 $15, children under 2 free. Hotel guests free. Daily 10 a.m.-8 p.m.

TITANIC: THE ARTIFACT EXHIBITION
Luxor, 3900 Las Vegas Blvd. S., Las Vegas, 800-288-1000; www.titanictix.com

This exhibit gives colorful insight into the 1912 tragedy, boasting an extensive collection of artifacts discovered two and a half miles under the sea, including snippets from the last night's dinner menu, luggage, floor tiles and other items salvaged from "the ship of dreams." The 25,000-square-foot exhibit even features a piece of the *Titanic's* hull and a full-scale replica of the grand staircase. We know the photo op will be tempting, but just try and keep your inner Leonardo DiCaprio to yourself.

Admission: adults $27, seniors $25, children 4-12 $20, children 3 and under free. Daily 10 a.m.-10 p.m.

VEGAS INDOOR SKYDIVING
200 Convention Center Drive, Las Vegas, 877-545-8093; www.vegasindoorskydiving.com

This indoor simulation skydiving gig is not for the faint of heart. First, you watch a video and sign a lengthy disclaimer. Then you step into a one-piece jumpsuit, put on your flight goggles and enter the chamber. Once inside an instructor works with you as you lie, facedown, on what feels like metal fencing. Then they start the DC-3 propeller, and it makes enough wind (up to 120 mph) for you to float. So if the thought of jumping from an airplane is too terrifying to stomach, you can still experience the (simulated) thrill of freefall at this unique attraction.

First flight $75, second flight on same day $40. Minimum weight to fly is 40 pounds. Daily 9:45 a.m.-8 p.m.

THE VOLCANO
The Mirage, 3400 Las Vegas Blvd. S., Las Vegas, 800-374-9000; www.mirage.com

For nearly two decades, The Volcano at the Mirage burbled and spewed its innards onto the surrounding lake thanks to some fancy lighting and special effects. It went dormant in February 2007, but after a complete renovation by WET Design, the company responsible for creating the Fountains of Bellagio, the Volcano is erupting yet again, this time with music to match. Thanks to the combined efforts of Grateful Dead drummer Mickey Hart and Indian tabla virtuoso Zakir Hussain, the new Volcano impresses Strip passersby with an exclusive soundtrack to match the erupting rhythms, soaring fireballs and fiery lava.

Daily 7 p.m., 8 p.m., 9 p.m., 10 p.m. and 11 p.m.

WYNN GOLF COURSE
3131 Las Vegas Blvd. S., Center Strip, 888-320-7122; www.wynnlasvegas.com

Built in 2003, Wynn Golf Course actually has a historic reputation. It's located on the former Desert Inn Golf Club site that for 50 years hosted PGA, Senior PGA and LPGA tournaments. Nearly 1,200 of the 50-year-old trees still stand on the 7,042-yard par-70 course, which was designed by Tom Fazio and Steve Wynn. A 37-foot waterfall is just one of the many water details that meander throughout the course. Wynn has something of the Midas touch when it comes to development, and Wynn Golf Club is no exception. To emphasize its exclusivity, the course was previously open to Wynn hotel guests and invited visitors only, though that requirement was lifted in November of 2007, and fees reach $500.

See website for fees and hours.

WHERE TO STAY

★★★BALLY'S LAS VEGAS

3645 Las Vegas Blvd. S., Las Vegas, 877-603-4390; www.ballyslasvegas.com

If Vegas conjures images of showgirls then look to Bally's, which offers the quintessential showgirl sensation, *Donn Arden's Jubilee!* Like the show, Bally's epitomizes classic Vegas with its center-Strip location and traditional-style guest rooms. The beige-on-beige décor can feel a bit dated, but the rooms are comfortable and the floor-to-ceiling windows provide nice views of the Strip. The North Tower rooms have been renovated more recently, so be sure to specify when you book. Eight tennis courts (illuminated for night play) and access to two nearby golf courses motivates those who thought they'd spend all their time at the pool (which isn't a bad plan B, especially if you secure one of the cabanas). Movie buffs may remember Bally's as the spot where the Flying Elvis' skydivers landed in the film *Honeymoon in Vegas*.

2,814 rooms. Restaurant, bar. Tennis. Fitness center. Pool. Spa. Business center. $151-250

★★★★BELLAGIO LAS VEGAS

3600 Las Vegas Blvd. South, Las Vegas, 888-987-6667; www.bellagio.com

With its world-class art offerings—from the Chihuly glass sculpture overlooking the lobby to the masterpieces gracing the walls of The Bellagio Gallery of Fine Art—the Bellagio continues to hail as the class act of the Strip. Water is the element of choice here, with the magical Fountains of Bellagio, Cirque du Soleil's awe-inspiring water-themed performance *O*, and five beautifully manicured courtyard pool areas. The guest rooms continue the aquatic adventure with Italian marble deep-soaking tubs and glass-enclosed showers. Flat-screen TVs, a fully stocked minibar and electronic drapes round out the contemporary décor. For those looking to raise the stakes, the Bellagio Tower suites flaunt deep, dark wood furnishings, extra-spacious floor plans and a striking panoramic view of the city.

3,933 rooms. Restaurant, bar. Fitness center. Pool. Spa. Business center. $251-350

★★★CAESARS PALACE

3570 Las Vegas Blvd. S., Las Vegas, 702-731-7110, 866-227-5938; www.caesarspalace.com

With a name like Caesars, you'd expect a bit of Roman excess—but that's an understatement, considering the Palace's 85 acres, 26 restaurants, five (soon to be six) towers and eight pools, including one for swim-up blackjack. Your only problem will be deciding where to go first. The original circular casino is still popular and offers a 14,000-square-foot poker room and a Pussycat Dolls-themed area with go-go dancers performing in bronze cages. No matter which of the towers you retreat to, your room is guaranteed to give a lesson in tasteful opulence with plush linens, modern décor, LCD TVs (including one embedded in the bathroom mirror) and oversized walk-in showers with dual rain showerheads. A sixth tower, the Octavius, was in the works at press time and is expected to feature 665 new guest rooms that include the latest in amenities. Until then, the Augustus Tower has the newest and most up-to-date rooms, with views of the newly renovated Garden of the Gods pool complex or the Strip.

3,400 rooms. Restaurant, bar. Fitness center. Pool. Spa. Business center. $151-250

★★★★ENCORE LAS VEGAS
3121 Las Vegas Blvd. S., Las Vegas, 888-320-7125, 702-770-8000; www.encorelasvegas.com

The newest resort in Steve Wynn's luxury Vegas repertoire, Encore delivers the same exceptional service and class as its flagship property with more of a boutique vibe. The casual elegance of the décor is both playful and intimate, from the vibrant red chandeliers in the casino to the alluring golden buddha in the spa to the signature butterfly motif fluttering throughout the property (said to portend good luck). Guest suites are awash in neutrals, reds and blacks, and have floor-to-ceiling windows with views of the Strip, swiveling flat-screen TVs, and limestone and marble baths. With five restaurants onsite, your taste buds will want for nothing. An evening at Sinatra will have you crooning between bites of house-made pasta, while Botero is sure to have you seeing food as a higher art form. The spa gets top billing in Las Vegas with 37 treatment rooms in which to enjoy a transformation ritual or fusion massage. And if the tables have been good to you, leaving you money to burn, book a VIP table at XS or Surrender, two of Vegas' hottest nightclubs. The Encore Beach Club features a three-tiered swimming pool, luxurious cabanas and bungalows.

1,767 rooms. Restaurant, bar. Fitness center. Pool. Spa. Business center. $351 and up

★★★★FOUR SEASONS HOTEL LAS VEGAS
3960 Las Vegas Blvd. S., Las Vegas, 702-632-5000; www.fourseasons.com

Tranquility isn't a word often used to describe the Las Vegas Strip, but it can be found at the Four Seasons. Located on floors 35 through 39 of the Mandalay Bay resort, this non-gaming hotel has its own entrance, restaurants and a pool with attendants at the ready to provide the requisite Evian spritz, fresh fruit and chilled water. They'll even provide you with a swimsuit to keep in case you hadn't planned on taking a dip during your trip. The elegance of the hotel extends to the guest rooms, which start at 500 square feet of luxury with down duvets and pillows, floor-to-ceiling windows overlooking the city and twice-daily housekeeping service. If this sybaritic lifestyle ever gets stale, Mandalay Bay's 135,000-square-foot casino is downstairs, and then it's back upstairs to your tranquil quarters.

424 rooms. Restaurant, bar. Fitness center. Pool. Spa. Business center. Pets accepted. $351 and up

★★★GOLDEN NUGGET LAS VEGAS
129 E. Fremont St., Las Vegas, 702-385-7111, 800-846-5336; www.goldennugget.com

More than $160 million has been spent on renovations to the Golden Nugget since it was purchased by the Landry's Restaurants company in 2005, and now the hotel—which originally opened in 1946 and retains its Gold Rush-kitsch design—is the closest thing to a Strip-style property in the downtown area. The most striking addition is the hotel's Tank pool, which features a 200,000-gallon aquarium filled with sharks—no more dangerous than the poker variety you'll find in the casino—and a 30-foot waterslide that runs right through it. The hotel is made up of four towers. Rooms in the Rush Tower are modern and sophisticated with plenty of space, feather beds, flat-screen televisions and great views. Rooms in the Spa Tower run 1,500 square feet on two levels and offer whirlpool baths, floor-to-ceiling windows, wet bars and even a shoeshine machine. Before getting cozy at the tables, pay a visit to the hotel's "Hand of Faith," a gold nugget found in 1980 with an estimated worth of $425,000 and a weight of 61 pounds, 11 ounces.

2,300 rooms. Restaurant, bar. Fitness center. Pool. Spa. Business center. $61-150

★★★HARD ROCK HOTEL & CASINO LAS VEGAS

4455 Paradise Road, Las Vegas, 702-693-5000, 800-473-7625;
www.hardrockhotel.com

If you've never jammed on air guitar in your basement, the charms of The Rock may be lost on you. This rock 'n' roll-themed hotel is awash in memorabilia, but it's the rockers themselves (plus actors, models and sports stars) who really pull in the crowds. A center for stag parties, the Hard Rock attracts a 20-something set that's eager to hang out at the Tahitian-style pool wearing as little as possible. The standard guest rooms offer Bose stereo systems, plasma TVs, lots of plush linens and French doors that open onto either a pool or a mountain view. The 1,300-square-foot Celebrity Suite features a lounge area with a wet bar and a pool table, while the Penthouse ups the ante even more by adding a single-lane automated bowling alley and a mosaic hot tub with a view of the Strip. The new HRH Tower Suites offers private check in, a spa, new custom suites and restaurants of its own.

1,493 rooms. Restaurant, bar. Fitness center. Pool. Spa. Business center. $151-250

★★★HARRAH'S LAS VEGAS

3475 Las Vegas Blvd. S., Las Vegas, 800-214-9110;
www.harrahs.com

Bill Harrah opened his first bingo parlor in Reno in 1937, but never lived to see his eponymous hotel-casino open in the middle of the Las Vegas Strip (it would have been a long wait; Harrah's opened as a replacement for the Holiday Casino in 1992). The rooms are pretty much what you'd expect from a hotel built in the early nineties (muted colors, standard-issue furniture) but they're spacious and clean, and some even have Nintendo (just don't expect Wiis). The most updated rooms are in the Mardi Gras Tower, but even these are frill-free. The Carnaval theme (think Rio pre-Lent) spills out onto the street, where the outdoor Carnaval Court Bar & Grill offers a stage with live bands, a busy bar featuring "flair" bartenders and blackjack tables (on weekends).

2,640 rooms. Restaurant, bar. Fitness center. Pool. Spa. Business center. $61-150

★★★LAS VEGAS HILTON

3000 Paradise Road, Las Vegas, 702-732-5111;
www.lvhilton.com

The place where Elvis Presley broke concert attendance records, and where Barry Manilow played for years most recently, the Hilton has a long history on the Strip. Sports fans should enjoy the Hilton's Race and Sports SuperBook, which is considered one of the best in town for those who love putting bets down on everything from ponies to pugilists. The guest rooms have been recently renovated with a neutral color scheme, contemporary furnishings and new beds. If you can, upgrade to a premium room, which has high-end linens and plasma TVs. Business travelers no longer have to worry about walking in the heat in their suits thanks to the addition of a skybridge connecting the hotel to the Las Vegas Convention Center.

2,957 rooms. Restaurant, bar. Fitness center. Tennis. Pool. Spa. Business center. $151-250

★★★LAS VEGAS MARRIOTT SUITES

325 Convention Center Drive, Las Vegas, 702-650-2000; www.marriott.com

A smoke-free non-gambling hotel set directly across from the Las Vegas Convention Center, the Las Vegas Marriott Suites offers a convenient location for those attending a conference. The adjacent Monorail Station affords easy access to several stops along the Strip for those who simply can't resist throwing down a few chips between meetings. Some of the newly renovated guest rooms have separate living and sleeping areas, while all offer work stations with high-speed Internet access, cotton-rich linens and custom duvets. Essentially, this is a very pleasant stay for those who want to be in Vegas without really being in Vegas.

278 rooms. Restaurant, bar. Fitness center. Pool. Business center. $61-150

★★★LUXOR

3900 Las Vegas Blvd. S., Las Vegas, 702-262-4444; www.luxor.com

Boasting the world's brightest beam of light, the Luxor's famous pyramid shape has become synonymous with the Strip. The hotel's 30 stories are serviced by "inclinators" that run at a 39-degree angle in each corner of the pyramid. The décor is contemporary and simple with warm colors, Egyptian-themed bedspreads and work spaces—just watch your head when you're near the window (that slanted wall will get you every time). The rooms in the twin 22-story towers are larger and offer better views of the city lights with floor-to-ceiling (non-slanted) windows. Luxor jumped on the Cirque bandwagon when they opened the Cirque du Soleil show featuring magician Criss Angel, *Believe*. The LAX Nightclub is one of the sultriest spots on the Strip.

4,400 rooms. Restaurant bar. Fitness center. Pool. Spa. Business center. $61-150

★★★★THE M RESORT SPA & CASINO LAS VEGAS

12300 Las Vegas Blvd. S., Las Vegas, 702-797-1000; www.themresort.com

The newest addition to Sin City, the M Resort provides a refreshing alternative to typical Vegas. Instead of the constant dinging of slot machines and flashing of neon signs, the M Resort is a study in natural light, trickling waterfalls and the subtle scent of eucalyptus, which is filtrated through the hotel. Lest you forget you're in Las Vegas, guest rooms offer views of the Strip through floor-to-ceiling windows, as well as Bose sound systems, flat-screen TVs and marble vanities. The sprawling 100,000-square-foot Villaggio Del Sole Pool and Entertainment Piazza includes two pools, cabanas, an outdoor cocktail lounge and a stage for live music performances. Nine onsite restaurants and bars ensure that you're well fed throughout your stay.

390 rooms. Restaurant, bar. Business center. Fitness center. Pool. Spa. $61-150

★★★MANDALAY BAY RESORT & CASINO

3950 Las Vegas Blvd. S., Las Vegas, 702-632-7777; www.mandalaybay.com

From the 14-foot-high salt-water aquarium in the lobby to the 11-acre Mandalay Bay Beach, which includes 2,700 tons of real sand, waves and a lazy river, this hotel offers more than most Las Vegas resorts for non-gamblers. Families traveling with kids are big business for Mandalay Bay, but the hotel covers the adult playground concept, too, with THEhotel at Mandalay Bay, a boutique-style hotel-within-a-hotel that has a separate entrance, check-in and spa. Space isn't an issue at this mega-resort, which almost feels like a small city—a city with its own 135,000-square-foot casino, 1.7 million-square-foot convention center and 12,000-seat event center that hosts everything from boxing to Beyoncé concerts. The guest rooms recently got a facelift and now are outfitted in classic neutral tones, chic modern furnishings and enormous marble baths. You can even pick your room—maybe an unobstructed Strip view, or one with a spa tub, or perhaps a room with a "playpen couch" that allows for face-to-face seating.

4,328 rooms. Restaurant, bar. Fitness center. Pool. Spa. Business center. $151-250

★★★★MANDARIN ORIENTAL, LAS VEGAS
3752 Las Vegas Blvd. S., Las Vegas, 702-590-8888; www.mandarinoriental.com/lasvegas

The smallest of the new CityCenter hotels, this 47-story, non-gaming hotel delivers the same sophisticated elegance and top-notch service that its namesake properties have been providing for years. Spacious guest rooms include floor-to-ceiling windows and state-of-the-art entertainment systems. The 27,000-square-foot spa includes 17 treatment rooms with seven couples suites, as well as a fitness center with yoga and Pilates studios. If you'd rather get your exercise outdoors, try one of the hotel's two lap pools before grabbing lunch at the café or one of the premier restaurants onsite, including Twist, the first U.S. restaurant by chef Pierre Gagnaire.

392 rooms. Restaurant, bar. Fitness center. Pool. Spa. Business center. $351 and up

★★★MGM GRAND HOTEL & CASINO
3799 Las Vegas Blvd. S., Las Vegas, 702-891-7777; www.mgmgrand.com

With more than 5,000 hotel rooms in four 30-story towers, 170,000-square-feet of casino space and a 6.6-acre pool complex, the MGM takes the "Grand" in its name seriously. Even the entrance looms large with its icon, a 45-foot-tall, 100,000-pound bronze lion (the largest bronze statue in the country), greeting guests from atop a 25-foot pedestal. Guest rooms vary based on the tower, but all include comfortable pillow-top mattresses, oversized bathrooms with marble vanities and work spaces. Rooms in the West Wing have been recently renovated and up the ante with Bose Wave radios, sleek modern furnishings and flat-screen TVs in the bathrooms. It's nearly impossible to choose from more than a dozen signature restaurants onsite, but Joël Robuchon should be at the top of any foodie's list. The Cirque du Soliel show, KÀ, is a must-see.

5,044 rooms. Restaurant, bar. Pool. Fitness center. Spa. Business center. $151-250

★★★THE MIRAGE
3400 Las Vegas Blvd. S., Las Vegas, 702-791-7111; www.mirage.com

The theme of the Mirage is that of a South Seas oasis dropped into the middle of the desert. As part of the tropical feel, Siegfried & Roy's Secret Garden and Dolphin Habitat features tigers, panthers, leopards and bottlenose dolphins (which you can swim with for a price). The Mirage's tropical theme continues at the pool complex where verdant gardens mix with freeform lagoons and a cascading waterfall. The poolside chaises are functional, but during the busy season, you'll be lucky to find an empty one. The "Bare" pool, where bikini tops are optional and an ID is required, is a more comfortable choice, if you're not shy (and willing to pay). When booking, ask for a deluxe or Tower deluxe room, as these recently underwent a $90 million renovation and now feature pillow-top mattresses, down comforters and LCD TVs, not to mention impressive views of the mountains, the Strip or the pool.

3,044 rooms. Restaurant, bar. Fitness center. Pool. Spa. Business center. $61-150

★★★MONTE CARLO RESORT & CASINO

3770 Las Vegas Blvd. S., Las Vegas, 702-730-7777; www.montecarlo.com

As the name suggests, Monte Carlo is all about the feeling of the Riviera. Water takes center stage with a 21,000-square-foot pool, waterfalls, a lazy river and wave pool. When the desert sun gets the best of you, retreat to one of the private cabanas, complete with a flat-screen TV, radio, phone and refrigerator. The Lido-like atmosphere carries into the monochromatic guest rooms with cherry wood furniture and Italian marble baths. For a more spacious experience, upgrade to a Monaco suite and enjoy a clean, modern design with black chrome and shades of gray, dark brown and white—essentially what you'd expect if you were to spend your holiday in Monte Carlo. Restaurant offerings include the BRAND Steakhouse, and for the all-night crowd, there's a 24-hour Starbucks in the lobby. The recently opened Hotel 32 occupies the top floor of the Monte Carlo and offers VIP airport transport service and sleek suites stocked with high-def TVs and iPod docking stations.

2,992 rooms. Restaurant, bar. Fitness center. Pool. Spa. Business center. $151-250

★★★NEW YORK-NEW YORK

3790 Las Vegas Blvd. S., Las Vegas, 702-740-6969; www.nynyhotelcasino.com

Only in Las Vegas can the Big Apple be so accessible. Best known for its checker-cab roller coaster, New York-New York whirls guests through the city's most recognizable monuments, including the Empire State Building and the Statue of Liberty, in a matter of minutes. Guest rooms are given appropriate names like Park Avenue and Broadway Deluxe, which offers nearly 450 square feet of space and includes marble counter tops and a glass tub enclosure. When space is available, you can upgrade to a spa suite for a nominal fee. Entertainment options run the gamut from dueling pianos at the Bar at Times Square to Cirque du Soleil's show Zumanity to rockin' DJs at the ROK Vegas nightclub.

2,024 rooms. Restaurant, bar. Fitness center. Pool. Spa. Business center. $151-250

★★★★THE PALAZZO LAS VEGAS RESORT HOTEL CASINO

3325 Las Vegas Blvd. S., Las Vegas, 702-607-7777; www.palazzolasvegas.com

This sister property of the Venetian opened in December 2007 at an estimated cost of $1.9 billion. The guest rooms in the 50-story tower start at 720 square feet and are decorated in a contemporary Italian style complete with remote-controlled Roman shades and curtains to block out that searing desert sun. The rooms also offer Egyptian linens from Anichini and have been reviewed by a feng shui master for proper energy flow (always good to have before hitting the slots). The swank Shoppes at Palazzo has more than 50 stores, including an 85,000-square-foot Barneys New York, with the New York vibe continuing in the Broadway musical Jersey Boys at the Palazzo Theater. Celebrity chefs such as Mario Batali, Wolfgang Puck, and Emeril Lagasse have all opened signature restaurants here, bringing with them a hip crowd of hungry, happy revelers.

3,066 rooms. Restaurant, bar. Fitness center. Pool. Spa. Business center. $251-350

★★★PALMS CASINO RESORT

4321 W. Flamingo Road, Las Vegas, 702-942-7777, 866-942-7777; www.palms.com

Home to Bravo's *Celebrity Poker Showdown*, the Palms is known for its Hollywood-hip credentials and its themed "fantasy" suites. Sports fans will enjoy the Hardwood Suite, which has its own basketball court, or Kingpin Suite, which offers two regulation bowling lanes. The Palms has also revived the classic Playboy Club, which includes a lounge and gaming venues and Playboy Bunnies wearing both vintage and updated Roberto Cavalli-designed attire. It's the closest thing you can get to a Sunset Strip hotel in Las Vegas, and it hits home with the 30-something hipster crowd. The three-acre pool complex features an air-conditioned gaming area and a catwalk for swimsuit shows. The Palms Place tower has 599 condominium suites (many of which are available to rent as hotel rooms) and is attached to the Palms by the SkyTube, an elevated, enclosed moving walkway (to avoid that oppressive desert heat).

1,359 rooms. Restaurant, bar. Fitness center. Pool. Spa. Business center. $151-250

★★★PARIS LAS VEGAS

3655 Las Vegas Blvd. S., Las Vegas, 702-946-7000; www.parislasvegas.com

With a half scale version of the Eiffel Tower (built using Gustav Eiffel's original drawings) dotting the skyline, Paris Las Vegas offers a Vegas version of the City of Lights. Francophiles will be either entranced or dismayed (the bar at the sports book is called Le Bar du Sport). The 34-floor tower is modeled after Paris's Hotel de Ville (the city hall) and features guest rooms ranging from 750 to 4,180 square feet in size and decorated using European-style furniture and fabrics in warm colors. The 85,000-square-foot casino is surrounded by Paris street scenes and features a ceiling painted to emulate the city's sky. At 100 feet up, the Eiffel Tower Restaurant offers skyline views of the Strip, while the street-side Mon Ami Gabi supplies a great vantage point for the Fountains of Bellagio.

2,916 rooms. Restaurant, bar. Fitness center. Pool. Spa. Business center. $151-250

★★★PLANET HOLLYWOOD RESORT & CASINO

3667 Las Vegas Blvd. S., Las Vegas, 702-785-5555; www.planethollywoodresort.com

Previously the Aladdin, this Sheraton-managed hotel brings a little Hollywood to Sin City. Focused on the cult of celebrity, there is plenty of movie memorabilia to go around in the rooms decorated in shades of yellow, purple, red, black and white. Three acres of gaming include the Playing Field race and sports book. Restaurants include Koi (a paparazzi favorite in Los Angeles) and the Strip House from New York. A newly constructed all-suites luxury tower opened in 2010, which features studios, and one- and two-bedroom suites with kitchenettes, floor-to-ceiling windows and spa tubs. The hotel often hosts movie premieres and is home to the popular Peepshow. Head to the Pleasure Pool for a party atmosphere.

2,600 rooms. Restaurant, bar. Fitness center. Pool. Spa. $151-250

★★★THE PLATINUM HOTEL & SPA

211 E. Flamingo Road, Las Vegas, 702-365-5000, 877-211-9211; www.theplatinumhotel.com

With no gaming and a no-smoking policy throughout the hotel, the sleek Platinum would seem almost anti-Vegas. But that doesn't mean it isn't hip. The guest rooms, which run between 900 and 2,200 square feet, are all residential-style suites and include living rooms, gourmet kitchens, sound systems, double vanities and whirlpool tubs in the bathroom and private balconies offering views of the Strip or the nearby mountains. Chef Jay Watson oversees the restaurant, which is on the fifth floor and adjoins a lounge and pool deck area with outdoor fire pits and cabanas.

255 rooms. Restaurant, bar. Fitness center. Pool. Spa. Business center. $151-250

★★★★THE SIGNATURE AT MGM GRAND LAS VEGAS

145 E. Harmon Ave., Las Vegas, 877-612-2121; www.signaturemgmgrand.com

Luxury properties have been popping up along the Las Vegas Strip for years, so it should come as no surprise that one of Sin City's biggest players has an über-luxe offering all its own. The Signature at MGM Grand consists of three separate towers that are connected to the MGM Grand via indoor walkway. The all-suite hotel has no casino and a no-smoking policy to ensure a relaxing getaway atmosphere for its guests. Whether you book a junior suite or a very large two-bedroom, you'll be treated to a deluxe king-sized bed, 300-count Anichini cotton sheets, a marble and granite bathroom with dual sinks and a spa tub, a kitchenette with Sub-Zero stainless steel appliances and wireless Internet throughout. But the perks go beyond the guest rooms; a 24-hour concierge is there to attend to your every request, private fitness centers for Signature guests only are outfitted with state-of-the-art equipment, and each tower boasts its own private pool with cabanas and cocktail service, so you'll never be vying for that last chaise lounge. There's also a cafe for breakfast and lunch, a cocktail lounge which serves food and a Starbucks. From the moment you enter through the grand private entrance, you'll be whisked away to a pleasantly quiet experience.

1,728 rooms. Restaurant, bar. Fitness center. Pool. Business center. $251-350

★★★★★SKYLOFTS AT MGM GRAND

3799 Las Vegas Blvd. S., Las Vegas, 877-711-7117; www.skyloftsmgmgrand.com

With thousands of guests streaming through the doors of the MGM Grand each day, it can be hard to get personalized attention, which is why the clever people at MGM created Skylofts, an ultra-luxury, stylish boutique hotel within the hotel. Occupying the top two floors of the MGM Grand, Skylofts is the brainchild of designer Tony Chi, and evokes an urban loft with modern furniture, steam rooms, flat-screen TVs in the bathrooms and custom Bang & Olufsen entertainment systems. A 24-hour butler is at your beck and call, offering everything from lifts from the airport in a custom Maybach limousine to custom chef-prepared gourmet room service to movies on demand. Check-in takes place in the privacy of your own room (rather than in line at the MGM below), a luxury that in Las Vegas is worth its weight in casino chips.

51 rooms. Fitness center. Spa. Business center. $351 and up

★★★THEHOTEL AT MANDALAY BAY

3950 Las Vegas Blvd. S., Las Vegas, 702-632-7777, 877-632-7800; www.mandalaybay.com

THEhotel's odd naming convention is just about its only showy, Vegas-style gimmick. This all-suite boutique hotel located within the Mandalay Bay is all about class. Its slicker-than-thou décor (minimalist with Art Deco touches and a Mid-Century modern aesthetic) seems to have been plucked from the pages of a magazine, and the sizable suites (they start at 725 square feet) feature elegant marble and granite bathrooms, down comforters and 42-inch flat-screen TVs, and stunning views of the Strip and the Las Vegas valley mountains. The clientele isn't far behind, either—you can find young and sophisticated types cutting through the gleaming black-and-white lobby to get to their suite or to Mix, a scenester's dream of a restaurant outfitted in stark white and a canopy of hanging glass globes. It's gorgeous enough to make you forget about any grammatical gambits.

1,117 rooms. Spa. Fitness center. Restaurant, bar. $251-350

★★★★★TOWER SUITES AT ENCORE LAS VEGAS

3121 Las Vegas Blvd. S., Las Vegas, 888-320-7125, 702-770-8000; www.encorelasvegas.com

Taking its cues from its flagship property (and next door neighbor), Tower Suites at Wynn Las Vegas, this exceptional hotel within a hotel delivers the utmost in luxury, making you feel more at home than ever—assuming your home includes panoramic views of the Strip and a flat-screen TV in the bathroom. A private entrance and registration lounge lets you bypass the mayhem of the casino floor before being whisked up to your hotel room. Suites are cosmopolitan and modern with neutral and black tones, signature Encore artwork, and high-tech features such as one-touch climate controls and wireless office equipment. Access to a private pool reserved for Tower Suites guests guarantees that you'll always find an empty chaise lounge with your name on it. Restaurants run by celebrity chefs, an electric club scene and ritzy shopping options on The Esplanade round out the Encore experience.

267 rooms. Restaurant, bar. Fitness center. Pool. Spa. Business center. $351 and up

★★★★★TOWER SUITES AT WYNN LAS VEGAS

3131 Las Vegas Blvd. S., Las Vegas, 877-321-9966, 702-770-7000; www.wynnlasvegas.com

Located within Wynn Las Vegas, the luxurious Tower Suites offers not only the ultimate in intimate hotel experiences, but also the amenities to round out the perfect stay (think fine cuisine, high-end shops, an exclusive golf club, a Ferrari dealership). Guests of the Tower Suites enter from the south gate entrance, which means no walking through a casino floor or fighting crowds to get to check-in. Instead, you're greeted by an army of smiling Wynn employees standing at attention to take care of your every desire. Additional amenities include a personal shopper, an exclusive restaurant and a private pool with personal cabanas outfitted with ceiling fans, lounge chairs, mini-bars and flat-screen TVs. Guest rooms have the feel of residential apartments and feature wall-to-wall and floor-to-ceiling windows; automatic drapery and lighting controls; the pillow-top Wynn Dream Bed featuring 100 percent Egyptian cotton linens with a 310 thread count; and enormous bathrooms with soaking tubs, glass-enclosed showers and nightlights under his and her sinks.

608 rooms. Restaurant. Fitness center. Pool. Spa. Business center. $351 and up

★★★TREASURE ISLAND (TI)

3300 Las Vegas Blvd. S., Las Vegas, 702-894-7111; www.treasureisland.com

While visitors to Treasure Island—now called simply TI—won't find any real pirates here, they will find a unique band of pirates frolicking about the front entrance every 90 minutes from 7 to 11:30 p.m. The free nightly show has been transformed from its earlier, more family-friendly incarnation into the more adult-themed Sirens of TI, but the swordplay and pyrotechnics are still cool for all ages. The guest rooms have all been renovated to include floor-to-ceiling windows, marble bathrooms and pillow-top beds. A new nightclub from designer Christian Audigier features rhinestone-encrusted skulls and an outdoor terrace facing the Siren show in case you don't want to fight the crowds that gather on the Strip. The hotel's tropical pool provides cabanas and the TI Party Tub, an over-sized hot tub that can hold up to 25 people.

2,885 rooms. Restaurant, bar. Fitness center. Pool. Spa. Business center. $151-250

★★★TROPICANA LAS VEGAS

3801 Las Vegas Blvd. S., Las Vegas, 702-739-2222; www.tropicanalv.com

An affordable alternative to neighboring hotels MGM Grand and New York-New York, the Tropicana delivers a prime location and brand-new upgrades. All the rooms were revamped in 2010. The Paradise Tower features 42-inch flatscreen televisions and warm colors, while the Island Tower has a tropical vibe with original artwork from Latin artists. Nikki Beach, the popular Miami beach club, is scheduled to open in the spring. The Vegas location will feature a restaurant, swim-up blackjack, sand volleyball courts, a private island in the center of the pool and outdoor concert space. For the novice gambler, the casino offers instruction (in case you want to brush up on your craps skills) and a casual, less-stressful environment in which to learn how to play—not to mention lower minimums.

1,876 rooms. Restaurant, bar. Fitness center. Pool. Spa. Business center. $61-150

★★★TRUMP INTERNATIONAL HOTEL LAS VEGAS

2000 Fashion Show Drive, Las Vegas, 702-982-0000, 866-939-8786;
www.trumplasvegashotel.com

Trump International Hotel Las Vegas has The Donald's signature panache written all over it—here in the form of the 24-karat gold glass windows that wrap around the 64-story building. Located just off the Strip adjacent to the Fashion Show mall, the non-gaming Trump is another jewel in a neighborhood that also houses Wynn. The elegant condominium suites (available for purchase) feature floor-to-ceiling windows offering panoramic views of the city, custom-designed furnishings in warm earth tones that play off the white duvets, and a luxe marble bathroom with a separate shower and jet-stream tub. Not only is the refrigerator custom-stocked, but each guest is assigned a Trump Attaché to make sure every whim is granted. If you're curious about what fills the Trump table at home, book a table at DJT, a lovely restaurant that offers modern American fare. Otherwise, you can request an in-room chef to prepare a meal in your personal kitchen—which has appliances by Sub-Zero, Wolf and Bosch—and serve them course by course. The Spa at Trump also comes with an attaché, who can customize everything from the infused elixir tonics to the music selections on your iPod.

1,282 rooms. Restaurant, bar. Fitness center. Pool. Spa. Business center. Pets accepted.
$251-350

★★★★THE VENETIAN RESORT HOTEL CASINO

3355 Las Vegas Blvd. S., Las Vegas, 702-414-1000; www.venetian.com

Built on the former site of the historic Sands Hotel in the center of the Las Vegas Strip, the Venetian takes the idea of a mega-resort to a new level. The Italy-themed property features two towers comprising more than 4,000 suites, more than 2.25 million square feet of meeting space, 80-some-odd stores in its Grand Canal Shoppes, and 20 restaurants from celebrated chefs such as Thomas Keller, Wolfgang Puck and Emeril Lagasse. The newest suites are found in the Venezia Tower, which has a separate check-in area and offers access to the private Venezia Garden Pool Deck. But the best part? The bathrooms. Nearly a third of the size of the room itself, each bathroom includes a Roman tub with a separate glass-enclosed shower, marble countertops and intricate gold detailing. Additional amenities include a private work area with fax/printer/copier, dual-line telephone, wireless Internet access and flat-screen TVs in both the bedroom and living room.

4,027 rooms. Restaurant, bar. Fitness center. Pool. Spa. Business center. $151-250

★★★THE WESTIN CASUARINA LAS VEGAS HOTEL CASINO & SPA

160 E. Flamingo Road, Off-Strip, 702-836-5900, 866-716-8132; www.westin.com

The Westin Casuarina offers a relaxing Westin experience just a block from the Strip. For businesspeople or meeting-goers, it's a mile from the Las Vegas Convention Center (in one direction) and the convention complex at Mandalay Bay (in the other), to leave you plenty of time to either relax by the pool or try your luck at the gambling tables before and after your business. The hotel's Heavenly Bed, Heavenly Bath and muted tones in the guest rooms and a Westin Kids Club onsite (in case you brought the kids along) make for a comfortable stay. The 20,000-square-foot casino in the lobby acts as a nice (and not-so-subtle) reminder that you're still in Vegas.

826 rooms. Restaurant, bar. Fitness center. Pool. Spa. Business center. Pets accepted. $151-250

★★★★WYNN LAS VEGAS

3131 Las Vegas Blvd. S., Las Vegas, 877-321-9966, 702-770-7000; www.wynnlasvegas.com

In his most personal resort to date, Steve Wynn has put his name, voice and signature on just about everything you could think of—including an 18-hole golf course attached to the back of the resort, designed by Tom Fazio and Wynn himself. Wynn's penchant for fusing nature, art and luxury is also on display, with flowers and trees, waterfalls and lagoons scattered about the property along with original fine art draping the walls. Resort rooms average 640-square-feet in space (nearly twice as large as standard Vegas hotel rooms) and, like the more expensive rooms in the Tower Suites, include wall-to-wall and floor-to-ceiling windows, the pillow-top Wynn Dream Bed (covered in 100 percent Egyptian Cotton and 300-plus-thread-count sheets) and Desert Bambu bath amenities. Entertainment includes the unique show Le Rêve ("the Dream") and the Blush Boutique Nightclub overlooking the casino, while shopaholics will enjoy window shopping along the Wynn Esplanade, which includes a Manolo Blahnik boutique and a Ferrari-Maserati dealership.

2,063 rooms. Restaurant, bar. Fitness center. Pool. Spa. Business center. Golf. $251-350

RECOMMENDED
EMBASSY SUITES LAS VEGAS
4315 Swenson St., Las Vegas, 702-795-2800; www.embassysuites.com

Embassy Suites is all about consistency; if you've stayed at an Embassy Suites in the past, you know what to expect: a free cooked-to-order breakfast, complimentary happy hour and a separate bedroom and sitting area in each room. This particular Embassy Suites was recently renovated and also offers flat-screen TVs, work spaces with ergonomic chairs, and sleek black and tan décor. The hotel is across from über-hip Hard Rock, the University of Nevada, Las Vegas campus and close to the gay-friendly district nicknamed "the Fruit Loop."

220 rooms. Complimentary breakfast. Restaurant, bar. Fitness center. Pool. Business center. $61-150

FLAMINGO LAS VEGAS
3555 Las Vegas Blvd. S., Las Vegas, 702-733-3111, 800-732-2111; www.flamingolasvegas.com

The Flamingo was Bugsy Siegel's dream project realized when it opened in 1946 and according to legend, the name comes from the long legs of his showgirl girlfriend, not the bird itself. Still, six-foot flamingos flank the European-style "GO" pool, while the newly renovated Flamingo Go Rooms feature retro furnishings that include white vinyl headboards and splashes of Flamingo pink throughout the space—those looking for a more subdued experience might be more comfortable in the less colorful deluxe rooms. Go rooms have also been updated with the latest in high-tech devices, such as iPod docking stations, flat-screen HDTVs and motorized drapes. Be sure to check out one of the shows in the Flamingo Showroom which have included such comedians as George Wallace and Vinnie Favorito, as well as popular acts including Donny and Marie.

3,545 rooms. Restaurant, bar. Fitness center. Tennis. Pool. Spa. Business center. $151-250

MAIN STREET STATION CASINO BREWERY & HOTEL
200 N. Main St., Las Vegas, 702-387-1896, 800-713-8933; www.mainstreetcasino.com

The Main Street Station is located, appropriately, on Main Street, where it connects with Fremont at the beginning of the Fremont Street Experience. The hotel has a Victorian theme and is filled with unique artifacts that include Buffalo Bill Cody's private rail car, a fireplace from Scotland's Prestwick Castle and a piece of the Berlin Wall (found in the men's bathroom off the casino floor). Guest rooms have been recently renovated with a few of the same Victorian touches as the casino, including sconces and dark mahogany headboards. The rooms are still basic and can feel cramped, though. Main Street also offers an RV park for anyone who wants to camp out in Sin City come winter.

406 rooms. Restaurant, bar. Pool. $61-150

RIO ALL-SUITE HOTEL & CASINO
3700 W. Flamingo Road, Las Vegas, 702-777-7777, 866-746-7671; www.riolasvegas.com

Although the Rio has an Off-Strip location that prohibits you from casino-hopping, you'll find there's plenty to keep you occupied here. People-watching takes the top spot on the list, thanks to the hundreds of sunglass-donning, stone-faced players flocking to the World Series of Poker tournaments. Penn & Teller entertain nightly and the Village Seafood Buffet gets high marks—as does the new adults-only pool that is open to the public (but charges a cover) and features DJ Madam Malixa spinning Top 40 and hip hop throughout the day. The guest rooms are all suites and while the décor leaves something to be desired, you'll have plenty of room to spread out with more than 600 square feet of space.

2,522 rooms. Restaurant, bar. Fitness center. Pool. Spa. Business center. $61-150

JUST OPENED
ARIA RESORT & CASINO
3730 Las Vegas Blvd. S., Las Vegas, 866-359-7757; www.arialasvegas.com

With more than 4,000 guest rooms and suites, Aria is Vegas' latest mega resort. Everything is big at Aria, from the three-story lobby to the gargantuan 215,000-square-foot pool area. Guest rooms offer modern décor and one-touch technology, controlling everything from the curtains to the room temperature. Entertainment options are equally enticing, from Haze Nightclub to The Gold Lounge. The casino incorporates natural sunlight into its design, and includes exclusive high-limit salons for VIP guests. Cirque du Soleil's newest theatrical sensation based on the life of Elvis Presley, Viva Elvis, has been playing here to rave reviews by Elvis fans.

4,004 rooms. Restaurant, bar. Fitness center. Pool. Spa. Business center. Casino. $251-350

ARIA SKYSUITES
3730 Las Vegas Blvd. S., Las Vegas, 866-359-7757; www.arialasvegas.com

Part of the Aria Resort and Casino in the massive CityCenter complex, the Aria Sky Suites are an ultra-exclusive experience. A limousine picks you up at the airport and whisks you to the private lobby, where drinks and hors d'oeuvres await upon check-in. (Bonus: Snacks as well as coffee, soda and libations are complimentary in the lobby throughout your stay. Who said free drinks were only for the gambling set?) Whether you choose a one- or two-bedroom suite or penthouse, or an expansive Sky Villa, the contemporary design won't disappoint—nor will the view. Electronic controls satisfy your every whim, from closing the shades for an early morning bedtime or afternoon nap to summoning the butler to draw a bath. Although you feel far removed from the Aria Casino and CityCenter offerings, they are only a quick elevator ride away. That is, if you ever desire to roam from your luxury confines.

312 rooms. Restaurant, bar. Fitness center. Pool. Spa. Casino. $351 and up.

THE COSMOPOLITAN OF LAS VEGAS
3700 Las Vegas Blvd., Las Vegas, 702-698-7000; www.cosmopolitanlasvegas.com

The only hotel to open on the Las Vegas strip in 2010, this newly constructed, gleaming glass and steel hotel and casino will bring another 2,995 rooms to the city. Part of Marriott's new Autograph Collection of independent hotels, the Cosmopolitan has studios and one-bedroom suites that are stocked with just-released technology (flat-screen TVs, entertainment systems, technology control panels) and spacious bathrooms with Japanese soaking tubs. The resort's arrival brings a chance for another roster of star chefs to open their first-ever Vegas restaurants, from Costas Spiliadis (with a Sin City branch of his New York-based Estiatorio Milos) to Scott Conant (Scarpetta). Joining the lineup is José Andrés, who will open tapas bar Jaleo and Mexican-Chinese concept China Poblano, and Los Angeles-based chef David Myers with his French brasserie concept Comme Ça. Pools have become big business in Vegas, and Cosmopolitan's gambit includes three, one of which, the Boulevard Pool, is the only to overlook the Strip. Rounding out the offerings at the resort are a spacious casino, a spa and a nightclub overseen by the Tao Group.

2,995 rooms. Restaurant, bar. Fitness center. Spa. Pool. $251-350

VDARA HOTEL & SPA

2600 W. Harmon Ave., Las Vegas, 866-745-7767; www.vdara.com

Guest suites with open-floor plans, custom-designed artwork and a champagne bar in the spa are just a few of the details that set this new non-gaming CityCenter property apart from the rest on the Strip. As one of the major players in the massive CityCenter venture, this all-suite hotel is modern and luxurious in design (the brainchild of famed architect Rafael Vinoly) with large picture windows and frameless glass-enclosed showers in each of the guest rooms. The Vdara Pool and Lounge, occupying space above the entrance to the hotel, is reserved for guests only and offers made-to-order cocktails and semi-private plunge pools alongside spa cabanas.

1,495 rooms. Restaurant, bar. Fitness center. Pool. Spa. Business center. $251-350

WHERE TO EAT

★★★★★ALEX

Wynn Las Vegas, 3131 Las Vegas Blvd. S., Las Vegas, 702-248-3463; www.wynnlasvegas.com

Perhaps it is the walls lined in mother of pearl and the 22 karat gold sand-casted candelabras at the entrance, or the custom-carved mahogany ceiling and boiserie wood marquetry. Whatever the secret, Alessandro Stratta's namesake restaurant has awed diners and garnered accolades since settling in at Wynn Las Vegas in 2005. The richly appointed dining room is only a hint of the luxury and grandeur that await you on the plate. The cuisine of the French Riviera is what Stratta focuses on, and he executes it with such style and grace you'll think you're in the South of France. You will find entrées such as roasted squab and seared foie gras or olive oil poached kanpachi that concentrate on enhancing

---

WHAT ARE THE BEST OVERALL RESTAURANTS IN LAS VEGAS?

Alex:
If the walls are lined in mother of pearl and the ceiling is made from custom-carved mahogany, imagine how much effort is put into the food. Alessandro Stratta's appreciation for natural flavors makes even the simplest of dishes shine.

Joël Robuchon:
You'll feel far removed from the Las Vegas Strip upon entering this epicurean palace. From the caviar to the blinis to the chocolate cake, your taste buds will want for nothing at the hands of this culinary master.

natural flavors with subtle touches and aromatic sauces. The seasonal tasting menu, which runs at $185 per person, or $295 if you include wine pairings, travels through seven courses from a tangy heirloom tomato and octopus carpaccio amuse-bouche to a rich Wagyu strip loin with wild mushrooms to a perfectly subtle toasted vanilla custard topped with maple-poached peaches. Service is attentive and pleasant, but not overwhelming. A meal at Alex will certainly be one of those long marathon dining evenings, where you'll likely leave fuzzy from the wine pairings and, above all, pleasantly satiated.

French. Dinner. Closed Sunday-Tuesday. Jacket requested. $86 and up

★★★ALIZÉ

Palms Casino Resort, 4321 W. Flamingo Road, Las Vegas, 702-951-7000; www.alizelv.com

André Rochat of Alizé is one of the first star chefs to bring his knives to Las Vegas. His restaurant at the top of the Palms features a 180-degree view of the Strip through 16-foot floor-to-ceiling windows. A two-story wine cellar in the middle of the dining room houses more than 1,700 selections, with a healthy mix of New World and Old, top dollar price points and affordable finds. The intimate bar isn't the place to sling cosmopolitans or Red-Bull- and-vodkas; serious spirits await you, including an impressive collection of cognac gathered by Rochat himself. The menu is a study in contemporary French cuisine and elegant presentation with dishes such as escargots Burgogne with garlic herb butter and pan-seared duck breast with sautéed foie gras in a raspberry vinaigrette. Tasting menus are available and are a nice place to start for those being initiated into French fine dining.

French. Dinner. $36-85

★★★AQUAKNOX

The Venetian Resort Hotel Casino, 3355 Las Vegas Blvd. S., Las Vegas, 702-414-3772; www.venetian.com

Contrary to what you might think, seafood is big business in the desert, especially at places like Aquaknox, which has its own selections flown in daily. The restaurant lets you know from start to finish that they're serious about underwater delicacies, from the lights bathing the whole space in aquatic blue hues to the water cascading down around the bottles in the wine wall. Though the menu varies between Mediterranean and Asian influences, both treatments take full advantage of beautiful seafood sourced from around the world. The signature fish soup, much more than a solution for leftover scraps, is chock full of the choicest lobster, John Dory, mussels and clams in a fragrant and rich tomato saffron broth.

Seafood. Lunch, dinner. $36-85

★★★★AUREOLE

Mandalay Bay Resort & Casino, 3950 Las Vegas Blvd. S., Las Vegas, 702-632-7401; www.mandalaybay.com

When you come to Aureole, come thirsty. The 42-foot steel and glass wine tower that greets you at the door holds 10,000 bottles of wine and comes complete with "Wine Angel Stewards," servers who float on wires to snag your bottle of choice from the towers. Throw in one of the foremost chefs in American contemporary cuisine and a soaring modern interior, and you've got

Aureole. But this restaurant isn't all big names and acrobatic wait staff; there's soul in the cooking, too. Charlie Palmer's menu treats fresh-off-the-farm ingredients with elegance and sophistication, evidenced in dishes such as the scallop sandwiches in a crisp potato crust and monkfish osso buco with chanterelles and pork belly stuffed cabbage. A handheld computer gives you access to the expansive wine list, which is sent directly to the aerialists in the tower. It's worth ordering a bottle just to watch the show, which is part Cirque du Soleil, part Mission: Impossible.

Contemporary American. Dinner. $86 and up

★★★B&B RISTORANTE
The Venetian Resort Hotel Casino, 3355 Las Vegas Blvd. S., Las Vegas, 702-266-9977; www.bandbristorante.com

Celebrity chef Mario Batali's restaurant empire has expanded to Las Vegas with a few new ventures. B&B Ristorante (the other "B" stands for his partner, winemaker Joe Bastianich) is a small space where you might bump elbows with your neighbors, but the coziness adds to the jovial atmosphere. Batali's menu at this spot is simple, rustic Italian with a gourmet edge. The salumi are a must-try—all are made fresh in house by executive chef Zach Allen or cured in house, with the exception of the prosciutto di San Danielle, which is imported from Italy. More adventurous options include a light and airy lamb's brain francobolli. A pasta tasting menu is available for those who can't decide on which dish to order. The wine list, featuring some Bastianich private label bottles, is extensive, especially as far as—you guessed it—Italian wines go.

Italian. Dinner. $36-85

★★★BOUCHON
The Venetian Resort Hotel Casino, 3355 Las Vegas Blvd. S., Las Vegas, 702-414-6200; www.bouchonbistro.com

Star chef Thomas Keller has dreamed up his version of a French bistro, and it's appropriately elegant and tasteful, yet completely comfortable (the original is in Napa Valley). The room, designed by Adam Tihany, is spacious and simple, trimmed in dark woods against white walls and brass rails, and feels like an authentic brasserie. The dress code is Las Vegas chic, meaning that just about anything goes. Men in suits sit next to tourists in jeans and flip-flops, and everyone focuses on the simple flavors of the food. It's not about pretentious, tiny eats at Bouchon; it's about a solid meal of bistro standards, from steak frites to roasted lamb in thyme jus. Every dish comes with pommes frites, which is a good thing, since these French fries are revered as some of the best in Las Vegas. A casual brunch on weekends on the patio overlooking the pool and its sunbathers is a good way to get some fresh desert air.

French bistro. Breakfast, dinner, Saturday-Sunday brunch. $36-85

★★★★BRADLEY OGDEN
Caesars Palace, 3570 Las Vegas Blvd. S., Las Vegas, 877-346-4642; www.harrahs.com

Located off the casino floor at Caesars Palace, chef Bradley Ogden's eponymous restaurant, with its décor accented by rich wood, feels a million miles away from the Strip. Ogden is best known for his farm-to-table culinary philosophy, as well as his passion for using organic products from sustainable resources.

Though the menu changes seasonally, you can be sure that you're getting the freshest ingredients prepared so that their true flavors shine through. This is definitely an upscale restaurant, but the affable waitstaff makes the experience comfortable, inviting and warm. The menu is an honest reflection of simple American cuisine, so dishes will be ones you recognize. The burger, available at the bar, is often cited as one of the best in Las Vegas. Another mainstay, the twice-baked Maytag blue cheese soufflé—fluffy, rich and savory—is divine and a necessary indulgence every time you find yourself in this dining room.
Contemporary American. Dinner. $86 and up

★★★CARNEVINO

The Palazzo Las Vegas Resort Hotel Casino, 3325 Las Vegas Blvd. S., Las Vegas, 702-789-4141; www.carnevino.com

If you love a good steak and great wine, you'll be happy at chef Mario Batali's Carnevino. While there are Italian dishes on the menu (such as pappardelle with porcini trifolati), made-in-the-Midwest meat is the main attraction. You're guaranteed a good cut, as the steaks are all-natural and free of hormones and antibiotics. The Italian villa-inspired dining room is decked out in dark wood, plump cushions, a marble bar and a big bronze bull, just in case you didn't know it was a steakhouse. Order a bottle from the never-ending wine list and share the slightly charred Florentine porterhouse, which is rubbed with sea salt, pepper and fresh rosemary. This succulent steak is one of the highlights of Mario Batali's menu.
Steak, Italian. Lunch, dinner. 36-85

★★★CRAFTSTEAK

MGM Grand Hotel & Casino, 3799 Las Vegas Blvd. S., Las Vegas, 702-891-7318; www.craftrestaurant.com

Meat purists will want to sink their teeth into the prime cuts here. Chef Tom Colicchio, who also moonlights as the exacting head judge on Bravo's *Top Chef*, goes by the philosophy that simpler is better. That goes for the dining room, too, which is plainly decorated with wooden tables without tablecloths, bare branches in vases and spare bulbs dangling from the ceiling. When it comes to food, Colicchio refuses to let fancy sauces or complicated preparations take away from the meat. But fewer ingredients don't mean fewer choices: You can have your piece of protein roasted, grilled or braised; you can get cuts from Idaho, New York or Australia; you can opt for corn-fed or grass-fed beef; and you'll have to pick from sizes ranging from six to 32 ounces. A solid option is the Kobe skirt steak. If you're not a meat fan, go for the shellfish sampler, a tempting platter teeming with fresh chilled lobster salad, Alaskan king crab, oysters and clams. At a back-to-basics restaurant like this, when it comes time for dessert, stick to the classics and get the sinful chocolate soufflé with espresso ice cream doused with caramel sauce.
Steak. Dinner. $86 and up

★★★CUT

The Palazzo Las Vegas Resort Hotel Casino, 3325 Las Vegas Blvd. S., Las Vegas, 702-607-6300; www.palazzolasvegas.com

Wolfgang Puck is at it again. This time it is in the form of a steakhouse at the Palazzo that some say is the best place for steak in Las Vegas. The 160-seat metallic dining room manages to feel simultaneously industrial and warm thanks to well-chosen appointments and lamp-lit chandeliers. In the adjacent bar, sample custom cocktails and dishes from the smaller "Rough Cuts" bar menu. The classic steakhouse offerings are given the Puck treatment, including the use of Wagyu and pure Japanese Kobe beef, but innovative dishes such as double thick pork chop atop an apple and nectarine moustarda allow the chef's true talents to shine through. Other hits from the menu include the Indian-spiced Kobe short ribs, slow cooked for eight hours and finished with a purée of curried corn.

Steak. Dinner. $86 and up

★★★DELMONICO STEAKHOUSE

The Venetian Resort Hotel Casino, 3355 Las Vegas Blvd. S., Las Vegas, 702-414-1992; www.venetian.com

Celebrity chef Emeril Lagasse is best known for his talent with Creole cuisine, and at Delmonico he brings this influence to the steakhouse concept. The dining room, with its high-backed chairs and padded banquettes, vaulted ceilings and track-lighting, is comfortable enough to enjoy the kind of meal Lagasse can provide. The steaks and chops themselves are standard steakhouse fare, but some options, such as bone-in rib eye or a chateaubriand for two, are carved and presented tableside. Don't overlook the appetizers: a Creole boiled gulf shrimp cocktail with a piquant horseradish sauce will call your taste buds to attention. To wash it all down, there is a spectacular wine list that has garnered many awards for its vast and high-quality selections.

Steak, Creole. Lunch, dinner. $36-85

★★★DJT

Trump International Hotel & Tower Las Vegas, 2000 Fashion Show Drive, Las Vegas, 702-982-0000; www.trumplasvegashotel.com

It's all about the art of the meal at this handsome restaurant inside Trump International Hotel & Tower. The dining room, with rich colors and intimate seating, recalls the glamour of the 1930s. The upscale and sophisticated contemporary American fare includes dishes such as the 28-day dry aged bone-in ribeye, slow roasted chicken with broken rice, spinach and adobo sauce, and buccatini carbonara. A three-course tasting menu is also available for $39, which includes a choice between two appetizers, three entrees and a dessert.

American. Breakfast, lunch, dinner. $36-85

★★★EMERIL'S

MGM Grand Hotel & Casino, 3799 Las Vegas Blvd. S., Las Vegas, 702-891-7374; www.mgmgrand.com

The restaurant that started the Emeril Lagasse empire in New Orleans now has a home at MGM Grand. The same spunk that Lagasse exudes on television is present in the fun dining room (complete with a 14-foot wrought-iron fish sculpture to greet you at the entrance), even if its namesake chef isn't always behind the burners. Focused heavily on Creole and Cajun flavors, the menu is both home-style and sophisticated, elevating low-country cuisine. The seafood gumbo is a standout starter, as is the signature New Orleans barbecue shrimp. A hearty lunch requires little more than the seafood pan roast, which is full of fresh seafood, jambalaya and a butter sauce spiked with Emeril's own herb essence.

Seafood, Cajun. Lunch, dinner. $36-85

★★★FIAMMA TRATTORIA

MGM Grand Hotel & Casino, 3799 Las Vegas Blvd. S., Las Vegas, 702-891-7600; www.mgmgrand.com

This cozy, chic trattoria encourages lingering. Clusters of bamboo form nests of lighting that hang above chocolate banquettes with honey-hued pillows. You'll want to sit near the undulating sculptural wave wall in front of the glass-enclosed, blazing fireplace, a nod to the restaurant's name, which means "flame" in Italian. The menu isn't as contemporary as the décor, but it updates old-school Italian faves. Spaghetti comes with Kobe meatballs, raviolini is stuffed with short ribs and splashed with Barbera wine sauce and sprinkled with pecorino romano, and gnocchi become puffs of lobster instead of potato. If you're not in the mood for pasta, choose entrées like the involtino di coniglio (roasted rabbit leg) or the brasato (Piemontese braised beef short ribs). Be sure to leave room for the Italian desserts. Cheesecake gelato and basil-lime sorbetto give fresh alternatives to the usual flavors, but a real treat is the crochette, crispy amaretti doughnuts that come with a trio of dunking sauces: chocolate ganache, vanilla bean glaze and strawberry jam. If you can't eat another bite, opt for a glass of Italian wine and huddle in front of the beautiful fireplace.

Italian. Dinner. $36-85

★★★HACHI

Red Rock Casino, Resort & Spa, 11011 W. Charleston Blvd., Summerlin, 702-797-7576; www.ilovehachi.com

Modern Japanese has found its way into the suburbs under the capable hands of Nobu alum chef Linda Rodriguez. One of the few female executive chefs at a major property in Las Vegas, Rodriguez's touch can be seen and felt throughout the dining room and in the kitchen. Hachi's décor is both modern and feminine, with Japanese cherry blossoms incarnated not only in photographs on the wall, but also in the form of 2,500 hand-blown glass blossoms hanging from the ceiling. Presentations of dishes are dynamic, yet delicate and thoughtful. Drawing on her training from Nobu as well as cultural influences from Europe and Latin America, the menu offers twists on classics like seared Kobe beef sashimi with yuzu soy and seared tuna tataki salad with warm bacon vinaigrette. With an outstanding sushi selection and amazing hot dishes under her belt, Rodriguez also is willing to do an omakase tasting menu for tables of six or fewer (a must if you have the time). With her making the decisions based on your personal likes and dislikes, you're in good hands.

Japanese. Dinner. $36-85

★★★JASMINE

Bellagio Las Vegas, 3600 Las Vegas Blvd. S., Las Vegas, 702-693-7223; www.bellagio.com

Going out for Chinese has never felt so refined. With a great view of Lake Bellagio, this dining room is regal and elegant with warm pastel tones and glowing chandeliers. Chef Phillip Lo's menu includes traditional Cantonese, Szechwan and Hunan fare as well as nouveau Hong Kong cuisine. Traditional dishes like hot and sour soup are done with panache. The Maine lobster dumplings with a ginger dipping sauce are excellent, as is the caramelized pork tenderloin. Be sure to specify that you'd like a table by the open windows to ensure an uninterrupted view of the famed Bellagio fountains.

Chinese. Dinner. $36-85

★★★★★JOËL ROBUCHON

MGM Grand Hotel & Casino, 3799 Las Vegas Blvd. S., Las Vegas, 702-891-7925; www.mgmgrand.com

One of the world's greatest chefs, Joël Robuchon has come to epitomize fine, French cuisine. The intimate dining room is regal, from the black and white tiled entryway to the chandelier in the middle of the room. There is even an indoor patio where a façade of flowing greenery transforms a windowless side room into a classical garden. The 16-course tasting menu will set you back $385, but it's worth it. What makes his food so special is the innovative ways he shows his respect for ingredients. Take Le Caviar Osciètre, one of Robuchon's signature dishes, for example. Elevating the ingredient beyond typical blinis and crème fraîche, he combines thin slices of warm scallops with lime zest, smooth cauliflower cream, avocado and Osetra caviar to create a total sensory explosion of surprisingly complementary textures and flavors. You'd never think to mix these ingredients yourself, but when you bite into his creations, they just make sense. Service is formal and flawless—exactly what you'd expect from a restaurant of this caliber.

French. Dinner. $86 and up

★★★L'ATELIER DE JOËL ROBUCHON

MGM Grand Hotel & Casino, 3799 Las Vegas Blvd. S., Las Vegas, 702-891-7358; www.mgmgrand.com

It might be safe to call L'Atelier ("workshop" in French) a more casual offering from master chef Joël Robuchon, as a meal here is somewhat more interactive than at the formal Joël Robuchon located right next door. The dining room, decorated in reds and blacks, features an open-air kitchen and counter seating where you can watch chefs prepare your food. No surprise here: The cuisine is all French, and signature dishes include a langoustine fritter with basil pesto and free-range quail stuffed with foie gras. Two tasting menus are available, though you can order à la carte to mix and match your own personal Robuchon experience.

French. Dinner. $36-85

★★★LAVO

The Palazzo Las Vegas Resort Hotel Casino, 3325 Las Vegas Blvd. S., Las Vegas, 702-791-1800; www.lavolv.com

Before the party crowd heads upstairs to club LAVO, they gather for dinner and drinks at this first-floor restaurant. Join the party and order up a bunch of dishes to share, such as the Kobe meatballs with whipped fresh ricotta, spagetti carbonara, cacciatore pizza and grilled New York prime strip with garlic gorgonzola butter. You'll want to keep dessert all to yourself; tasty treats include the delectable chocolate bread pudding with silky dulce de leche and vanilla ice cream, or the warm apple crisp, which updates plain old apple pie with cinnamon ice cream and a bowl made of hazelnut streusel. You'll want to linger in this dining room; the high ceilings with coned chandeliers, low leather booths and tables make it a cozy social spot. If you feel like continuing the evening, make your way to the gorgeous glass-and-wood-screened bridge that leads to the lively nightclub.

Italian. Dinner. $36-85

★★★★LE CIRQUE

Bellagio Las Vegas, 3600 Las Vegas Blvd. S., Las Vegas, 702-693-7223; www.bellagio.com

The original Le Cirque in New York City is legendary because the food is spectacular, and because the service, often led by family patriarch Sirio Maccioni himself, is stellar and welcoming. Le Cirque at Bellagio holds to the same principles. Maccioni's sons run the restaurant to the same exacting standards as its East Coast sibling. In the vibrantly colored, circus-tent-like dining room, expertly executed French cuisine is served. Le Cirque's signature dish, the potato-crusted sea bass with a red wine reduction, lives up to its reputation as an outstanding offering. The three-course, $98 prix fixe menu is a smart choice.

French. Dinner. $86 and up

★★★MARCHÉ BACCHUS

2620 Regatta Drive #106, Summerlin, 702-804-8008; www.marchebacchus.com

You don't have to be relegated to the Strip to find excellent French bistro fare. Marché Bacchus, located in the community of Summerlin, 10 miles from downtown, is a perfect way to get a feel for just how good the locals have it here. The restaurant is part wine shop, part restaurant, and diners can select from the shop's 950 labels and have the bottle with their meal at only $10 over the retail price. The outdoor patio sits alongside one of the city's many man-made lakes, and cooling misters and rustic trellises offer a nice respite from the Vegas heat. Executive chef Jean Paul Labadie recently joined the restaurant after stints as head chef at Emeril's in the MGM Grand and Table 10. Labadie's menu features French bistro favorites such as croque monsieur sandwiches, steak frites (which they call "La Piece de Boeuf du Boucher") and baked escargot in garlic herb butter. With a selection of wine platters offering everything from imported cheeses and olives to pâté and French salami, Marché Bacchus is also a stellar pick if you're looking to get away from the casinos for an afternoon.

French. Lunch, dinner, Sunday brunch. $36-85

★★★★MICHAEL MINA

Bellagio Las Vegas, 3600 Las Vegas Blvd. S., Las Vegas, 702-693-7223; www.bellagio.com

Tucked behind the Bellagio's stunning Conservatory, Michael Mina feels like a nice little secret. The restaurant is the perfect storm of design and cuisine, from its chic décor with floor-to-ceiling blond wood shelves to its innovative menu and equally sleek wine collection. Michael Mina, one of the few restaurants on the Strip that does a vegetarian tasting menu, is well-known for its tasting trios, which feature a singular product presented three different ways, ideal for those who want to expand their palates. Ingredients such as boneless Colorado rack of lamb, American Kobe rib eye and Nantucket Bay scallops get Mina's signature trio treatment. Seafood also factors in heavily on this menu, done primarily in the style of contemporary California cuisine. If you have a soft spot for foie gras, order a dish of whole foie gras, which is carved tableside and proves as savory for the eyes as the taste buds. Mina's signature root beer float, a swimmingly icy blend of sassafras ice cream and root beer sorbet, seals the deal on this American classic.

Contemporary American. Dinner. Closed Wednesday. $86 and up

★★★★MIX IN LAS VEGAS

Mandalay Bay Resort and Casino, 3950 Las Vegas Blvd. S., Las Vegas, 702-632-9500; www.mandalaybay.com

Alain Ducasse's artful restaurant atop THEHotel at Mandalay Bay offers one of the most stunning views of the Strip. Walking into the restaurant is like entering into a modern art museum with its sleek, white décor and enormous chandelier, made of 15,000 hand-blown Murano glass balls. With the glitter of the lights of the Mandalay Bay sign outside the windows and surrounded by the glass bubbles, you'll feel like you've entered a flute of champagne. The chic design of the restaurant is reflected on the plate as well. American cuisine is interpreted using contemporary haute French technique, producing dishes such as lobster salad served with a tangy apple and vegetable mosaique, and surf and turf made with halibut and foie gras rather than the standard lobster and steak.

Contemporary French. Dinner. $86 and up

★★★N9NE STEAKHOUSE

Palms Casino Resort, 4321 W. Flamingo Road, Las Vegas, 702-933-9900; www.n9negroup.com

It may feel like a nightclub when you walk in, complete with loud, thumping music and a modern metal décor lit by blacklights, but if you can get past the trendy aspect, you're in for a good meal. Starters such as the N9NE rock shrimp are always fun to munch on, and are served in a carnival-style cardboard box with two dipping sauces. Prime aged steaks are expertly done and sides, such as macaroni and cheese and loaded baked potatoes, are above average. There's a high likelihood of a celebrity sighting as sports stars like to drop by before heading out to the big parties. So if part of your Vegas experience includes a solid steak and some star gazing, you'd better get used to the pulsating house music.

Steak. Dinner. $36-85

★★★NOBHILL TAVERN

MGM Grand Hotel & Casino, 3799 Las Vegas Blvd. S., Las Vegas, 702-891-7337; www.mgmgrand.com

San Francisco chef Michael Mina's Nobhill Tavern is one of the great contemporary American restaurants on the Strip. Many ingredients on the menu are sourced from the Bay Area and all over the country, including poultry and organic produce. Try one of Mina's specialties, such as the San Francisco cioppino with steamed shellfish, tomato broth and basil oil, or chicken and dumplings served with roasted cauliflower, carrots and baby leeks. If you're looking for a bite at the bar, try the cheeseburger sliders or dig into Mina's famous lobster pot pie. Finish with desserts such as a pecan-praline sundae or apple crisp with cinnamon ice cream. The restaurant's design takes its cues from the best Bay City spots, complete with dark wood accents, intimate booths and a soothing, earthy color palette.

Contemporary American. Dinner. $86 and up

★★★NOBU

Hard Rock Hotel, 4455 Paradise Road, Las Vegas, 702-693-5090; www.hardrockhotel.com

There's sushi in Las Vegas, and then there's Nobu. One of the pioneers of modern Japanese cuisine, chef Nobu Matsuhisa takes traditional Japanese ingredients and technique and applies to them the knowledge he acquired while working in South America. There may now be about 20 versions worldwide of Matsuhisa's original restaurant, but this outpost at the Hard Rock Hotel is particularly welcoming, with calming green walls behind bamboo stalks, small birch trees and an onyx-tiled sushi bar. The yellowtail sashimi with jalapeños simply melts in your mouth and the lobster salad includes a spicy lemon dressing that will kick-start any meal. You know that black cod with miso that you find on every menu in every trendy Japanese restaurant across the country? This is one of Matsuhisa's original signature dishes, and there's nothing quite like the original.

Japanese. Dinner. $36-85

★★★OLIVES

Bellagio Las Vegas, 3600 Las Vegas Blvd. S., Las Vegas, 702-693-7223; www.bellagio.com

Celebrity chef Todd English is best known for his take on rustic Italian and Mediterranean cuisine. His dim and sexy Jeffrey Beers-designed restaurant at the Bellagio overlooks the famed fountains, and features outdoor patio seating for those wanting an even closer look. Like the original Olives in Boston, the menu focuses on the best of his Italian cooking, including brick-oven flatbreads and pastas made in-house. The brick oven roasted chicken with avocado purée and fried polenta is particularly tasty and surprisingly light. This is one of those restaurants that is not only consistent every time you have a meal at the same outpost, but state to state as well. The waitstaff is upbeat and knowledgeable, so they feel like family and strive to help you feel the same way.

Mediterranean. Lunch, dinner. $36-85

★★★THE PALM

The Forum Shops at Caesars Palace, 3500 Las Vegas Blvd. S., Las Vegas, 702-732-7256; www.thepalm.com

The Palm has that classic steakhouse vibe and a staff that remembers your name. But you don't have to be a regular to enjoy a meal here. There are no frills, no fancy presentations, just honest-to-goodness solid steakhouse fare, as well as some traditional Italian-American dishes, staying true to the original New York City concept. The veal scallopini with Milanese, piccata or Marsala sauce is consistently wonderful. Of course, if you're more inclined to have a steak, you're in good company. The 32-ounce prime rib for two is fantastic; smaller appetites are well sated with the 9-ounce filet mignon. And since you were always taught to eat your vegetables, a side of creamed spinach balances out the meal.

Steak. Lunch, dinner. $36-85

★★★★PICASSO

Bellagio Las Vegas, 3600 Las Vegas Blvd. S., Las Vegas, 702-693-7223; www.bellagio.com

Only in Las Vegas can you sit and eat a full meal among priceless works of art by a legendary artist. Picasso, with its stunning view of the Fountains of Bellagio, is by far one of the most elegant and awe-inspiring dining rooms in the world. And if all the Picassos surrounding you aren't enough, culinary artist Julian Serrano prepares his own masterpieces for you to enjoy. The sublime degustation and prix fixe menus are predominantly French and Spanish influenced, and the wines, with more than 1,500 selections to choose from, are sourced exclusively from European vineyards. The menu changes almost daily based on what's fresh each morning. If you can catch the pan-seared sea scallops with potato mousseline and leeks, you're in for a culinary treat.

French, Spanish. Dinner. Closed Tuesday. $86 and up

★★★POSTRIO BAR & GRILL

The Venetian Resort Hotel Casino, 3377 Las Vegas Blvd. S., Las Vegas, 702-796-1110; www.wolfgangpuck.com

Located in St. Mark's Square at the Grand Canal Shoppes at The Venetian, Postrio is a perfect spot to enjoy a casually elegant meal, with some priceless people-watching to boot. The interior of the restaurant is subtle, with intimate booths and soothing colors. Sitting on the faux patio (you're still inside a mall) allows you to watch not only passers-by, but also the entertainment (in the way of jugglers, singers and musicians) that roams around the plaza. Postrio is Wolfgang Puck's blend of American and Mediterranean cuisine, so expect plenty of fresh flavors and ingredients prepared in unexpected ways. Try the lobster club sandwich; it's one of the best on the Strip. For a heartier dish, opt for the kurobuta pork schnitzel with Austrian potatoes. If you're in luck, Puck's famous 13-layer tiramisu with coffee anglaise and chocolate sorbet will be available.

American. Lunch, dinner. $36-85

★★★PRIME STEAKHOUSE

Bellagio Las Vegas, 3600 Las Vegas Blvd. S., Las Vegas, 702-693-7223; www.bellagio.com

A concept by celebrity chef and restaurateur Jean-Georges Vongerichten, Prime delivers a true luxury steakhouse experience. From its plush brown and blue décor to the contemporary art hanging on the walls, the room sings decadence. The menu offers standard steakhouse dishes, but it's the detailed presentation that sets it apart from other steak places. Vongerichten is known for the Asian influences and flavors in his dishes, and he continues this theme in dishes such as grilled diver scallops in a soy-yuzu broth, or filet mignon over shishito peppers. The wine list is impressive, featuring the best of the big reds of California. If you forgot to secure a reservation weeks in advance, try your luck on the outdoor terrace, where you can sample tasty appetizers and desserts without calling ahead.

Steakhouse. Dinner. $36-85

★★★★RESTAURANT GUY SAVOY

Caesars Palace, 3570 Las Vegas Blvd. S., Las Vegas, 702-731-7385; www.harrahs.com

Located in the Augustus Tower of Caesars Palace, Guy Savoy's only American venture is quiet, cool and sophisticated. Run by Guy's son Franck, you can be assured that you'll get the same quality treatment and meal here that you would at the original Guy Savoy in Paris—minus the Eiffel Tower view. Two tasting menus (one 10-course and one four-course) are available, and both offer Savoy's signature dish of artichoke and black truffle soup, a divine concoction served with toasted mushroom brioche and an earthy truffle butter. For a more casual experience, grab a seat at the Bites & Bubbles bar where you can order smaller tasting portions of the menu as well as fantastic champagnes by the glass.

French. Dinner. Closed Monday-Tuesday. Bar. $86 and up

★★★SEABLUE

MGM Grand Hotel & Casino, 3799 Las Vegas Blvd. S., Las Vegas, 702-891-3486; www.mgmgrand.com

Delicious seafood is the theme at Seablue, one of two Michael Mina-helmed restaurants at MGM Grand. Watch the chefs in the open-air kitchen from the aquatic-themed dining room, complete with water cascading down the walls. The menu changes with the season, and all the seafood is caught wild and flown in daily. The kitchen draws from traditional Mediterranean cooking techniques, including the use of tagines (Moroccan clay ovens), and simple grilling to make the seafood shine. The Seablue paella is not traditional Spanish paella, but it is loaded with fresh seafood, rabbit, and chorizo and finished with a saffron risotto. One of the biggest hits on the menu is the lobster corndog, a luxurious version that puts the original to shame. Delicate lobster sausage is dipped in batter, fried and served with a pungent but refreshing mustard crème fraîche.

Seafood. Dinner. $86 and up

★★★SHIBUYA

MGM Grand Hotel & Casino, 3799 Las Vegas Blvd. S., Las Vegas, 702-891-3001; www.mgmgrand.com

MGM Grand's Japanese restaurant is so much more than just a sushi bar. Taking its name from a popular neighborhood in Tokyo, Shibuya features traditional Japanese cuisine executed with contemporary twists and techniques. The interior is chic and almost clubby; the cool physique of the glass cube wall behind the sushi bar at the entrance is balanced by the appearance of natural woods throughout the space. High quality ingredients make for interesting preparations, including the toro tartare, which features gorgeous tuna belly enhanced with achiote oil and made more decadent with the addition of caviar and gold leaf. If you're feeling adventurous, opt for the live Maine lobster served three ways: the tail as sashimi, the claws as tempura and the rest in a silky miso soup. Boasting the only certified sake sommelier in Las Vegas, Shibuya has the Japanese fine dining experience covered from all angles.

Japanese. Dinner. $86 and up

★★★TABLE 10

The Palazzo Las Vegas Resort Hotel Casino, 3327 Las Vegas Blvd. S., Las Vegas, 702-607-6363; www.emerils.com

Enter the French Quarter-inspired iron gates of Table 10 to get a taste of Emeril "Bam!" Lagasse's Cajun flavors and his seafood-heavy comfort cuisine. Watch all of the action at the Food Bar, which gives you a glimpse of the chefs manning the grills and flitting about the busy kitchen. Watching them cook will make your stomach rumble, so start off with the traditional gumbo with bits of andouille sausage or the crab trinity, a holy union of snow crab cocktail, lump crab rémoulade and jumbo lump citrus onion salad. Keep the fresh-from-the-ocean theme going with the to-die-for lobster dome, with chunks of Maine lobster, sweet corn, mushrooms, leeks and spinach in truffle-sherry cream sealed in a flaky crust. For dessert, get the white chocolate malassadas, doughnut-like cousins to native-to-New-Orleans beignets, with cinnamon sugar and vanilla bean crème anglaise.

Cajun, American. Lunch, dinner. $36-85

★★★TAO

The Venetian Resort Hotel Casino, 3355 Las Vegas Blvd. S., Las Vegas, 702-388-8338; www.taolasvegas.com

Part nightclub, part Asian restaurant, Tao packs crowds in nightly with its alluringly sexy Buddha-filled décor, a koi pond and weathered wood, a harmonious combination of ancient culture and contemporary life. You'll find a pan-Asian menu with elements of Chinese, Japanese and Thai cuisine figuring prominently. Sushi is a good choice, and the menu is heavy on trendy maki creations. Entrées are boldly flavored but still familiar, including the wasabi-crusted filet mignon. If you want to linger after your meal, head upstairs to the nightclub—it's one of the hottest Vegas spots for bass-thumping music and celebrity sightings.

Asian. Dinner. $36-85

★★★TOP OF THE WORLD

Stratosphere Las Vegas, 2000 Las Vegas Blvd. S., Las Vegas, 702-380-7777; www.topoftheworldlv.com

It may not literally be the top of the world, but when the Strip includes the Empire State Building, the Eiffel Tower and the Great Pyramids of Giza, you might think it is. Perched atop the Stratosphere, the tallest point in Las Vegas, Top of the World is best known for its revolving dining room, which offers a complete 360-degree view of the city. On a clear day, you can see straight to Nellis Air Force Base, and at night spy one of the best views of downtown Las Vegas. You'll find classic continental cuisine on the menu, executed with quality ingredients, including the veal chop served with roma artichoke and mushroom demi-glace. Old favorites such as surf and turf are a big hit. But in Vegas you get what you pay for, so don't expect the food to be quite as good as some of the celeb-chef haunts down below. Top of the World can also get a tad tourist-heavy, with gawkers wanting to see that perfect view of Vegas.

American. Lunch, dinner. $36-85

★★★★TWIST BY PIERRE GAGNAIRE

Mandarin Oriental, Las Vegas, 3752 Las Vegas Blvd. S., Las Vegas, 888-881-9367; www.mandarinoriental.com

Following in the footsteps of fellow legendary French chefs Joël Robuchon, Guy Savoy and Alain Ducasse, Pierre Gagnaire opened Twist as his first stateside foray. Located on the 23rd floor of the opulent Mandarin Oriental, the views from Twist's 20-foot-high windows are as noteworthy as the chef. But there's plenty to gaze at inside the restaurant as well, particularly the 300 suspended illuminated globes floating throughout the space. Don't-miss dishes include chicken chiffonade with three kinds of tender gnocchi, as well as the signature langoustine five ways, including a seared tail of langoustine with salty ham; a lightly grilled version with creamy avocado; a mousseline with manzanilla; a gelée made with lobster innards; and then tartare with pomegranate. Close with the Grand Dessert Pierre Gagnaire, a twist on traditional French pastries and a meal unto itself. The five-course indulgence features inventive dishes like the savory Evil, a saffron-tequila bavaroise with a scoop of peppered mozzarella ice cream.

French. Dinner. Closed Sunday-Monday. $86 and up

★★★VALENTINO LAS VEGAS

The Venetian Resort Hotel & Casino, 3355 Las Vegas Blvd. S., Las Vegas, 702-414-3000; www.venetian.com

Italian cuisine can either be very humble and rustic, or it can be highly refined and extravagant. Sometimes, however, there is a pleasant blending of the two, and Valentino is it. This signature Venetian spot is spacious and beautifully appointed and has six private dining rooms in addition to the main rooms, including an intimate wine cellar room that can seat four and an exclusive chef's table for up to six people. The menu is, of course, Italian, concentrating on traditional flavors with elegant presentations. Many ingredients are imported directly from Italy for optimum authenticity in flavor, and the menu changes seasonally. One of the mainstays, the pollo al mattone, a simple, flavorful roast chicken butterflied and cooked flat under a brick, served with a creamy spinach risotto. While you're piling on the carbs, go for the three-color gnocchi with rabbit sausage, mushrooms and a cream demi-glace sauce—it's actually lighter than it sounds. The wine list is staggering–with about 2,500 selections—and service is impeccable.

Italian. Dinner. $86 and up

★★★VERANDAH

Four Seasons Hotel Las Vegas, 3960 Las Vegas Blvd. S., Las Vegas, 702-632-5000; www.fourseasons.com

Four Seasons Hotel Las Vegas is one of those rare spots on the Strip where you don't feel like you're on the Strip at all. Verandah, an open, airy restaurant with plenty of lush greenery and overlooking the exclusive Four Seasons pool is a common destination for both ladies who lunch and those looking for a little break from daily Las Vegas shenanigans. Afternoon tea (you can opt for champagne as well), complete with tiered platters of delicate finger sandwiches, scones and pastries, is popular, as Verandah is one of the few places where you can enjoy this genteel activity without the sound of slot machines in the background. Though the restaurant serves breakfast, lunch and dinner, the weekend breakfast buffet, with its create-your-own-doughnut station, is most popular. Instead of focusing on quantity for the masses, the staff delivers quality for those who are smart enough to dine here rather than the cattle calls that can be found at other hotel buffets.

American. Breakfast, lunch, dinner, Saturday-Sunday brunch, afternoon tea. $36-85

RECOMMENDED

AMERICAN FISH

Aria Resort & Casino, 3730 Las Vegas Blvd. S., Las Vegas, 702-590-8610; www.michaelmina.net

Yet another Michael Mina restaurant (this marks his 17th, and fifth in Las Vegas alone), American Fish focuses on simply prepared seafood dishes in a clean-lined modern space with an intriguing steel ceiling sculpture. Of course, Mina doesn't really do simple; he cooks up a bounty of regional seafood in four signature preparations, including salt baked, wood grilled, cast-iron grilled and ocean-water poached. The ocean water is flown in from Hawaii and used to lightly poach a daily shellfish selection or two other fish filets, like halibut and bass. A highlight is the old-fashioned cornmeal-crusted rainbow trout, which comes from the cast-iron portion of the menu. Sides are required ordering here, including malt vinegar french fries with tartar dipping sauce, truffled mac and cheese and sweet corn with bacon. An extensive wine list is offered, but classic American cocktails like Singapore slings and gimlets are the draw.

Seafood. Dinner. Closed Tuesday. Bar. $36-85

BAR MASA

Aria Resort and Casino, 3730 Las Vegas Blvd., Las Vegas, 877-230-2742; www.arialasvegas.com

Chef Masa Takayama follows up his New York success with Bar Masa, located within Aria at CityCenter. The restaurant is actually two in one. At Bar Masa, guests can dine on simply prepared, traditional Japanese fare in a sleek and open space that resembles a large airport hangar. The menu changes seasonally and includes a variety of sushi and sashimi, as well as dishes such as uni risotto with truffles and Peking duck with foie gras. The more intimate Shaboo seats just 54 and offers an omakase menu that focuses on the Japanese variant of a "hot pot," known as shabu-shabu, where guests cook meats and vegetables in a shared pot of bubbling broth. It's an exclusive, tranquil and rare dining experience. Masa's unique talent for omakase will appeal to a variety of discerning palettes.

Japanese. Dinner. Reservations recommended. $86 and up

BARTOLOTTA RISTORANTE DI MARE

Wynn Las Vegas, 3131 Las Vegas Blvd. S., Las Vegas, 702-248-3463; www.wynnlasvegas.com

Italian preparations of seafood usually revolve around the freshest fish available, treated with the simplest of ingredients. Bartolotta Ristorante di Mare upholds that practice by flying in shellfish and seafood daily straight from the Mediterranean, which means you're most likely getting choices that aren't available elsewhere on the Strip. The warm and friendly waitstaff walks diners through chef Paul Bartolotta's newest creations and can aptly suggest the perfect wine pairing to complete any meal. The elegant dining room overlooks a romantic lagoon, and the mood is further enhanced by dim lighting and sparkling crystal chandeliers. If the weather is nice, and you can secure a table, dine in one of the chic outdoor private cabanas overlooking the lagoon. Serene, quiet and secluded, this intimate space is a breath of fresh air in Las Vegas. Combine the impossibly fresh seafood with the homemade pastas, or opt for a whole fish simply grilled with minimal accoutrement and a glass of wine, and it's the perfect light, yet still decadent, Italian meal.

Italian, seafood. Dinner. $36-85

BLUE AGAVE

Palms Casino Resort, 4321 W. Flamingo Road, Las Vegas, 702-942-7777; www.palms.com

Latin flavors collide with prime raw seafood at the Palms' Blue Agave. Top that off with a margarita made from any one of their 150 tequilas behind the bar and you've got yourself the perfect Mexican meal. The circular bar is festive, with stars hanging from the ceiling, and always draws a crowd (we assume the tequila has something to do with it). Expect bold tastes in almost everything that comes out of the kitchen, from the pastas to the roasted seafood, including our favorite: the spicy lobster, shrimp, crab and scallop gumbo. Be sure to utilize the chile bar, a wide assortment of fresh chilies and salsas to add extra heat and even more flavor to your plate.

Mexican. Lunch, dinner, Sunday brunch. $16-35

BOTERO

Encore Las Vegas, 3121 Las Vegas Blvd. S., Las Vegas, 702-248-3463; www.encorelasvegas.com

If you ever doubted the link between food and fine art, an evening spent at Botero is certain to change your mind. This poolside space is visually stunning, with a soaring arched ceiling, padded white columns and, of course, lots of original works of art by Fernando Botero. Celebrity chef Mark LoRusso ensures that the food is equally artistic. Ahi tuna tartare is a study in color and texture with creamy avocado and crispy ginger, while the pinwheel of wild salmon is almost too pretty to eat. There is no lack of masterpieces on the dessert menu either. The signature ice cream cupcakes will have you reminiscing back to your early days, as will the PB & J brioche doughnuts.

Contemporary American. Lunch (Friday-Saturday), dinner. $86 and up

THE COUNTRY CLUB

Wynn Las Vegas, 3131 Las Vegas Blvd. S., Las Vegas, 702-248-3463; www.wynnlasvegas.com

Down a long hallway far away from the casino, The Country Club feels exactly as it should: exclusive. But that doesn't mean the space is stuffy. With gorgeous views of the waterfalls on the 18th hole of the Wynn golf course, the restaurant has a supper club vibe to it, with dark woods, plaid carpeting and low lighting. The friendly staff makes you feel like a long-standing member from the moment you enter to your last sip of wine. For lunch, you'll find excellent burgers and more casual offerings such as a French dip and a grilled hot dog. Dinner is more subdued and slightly more formal, with a variety of steaks including a charbroiled 20-ounce rib chop and a veal T-bone.

Steak. Lunch (Monday-Friday), dinner (Wednesday-Saturday), Saturday-Sunday brunch. $86 and up

DIEGO

MGM Grand Hotel & Casino, 3799 Las Vegas Blvd. S., Las Vegas, 702-891-3200; www.mgmgrand.com

With hues of red, pink and orange, Diego's atmosphere is vivacious and sexy, adding excitement to your impending night out. You'll find traditional Mexican flavors and dishes given contemporary twists, such as the Diego carne asada, a rib eye steak marinated in red chile adobo and topped with tequila-laced roasted cactus and tangy onion salsa. Guacamole custom-prepared tableside isn't only entertaining, but tasty, too. With an unparalleled tequila selection, Diego makes going out for a taco a livelier experience. After dinner, try the Mexican coffee with Herradura Reposado tequila, Kahlua and fresh whipped cream.

Mexican. Dinner. $36-85

HAMADA OF JAPAN

365 E. Flamingo Road, Las Vegas, 702-733-3005; www.hamadaofjapan.com

With three locations close to each other by the Las Vegas Strip, Hamada of Japan must be doing something right. Sure, it might play into the stereotypes of what a Japanese restaurant looks like, in addition to pushing specialty cocktails with names like "Geisha" and "Banzai," but they definitely do traditional Japanese cuisine well, if not a little kitschy. Favorites such as teriyaki, tempura and sushi dinners are popular, and special platters groaning under the weight of seafood or shabu shabu prepared tableside can be ordered for two or more to share. With private, low-seated tatami rooms and teppanyaki dinner grilled tableside, Hamada of Japan is great for groups who want to have a good time during their meal at a decent price point.

Japanese. Lunch, dinner. $36-85

JEAN GEORGES STEAKHOUSE

Aria Resort & Casino, 3730 Las Vegas Blvd. S., Las Vegas, 877-230-2742; www.jean-georges.com

Chef Jean-Georges Vongerichten has another modern steakhouse, Prime, nearby at the Bellagio, but his homage to meat at Aria stands out by featuring cuts from all over the world, including Japan, Argentina and Uruguay. The striking space nestled in the promenade level of the casino resort is done up in a bold palette of black, white and gold. Of course steak is the star on the menu, but go for an innovate meat-free appetizer like black pepper beignets with Asian pear as well as rice-cracker-crusted tuna. Not in the mood for steak? The Kobe cheeseburger provides a juicy alternative. Just be sure to finish with Jean George's signature dessert, warm chocolate cake with vanilla ice cream.

American. Dinner. Reservations recommended. Bar. $36-85

JULIAN SERRANO

Aria Resort & Casino, 3730 Las Vegas Blvd. S., Las Vegas, 877-230-2742; www.arialasvegas.com

You can do some great people-watching at Julian Serrano. The restaurant opens right into Aria's lobby, where hordes of tourists come and go, but your eyes will be fixed on the innovative Spanish tapas. Try signature dishes like a lobster-pineapple skewer, salmon with truffle béchamel sauce and portobello mushrooms, as well as a refreshingly simple apple-manchego salad with chives. Go with a group of high rollers and order away; these plates are meant to be shared. Adding to the convivial atmosphere is the autumn-inspired décor: the dining room's decked out in inviting reds and golds with tall glossy black tree sculptures sprouting between tables. There's also a hopping bar scene, where Spanish wines and housemade sangria keep the mood light and fun.

Spanish. Lunch, dinner. Bar. $36-85

MING'S TABLE

Harrah's Las Vegas, 3475 Las Vegas Blvd. S., Las Vegas, 702-369-5000; www.harrahslasvegas.com

For hearty Chinese classics, head to Ming's Table. The restaurant provides a casual and authentic Chinese dining experience in a comfortable setting. The bright room takes on a minimalist mystique with a few Asian accents mixed in, but the food is decidedly authentic. Favorites include crab Rangoon, roast duck with plum sauce, Peking duck, spicy hot and sour soup, and kung pao shrimp and scallops. You'll also find dan dan noodles and shark's fin stir fried with black bean or ginger scallion sauce. Sushi and Southeast Asian cuisine are available, but the Chinese fare is definitely the way to go.

Asian. Lunch, dinner. Closed Wednesday-Thursday. $36-85

OKADA

Wynn Las Vegas, 3131 Las Vegas Blvd. S., Las Vegas, 702-248-3463; www.wynnlasvegas.com

Japanese cuisine is traditionally elegant, precise and simple, and the food served at Okada at Wynn Las Vegas falls in line with those aesthetics. The dining room has an excellent flow to it and is accented by blond woods and natural stone, with a giant window offering a view of the waterfall just outside. Sushi is the main attraction, with expert sushi chefs behind the bar preparing some of the freshest raw fish available in Las Vegas. Teppanyaki-style cooking is also a good bet, but don't expect these chefs to theatrically clang their knives against the grill—this is a much more reserved forum, ideal for group dinners.

Japanese. Dinner. $36-85

OSTERIA DEL CIRCO

Bellagio Las Vegas, 3600 Las Vegas Blvd. S., Las Vegas, 702-693-7223; www.bellagio.com

The famed Maccioni family may have made their mark with French cuisine in New York, but at Osteria del Circo, they return to their Italian roots with a Tuscan menu inspired by their matriarch, Egidiana Maccioni. Circo is referred to as the more "casual" sister to Le Cirque next door, but it's still fine dining in our book. The whimsical, colorful décor adds an air of playfulness, making the ambience less stuffy. The menu may look intimidating but in reality, this is pure, honest Italian food at its best. Simple preparations of seafood, such as grilled sea bass served with fennel, cherry tomatoes and zucchini, are presented with style and elegance, allowing the flavors of the dish to shine. If you think all pizza is created equal, forgo the heartier dishes and opt for pizza alla crema bianca, which incorporates Norwegian smoked salmon, onions, capers, crème fraîche and American caviar into a clay-oven-baked, thin-crust masterpiece. Overlooking Lake Bellagio, Circo makes you feel as if you're on Lake Como itself, complete with the authentic Tuscan aromas streaming from the kitchen.

Italian. Dinner. $36-85

PEARL

MGM Grand Hotel & Casino, 3799 Las Vegas Blvd. S., Las Vegas, 702-891-7380;
www.mgmgrand.com

True elegance and sophistication is what Pearl exudes in both its traditional
menu and minimalist, but stunning décor. With red lanterns hanging from
the ceiling, black lacquered tables and serene blue walls, it demonstrates a
combination of modern and classic Asian aesthetics. Here you'll discover
that Chinese food is more than egg foo young and General Tso's chicken.
Fresh seafood is exceptional, dispatched only before it's going to be cooked,
and prepared simply to allow the ingredients' true flavors to surface. Signature
items such as spider prawn dumplings and roasted Peking duck showcase the
chef's talent for Cantonese and Beijing cuisine.

Chinese. Dinner. $36-85

PINOT BRASSERIE

The Venetian Resort Hotel Casino, 3355 Las Vegas Blvd. S., Las Vegas, 702-414-8888;
www.patinagroup.com

As a classically-trained French chef, Eric Lhuillier feels right at home with the
traditional brasserie fare on the menu here. The charming space looks as if it
came straight from Paris, with its red leather chairs and banquettes, brass rails
and wood walls. Like the décor, the bistro menu is comfortable, yet elegant.
Dishes such as the roasted chicken with garlic French fries and braised short
rib with potato mousseline are comfort foods at their best. If your evenings
are already booked up, try Pinot Brasserie for lunch, as there are hearty sandwiches, including a croque monsieur, that, hit the right note every time.

French. Lunch, dinner. $36-85

RAKU

5030 W. Spring Mountain Road, LasVegas, 702-367-3511; www.raku-grill.com

Located way off the Strip within a seedy strip mall in the heart of Chinatown,
Raku doesn't look like a great spot for dinner. But it's where many big-name
Vegas chefs head to eat after cooking all night in their own restaurants. Ignore
the underwhelming exterior (and massage parlors) and step inside for some
of the most innovative and addictive food the city has to offer. This authentic
Japanese charcoal grill restaurant serves an extended menu of small bites
that are perfect for sharing while sipping ice-cold Sapporo drafts. The staff
is friendly and welcoming and willing to steer novices in the right direction.
Grilled asparagus, tomatoes and mushrooms are deceptively simple but
delicious, and the fresh tofu in hot broth is a house specialty. The menu offers
some delicious surprises you wouldn't ordinarily find at a Japanese eatery, such
as a delicious fried chicken and a fluffy cheesecake dessert. Go late at night (it
serves until 3 a.m.) to see many of Vegas' top chefs chowing down on the tasty
mix of traditional and untraditional eats.

Japanese. Dinner. Closed Sunday. $16-35

RED 8

Wynn Las Vegas, 3131 Las Vegas Blvd. S., Las Vegas, 702-770-3380; www.wynnlasvegas.com

Red 8 is the more casual Asian restaurant at Wynn, offering a wider variety of cuisines, but that doesn't mean it resembles your average Chinese take-out place. The red and black dining room is often bustling, as guests schmooze around cozy booths and polished stone tables. In case there's any doubt left as to the cuisine of choice here, a large red lantern hangs majestically in the middle of the restaurant, with tiny lamps around the perimeter of the space. Red 8 offers heartier, more common dishes than its shark's fin-serving counterparts, including Hong Kong-style barbecued beef and soups containing fresh noodles and meaty dumplings. Don't miss the dim sum menu, offering 20 choices of deliciously dense dumplings. And with this more casual dining experience comes a smaller bill—in case you haven't had luck at the tables.

Asian. Lunch, dinner. $36-85

SAGE

Aria Resort and Casino, 3730 Las Vegas Blvd S., Las Vegas, 877-320-2742; www.arialasvegas.com

You might think of bypassing Sage for one of the splashier, celebrity-chef driven restaurants in Aria, but you'd be missing out on a great meal. Sage is a serious restaurant serving provocative farm-driven cuisine in a lively and boldly decorated space that feels worlds away from the slot machines. Chef Shawn McClain is an acclaimed Chicago-based chef, and his experience shows in signature dishes such as savory foie gras brûlée. This unique take of the requisite goose liver dish will have you doing a double take if you are used to the more familiar seared foie gras popular around town. Vegetarians and non-vegetarians alike would be amiss to overlook the slow-poached organic farm egg with smoked potato and black truffle. Desserts are a highlight as well, particularly the warm sugared beignets with the freshest fruit of the season. Time your dinner so you can enjoy one of the inventive housemade cocktails or intriguing beers at the large bar and lounge area before settling down for a modern farm dinner.

American. Dinner. Closed Sunday. Bar. $36-85

SHANGHAI LILLY

Mandalay Bay Resort and Casino, 3950 Las Vegas Blvd. S., Las Vegas, 702-632-7409; www.mandalaybay.com

With long curtains and walls adorned with vintage photos of Chinese beauties, Shanghai Lilly simultaneously examines the past while looking forward to the future. They don't tell you if Shanghai Lilly was an actual woman or not, but the black and white 1920s-era portraits of anonymous ladies hanging throughout the space make you hope she was. The award-winning design of the room was imagined by Tony Chi, who sought to simulate the elegance and ease of ancient Chinese luxury. The Imperial Peking duck is second to none, as are the lobster lettuce wraps. If you're more of a traditionalist, go for the black-peppered beef tenderloin or kung pao chicken; you won't be disappointed. The four private dining rooms, apart from the main dining area, are ideal for a private affair or a special celebration—just book months out because those tables are often hard to nab.

Chinese. Dinner. Closed Tuesday-Wednesday. $36-85

SILK ROAD

Vdara Hotel & Spa, 2600 W. Harmon Ave., Las Vegas, 866-745-7767; www.vdara.com

Silk Road offers a sleek and sunny spot for breakfast and lunch, thanks to a bold indigo color scheme, undulating waves on everything from the walls to the booths, and bright, natural light that flows inside. Executive chef Martin Heierling has crafted a balanced menu of savory and sweet selections, such as delectable sliders with beef tenderloin, fried egg, bacon and tomato confit as well as addicting blueberry and ricotta pancakes with honeycomb butter and candied rose petals. If you have trouble deciding, try the signature Eggs, Eggs and Eggs, which offers poached, scrambled and fried eggs all in one dish. During lunch, go for the Southern-inspired chicken and waffle basket or the refreshing popcorn shrimp lettuce wraps with mango slaw.

American, Asian. Breakfast, lunch, Sunday brunch. $16-35

SINATRA

Encore Las Vegas, 3121 Las Vegas Blvd. S., Las Vegas, 702-248-3463;
www.encorelasvegas.com

Encore's signature restaurant pays homage to Ol' Blue Eyes in more than name alone. Framed images of the famous crooner line the cream colored walls and his voice provides a pleasant backdrop for dinner conversation. Celebrated chef Theo Schoenegger continues the salute with sophisticated Italian fare fit for the Rat Packer himself. Pastas read simple and straightforward, though taste anything but. The lasagna Bolognese incorporates veal, pork and beef between layers of heavenly hand-rolled pasta, and the agnolotti stuffed with bufala ricotta is surprisingly light and airy. The chicken saltimbocca is another sure bet, only improved upon with a side of herb-potato gnocchi. The intimate dining room is often filled with two-tops looking for a romantic alternative to the frenzied pulse of Vegas. And what's more romantic than spending a night with Ol' Blue Eyes?

Italian. Dinner. $86 and up

SIRIO RISTORANTE

Aria Resort & Casino, 3730 Las Vegas Blvd. S., Las Vegas, 877-230-2742;
www.arialasvegas.com

Sirio Maccioni of New York's famed Le Cirque created this restaurant to show off the rustic dishes of his Tuscan childhood. The Italy-inspired design—with proscenium arches, travertine floors, a silver-leaf-patterned inverted dome ceiling and black-and-white photographic murals of Italian architecture—provides the perfect setting for the simple appetizers, pastas and main courses, such as the white-truffle-scented beef carpaccio and the traditional Tuscan tomato bread soup. For a hearty entrée, try the pistachio-crusted lamb with semolina gnocchi. There's no better way to end a traditional Italian meal than with some cannoli. Here, the housemade Sicilian treats are filled with imported buffalo ricotta, candied citrus, pistachios and chocolate chips.

Italian. Dinner. Bar. $36-85

SOCIETY CAFÉ

Encore Las Vegas, 3121 Las Vegas Blvd. S., Las Vegas, 702-770-5300; www.encorelasvegas.com

This popular restaurant at Encore Las Vegas is the perfect place to dine at any time of the day. Lavish décor makes you feel like high society, but the casual vibe makes you feel comfortable. With inspiration taken from London during the Victorian era, you'll see high ceilings, archways with black and white striped drapes, bright green light fixtures, oversized hot pink couches that serve as banquette seating and black crocodile chairs. Chef Kim Canteenwalla serves up classic American fare with a fun twist like frosted flake French toast and steak and egg sliders at breakfast, and lollipop chicken wings at lunch. At dinner, warm pretzel bread is brought out with mustard butter while you peruse the menu. Start with tasty tuna tacos or one of their many salads and then move on to an entrée such as the jidori chicken, Mediterranean seabass or build your own burger. For dessert, try the warm donut bites with chocolate, caramel and raspberry dipping sauces.

American. Breakfast, lunch, dinner, late-night. $36-85

STRATTA

Wynn Las Vegas, 3131 Las Vegas Blvd. S., Las Vegas, 702-770-3463; www.wynnlasvegas.com

Chef Alessandro Stratta's second restaurant at the Wynn is his more-casual concept of rustic, regional Italian fare. Red-backed chairs, an open fire hearth and a clear view into the kitchen create an atmosphere that is laid back and welcoming. The restaurant's lounge is a smart place to meet for drinks, and the location makes it an ideal spot to grab a bite before or after catching a show at Wynn. The wood-fired pizzas are great picks (we particularly liked the Bosco, with roasted mushroom purée, white truffle oil and Bel Paese cheese), and the pastas definitely have enough variety to make everyone in your group happy. For a more substantial meal, the roasted pork chop stuffed with fontina cheese and prosciutto is heavenly.

Italian. Lunch (Friday-Sunday), dinner. $36-85

SW STEAKHOUSE

Wynn Las Vegas, 3131 Las Vegas Blvd. S., Las Vegas, 702-248-3463; www.wynnlasvegas.com

SW at Wynn Las Vegas rises above and beyond a classic Vegas steakhouse. You won't find a dimly lit, smoky room here. Instead, an airy dining room opens onto the Lake of Dreams, where light and music shows play nightly. The prime steaks come from corn-fed Nebraskan cows, which results in great tasting beef. Side dishes are where steakhouses always differentiate themselves, and SW's offerings—truffled creamed corn, crisp potato tots with herb cream—are what set it apart. The fairground-gone-luxe funnel cake is a good way to end an indulgent experience—crisp, fluffy funnel cake slices are presented on the branches of a metal tree, and served with sauces of crème anglaise, salty caramel and fudge.

Steak. Dinner. $86 and up

SWITCH

Encore Las Vegas, 3121 Las Vegas Blvd. S., Las Vegas, 702-248-3463; www.encorelasvegas.com

If anything at Encore is kitschy, this restaurant might be it. But as with all things Wynn, even kitsch is done with style, sophistication and a touch of playfulness. The concept behind Switch is that the walls constantly rotate to provide changing ambience throughout your meal. You won't get through dessert without seeing a few repeats, but at that point your full attention will be on your plate, not the walls around you. Chef René Lenger has created a menu that is as animated as the décor. Jumbo lump crab cakes come alongside a quail egg and fried pickles, while the salmon filet is bathed in a champagne sauce. Serious carnivores will appreciate the charbroiled steak selection, and the black truffle creamed spinach is a side worth splurging on. The service is warm and informed, especially on questions regarding the lengthy wine list.

American. Dinner. $86 and up

TABLEAU
Wynn Las Vegas, 3131 Las Vegas Blvd. S., Las Vegas, 702-248-3463; www.wynnlasvegas.com

Don't think you can't secure a table at Tableau just because it's tucked away in the Tower Suites at Wynn. This spacious, airy dining room offers American cuisine for breakfast, lunch and weekend brunch, along with prime views of the Tower Suites pool and gardens. You won't find any frilly nouveau fare here— deep down the menu is meat and potatoes, albeit more elegantly presented. The organic roast chicken BLT sandwich is far from your run-of-the-mill lunch option, with cipolini onions and a warm bacon-shallot dressing. For sweeter palates, the wild blueberry buttermilk pancakes slathered in orange blossom butter is the perfect way to start the day. Service is personable and outgoing, but not obsequious. Tableau certainly offers fine dining, but it's not hard to feel comfortable here.

American. Breakfast, lunch, Saturday-Sunday brunch. $36-85

VOODOO STEAK & LOUNGE
Rio Hotel & Casino, 3700 W. Flamingo Road, Las Vegas, 702-777-7923; www.riolasvegas.com

As if the nightclub at the top of the Rio wasn't enough, you can have a good steak up there as well. Formerly known as VooDoo Café, VooDoo Steak has a more refined menu, with premium reserve and dry-aged beef as the specialties. With a gorgeous view of the entire Strip, the restaurant features Creole and Cajun bites such as ham and andouille sausage beignets and delta frog legs and mussels. The VooDoo "Menage a Trois," a surf and turf offering of petite filet mignon, prawns and lobster, puts a sexy spin on your meal. Head out on to the terrace for an after-dinner cocktail, but don't look down (the view of the ground below is not for the weak).

Steak/Cajun/Creole. Dinner. $36-85

WING LEI
Wynn Las Vegas, 3131 Las Vegas Blvd. S., Las Vegas, 702-248-3463; www.wynnlasvegas.com

The meaning of the Chinese characters that represent Wing Lei is twofold: not only does it mean "forever prosperous" but it also represents "Wynn" itself (Wing in English is "Wynn"). This upscale Chinese offering pulls out all the stops with its decadent menu and French- and Chinese-inspired décor. Red, the color of luck in China, accents the room in the form of curtains and on the backs of chairs, emphasizing the handcrafted black onyx bar in the corner. Executive chef Ming Yu's menu is a blend of traditional Shanghai, Szechwan and Cantonese cuisines, including a five-course Peking duck extravaganza which starts with Peking duck salad with orange truffle vinaigrette and wild duck soup and carries into pan-seared duck noodles and the famed table-carved roasted duck presentation. The Mongolian beef and Sichuan chili prawns are solid entrées. If you simply can't decide (the menu is lengthy), the chef's signature dinner is a five-course affair with dishes like grilled black cod, wok-tossed Maine lobster and braised Kobe sirloin with black pepper au jus. *Chinese. Dinner. $86 and up*

SPAS

★★★THE BATHHOUSE

THEhotel at Mandalay Bay Resort & Casino, 3950 Las Vegas Blvd. S., Las Vegas, 877-632-9636; www.mandalaybay.com

The Bathhouse makes its home inside Mandalay Bay's boutique sidekick THEhotel, giving the spa a very intimate feel (by Vegas standards, at least). Designed with simple stripped-down European aesthetics in mind, the imposing slate-gray walls throughout the space have an almost-industrial, gallery-like vibe. Luxuriating in the Jacuzzi pool, for instance, you feel almost as if you've sneaked into a heated museum fountain. Even the Jacuzzi warnings look artistic and cool, printed on the wall in an interesting typeface. Every once in a while, though, a bright, geometric-patterned pillow or flower arrangement offers a pop of color. Crème brûlée body treatments and hot spiced rum stone massages demonstrate a propensity towards intermingling the senses (taste, smell and touch). If you need to look bikini-ready upon arrival, treatments like the Cell-U-Less Herbal Wrap offer a boost.

★★★★CANYON RANCH SPACLUB

The Palazzo Resort Hotel Casino/The Venetian Resort Hotel Casino, 3355 Las Vegas Blvd. S., Las Vegas, 877-220-2688; www.canyonranchspaclub.com

The newly renovated and expanded Canyon Ranch SpaClub—at 134,000 square feet—is enormous. In fact, as you wander past the impressive Palazzo into the Venetian and toward the neutral-toned spa (festooned with raw organic design elements like bamboo) you'll enter the biggest spa in North America (with more than 100 treatment rooms). Canyon Ranch's wellness reputation—as the foremost pioneer of modern day ultra-luxury health resorts—precedes the Sin City addition (the first Canyon Ranch opened in 1979 in Tucson, Arizona). And it has unveiled something exclusive and brand new: The Aquavana pre-treatment plunging experience allows guests to move between invigorating spaces such as a Wave Dream, Salt Chamber, Igloo, Rasul mud room and Snow Cabin, in addition to the usual steam and sauna. No appointment is necessary, as long as you buy a day pass to the spa ($35 or less per pass if purchased for several days). Not for cynics are new-age signatures like Vibrational Therapy, which combines crystal sounding bowls, essential oils, Chakra stone placements, acupoints and negative ionization of the Cavitosonic chamber to balance the body's energy fields. A Yamuna Hands-On Treatment, in which muscles are massaged with a special ball, may offer more tangible satisfaction. And while the fitness center is an afterthought at many spas, Canyon Ranch SpaClub offers holistic wellness programs. The multi-colored climbing wall is also the spa's aesthetic centerpiece, so be aware that if you scale it you might attract some attention.

FOUR PRESTIGIOUS AWARDS.
ONE DISTINCT EXPERIENCE.

Joël Robuchon
RESTAURANT

GET THE EXPERIENCE OF A LIFETIME AT MGM GRAND.

maximumVegas. MGM GRAND.

Go all out at MGM Grand. Kick off the excitement with KÀ™ by *Cirque du Soleil*®, an unprecedented theatrical event. Enjoy cuisine from casual to upscale at a variety of gourmet restaurants. Feel the nightlife pulse at Tabú Ultra Lounge, Studio 54®, or the red-hot Rouge. Unwind with a treatment at the Grand Spa. Take a dip in the lazy river, or at one of five pools at our 6.6-acre Grand Pool complex. Then start all over. After all, this is maximum Vegas℠

★★★QUA BATHS & SPA

Caesars Palace, 3570 Las Vegas Blvd. S., Las Vegas, 866-782-0655; www.caesarspalace.com

Mile-high ceilings and lavish azure décor—mimicking an underwater world—welcome you to Qua Baths & Spa at Caesars Palace. After slipping on your robe, stroll around the corner to the sizeable relaxation lounge. If you're thirsty, head to the Tea Room, where an herbal sommelier will find the perfect concoction to ease you into a mellow mood before your treatment. Signature experiences like the Hawaiian Lomi Lomi and Chakra Balancing—with aromatherapy oil dripped onto the third eye (that's "forehead" to you) and energetic stones arranged on your back—may seem a bit far-fetched but are actually very relaxing. "Social spa-ing" is also a priority here and shared amenities truly deliver: Three Roman baths (separate pools ranging in temperature from 76° to 104°) sit poised atop polished stone steps and are surrounded by opalescent walls, just waiting for a group to soak and chit-chat. But a favorite is the amazing Arctic Ice Room (best used as cooling relief after a sauna and/or a Laconium steam), where a water and moisturizer mix, posing as snow, falls upon heated seats and floors—a truly refreshing winter wonderland.

★★★★★THE SPA AT ENCORE LAS VEGAS

Encore Las Vegas, 3121 Las Vegas Blvd. S., Las Vegas, 702-693-7472; www.encorelasvegas.com

The wow-factor is certainly in play at this ritzy rejuvenation center. Taking pointers from the Spa at Wynn, Encore carries the Asian theme further with glowing gold lanterns, life-size Buddhas and blossoming orchids. The expansive reception area looks like the lobby of a luxury hotel rather than a sterile spa environment (with plenty of pillow-laden couches for lounging), while the locker rooms are unusually bright and airy. The separate men's and women's spaces are sprawling in size, with large saunas and steam rooms, as well as just about any amenity you might need to refresh post-treatment. But it's not just about the décor; technology plays a part as well. State-of-the-art waterfall showers use digital screens to let you control water temperature, water pressure from the six shower heads, and mood lighting, and the personal lockers don't require keys. A transformation ritual might be just what you need after a long losing battle in the casino. Try the Lavender Stone Ritual, which incorporates lavender and sea salt to calm frayed nerves, or the Vitamin Infusion Facial, giving your system a boost of vitamins and collagen to heal damaged skin. The onsite salon offers everything from manicures and pedicures to cuts and colors, as well as a full menu of traditional barbershop services. You can also buy a day pass and enjoy all of the outrageous amenities of the spa without a treatment. It may be the best $30 you spend in Vegas.

★★★★THE SPA AT THE FOUR SEASONS HOTEL LAS VEGAS

Four Seasons Hotel Las Vegas, 3960 Las Vegas Blvd. S., Las Vegas, 702-632-5000; www.fourseasons.com/lasvegas

You'd never know you were in Sin City at The Spa at The Four Seasons Hotel Las Vegas, as there's no casino and, hence, no stroll—on the road to relaxation—through intentionally disorienting chaos. Once you wander into the hotel's tasteful lobby, a representative immediately leads you to your destination. The Spa's subdued décor is seamless. This intimate refuge swathed in mild tones is on the smaller side, so personal attention (in concert with The Four

Seasons' usual impeccable service) is a plus. Shuffling to the Zen lounge in one of the city's plushest robes, you sip cucumber water or herbal tea and nibble on an array of treats from dried fruit to pastries. Don't be surprised by the smell of fresh-baked goods either; fresh doughnuts are served in the lobby café, and sinful mini-chocolate muffins are omnipresent in the spa (finally, snacks you actually want to eat). The Spa's services are some of the most effective and clinical of the Vegas bunch, so you're asked to fill out a health information form at onset. Opt for a unique results-oriented facial like the signature Vitality of the Glaciers, an anti-aging RNA, DNA and collagen treatment that jump starts your cellular metabolism. Think you liked hot rocks on your back? You'll leave the new Everlasting Flower Stone facial, with poppy seed exfoliation, hibiscus extract and rhodochrosite rocks, feeling relaxed.

★★★★★THE SPA AT MANDARIN ORIENTAL, LAS VEGAS
Mandarin Oriental Las Vegas, 3752 Las Vegas Blvd. S. Las Vegas, 888-881-9530; www.mandarinoriental.com/lasvegas

Located within the serene Mandarin Oriental, this spa is luxuriously designed with dark woods and exotic Shanghai undertones, making it a welcome respite from the bustle of the Strip immediately below. Guests are greeted with tea and a cool towel before being whisked away to the elegantly appointed locker rooms and relaxation area. Be sure to budget enough time to take full advantage of the steam room, dry sauna, vitality pool and Laconium room. An ice fountain and experience showers provide luxurious means to cool down. The relaxation lounge is inviting, with plush chairs and panoramic views of the Strip, and heated Tepidarium chairs to soothe aching muscles. Each guest receives their own attractive souvenir amenities kit with razor, toothbrush and other necessities. Many of the massage rooms are designed with couples in mind. While a variety of treatments are offered, the highlight may just be the Chinese Foot spa, which offers authentic and luxurious foot massages. Be sure to take a dip in one of the outdoor pools located just outside the spa area with incredible views of the Strip.

★★★THE SPA AT RED ROCK
Red Rock Casino, Resort & Spa, 11011 West Charleston, Summerlin, 866-767-7773; www.redrocklasvegas.com

As Red Rock is situated closer to a national park than the Strip, spa services extend outside their casino-adjacent digs and into the great outdoors. "Adventure Spa" activities include horseback riding and rock climbing, as well as location-specific experiences like rafting down the Colorado River and hiking to natural hot springs. Inside, mosaic pebble fountains, a bright red relaxation area with a faux snakeskin centerpiece and a chocolate and turquoise color scheme lend a "boutique" feel to the ultra-modern (yet-retro '60s/ mod-style) spa. If you're up for something different, try the Ashiatsu massage, where a masseuse actually suspends from the ceiling to walk on your back, or the radiance facial, which uses a cinnamon enzyme peel and active protein enzymes to improve skin's elasticity.

★★★★THE SPA AT TRUMP

Trump International Hotel Las Vegas, 2000 Fashion Show Drive, Las Vegas, 702-797-7878; www.trumplasvegashotel.com

The Spa at Trump International Hotel is among Vegas' most intimate and, of course, swankiest refuges. A spa attaché guides you through 11,000 square feet of Rain Shower and eucalyptus steam-laden space to help discern your signature intention: Calm, Balance, Purify, Heal or Revitalize. Special gemstone-infused oil massages are meant to heal internally and externally. To get event-ready, try the Dermal Quench: hydration with oxygen and hyaluronic serum delivered with hyperbaric pressure for extra absorption. Or, for long-lasting benefits, sample the Dermalucent with LED skin rejuvenation; or a hotel-exclusive Ultimate Kate facial (combining both of the above and a foot massage). Late-night partiers flock to the Morning-After Eye Cure to refresh before starting the cycle again. Of course, The Donald wouldn't open a spa without some kind of service for luscious locks, so try an Espresso Yourself hair treatment for damage control.

★★★★★THE SPA AT WYNN LAS VEGAS

Wynn Las Vegas, 3131 Las Vegas Blvd. S., Las Vegas, 702-770-3900; www.wynnlasvegas.com

No need to feel a pang of guilt as you pass exercise bikes between treatments. At The Spa at Wynn, the fitness center sits outside the pampering area, unlike at many other spas. The décor is plush, and the waiting room—adorned with a large "fire and ice" fireplace—is comfortable and relaxing. You could lounge here on one of the ultra-comfortable couches sipping herbal tea and flipping through magazines for hours post-treatment. The lovely Jacuzzi room harkens to a mermaid's lair, with its lily pad-covered walls inset with stones, Deluge showers that simulate waterfalls, and a central soaking bath. Exotic Asian- and Middle Eastern-inspired treatments are signatures here, but the real attraction is the ultra-indulgent, 80-minute Stone Ritual, a soothing full-body massage using heated stones to melt the knots in overworked muscles. Other treatments include Thai massage, shiatsu, and facials that will do everything from boost the collagen in your visage to impart a glow to tired, dull skin. Male estheticians are plentiful here, so make sure to specify if you have a gender preference. If the views in your room at Wynn are too difficult to pull yourself away from (and at night, they are alluring, no matter which direction your room faces), you can opt to have a massage performed in the privacy of your own retreat. Manicures and pedicures at the onsite salon are performed in comfortable chairs cordoned off by curtains that provide extra privacy. An army of black-clad, top-notch stylists are on hand to offer cuts, coloring and even makeup application, which makes the salon a favorite for visiting brides and their bridal parties celebrating their big day.

★★★★SPA BELLAGIO LAS VEGAS

Bellagio Las Vegas, 3600 Las Vegas Blvd. S., Las Vegas, 888-987-6667; www.bellagio.com

Bellagio's spa is a well-oiled machine, albeit a large machine that runs well thanks to the efficiency of its technology-aided staff, who don headsets to subtly communicate with each other as they whisk you into the spa. Once checked in at the second story spa (having wandered past the full-service salon, enormous manicure/pedicure area and a gentlemen's "Barber Shop"), disrobe and re-robe in the large changing area, then head to the coed waiting area. (At last, you can sit with your significant other before a couple's treatment.) The designers adorned the space with spectacular natural elements like wall-mounted orchid installations complete with waterfalls; enormous terra cotta pots; and backlit jade inlaid in fossilized sandstone floors. An extensive menu offers options from the luscious Deep Coconut Surrender massage, which features warm coconut milk drizzled on your back amidst hot stones, to more experimental treatments like spinal realignment essential oil Raindrop Therapy. But the mosaic Watsu massage is the spa's major claim to fame: In a large, steamy, sea blue- and green-tiled private space, submerged in 94-degree water, you experience a Zen Shiatsu-technique massage, which some say mirrors the experience of being born.

★★★★SPA MIO
The M Resort Spa & Casino Las Vegas, 12300 Las Vegas Blvd. S., Las Vegas, 702-797-1800; www.themresort.com

Natural wood and exposed brick, eucalyptus-scented air and the soothing sound of grasshoppers as you step off the elevators are just a few of the defining elements of Sin City's newest oasis. The 23,000-square-foot space has all the usual amenities—sauna, steam room, Jacuzzi—but it's the organic slant that draws the biggest buzz. The 50-minute Organic facial incorporates organic orchard fruits like papaya and apricots to nourish and hydrate the skin. The 80-minute Wild Flower and Earth wrap starts with a vigorous exfoliation before the body is painted with a blend of mineral-rich mud from the Atlas Mountains (apparently, it's an old beauty secret from Morocco) and your choice of essential oils. The fitness center boasts some of the best desert views in Vegas through its floor-to-ceiling windows, making even a workout an organic experience.

WHERE TO SHOP

THE ATTIC
1018 S. Main St., Las Vegas, 702-388-4088; www.atticvintage.com

You may have seen the credit card ads and other glimpses in glossy magazines of this self-proclaimed world's largest vintage clothing store. With its '60s retro décor and multi-tiered main room stuffed with feathers, fedoras and full suits from the past, you could spend hours playing dress-up and trying on new personas for your Vegas vacation. The clerks are very helpful in throwing together a cool look.
Tuesday-Saturday 10 a.m.-6 p.m.

BELLAGIO LAS VEGAS
Bellagio Las Vegas, 3600 Las Vegas Blvd. S., Las Vegas, 702-693-7111; www.bellagiolasvegas.com

Overlooking the Bellagio lake where the famed fountain show blasts off throughout the day, Via Bellagio offers a wide selection of luxury shopping options. When you seek out the roster here—Bottega Veneta, Christian Dior, Prada, Giorgio Armani, Gucci, Tiffany & Co., Yves Saint Laurent, Chanel and Fendi—you can pretty much guarantee that dropping your winnings won't be hard to do. After browsing the shops of Via Bellagio, head to the Via Fiore shops outlining the Conservatory and Botanical Gardens. For luminous artwork, Chihuly offers paintings and original glass blown by artist Dale Chihuly, who created the glass chandelier in the hotel's lobby. Or put a bit of beauty in your yard with a decorative gift from the Giardini Garden Store. If you can't resist some hotel gear, visit Essentials, which sells Bellagio-themed clothing, accessories and gifts. Not only can you pick up the typical tourist T-shirt, but there are hand towels and other household items to remember your travels.

Daily 10 a.m.-midnight. Essentials is open 24 hours a day, daily.

CRYSTALS RETAIL AND ENTERTAINMENT

3720 Las Vegas Blvd., S., Las Vegas, 866-754-2489; www.crystalsatcitycenter.com

The gorgeous Crystals shopping center—designed to look like an outdoor park—within CityCenter is devoted to high-end retailers including Louis Vuitton, Roberto Cavalli, Lanvin, Cartier and Prada, as well as new-to-Las Vegas outposts of Paul Smith, Tom Ford and Miu Miu. An impressive wooden tree house structure at the center of the complex contains the concierge desk on the lower level and a dining terrace for Mastro's Ocean Club above. Other restaurants include Wolfgang Puck Pizzeria & Cucina, the pan-Asian Social House and Beso, a dazzling venue from actress Eva Longoria Parker and celebrity chef Todd English. Eve Nightclub is located on the second floor of the restaurant. The Gallery showcases work by renowned artist Dale Chihuly.

Sunday-Thursday 10 a.m.-11 p.m., Friday-Saturday 10 a.m.-midnight.

ENCORE ESPLANADE

Encore Las Vegas, 3121 Las Vegas Blvd. S., Las Vegas, 702-770-8000; www.encorelasvegas.com

Sure, the Encore Esplanade is a thoroughfare, taking you from Wynn Las Vegas to Encore Las Vegas and vice versa. But what a thoroughfare it is. The sprawling indoor boulevard exudes class with latticed archways, elaborate chandeliers and verdant greenery. The boutiques aren't shabby either. Encore Esplanade has all the luxury of its sophisticated neighbor with a touch more edge. Case in point: Chanel or Hermès will have you ready for the high-rollers room, while Rock & Republic and Shades will get you decked to hit the clubs afterwards— convenient since Vegas's hottest club, XS, is located in the Esplanade. If you can't get enough of the Wynn lifestyle, stop by Homestore, an interiors store featuring many of the items used to decorate the hotel.

Sunday-Thursday 10 a.m.-11 p.m., Friday-Saturday 10 a.m.-midnight.

FASHION SHOW

3200 Las Vegas Blvd. S., Las Vegas, 702-784-7000; www.thefashionshow.com

One of the first malls on the Strip to feature high-end retailers, the Fashion Show underwent a multimillion-dollar expansion in 2002 to keep up with its neighbors. And we're not talking typical upgrades here. An 80-foot-long runway and stage were built right down the center of the two-story mall to host live fashion shows, and it's already been put to use during press conferences by Mayor Oscar Goodman, flanked by his usual entourage of showgirls, and for local charity fundraisers. You can rent it out for private events and have the guest of honor rise from below the floor on a sunken podium (really). But it's the shopping that attracts fashionistas from around the world. The nearly two million-square-foot mall has six anchor stores: Neiman Marcus, Saks

Fifth Avenue, Macy's, Dillard's, Nordstrom and Bloomingdale's Home. Other shopping-mall standbys include J. Crew, Banana Republic, Lacoste and Gap. A massive food court boasts everything from pizza to Mediterranean food, as well as the usual Wendy's and KFC. These may not be the pick of high-rolling foodies, but they'll keep you satiated through your shopping spree. For a classier (and quieter) alternative, try the Nordstrom Marketplace Café.
Monday-Saturday 10 a.m.-9 p.m., Sunday 11 a.m.-7 p.m.

THE FORUM SHOPS AT CAESARS PALACE
Caesars Palace, 3500 Las Vegas Blvd. S., Las Vegas, 702-893-4800; www.caesarspalace.com

The cobblestone faux-Roman streets that intersect inside Caesars' Forum Shops carry travelers from around the world to such retail meccas as Harry Winston, Baccarat, Gucci, Louis Vuitton, Versace and Jimmy Choo. This is one of the more upscale malls in the Las Vegas valley, but calling it a mall is not giving it all its due. Aside from shopping at this tony spot, there's the entertainment. The free Atlantis Show brings Roman gods and a simple story to life with animatronic "actors" that spring to action every hour. A Festival Fountain show also entertains guests; but don't miss the restaurants. Although there is much to choose from in Vegas, many stars still go back to their favorites at the Forum Shops. Singer Mariah Carey makes sure to stop in at Spago every time she is in Sin City—she loves the food so much, she has her favorite pasta dishes delivered to her hotel room, and has twice reserved the back room for a post-show feast. The Palm, BOA Steakhouse and Joe's Seafood, Prime Steak & Stone Crab are a few of the many fine-food finds scattered throughout this 636,000-square-foot mall. A winding circular escalator carries shoppers from the marbled first floor to the top third floor (parading you past all the window displays), where you will find some of the best views of the Strip at Sushi Roku.
Sunday-Thursday 10 a.m.-11 p.m., Friday-Saturday 10 a.m.-midnight.

THE GRAND CANAL SHOPPES AT THE VENETIAN
The Venetian Resort Hotel Casino, 3377 Las Vegas Blvd. S., Las Vegas, 702-414-4500; www.venetian.com

This elegant space sings of Italy: It boasts painted frescos, polished marble, gondoliers and, of course, exceptional shopping. Aside from the luxury retailers you'll find at other shopping destinations such as Venezia and Movado, there is also a nice array of independent boutiques. History buffs can have their pick of authentic Spanish galleons, coins and other finds at Ancient Creations; delicate, hand-blown Venetian glass sits pretty at Ripa de Monti; handmade Venetian masks and period pieces await you at Il Prato, and Ca'd'Oro is the place to go for exquisite jewelry. A winding indoor canal below the cobblestoned walkways links the shops together, and if you've always dreamed of having a gondolier steer you from storefront to storefront, now's the time to make it a reality, as rides with singing gondoliers are available. Throughout St. Mark's Square–the center of the Grand Canal Shoppes–actors, musicians and strolling singers entertain guests, and living statues come to life. If cash is tight after one too many rounds on the roulette wheel, the Grand Lux Café offers solid comfort food at affordable prices. Or if you want to splurge, try Canaletto in St. Mark's Square.
Sunday-Thursday 10 a.m.-11 p.m., Friday-Saturday 10 a.m.-midnight.

LE BOULEVARD SHOPS

Paris Las Vegas, 3655 Las Vegas Blvd. S., Las Vegas, 702-946-7000; www.parislasvegas.com

They've tried very hard to give an authentic feel to Le Boulevard, and they've nearly pulled it off. Stroll through the cobbled streets and take in the French-style shops that line this shopping center and you might feel like you are in the City of Lights, albeit in miniature. Small in comparison to other hotel shopping areas along the Strip, Le Boulevard is impressive for its attention to detail. From Les Enfants children's shop, where you can pick up soft little shirts and stuffed toys, to the Parisian décor store Les Eléments, Le Boulevard is drenched in decadent French culture. Grab an imported cheese and pair it with a fine wine from La Cave. If you are walking the Strip from casino to casino, duck into Le Boulevard to get from Paris to Bally's inside. It's a nice diversion, even if you aren't a Francophile.

Hours vary; walkway is open 24 hours.

MAIN STREET ANTIQUES, ART & COLLECTIBLES

500 S. Main St., Las Vegas, 702-382-1882; www.mainstreetantiqueslv.com

This cavernous string of buildings connects collectibles in a dizzying selection that you can't imagine. Antique hunters from around the world stop by regularly to check out the latest from more than 40 dealers who dabble in vintage Vegas. We picked up a 1950s-era ebony puzzle box with ivory detail for $20. The box unfolds to reveal two trays with grooves for cigarettes. Furniture, obscure odds and ends, pottery, slot signage and much more make for an interesting afternoon wandering through the past. The store ships worldwide, so you don't have to worry about paying the airlines an extra bag fee if you find something you just can't pass up. Don't be afraid to haggle, either; vendors expect nothing less. You can get quite a deal from tired sellers who want to move items.

Tuesday-Sunday 10 a.m.-6 p.m.

MIRACLE MILE SHOPS

Planet Hollywood Resort & Casino, 3663 Las Vegas Blvd. S., Las Vegas, 888-800-8284; www.miraclemileshopslv.com

Recently redesigned with a contemporary flair, this meandering mall is filled with 170 stores, including French Connection, Ann Taylor Loft, Bebe and Lucky Brand Jeans. You'll notice many shoppers with Alpaca Imports shopping bags, from an odd little store filled with the softest alpaca (a cousin of the llama) sweaters and slippers, as well as sheepskin rugs, car seat covers and home décor from around the world. Catch the free entertainment at small podiums around the mall, or at the V Theater in the middle of the mall, while you sip a coffee or eat gelato from the Aromi d'Italia. A favorite attraction for families is the live indoor rainstorm near Merchants' Harbor. Thunder, lightning and a light rain that turns torrential create a dramatic effect as you pass. If you're hungry, you won't find the usual food court choices here. Instead they've concentrated on restaurants such as Pampas Churrascaria Brazilian Grille or Sin City Brewing Co. If you just want a quick bite, you can pop into La Salsa Cantina, Sbarro pizza or the fun, frenzied Cheeseburger Las Vegas.

Sunday-Thursday 10 a.m.-11 p.m., Friday-Saturday 10 a.m.-midnight.

NOT JUST ANTIQUES MART

1422 Western Ave., Las Vegas, 702-384-4922; www.notjustantiquesmart.com

You can grab a nice little lunch and a piece from the past at this charming mart. Small in comparison to some of the others, this 12,000-square-foot mall is home to dozens of dealers who specialize in everything from gaming memorabilia to period furniture and glassware. Every item has a story, and the vendors are more than happy to tell you if they know the history of a particular piece. If you're a new collector or want to start, this is the place to get your feet wet as the pool of knowledge here is huge. A tea-room gallery upstairs takes reservations for high tea parties, perfect for mothers and daughters, family reunions or a bachelorette breather before or after a night on the town. Located in the Arts District just off Charleston Boulevard, you can ask for directions to the latest art installations or gallery shows within walking distance of the antique mart.

Monday-Saturday 10:30 a.m.-5:30 p.m., Sunday noon-5 p.m. First Friday of every month open until 10 p.m.

THE SHOPPES AT THE PALAZZO

The Palazzo Resort Hotel Casino, 3325 Las Vegas Blvd. S., Las Vegas, 702-607-7777; www.palazzolasvegas.com

One of the newest shopping complexes on the Strip, the Shoppes at the Palazzo houses the first Barneys New York in Vegas. At 85,000 square feet, it's a destination unto itself, complete with its own valet and entrance on the Strip. If that's not enough to lure you in, there are also boutiques by Christian Louboutin, Catherine Malandrino, Diane von Furstenberg and Michael Kors. If you find yourself parched after all that hanger-lifting, swing by the Double Helix Bar for some wine; there are more than 50 wines by the glass to choose from. Or down a few tasty bites at Emeril's Table 10 before hopping back on the shopping circuit.

Sunday-Thursday 10 a.m.-11 p.m., Friday-Saturday 10 a.m.-midnight.

TOWN SQUARE

6605 Las Vegas Blvd. S., Las Vegas, 702-269-5000; www.townsquarelasvegas.com

Designed to look like a quaint Italian village, Town Square is lined with cobbled avenues that wind through this stunning shopping, dining and entertainment mecca. The open air space, located at the corner of Sunset Road and Las Vegas Boulevard, is home to numerous shops, including Steve Madden, BCBG Max Azria, Robb & Stucky furniture and H&M (which is the one of the few places to find inexpensive fashion in this tony town). You could spend an entire day here and not get bored. Free shows in the park in the middle of Town Square are family-friendly and concerts are held in the evening. Aside from the eclectic mix of retail and restaurants, there's also an 18-screen movie theater, a sprawling children's park, a picnic area and restaurants. Recently, Brio Tuscan Grille opened inside Town Square, as well as California Pizza Kitchen and the Blue Martini bar. (There's usually a one- or two-hour wait to get into the Blue Martini on weekends after 10 p.m., so don't show up too famished.)

Sunday 11 a.m.-8 p.m., Monday-Thursday 10 a.m.-9 p.m., Friday-Saturday 10 a.m.-10 p.m., with bars and restaurants open later.

WYNN LAS VEGAS ESPLANADE

Wynn Las Vegas, 3131 Las Vegas Blvd. S., Las Vegas, 702-770-7000, 888-320-7123; www.wynnlasvegas.com

Since opening in 2005, Wynn has added even more luxury to its list of high-end boutiques. Some of the most exclusive names in haute couture have found a home in Wynn's elegant Esplanade. Owner Steve Wynn first brought high-end shops to Las Vegas when he opened the Bellagio more than a decade ago, and he's continued that trend in his eponymous luxe resort. Shops include Oscar de la Renta, Alexander McQueen, Manolo Blahnik, as well as Vertu, the luxury-phone creator that starlets covet (at up to $20,000 each). For $10 you can wheel around the Ferrari-Maserati dealership to check out some of the most expensive cars in the country. Louis Vuitton makes sure to stock the latest designs of its handbags here, and a walk through Cartier offers an impressive sight of diamonds and jewelry design that you won't soon forget. Even if you're not in Vegas to shop, the Wynn Esplanade is worth the trip for its beauty. Skylights bathe shoppers in soft, natural light in this high-ceilinged posh palace, and stained-glass accents round out the experience. Can't make it down to the Esplanade? The powers that be have thought of that, too, offering a complimentary personal shopping service for guests of Wynn Las Vegas.

Sunday-Thursday 10 a.m.-11 p.m., Friday-Saturday 10 a.m.-midnight.

WELCOME TO NEW MEXICO

NEW MEXICO IS A LAND OF CONTRASTS. ITS HISTORY

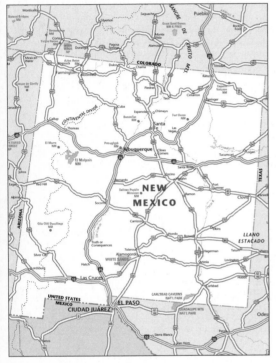

dates back far before the first Spanish explorers arrived in 1540 in search of gold. One day you might be on a Native American reservation, the next you may be taking in the many art galleries and restaurants in Santa Fe.

New Mexico was first occupied by Native Americans and had been a territory of Spain and then Mexico before becoming a state in 1912. Today, it still has the highest percentage of Hispanic Americans and the second-highest population of Native Americans, making for a unique culture.

The landscape ranges from desert in the south to forest and mountain country with clear streams and snow in the north. The Sangre de Cristo (Blood of Christ) Mountains run north and south along the east side of the Rio Grand in the north. There are many national parks in New Mexico and several reservations, which are popular with tourists. During World War II, the government built the Los Alamos Research Center, where the atomic bomb was developed and first detonated in the desert in 1954. There are atomic museums in Albuquerque. The capital, Santa Fe, has a large artistic community. There are many art galleries and museums, including one honoring New Mexico's own Georgia O'Keeffe.

NORTHERN NEW MEXICO

From extraordinary eroded rocks to striking volcanic formations, it's no wonder that the Northern New Mexico landscape inspired artist Georgia O'Keeffe. Aside from its aesthetic value the region also reveals a lot of Native American history, with numerous pueblos, reservations and other noteworthy sites. The most prominent of the cities is the state's largest, Albuquerque. The city celebrates the cultural heritage of groups like the Pueblo, the Anasazi and other tribes. Dry air and plenty of sunshine (more than 75 percent of the time) have earned Albuquerque a reputation as a health center. Adding to that reputation is the Lovelace Medical Center (similar to the Mayo Clinic in Rochester, Minnesota), which gave the first U.S. astronauts their qualifying examinations.

The Navajos gave Farmington the nickname Totah, the meeting place at the convergence of three rivers in the colorful land of the Navajo, Ute, Apache and Pueblo. Once the home of the ancient Anasazi, Farmington is now the largest city in the Four Corners area and supplies much of the energy to the Southwest. From Farmington, you can explore Mesa Verde, Chaco Canyon and the Salmon and Aztec ruins.

Taos is actually three towns: the Spanish-American settlement into which Anglos have infiltrated, which is Taos proper; Taos Pueblo, two and a half miles north; and Ranchos de Taos, four miles south. Many farming communities and fishing resorts can be found in the surrounding mountains. Taos Ski Valley, 19 miles northeast, is a popular spot for winter sports. The town has a few famous residents, including Julia Roberts, Val Kilmer and Donald Rumsfeld.

WHAT TO SEE

ALBUQUERQUE
ALBUQUERQUE BIOLOGICAL PARK
903 10th St. S.W., Albuquerque, 505-764-6200; www.cabq.gov

This biological park consists of the Albuquerque Aquarium, the Rio Grande Botanic Garden and the Rio Grande Zoo. The aquarium features a shark tank, an eel tunnel and a shrimp boat. The botanic garden displays formal walled gardens and a glass conservatory. The zoo exhibits include koalas, polar bears, sea lions and shows.

Admission: zoo/aquarium/botanic garden individually: adults $7, seniors and children 3-12 $3; combo ticket: adults $12, seniors and children 3-12 $5. Daily 9 a.m.-5 p.m., summer weekends 9 a.m.-6 p.m.

ALBUQUERQUE LITTLE THEATRE
224 San Pasquale Ave. S.W., Albuquerque, 505-242-4750; www.albuquerquelittletheatre.org

This historic community theater troupe stages Broadway productions like *Chicago*.
September-May.

ALBUQUERQUE MUSEUM
2000 Mountain Road N.W., Albuquerque, 505-243-7255; www.cabq.gov

Located in a solar-heated building across from the New Mexico Museum of Natural History and Science, this museum displays regional art and history.
Admission: adults $4, seniors $2, children 4-12 $1, children 3 and under free. Free every Sunday 9 a.m.-1 p.m. and the first Wednesday of the month. Tuesday-Sunday 9 a.m.-5 p.m.

HIGHLIGHTS

WHAT ARE SOME OF THE BEST PLACES FOR OUTDOOR FUN IN NEW MEXICO?

EXAMINE THE GROUNDS OF THE BISTI BADLANDS

Check out the unusual geologic formations, large petrified logs and other fossils in this protected wildlife area. It's a scenic spot, so bring your camera to take pictures of the odd-shaped eroded rocks.

STAND AT FOUR CORNERS MONUMENT

If you stand at this monument on the Navajo Reservation, you'll be in Arizona, Colorado, New Mexico and Utah simultaneously. It's the only place in the country common to four states.

EXPLORE THE CASAMERO PUEBLO RUINS

These pueblo ruins date back to A.D. 1000 and are on the World Heritage List. The structure originally was used for social and religious activities to create a sense of community among the families who lived there.

HIKE THE EL MALPAIS NATIONAL MONUMENT AND NATIONAL CONSERVATION AREA

You'll find 376,000 acres of volcanic formations and sandstone canyons at these two areas. Walk through the 17-mile-long lava tubes surrounding the monument and see one of New Mexico's largest freestanding natural arches.

VISIT THE TAOS PUEBLO

This is one of the most famous Native American pueblos. After 1,000 years, people still live here. The pueblo doesn't have electricity or plumbing, but the structure is a spectacular piece of architecture.

CIBOLA NATIONAL FOREST

2113 Osuna Road N.E., Albuquerque, 505-346-3900; www.fs.fed.us

This forest has more than 1.5 million acres and stretches throughout Central New Mexico. The park includes Mount Taylor (11,301 feet), several mountain ranges and four wilderness areas: Sandia Mountain (where you'll see bighorn sheep), Manzano Mountain, Apache Kid and Withington.

FINE ARTS CENTER, UNIVERSITY OF NEW MEXICO

Central Avenue and Stanford Drive, Albuquerque, 505-277-4001; www.unm.edu

The Fine Arts Center houses the University Art Museum, which features more than 23,000 pieces in its collection. It also has a Fine Arts Library, which contains the Southwest Music Archives; the Rodey Theatre; and Popejoy Hall, home of the New Mexico Symphony Orchestra and host of the Best of Broadway International Theatre seasons of plays, dance and music.

Admission: free; $5 donation suggested. Tuesday-Friday 9 a.m.-4 p.m., Sunday 1-4 p.m.

INDIAN PUEBLO CULTURAL CENTER

2401 12th St. N.W., Albuquerque, 505-843-7270, 866-855-7902; www.indianpueblo.org

Owned and operated by the 19 pueblos of New Mexico, the museum offers exhibits that tell the story of the Pueblo culture. The gallery showcases handcrafted art, and you can see Native American dance and craft demonstrations on the weekends.

Admission: adults $6, seniors $5.50, students and children 5-17 $3, children 4 and under free. Daily 9 a.m.-5 p.m.

MUSEUM OF GEOLOGY AND INSTITUTE OF METEORITICS METEORITE MUSEUM

Northrop Hall, 200 Yale Blvd. N.E., Albuquerque, 505-277-4204

The Museum of Geology contains numerous samples of ancient plants, minerals, rocks and animals while the meteorite museum has a major collection of more than 550 meteorites.

Admission: free. Geology Museum: Monday-Friday 7:30 a.m.-noon, 1-4:30 p.m. Meteorite Museum: Monday-Friday 9 a.m.-4 p.m.

NATIONAL ATOMIC MUSEUM

1905 Mountain Road N.W., Albuquerque, 505-245-2137; www.atomicmuseum.com

This nuclear energy science center, the nation's only such museum, features exhibits depicting the history of the atomic age, including the Manhattan Project, the Cold War and the development of nuclear medicine. See replicas of Little Boy and Fat Man, the world's first two atomic weapons deployed in Japan in World War II, as well as B-52 and B-29 aircraft. Guided tours and audiovisual presentations are offered.

Admission: adults $8, seniors and children 6-17 $7, military personnel $6, children 5 and under free. Daily 9 a.m.-5 p.m.

NEW MEXICO MUSEUM OF NATURAL HISTORY AND SCIENCE

1801 Mountain Road N.W., Albuquerque, 505-841-2800; www.museums.state.nm.us

Those interested in dinosaurs, fossils and volcanoes will love this museum, with exhibits on botany, geology, paleontology and zoology. The LodeStar Astronomy Center gives you a view of the heavens in its observatory.

Admission: adults $7, seniors $6, children $4. Daily 9 a.m.-5 p.m.

NEW MEXICO SYMPHONY ORCHESTRA

University of New Mexico, Popejoy Hall, 4407 Menaul Blvd., Albuquerque, 505-881-9590, 800-251-6676; www.nmso.org

The NMSO tackles the work of traditional classical musicians like Dvořák and some not-so-traditional artists like Queen.

September-May.

OLD TOWN

Old Town and Romero roads, Albuquerque

The original settlement is one block north of Central Avenue, the city's main street, at Rio Grande Boulevard. Old Town Plaza retains a lovely Spanish flavor with many interesting shops and restaurants.

PETROGLYPH NATIONAL MONUMENT

6001 Unser Blvd., Albuquerque, 505-899-0205; www.nps.gov

This park contains concentrated groups of rock drawings that experts believe ancestors of the Pueblo carved on lava formations. Three hiking trails wind along the 17-mile escarpment.

Daily 8 a.m.-5 p.m.

RIO GRANDE NATURE CENTER STATE PARK

2901 Candelaria Road N.W., Albuquerque, 505-344-7240; www.emnrd.state.nm.us

The highlight here is a glass-enclosed observation room overlooking a 3-acre pond that is home to birds and other wildlife. There are also interpretive displays on the wildlife of the bosque (cottonwood groves) along the Rio Grande and two miles of nature trails.

Daily 8 a.m.-5 p.m.

RIO GRANDE ZOO

903 10th St. S.W., Albuquerque, 505-764-6200; www.cabq.gov

Visit more than 1,200 exotic animals, including white tigers, at this 64-acre park.

Daily 9 a.m.-5 p.m., summer weekends 9 a.m.-6 p.m.

SANDIA PEAK AERIAL TRAMWAY

Albuquerque, 505-856-7325; www.sandiapeak.com

The tram travels almost three miles up the west slope of the Sandia Mountains to 10,378 feet, with amazing 11,000-square-mile views. It also has a hiking trail, a restaurant at the summit and a Mexican grill at the base.

Memorial Day-Labor Day, daily 9 a.m.-9 p.m.; shorter hours rest of year; closed two weeks in April and two weeks in October.

SANDIA PEAK TRAMWAY SKI AREA

Albuquerque, in Cibola National Forest, Crest Scenic Byway, Sandia Mountains, 505-856-7325; www.sandiapeak.com

The ski area has four double chairlifts, a surface lift, a patrol, a school, rentals and snowmaking. An aerial tramway on the west side of the mountain meets lifts at the top. The longest run is more than two miles with a vertical drop of 1,700 feet.

Mid-December-March, daily. Chairlift also operates July-Labor Day, Friday-Sunday.

TELEPHONE PIONEER MUSEUM
110 Fourth St. N.W., Albuquerque, 505-842-2937

Displays trace the development of the telephone from its 1876 beginnings to the present-day smart phone. You can check out more than 400 types of telephones, plus switchboards, early equipment and old telephone directories.

Admission: adults $2, children 12 and under $1. Monday, Wednesday, Friday 10 a.m.-2 p.m.

FARMINGTON
BISTI BADLANDS
Highway 371, Farmington, 505-599-8900

A federally protected wilderness area of strange geologic formations, large petrified logs and other fossils are scattered among a few scenic landforms. No vehicles are permitted beyond the boundary.

FOUR CORNERS MONUMENT
Navajo Reservation, Farmington, 64 miles northwest via Highway 64, Highway 504, Highway 160, 928-871-6647; www.navajonationparks.org

This is the only point in the country common to four states: Arizona, Colorado, New Mexico and Utah.

GRANTS
EL MALPAIS NATIONAL MONUMENT & NATIONAL CONSERVATION AREA
123 E. Roosevelt Ave., Grants, 505-783-4774; www.nps.gov

These two areas total 376,000 acres of volcanic formations and sandstone canyons. The monument features splatter cones and a 17-mile-long system of lava tubes. The conservation area, which surrounds the monument, includes La Ventana Natural Arch, one of the state's largest freestanding natural arches; Cebolla and West Malpais wildernesses; and numerous Anasazi ruins. The Sandstone Bluffs Overlook, off Highway 117, offers an excellent view of the lava-filled valley and surrounding area. Facilities include hiking, bicycling, scenic drives, primitive camping (acquire a Backcountry Permit at the information center or ranger station). Most of the lava tubes are accessible only by hiking trails; check with the information center in Grants before attempting any hikes. The information center and visitor facility are on Highway 117.
Daily.

ICE CAVE AND BANDERA VOLCANO
Highway 53, 28 miles southwest of Grants, 888-423-2283; www.icecaves.com

See an example of volcanic activity and hike on lava trails. The ice cave is part of a collapsed lava tube. The temperature never rises above 31 F, but reflected sunlight creates beautiful scenery. A historic trading post displays and sells artifacts and Native American artwork.
Daily 8 a.m.-one hour before sunset.

NEW MEXICO MINING MUSEUM
100 N. Iron Ave., Grants, 505-287-4802, 800-748-2142; www.grants.org

This is the only underground uranium mining museum in the world. It also carries Native American artifacts and relics as well as a native mineral display.
Admission: adults $3, seniors and children 7-18 $2, children 6 and under free. Monday-Saturday 9 a.m.-4 p.m.

LOS ALAMOS
BRADBURY SCIENCE MUSEUM
1350 Central Ave., Los Alamos, 505-667-4444; www.lanl.gov

The science museum displays artifacts relating to the history of the laboratory and the atomic bomb. You'll find exhibits on modern nuclear weapons, life sciences, materials sciences, computers, particle accelerators as well as geothermal, fusion and fission energy sources.

Admission: free. Tuesday-Saturday 10 a.m.-5 p.m, Sunday-Monday 1-5 p.m.

PAJARITO MOUNTAIN SKI AREA
397 Camp May Road, Los Alamos, 505-662-5725; www.skipajarito.com

Despite being a small resort (280 acres), Pajarito offers some excellent and challenging terrain, making it a well-kept secret for local ski buffs.

Friday-Sunday 9 a.m.-4 p.m.

SANTA ROSA
BILLY THE KID MUSEUM
1435 E. Sumner Ave., Fort Sumner, 575-355-2380; www.billythekidmuseumfortsumner.com

This museum is dedicated to the famous Wild West outlaw Billy the Kid. It contains 60,000 items, including relics of the Old West, Billy the Kid and Old Fort Sumner.

Admission: adults $5, seniors $4, children $3, children under 7 free. May 15-October 1, daily 8.30 a.m.-5 p.m.; October 1-May 15, Monday-Saturday 8:30 a.m.-5 p.m.

BLUE HOLE
Blue Hole Road, Santa Rosa; www.santarosanm.org

This clear blue lake set in a rock setting is fed by a natural artesian spring. Many people enjoy scuba diving here.

TAOS
CARSON NATIONAL FOREST
208 Cruz Alta Road, Taos, 575-758-6200; www.fs.fed.us

This forest occupies 1 million acres and includes Wheeler Peak, New Mexico's highest mountain at 13,161 feet. Lots of small mountain lakes and streams provide good fishing. There's also hunting, hiking, winter sports, picnicking and camping.

Daily.

GOVERNOR BENT HOUSE MUSEUM AND GALLERY
117 Bent St., Taos, 505-758-2376; www.laplaza.org

Visit the home of New Mexico's first American territorial governor (and the scene of his death in 1847). It includes Bent family possessions, Native American artifacts and Western American art.

Admission: adults $1, children $.50. Summer, daily 9 a.m.-5 p.m.; winter, daily 10 a.m.-4 p.m.

HARWOOD MUSEUM OF ART
238 Ledoux St., Taos, 505-758-9826; www.harwoodmuseum.org

Founded in 1923, this museum features paintings, drawings, prints, sculptures and photographs by artists of Taos from 1800 to the present.

Admission: adults $8, seniors and students $7, children free. Tuesday-Saturday 10 a.m.-5 p.m., Sunday noon-5 p.m.

KIT CARSON HOME AND MUSEUM

113 Kit Carson Road, Taos, 505-758-4945; www.kitcarsonroad.com/museum

The restored 1825 home of the famous frontiersman showcases artifacts, including a gun exhibit.

Admission: adults $4, seniors $4, children 13-18 $3, children 6-12 $2, children 5 and under free. Summer: daily 9 a.m.-5 p.m., call for winter hours.

KIT CARSON PARK

211 Paseo del Pueblo Norte, Taos, 575-758-8234

This 25-acre park includes a bicycle and walking path, picnic tables, a playground and a sand volleyball pit. No camping is allowed. The graves of Kit Carson and his family are also here.

ORILLA VERDE RECREATION AREA

Highway 570 and Highway 68, Taos, 505-758-8851; www.blm.gov

This park runs along the banks of the Rio Grande, offering some of the finest trout fishing in the state as well as white-water rafting. Enjoy hiking, picnicking and spectacular views.

Daily.

RANCHOS DE TAOS

60 Ranchos Plaza Road, Taos, 575-758-2754

This adobe-housed farming and ranching center has one of the most beautiful churches in the Southwest—the San Francisco de Asis Church. Its huge buttresses and twin bell towers echo the beauty of its interior.

Monday-Saturday 9 a.m.-4 p.m.

SIPAPU SKI & SUMMER RESORT

Highway 518, three miles west of Tres Ritos, 800-587-2240; www.sipapunm.com

The resort has two triple chairlifts, two Pomalifts, a patrol, a school, rentals and snowmaking. Of the 39 runs, the longest is two miles with a vertical drop of 1,055 feet.

Mid-December-March, daily.

TAOS PUEBLO

Taos, 505-758-1028; www.taospueblo.com

With a full-time population of 150, this is one of the most famous Native American pueblos and has been continuously inhabited for more than 1,000 years. Within the pueblo is a double apartment house. The north and south buildings, separated by a river, are five stories tall and form a unique communal dwelling. Small buildings and corrals are scattered around these impressive architectural masterpieces. The residents here live without modern utilities, such as electricity and plumbing, and get their drinking water from the river. The people are independent, conservative and devout in their religious observances. There are fees for parking and photography permits. In order to photograph individual Native Americans, you must get their consent first.

Daily 8 a.m.-4 p.m.; closed for special occasions in spring.

TAOS SKI VALLEY

103A Suton Place, Taos Ski Valley, 866-968-7386; www.skitaos.org
The ski area has 12 chairlifts, two surface lifts, a patrol, a school, rentals, a cafeteria, restaurants, a bar, a nursery and lodges. The longest run is more than four miles with a vertical drop 2,612 feet.
November-April, daily.

WHERE TO STAY

ALBUQUERQUE

★★★HILTON ALBUQUERQUE

1901 University Blvd. N.E., Albuquerque, 505-884-2500, 800-445-8667; www.hilton.com
With its arched doorways, Native American rugs and local art, this hotel on 14 acres near the university fits right in among its surroundings. The hotel includes indoor and outdoor heated pools, a sauna and lighted tennis courts. Rooms feature sliding glass doors and balconies with great views of the high desert.
261 rooms. Restaurant, bar. Business center. Fitness center. Pets accepted. Pool. $61-150

★★★HOTEL ALBUQUERQUE AT OLD TOWN

800 Rio Grande Blvd. N.W., Albuquerque, 505-843-6300, 800-237-2133; www.hhandr.com
With its large, open lobby and tiled floors, this hotel offers a casual yet elegant environment. Located in historic Old Town across from the New Mexico Museum of Natural History, it is close to more than 200 specialty stores. All guest rooms feature furniture made by local artists.
188 rooms. Restaurant, bar. Business center. Fitness center. Pool. Spa. Pets accepted. $61-150

★★★HYATT REGENCY ALBUQUERQUE

330 Tijeras N.W., Albuquerque, 505-842-1234, 800-233-1234; www.hyatt.com
Adjacent to the convention center, this 22-story tower is centrally located near Old Town and the Rio Grande Zoo and is only five miles from the airport. One of the city's newest high-rise hotels, the property offers a health club, sauna and outdoor pool. Business rooms include separate work areas and dual line phones. All rooms have Southwestern décor and views of the city or mountains.
395 rooms. Restaurant, bar. Business center. Fitness center. Pool. $151-250

ESPAÑOLA

★★★RANCHO DE SAN JUAN COUNTRY INN

Highway 285, Española, 505-753-6818; www.ranchodesanjuan.com

Situated between Taos and Santa Fe, this inn is spread over 225 scenic acres. Designed in the Spanish tradition, the décor is both rustic and refined with wildflower-filled courtyards, exposed beams, tile floors and Southwestern art and antiques. Rooms feature views of the mountains and river valley, as well as wood-burning fireplaces.

17 rooms. Restaurant. Spa. No children under 8 years. $151-250

TAOS

★★★EL MONTE SAGRADO

317 Kit Carson Road, Taos, 505-758-3502, 800-828-8264; www.elmontesagrado.com

This unique resort, tucked away in alluring Taos, celebrates the natural beauty of New Mexico while highlighting its rich Native American heritage. The themed guestrooms and suites, which display local and international artwork, are seductive retreats. Taos, well known for its world-class skiing, is a year-round playground, offering everything from rock climbing and fly-fishing to llama trekking and mountain biking. The onsite spa focuses on renewal of body and mind. The award-winning De La Tierra restaurant is a feast for the eyes and the palate.

36 rooms. Restaurant, bar. Business center. Fitness center. Spa. Pool. $351 and up

★★★THE HISTORIC TAOS INN

125 Paseo Del Pueblo Norte, Taos, 505-758-2233, 888-518-8267; www.taosinn.com

The likes of Greta Garbo, D.H. Lawrence and Robert Redford have hung out at this inn. It offers a comfortable Old West atmosphere and modern amenities. The grounds include an outdoor heated pool and greenhouse whirlpool. The unique guest rooms feature Southwestern décor and many offer kiva fireplaces. Be sure to dine at the acclaimed Doc Martin's Restaurant for delicious regional contemporary American cuisine.

44 rooms. Restaurant, bar. Pool. $61-150

★★★SAGEBRUSH INN

1508 Paseo Del Pueblo Sur, Taos, 505-758-2254, 800-428-3626; www.sagebrushinn.com

Built in 1929, this 100-room adobe inn houses a large collection of paintings, Native American rugs and other regional art. The most recent addition, an 18,000-square-foot conference center, features hand-hewn vigas and fireplaces. Visitors will enjoy the outdoor pool and two whirlpools. Guest rooms have handmade furniture.

100 rooms. Restaurant, bar. Complimentary breakfast. Pets accepted. Pool. $61-150

WHERE TO EAT

ALBUQUERQUE

★★★ARTICHOKE CAFÉ

424 Central St., Albuquerque, 505-243-0200; www.artichokecafe.com

This pleasant eatery, which has tables set with fresh flowers, serves a mix of French, Italian and creative American cuisine. Dishes include steamed

WHAT ARE
THE BEST
RESTAURANTS
SERVING
SOUTHWESTERN
CUISINE IN
NORTHERN NEW
MEXICO?

De la Tierra:

This restaurant avoids Southwestern kitsch in favor of Southwestern sleek with wrought-iron chandeliers and tapestry-covered chairs. It serves dishes with regional flair like bison filet with blue corn posole and warm sopapillas.

Doc Martin's:

At Doc Martin's, you'll find unusual regional fare that you won't encounter elsewhere, like rattlesnake sausage. If you're not an adventurous eater, stick with the tasty chile rellenos with salsa fresca, pumpkin seeds and goat cheese cream.

artichokes with three dipping sauces, or housemade pumpkin ravioli and scallops wrapped in prosciutto. Be sure to order some vino with your meal; the restaurant has an excellent wine program.

American. Lunch, dinner. Reservations recommended. $16-35

★★★SCALO NOB HILL

3500 Central Ave. S.E., Albuquerque, 505-255-8781; www.scalonobhill.com

Chef Steven Lemon has taken over the kitchen of this more than 20-year-old Italian grill that offers dining areas on several levels. From the wood-fired pizzas, like the basil-pesto pie with smoked chicken and roasted peppers, to the freshly made pastas, like the lobster ravioli with herb-mascarpone cheese, Lemon relies on organic, seasonal local ingredients. Classic Italian desserts such as tiramisu and bread pudding make for a sweet end to a meal.

American. Lunch, dinner. Closed Monday. Reservations recommended. Outdoor seating. Bar. $16-35

ESPAÑOLA

★★★RANCHO DE SAN JUAN

Highway 285, Española, 505-753-6818; www.ranchodesanjuan.com

The elegant, cheerful dining room of this inn overlooks the Ojo Caliente River Valley and the Jemez Mountains. The tranquil setting is an attractive backdrop for chef/owner John Johnson's Southwest-inspired international cuisine, including dishes such as roasted coriander quail and coconut-crusted white shrimp.

International. Dinner. Closed Sunday-Monday. Reservations recommended. Outdoor seating. Bar. $36-85

TAOS

★★★DE LA TIERRA

El Monte Sagrado, 317 Kit Carson Road, Taos, 505-758-3502, 800-828-8267; www.elmontesagrado.com

From its unique décor to its Southwestern cuisine, De la Tierra, located inside Taos' El Monte Sagrado resort, practically begs for special occasions. Towering ceilings capped by an enormous wrought-iron chandelier and high-backed, tapestry-covered chairs make this dining room romantic. Chef John Cox focuses on creative international farm-to-table dishes. Everything from roasted bison filet with blue corn posole and warm sopapillas; and lamb with barbecued eggplant, goat cheese timbale, arugula, olives and lemon is given his unique stamp.

Southwestern, International. Dinner. Reservations recommended. $36-85

★★★DOC MARTIN'S
The Historic Taos Inn, 125 Paseo Del Pueblo, Taos, 505-758-1977; www.taosinn.com

Chef Zippy White serves organic Southwestern cuisine in an adobe setting. Specialties include grilled shrimp on blue corn cakes with green onion and pineapple firecracker sauce; the chef's mixed grill of rattlesnake sausage, buffalo steak, whole quail and ancho chile sauce; and Doc's classic chile rellenos with green chile, salsa fresca, pumpkin seeds and goat cheese cream. The wine list, with more than 400 selections, is one of the best in the area.

American, Southwestern. Breakfast, lunch, dinner, Saturday-Sunday brunch. Reservations recommended. Outdoor seating. Children's menu. Bar. $36-85

★★★LAMBERT'S OF TAOS
309 Paseo Del Pueblo Sur, Taos, 505-758-1009; www.lambertsoftaos.com

Zeke and Tina Lambert came to Taos years ago on their honeymoon and never left. Instead, they opened this restaurant, which serves contemporary cuisine. The produce is local when possible and all the sauces are made from scratch. Dishes include breaded Kurobuta pork cutlet with chipotle cream sauce, braised red cabbage and apples with smashed sweet potatoes; and grilled filet mignon with horseradish crème, steak fries and grilled asparagus. The extensive wine list is primarily from California.

Contemporary American. Dinner. Reservations recommended. Outdoor seating. Children's menu. Bar. $36-85

SANTA FE

This picturesque city, the oldest capital in the United States, is set at the base of the Sangre de Cristo Mountains. A few miles south, these mountains taper down from a height of 13,000 feet to a rolling plain, marking the end of the North American Rockies. Because of the altitude, the climate is cool and bracing. There's much to do and see here all year.

In addition to its own attractions, Santa Fe is also the center of a colorful area, which can be reached by car. The Pueblos, farmers for centuries, are also extremely gifted craftworkers and painters. Their pottery, basketry and jewelry are especially beautiful. At various times during the year, especially on the saint's day of their particular pueblo, they present dramatic ceremonial dances. Visitors are usually welcome.

WHAT TO SEE

ATALAYA MOUNTAIN HIKING TRAIL
St. John's College, 1160 Camino Cruz Blanca, Santa Fe

The Atalaya Mountain Trail, accessible from the parking lot at St. John's College, is one of the most popular and easily accessible hiking trails in Santa Fe. Hikers have the option of taking the longer route (Trail 174), which is approximately seven miles round-trip, or parking further up near the Ponderosa Ridge development and doing a 4.6-mile loop (Trail 170). Both trails eventually join and take you toward the top of Atalaya Mountain, a 9,121-foot peak. The first few miles of the trail are relatively easy, but it becomes increasingly steep and strenuous as you near the summit, which offers great views of the Rio Grande valley and the city below.

HIGHLIGHTS

WHAT ARE SANTA FE'S TOP MUSEUMS?

GEORGIA O'KEEFFE MUSEUM

Brilliant painter Georgia O'Keeffe is synonymous with the New Mexico landscape. This museum houses the world's largest collection of her artwork. But it also shines a light on the American Modernism movement.

MUSEUM OF INTERNATIONAL FOLK ART

With a collection of more than 130,000 pieces, this museum has given itself the title of world's largest folk museum dedicated to the study of traditional cultural art. You'll find everything from toys to religious art among the offerings.

WHEELWRIGHT MUSEUM

This museum was created to preserve Navajo Nation's art and traditions. While those still remain a priority, the Wheelright has expanded its mission to host exhibits from Native American artists from tribes all over North America.

CANYON ROAD TOUR
Canyon Road, Santa Fe

Many artists live on this thoroughfare, and there is no better way to savor the unique character of Santa Fe than to travel along its narrow, picturesque old streets, which includes the famous Camino del Monte Sol. Stop in the Cristo Rey Church, the largest adobe structure in the U.S., with beautiful ancient stone reredos (altar screens).

Monday-Friday.

CATHEDRAL OF ST. FRANCIS
Santa Fe Plaza, 231 Cathedral Place, Santa Fe, 505-982-5619

This French Romanesque cathedral was built in 1869 under the direction of Archbishop Jean-Baptiste Lamy, the first archbishop of Sante Fe (the novel *Death Comes for the Archbishop* is based on his life). Also here is La Conquistadora Chapel, said to be the country's oldest shrine to the Virgin Mary. Tours are available in the summer.

Daily 8 a.m.-5:45 p.m., except during Mass.

CROSS OF THE MARTYRS

Paseo de la Loma, 545 Canyon Road, Santa Fe, 505-983-2567; www.historicsantafe.org

This large, hilltop cross weighs 76 tons, stands 25 feet tall and honors the memory of more than 20 Franciscan priests and numerous Spanish colonists who were killed during the 1680 Pueblo Revolt against Spanish dominion. Dedicated in 1920, this cross shouldn't be confused with the newer one at nearby Fort Marcy Park. Vistas from the old cross include those of the Sangre de Cristos mountain range immediately northeast, the Jemez about 40 miles west and the Sandias, 50 miles south near Albuquerque.

EL RANCHO DE LAS GOLONDRINAS

334 Los Pinos Road, Santa Fe, 505-471-2261; www.golondrinas.org

This living history museum is set in a 200-acre rural valley and depicts Spanish-colonial life in New Mexico from 1700 through 1900. It was once a stop on El Camino Real and is one of the most historic ranches in the Southwest. Original colonial buildings date from the 18th century. Special festivals offer a glimpse of the music, dance, clothing, crafts and celebrations of Spanish-colonial New Mexico. *June-September, Wednesday-Sunday 10 a.m.-4 p.m.*

GEORGIA O'KEEFFE MUSEUM

217 Johnson St., Santa Fe, 505-946-1000; www.okeeffemuseum.org

One of the most important American artists of the 20th century, Georgia O'Keeffe lived and worked at Ghost Ranch near Abiqui for much of her career, drawing inspiration from the colors and forms of the surrounding desert environment. This museum houses the world's largest permanent collection of her artwork and is also dedicated to the study of American Modernism, displaying special exhibits of many of her contemporaries.

Admission: adults $10, seniors and students $8, children 18 and under free. First Friday of the month 5-8 p.m. free. November-June, Monday-Tuesday, Thursday, Saturday-Sunday 10 a.m.-5 p.m., Friday 10 a.m.-8 p.m.; daily rest of year.

HYDE MEMORIAL STATE PARK

740 Hyde Park Road, Santa Fe, 505-983-7175; www.emnrd.state.nm.us

Perched 8,500 feet up in the Sangre de Cristo Mountains near the Santa Fe Ski Basin, this state park serves as a base camp for backpackers and skiers in the Santa Fe National Forests. You can do cross-country skiing, picnicking and camping here.

HYDE PARK HIKING/BIKING TRAILS

Hyde Memorial State Park, Santa Fe; www.emnrd.state.nm.us

One of the closest hiking opportunities to Santa Fe is available in the Hyde Park area on the road to the ski basin. From the Hyde Park parking lot, you can access a loop covering three different trails. It offers easy hiking that's popular with dog walkers and locals on weekends. The loop consists of switchbacks, moderate grades and creek crossings and has good views of the mixed conifer forest. If you come during the fall, you can view the spectacularly colorful changing of the aspen leaves. Start with the common trailhead at the far side of the parking lot. Look for the Borrego Trail (150), Bear Wallow Trail (182) and Winsor Trail (254) markings. A loop covering all three is about four miles long.

INSTITUTE OF AMERICAN INDIAN ARTS MUSEUM

108 Cathedral Place, Santa Fe, 505-983-8900; www.iaiancad.org

The Institute of American Indian Arts, established in 1962, runs a college in south Santa Fe in addition to a museum just off the Plaza. The museum is the only one in the country dedicated solely to collecting and exhibiting contemporary Native American art, much of it produced by the staff and faculty of the college.

June-September, daily 9 a.m.-5 p.m.; October-May, daily 10 a.m.-5 p.m.

KOKOPELLI RAFTING ADVENTURES

551 W. Cordova Road, Santa Fe, 505-983-3734, 800-879-9035; www.kokopelliraft.com

Kokopelli Rafting offers a full range of white-water rafting trips to the Rio Grande and Rio Chama rivers, as well as kayaking trips to Cochiti and Abiqui lakes and Big Bend National Park in Texas. Excursions include half-day, full-day, overnight and two- to eight-day wilderness expeditions. Transportation from Santa Fe is included.

April-September.

LENSIC PERFORMING ARTS CENTER

211 W. San Francisco St., Santa Fe, 505-988-1234; www.lensic.com

The Lensic Theater is one of Santa Fe's historical and architectural gems, reopened after a full restoration in 2001. The structure was first built in 1931 in a Moorish/Spanish Renaissance style and has always been Santa Fe's premier theater space, having played host to celebrities such as Roy Rogers and Judy Garland over the years. Since reopening, it has provided a constantly changing schedule of theater, symphony and performing arts events.

LORETTO CHAPEL

207 Old Santa Fe Trail, Santa Fe, 505-982-0092; www.lorettochapel.com

Modeled after St. Chapelle Cathedral in Paris, this chapel, built in 1873, was the first Gothic building created west of the Mississippi. The chapel itself is not particularly impressive, but what draws countless tourists is the miraculous stairway, a two-story spiral wooden staircase made without any nails or central supports that seems to defy engineering logic.

Summer, Monday-Saturday 9 a.m.-6 p.m., Sunday 10:30 a.m.-5 p.m.; winter, Monday-Saturday 9 a.m.-5 p.m., Sunday 10:30 a.m.-5 p.m.

MUSEUM OF INDIAN ARTS AND CULTURE

710 Camino Lejo, Santa Fe, 505-476-1250; www.indianartsandculture.org

When the Spanish arrived in the Southwest in the 16th century, they found many sprawling towns and villages, which they referred to as pueblos, a name that is still used to identify Native American communities here. The Museum of Indian Arts and Culture houses an extensive collection of historic and contemporary Pueblo art from throughout the Southwest. The highlight is an excellent interpretive section where you can encounter Pueblo cultures from the viewpoint and narrative of modern-day natives and exhibit designers. The museum itself is in a large adobe-style building that blends architecturally into the surroundings and also showcases many outstanding examples of Pueblo textiles, pottery, jewelry, contemporary paintings and other rotating exhibits.

Admission: New Mexico residents $6 (Sunday free), $9 non-residents, children 16 and under free. Labor Day-Memorial Day, Tuesday-Sunday 10 a.m.-5 p.m.; Memorial Day-Labor Day, daily 10 a.m.-5 p.m.

MUSEUM OF INTERNATIONAL FOLK ART
706 Camino Lejo, Santa Fe, 505-476-1200; www.moifa.org

The Museum of International Folk Art, first opened in 1953, contains more than 130,000 objects, billing itself as the world's largest folk museum dedicated to the study of traditional cultural art. Much of the massive collection was acquired when the late Italian immigrant and architect/designer Alexander Girard donated his 106,000-object collection of toys, figurines, figurative ceramics, miniatures and religious/ceremonial art, which he had collected from more than 100 countries around the world. This is a rich museum experience and can easily take several hours to explore. Two museum shops offer a wide variety of folk-oriented books, clothing and jewelry from which to choose so that you can start your own collection at home.

Admission: New Mexico residents $6 (Sunday free), $9 non-residents, children 16 and under free. Labor Day-Memorial Day, Tuesday-Sunday 10 a.m.-5 p.m.; Memorial Day-Labor Day, daily 10 a.m.-5 p.m.

MUSEUM OF SPANISH COLONIAL ART
750 Camino Lejo, Santa Fe, 505-982-2226; www.spanishcolonial.org

This small museum, housed in a building designed in 1930 by famous local architect John Gaw Meem, holds some 3,000 objects showcasing traditional Hispanic art in New Mexico dating from conquest to present day. The collection includes many early works in wood, tin and other local materials, as well as numerous works by contemporary New Mexican artists.

Admission: adults $8, residents $4, children 16 and under free. Labor Day-Memorial Day, Tuesday-Sunday 10 a.m.-5 p.m.; Memorial Day-Labor Day, daily 10 a.m.-5 p.m.

NEW MEXICO MUSEUM OF ART
107 W. Palace Ave., Santa Fe, 505-476-5072; www.museumofnewmexico.org

Designed by Isaac Hamilton Rapp in 1917, this facility is one of Santa Fe's earliest Pueblo revival structures and its oldest art museum. It contains more than 20,000 holdings, with an emphasis on Southwestern regional art and the artists of Santa Fe and Taos from the early 20th century. The St. Francis Auditorium inside the museum also presents lectures, musical events, plays and various other performances.

Admission: New Mexico residents $6 (Sunday free), $9 non-residents, children 16 and under free. Friday 5-8 p.m. free. Labor Day-Memorial Day, Tuesday-Sunday 10 a.m.-5 p.m.; Memorial Day-Labor Day, daily 10 a.m.-5 p.m.

PALACE OF THE GOVERNORS
105 Palace Ave., Santa Fe, 505-476-5100; www.palaceofthegovernors.org

Built in 1610, this is the oldest public building in continuous use in the U.S. It was the seat of government in New Mexico for more than 300 years. Lew Wallace, governor of the territory (1878-1881), wrote part of *Ben Hur* here in 1880. It is now a major museum of Southwestern history. The Palace, Museum of Fine Arts, Museum of Indian Arts and Culture and Museum of International Folk Art all make up the Museum of New Mexico. Tours are available.

Admission: New Mexico residents $6 (Sunday free), $9 non-residents, children 16 and under free. Friday 5-8 p.m. free. Labor Day-Memorial Day, Tuesday-Sunday 10 a.m.-5 p.m.; Memorial Day-Labor Day, daily 10 a.m.-5 p.m.

PLAZA

100 Old Santa Fe Trail, Santa Fe

The Santa Fe Plaza, steeped in a rich history, has been a focal point for commerce and social activities in the city since the early 17th century. The area is marked by a central tree-lined park surrounded by some of Santa Fe's most important historical landmarks, many of which hail from Spanish-colonial times. The most important landmark is the Palace of the Governors. Native American artists from nearby pueblos sell handmade artwork in front of the Palace and various museums, shops and dining establishments surround the Plaza, making it the top tourist destination in Santa Fe. Numerous festivals and activities are held here throughout the year.

SAN ILDEFONSO PUEBLO

Santa Fe, 505-455-2273; www.indianpueblo.org

This pueblo is famous for its beautiful surroundings and its black, red and polychrome pottery made famous by Maria Poveka Martinez. Various festivals take place here throughout the year. The circular structure with the staircase leading up to its rim is a kiva, or ceremonial chamber. There are two shops in the pueblo plaza and a tribal museum adjoins the governor's office.

Admission: $4 per person(for groups of 10 or more); reservations required.

SAN MIGUEL MISSION

401 Old Santa Fe Trail, Santa Fe, 505-983-3974

Built in the early 1600s, this is the oldest church in the U.S. still in use. Construction was overseen by Fray Alonso de Benavidez, along with a group of Tlaxcala Indians from Mexico, who did most of the work. The original adobe still remains beneath the stucco walls and the interior has been restored along with Santa Fe's oldest wooden reredos (altar screens). Church services are held on Sundays.

Sunday 1-4:30 p.m.; summer, Monday-Saturday 9 a.m.-4:30 p.m.; winter, Monday-Saturday 10 a.m.-4 p.m.

SANTA FE CHILDREN'S MUSEUM

1050 Old Pecos Trail, Santa Fe, 505-989-8359; www.santafechildrensmuseum.org

The hands-on exhibits invite kids to make magnetic structures, route water streams, create paintings, illustrate cartoon movies, discover plants on a greenhouse scavenger hunt, scale an 18-foot-high climbing wall, use an old-fashioned pitcher pump and weave beads and fabric on a loom. Local artists and scientists make appearances.

Admission: New Mexico residents $5, non-residents $9; residents $2, non-residents $5 on Sunday. Wednesday, Saturday 10 a.m.-5 p.m., Thursday noon-8 p.m., Friday 9 a.m.-5 p.m., Sunday noon-5 p.m.

SANTA FE NATIONAL FOREST

1474 Rodeo Road, Santa Fe, 505-438-7840; www.fs.fed.us

This forest covers more than 1.5 million acres. Fishing is excellent in the Pecos and Jemez rivers and tributary streams, and hiking trails are close to unusual geologic formations. You'll find hot springs in the Jemez Mountains. Four wilderness areas within the forest total more than 300,000 acres. Campgrounds are provided by the Forest Service at more than 40 locations.

SANTA FE RAFTING COMPANY

1000 Cerrillos Road, Santa Fe, 505-988-4914, 888-988-4914; www.santaferafting.com

The Rio Grande and Rio Chama rivers north of Santa Fe provide excellent opportunities for river running and white-water rafting. Santa Fe Rafting Company offers several rafting trips, including half-day, full-day and multi-day camping excursions, some of which include a boxed lunch. The biggest rapids are found on the Taos Box full-day trip, open to anyone over age 12. All trips include roundtrip transportation from Santa Fe.

April-September.

SHIDONI BRONZE FOUNDRY AND GALLERY

1508 Bishop's Lodge Road, Santa Fe, 505-988-8001; www.shidoni.com

A fantastic resource for art collectors and sculptors, Shidoni consists of a bronze foundry, art gallery and outdoor sculpture garden set in an 8-acre apple orchard. Artists from around the country come to work at Shidoni's 14,000-square-foot foundry, open to the public for self-guided tours. Explore the lovely sculpture garden during daylight or shop for works of bronze and metal in the adjacent gallery.

Gallery: Monday-Saturday 9 a.m.-5 p.m. Foundry: Monday-Friday noon-1 p.m., Saturday 9 a.m.-5 p.m.

SKI SANTA FE

2209 Brothers Road, Santa Fe, 505-982-4429; www.skisantafe.com

World-class skiing and snowboarding in the majestic Sangre de Cristo Mountains is only a 20-minute drive from the downtown Santa Fe Plaza. Ski Santa Fe is a family-owned resort catering to skiers and snowboarders of all levels. In addition to great views of the city, the 12,075-foot summit offers six lifts and 67 runs (20 percent easy, 40 percent more difficult, 40 percent most difficult), with a total of 660 acres of terrain. The longest run is three miles and the mountain offers a vertical drop of 1,725 feet. The average yearly snowfall is 225 inches. A PSIA-certified ski school offers group and private lessons for adults and children and there are restaurants, rental shops and a clothing boutique onsite. The Chipmunk Corner offers activities and lessons for children ages 4-9.

Late November-early April, daily.

TEN THOUSAND WAVES

3451, Hyde Park Road, Santa Fe, 505-982-9304; www.tenthousandwaves.com

This exquisite Japanese-themed spa and bathhouse is a genuine treat. Located in a unique Zen-like setting in the Sangre de Cristo Mountains, Ten Thousand Waves offers soothing hot tubs, massages, facials, herbal wraps and other treatments. Services include coed public hot tubs (where clothing is optional before 8:15 p.m.), a women-only tub, secluded private tubs and large private tubs that can accommodate up to 20. All the tubs are clean and chlorine-free, and amenities such as kimonos, towels, sandals, lotion and lockers are provided for you. Be sure to call ahead for reservations, especially for massage services.

TURQUOISE TRAIL
Highway 14, Santa Fe; www.turquoisetrail.org

Undeniably the most interesting path between Albuquerque and Santa Fe, this poetically named route is the 50-mile reach of New Mexico 14 that parallels Interstate 25 north from Interstate 40; the road is a National Scenic Byway. Cutting a course along the backside of the Sandias just north of Albuquerque, the trail winds through a rolling countryside of sumptuous, cactus-lined hills populated by tiny burgs. Along the way, watch for crumbling rock houses, ancient family cemeteries and long-abandoned ranch houses and barns. Stops include the town of Golden, where the first discovery of gold west of the Mississippi was made and where a silver boom once employed more than 1,200 workers, and Madrid, once rich in coal mines but today the refuge of artists whose galleries and shops have become lucrative businesses. The wonderful Mine Shaft Tavern offers burgers, buffalo steaks and cold beer, along with live entertainment on weekends.

WHEELWRIGHT MUSEUM
704 Camino Lejo, Santa Fe, 505-982-4636, 800-607-4636; www.wheelwright.org

Founded in 1937 by Mary Cabot Wheelwright and Navajo singer/medicine man Hastiin Klah to help preserve Navajo art and traditions, the Wheelwright now devotes itself to hosting major exhibits of Native American artists from tribes throughout North America. The Case Trading Post in the basement sells pottery, jewelry, textiles, books, prints and other gift items.

Admission: free. Monday-Saturday 10 a.m.-5 p.m., Sunday 1-5 p.m.

WHERE TO STAY

★★★THE BISHOP'S LODGE RANCH RESORT & SPA
1297 Bishop's Lodge Road, Santa Fe, 505-983-6377, 800-419-0492; www.bishopslodge.com

This lodge is a Santa Fe treasure. The historic resort dates back to 1918 and its chapel, listed on the National Register of Historic Places, remains a popular site for weddings. This resort is vintage chic, with rooms decorated either in an old Sante Fe style or with more modern décor. The ShaNah Spa and Wellness Center is influenced by Native American traditions—each treatment begins with a soothing drumming and blessing. Modern seasonal American cuisine is the focus at the lodge's restaurant, Las Fuentes Restaurant & Bar.

111 rooms. Restaurant, bar. Fitness center. Pool. Spa. Pets accepted. Tennis. $251-350

★★★ELDORADO HOTEL & SPA
309 W. San Francisco St., Santa Fe, 505-988-4455, 800-955-4455; www.eldoradohotel.com

The Pueblo Revival-style building is one of Santa Fe's largest and most important landmarks. Its lobby and interiors are lavishly decorated with an extensive collection of original Southwest art. Rooms have private balconies and kiva fireplaces. Head over to the Nidah Spa (nidah is the Native American word for "your life") to get treatments such as the turquoise gem massage or the blue corn and Anasazi bean cleansing body wrap. The Eldorado Court and Lounge, near the main lobby, is a great spot for snacking, people-watching and enjoying live entertainment.

219 rooms. Restaurant, bar. Business center. Fitness center. Pool. Spa. Pets accepted. $251-350

★★★★ENCANTADO RESORT

198 State Road 592, Santa Fe, 505-988-9955;
www.encantadoresort.com

Tucked in the foothills of the Sangre de Cristo Mountains, Encantado is an oasis of serenity, privacy and luxury. Tapping into the mystic energies that New Mexico is known for, it was designed as a destination for wellness and rejuvenation. And you can find just that at the new Spa at Encantado, which provides treatments from massage to ayurvedic rituals, Eastern medicine and aesthetic arts. Complementing the New Mexico landscape, Encantado has a main lodge and 65 private and cozy casitas with kiva fireplaces and outdoor terraces, which are scattered throughout the 57-acre property. Terra, Encantado's signature restaurant, features American cuisine made with organic ingredients—much of it is also local—and offers alluring views of the surrounding vistas.

65 rooms. Restaurant, bar. Fitness center. Pool. Spa. $351 and up

★★★HILTON SANTA FE HISTORIC PLAZA

100 Sandoval St., Santa Fe, 505-988-2811, 800-445-8667;
www.hiltonofsantafe.com

Located just two blocks from the historic Plaza, this hotel is in a 380-year-old family estate, and takes up an entire city block. The Hilton has the city's largest pool, which is a savior during those scorching summers. Guest rooms feature locally handcrafted furnishings.

157 rooms. Restaurant, bar. Business center. Fitness center. Pool. Pets accepted. $151-250

★★★HYATT REGENCY TAMAYA RESORT & SPA

1300 Tuyuna Trail, Santa Ana Pueblo, 505-867-1234,
800-554-9288; www.tamaya.hyatt.com

Located on 500 acres of unspoiled desert, the Hyatt Regency Tamaya Resort & Spa has striking views of the Sandia Mountains. The property blends right in with its pueblo-style buildings and open-air courtyards and includes punches of turquoise and bright oranges throughout the public and private spaces. Golf, tennis and hot-air ballooning are among the activities available at this family-friendly resort, where programs for kids are available. The restaurants are a showcase of Southwestern flavors, offering sophisticated takes on local favorites.

350 rooms. Restaurant, bar. Business center. Fitness center. Spa. Pets accepted. Golf. Tennis. $151-250

WHAT ARE THE BEST HOTELS IN SANTA FE FOR A QUIET ESCAPE?

Encantado Resort: If you are looking for an escape, Encantado is your place. It was designed as a place for wellness and rejuvenation, so you'll have peace and quiet as well as privacy. For more serenity, visit the spa and indulge in one of the many treatments.

Sunrise Springs: This hotel promises that you'll find solitude on its 70 acres of ponds, gardens and wildlife. But if that doesn't work, try the Japanese-inspired spa, yoga and tai chi classes or release your tensions in the raku clay studio.

★★★INN AND SPA AT LORETTO

211 Old Santa Fe Trail, Santa Fe, 505-988-5531, 800-727-5531; www.hotelloretto.com

This boutique hotel, which rests at the end of the Sante Fe Trail, is a re-creation of an ancient adobe. Rooms feature a charming Southwestern motif with hand-carved furniture and Native American art. The property includes a heated pool and 12 specialty stores, including many art galleries.

129 rooms. Restaurant, bar. Spa. Fitness center. Pool. $151-250

★★★INN OF THE GOVERNORS

101 W. Alameda St., Santa Fe, 505-982-4333, 800-234-4534; www.innofthegovernors.com

First-rate amenities are the draw at this cozy inn. Guests are treated to a complimentary full breakfast each morning and a heated outdoor pool with poolside service. Rooms are decorated Southwestern style and feature handcrafted furniture, Spanish artwork, fireplaces and French doors that open to a patio. Perks include wireless Internet access, feather pillows, down comforters and plush towels and robes. The rustic Del Charro Saloon, a popular gathering place for locals and tourists alike, offers cocktails and a full bar menu, including what many say are the best burgers in town.

100 rooms. Restaurant, bar. Complimentary breakfast. Pool. $151-250

★★★LA POSADA DE SANTA FE RESORT AND SPA

330 E. Palace Ave., Santa Fe, 505-986-0000, 866-331-7625; www.rockresorts.com

Located on six landscaped acres, La Posada easily blends past and present. The attractive Spanish colonial-style rooms and suites are scattered throughout the gardens in a village setting. The fantastic Avanyu Spa features Native American-themed treatments using local ingredients. Fuego Restaurant is a standout for its innovative food with Spanish and Mexican inflections, while the historic Staab, dating to 1870, is the focal point of the resort and provides an inviting setting for American classics.

157 rooms. Restaurant, bar. Fitness center. Pool. Spa. $251-350

★★★★ROSEWOOD INN OF THE ANASAZI

113 Washington Ave., Santa Fe, 505-988-3030; www.innoftheanasazi.com

Just off the historic Plaza, the inn was designed to resemble the traditional dwellings of the Anasazi tribe. Enormous handcrafted doors open to a world of authentic artwork, carvings and textiles synonymous with the Southwest. The lobby sets a sense of place for arriving guests with its rough-hewn tables, leather furnishings, unique objects and huge cactus plants in terra cotta pots. The region's integrity is maintained in the guest rooms, where fireplaces and four-poster beds rest under ceilings of vigas and latillas and bathrooms are stocked with toiletries made locally with native cedar extract. The restaurant earns praise for honoring the area's culinary heritage.

58 rooms. Restaurant, bar. Business center. Fitness center. Pets accepted. $251-350

★★★SUNRISE SPRINGS

242 Los Pinos Road, Santa Fe, 505-471-3600, 800-955-0028; www.sunrisesprings.com

Get your chakras in order at Santa Fe's Zen-chic Sunrise Springs. This eco-conscious resort proves that it's easy being green with biodynamic gardens, organic produce and locally harvested spa products. Sunrise Springs takes its cues from the East for its activity menu, offering tai chi, raku ceramics and yoga, as well as traditional tea ceremonies in its authentic Japanese teahouse, but the guestrooms and casitas are definitively Southwestern.

56 rooms. Fitness center. Pool. Spa. $151-250

WHERE TO EAT

★★★THE ANASAZI RESTAURANT & BAR

Rosewood Inn of the Anasazi, 113 Washington Ave., Santa Fe, 505-988-3236; www.innoftheanasazi.com

The creators of the memorable cuisine at this Plaza mainstay like to point out that the Navajo definition of Anasazi has come to embody an ancient wisdom that encourages living in peace with the environment. That philosophy is translated in the petroglyph-inspired art on the walls. Executive chef Oliver Ridgeway devotes himself to finding inventive uses for organic, locally grown products in dishes such as chile and mustard braised rabbit with spring pea fettuccine, baby heirloom carrots and lemon thyme gremolata, and blue-corn-crusted salmon with crimini mushroom, spring squash succotash and citrus jalapeño sauce.

Southwestern. Breakfast, lunch, dinner, Sunday brunch. Bar. $36-85

★★★THE COMPOUND RESTAURANT

653 Canyon Road, Santa Fe, 505-982-4353; www.compoundrestaurant.com

The setting of this landmark restaurant is casual yet elegant, with minimalist décor, neutral tones and white-clothed tables. Patios surrounded by flower gardens and a marble fountain make for a relaxing outdoor dining experience. The contemporary American menu features specialties such as grilled beef tenderloin and tuna tartare topped with Osetra caviar and preserved lemon. The warm bittersweet liquid chocolate cake is a star dessert.

American. Lunch (Monday-Saturday), dinner. Outdoor seating. Bar. $16-35

★★★COYOTE CAFE

132 W. Water St., Santa Fe, 505-983-1615; www.coyotecafe.com

Famed cookbook author and Southwestern cuisine pioneer Mark Miller enjoyed nothing but success at this super-cool restaurant decorated with folk art and located just a block off the Plaza. But when he decided to sell it, chef Eric DiStefano (who was the executive chef of Santa Fe hot spot Geronimo) stepped in to save the popular spot. Although the menu changes seasonally, regulars know they'll find a whimsical mingling of the cuisines of New Mexico, Mexico, Cuba and Spain. Look for slow-braised prime beef short ribs with red pepper risotto and brandy shallot sauce, and elk tenderloin with roasted garlic potatoes, applewood-smoked bacon and brandied mushroom sauce. The rooftop Cantina is a festive spot to enjoy cocktails and lighter fare.

Southwestern. Dinner. Reservations recommended. Outdoor seating. Children's menu. Bar. $36-85

★★★★GERONIMO

724 Canyon Road, Santa Fe, 505-982-1500; www.geronimorestaurant.com

Housed in a restored 250-year-old landmark adobe building, Geronimo (the name of the restaurant is an ode to the hacienda's original owner, Geronimo Lopez) offers robust Southwestern-spiked global fusion fare in a stunning and cozy space. Owners Cliff Skoglund and Chris Harvey treat each guest like family. The interior is like a Georgia O'Keeffe painting come to life, with its wood-burning cove-style fireplace, tall chocolate-and-garnet-leather seating and local Native American-style artwork decorating the walls. The food is remarkable, fusing the distinct culinary influences of Asia, the Southwest and the Mediterranean. Vibrant flavors, bright colors and top-notch seasonal and regional ingredients come together in such dishes as peppery elk tenderloin and applewood-smoked bacon with roasted garlic fork-mashed potatoes, sugar snap peas and creamy brandied mushroom sauce; or sweet chile and honey grilled Mexican white prawns with Jasmine-almond rice cakes and frisée red onion salad. When it's warm outside, sit on the patio for prime Canyon Road people-watching.

International. Dinner. Reservations recommended. Outdoor seating. Bar. $36-85

★★★LAS FUENTES RESTAURANT & BAR

The Bishops Lodge Ranch Resort & Spa, 1297 Bishop's Lodge Road, Santa Fe, 505-983-6377, 800-419-0492; www.bishopslodge.com

Executive chef Brian Shannon brings an explosion of continental American cuisine to the Bishop's Lodge at this inviting restaurant. Standout dishes include tomatillo-chipotle-glazed pork ribs with mango slaw and grilled sweet corn succotash and grilled ruby trout with tagliatelle pasta with lemon, olives, artichoke hearts, capers, piquillo peppers and fresh oregano. The interior has ranch-like Southwestern décor, Navajo rugs and murals by a local Santa Fe artist.

American. Breakfast, lunch, dinner, Sunday brunch. Outdoor seating. Bar. $36-85

★★★THE OLD HOUSE RESTAURANT

Eldorado Hotel & Spa, 309 W. San Francisco St., Santa Fe, 505-988-4455, 800-955-4455;
www.eldoradohotel.com

Located in the Eldorado Hotel & Spa, the Old House Restaurant serves up international cuisine with a Southwestern twist. For example, try the bistro steak served with duck fat fries and creamed spinach or the chicken with wild mushrooms, green chile and corn flan and chicken jus. Steal a moment to look up and take in the candlelit stucco room, part of one of the city's oldest buildings, which is adorned with Mexican folk art and bold, oversized paintings. To enjoy your meal somewhere more intimate, reserve the private wine room.

Southwestern. Dinner. Reservations recommended. Bar. $36-85

★★★SANTACAFÉ

231 Washington Ave., Santa Fe, 505-984-1788; www.santacafe.com

Situated a block from the Plaza in the restored Padre Gallegos House, Santacafé offers dishes such as shiitake and cactus spring rolls with Southwestern ponzu; shrimp-spinach dumplings in a tahini sauce; filet mignon with asparagus, green chile mashed potatoes and truffle oil butter; or roasted free-range chicken with creamy gorgonzola polenta, applewood-smoked bacon, capers, olives and sage. The patio dining in warmer weather is a treat.

American, Southwestern. Lunch, dinner, Sunday brunch. Reservations recommended. Outdoor seating. Children's. Bar. $36-85

★★★TERRA

Encantado Resort, 198 State Road 592, Santa Fe, 877-262-4666; www.encantadoresort.com

Terra is the signature restaurant at the Encantado Resort. The minimalistic and modern design uses natural materials such as stone, leather and wood, as well as poured concrete and steel, which contrast nicely with the crisp white linens topping the tables. Executive chef Charles Dale uses many ingredients from the restaurant's own 10,000-square-foot onsite biodynamic garden to create dishes such as miso-baked wild Tasmanian salmon with bamboo rice, poached shiitake mushrooms and soy vinaigrette, as well as the Three Little Pigs, which consists of grilled tenderloin in adobo, crispy belly over edamame purée and pork cheek casuela with pumpkin seed mole. A well-edited list of specialty cocktails and wines rounds out the offerings.

American. Breakfast, lunch, dinner. Bar. $35-86

★★★TRATTORIA NOSTRANI

304 Johnson St., Santa Fe, 505-983-3800; www.trattorianostrani.com

You can dine in one of four semi-private dining rooms at Trattoria Nostrani, a northern Italian restaurant housed in an 1883 territorial-style house. The interior retains much of its historical atmosphere, with tin ceilings and adobe archways. Entrées include diver scallops with quail porchetta, white wine and tomatoes; roasted chicken with mushrooms and marsala wine; and duck ravioli with plums and red wine. If all that talk of wine-infused food has you thirsty, there's more than 400 pours on the extensive European wine list and a knowledgeable staff will assist in selecting the perfect one.

Italian. Dinner. Closed Sunday. Reservations recommended. $36-85

SPAS

★★★THE SPA AT ENCANTADO
198 State Road 592, Santa Fe, 877-262-4666; www.encantadoresort.com

Reflecting the uniquely modern and earthy décor of the resort, The Spa at Encantado is a peaceful and luxurious retreat. If you're with someone special, book one of the two couple's massage rooms, which are more like private retreats that feature their own personal Jacuzzi, steam bath and shower. With or without a private treatment room, allow enough time to take full advantage of the elegant and inviting Warming Room. Here, guests can relax by the fire while enjoying some tea, hot chocolate, appetizers and a good book before or after a treatment. Signature services are inspired by the surroundings. The Blue Corn and Honey Renewal, for example, uses native blue corn and wildflower honey to exfoliate and revive tired skin. Prior to beginning any treatment, follow the spa's well-detailed purification ritual to maximize your enchanting spa experience at this foothill retreat.

WHERE TO SHOP

SANTA FE FASHION OUTLETS
8380 Cerrillos Road, Santa Fe, 505-474-4000; www.fashionoutletssantafe.com

This is New Mexico's only outlet center, so if you are looking to do some serious shopping, bring your credit cards here. It has more than 40 stores, including Coach, Nike, Eddie Bauer and Brooks Brothers.

Monday-Saturday 10 a.m.-7 p.m., Sunday 11 a.m.-6 p.m.

WELCOME TO TEXAS

BRASH, BOLD AND UNDENIABLY UNIQUE, TEXAS EMBODIES

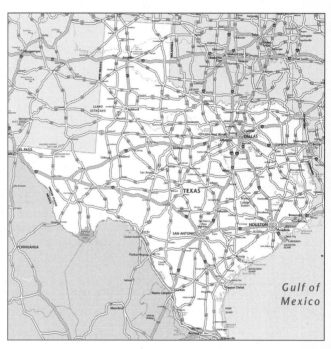

the pioneer spirit of America. Once its own republic, this Southern state (which natives consider distinct from the South, even though it fought for the Confederacy in the Civil War) is fiercely independent. In Texas, you'll find country music, rodeos, rock 'n' roll and the space race. A Texan lived in the White House for 12 of the past 22 years, and some of the country's most innovative—and lucrative—industries are headquartered here, from technology to oil.

The character of Texas changes markedly from region to region. West Texas is made up of open range, while East Texas is home to Houston and acres of rolling, wooded ranchland. Northern Texas is home to Dallas, a cosmopolitan city, and the Western-flavored Fort Worth—together they boast an impressive art scene and world-class restaurants. South Texas is lined with citrus groves that thrive in its semitropical climate and beaches with hundreds of miles of sand along the Gulf Coast and the barrier islands. Central Texas has a booming music scene in the state's capital, Austin, which hosts the South by Southwest Music Festival and has more live music venues per capita than any other U.S. city.

HIGHLIGHTS

TEXAS' BEST ATTRACTIONS

AUSTIN
Austin is the hippest city in Texas. Music fans head there for the yearly South by Southwest Festival and to hear bands jam, since Austin has more live music venues per capita than any other U.S. city.

DALLAS
You won't find cowboys lassoing cows in this Texas city. Dallas is a sophisticated, hopping city. Visit Deep Ellum's hot music venues, the Dallas Museum of Art or upscale shopping center Highland Park Village.

HOUSTON
Choose your own adventure in Houston: Peruse the Museum District, see a game at Minute Maid ballpark, visit NASA headquarters or catch a musical at Hobby Center. Whatever you do, don't leave without tasting some barbecue.

SAN ANTONIO
History buffs will put San Antonio on their itineraries. After all, it's the home of the Alamo and the Fort Sam Houston Museum. Other tourists will opt for ambling down the popular river walk and shopping at Market Square.

AUSTIN

Consistently topping celebrated "best places to live" and "greenest city in America" lists, Austin has experienced a population boom in recent years thanks in part to its strong high-technology industry, diverse cultural scene, laid-back and friendly vibe, great weather and favorable reputation for outdoor sports. The surrounding area offers rolling hills and lakes suited for mountain biking, hiking and kayaking.

Home to the University of Texas and its thousands of students, professors and researchers, this is more than just a college town; it's also the center of Texas' raucous political scene. With 12 of the last 22 years of the American presidency held by the Texas-based Bush family, the city remains at the forefront of the country's politics.

But with George W. out of the White House, Austin's spotlight has shifted to its diverse music, film and art scenes. The self-proclaimed "Live Music Capital of the

World," Austin celebrates music at venues citywide. It also hosts *Austin City Limits*, the longest-running live concert music program on American television and annual festival, and South by Southwest (SXSW), a wildly popular film and music fest.

Dining also puts Austin on the map, with some of the country's best Tex-Mex and Southwestern-influenced fare created here by the city's finest chefs. The dress code at most restaurants is decidedly relaxed—jeans can be worn just about everywhere. This attitude is no doubt what attracts celebrities such as Lance Armstrong, Matthew McConaughey and Sandra Bullock, all of whom call Austin home.

WHAT TO SEE

AUSTIN CHILDREN'S MUSEUM

201 Colorado St., Austin, 512-472-2499; www.austinkids.org

Through its interactive galleries, this 7,000-square-foot museum aims to entertain and educate the younger set (although there are also activities suited to older kids). In its "Global City" exhibit, children take on the roles of adults—going to the grocery store, ordering lunch at the diner and working as doctors or construction workers, among other things. Austin's history is also on display; kids learn what it's like to live and work on a Texas ranch.

Admission: adults and children 2-18 $6.50, children 1-2 $4.50, children under 1 free. Tuesday-Saturday 10 a.m.-5 p.m., Wednesday until 8 p.m., Sunday noon-5 p.m.

AUSTIN LYRIC OPERA

901 Barton Springs Road, Austin, 512-472-5992; www.austinlyricopera.org

Since 1986, this opera company has won critical acclaim for its lyrical presentations. International artists and rising young singers often team up to stage the company's three-opera season. The variety in its productions is vast, presenting tragedy to comedy, conventional to modern. No matter the script, the performance is always an innovative and stimulating experience.

Admission: prices vary. November-March, showtimes vary.

AUSTIN MUSEUM OF ART

823 Congress Ave., Austin, 512-495-9224; 3809 W. 35th St., West Austin, 512-458-8191; www.amoa.org

With two disparate locations, one on the main drag in downtown Austin and the other in West Austin, there is always something new on exhibit. Modern and contemporary art takes center stage downtown with works by such famed artists as Dale Chihuly, Chuck Close and Robert Rauschenberg. There is also a focus on regional artists. The West Austin branch of AMOA was the museum's original home and is housed in a stunning 1916 Italianate-style villa surrounded by 12 acres of verdant gardens and rolling hills overlooking Lake Austin. The art school is located here, and it offers more than 400 classes and lectures open to the public.

Admission: adults $5, seniors and students $4, children under 12 free. Tuesday-Friday 10 a.m.-5 p.m., Thursday 10 a.m.-8 p.m., Saturday 10 a.m.-6 p.m., Sunday noon-5 p.m.

AUSTIN ZOO

10807 Rawhide Trail, Austin, 512-288-1490; www.austinzoo.org

The Austin Zoo specializes in rehabilitating animals in need of rescue. Starting

HIGHLIGHTS

WHAT ARE THE TOP THINGS TO DO IN AUSTIN?

SWIM IN BARTON SPRINGS POOL

Take a plunge into the Barton Springs Pool, one of the city's best attractions. This 3-acre pool rests above springs that maintain a temperature of 68 F. Bring your bathing suit because the pool is open year round.

EXPLORE THE LADY BIRD JOHNSON WILDFLOWER RESEARCH CENTER

The botanical garden got its start with a grant from the former first lady. Now it boasts 16 gardens. Stop and smell the flowers at the South Meadow, which has native Central Texas blooms.

IMBIBE AT MANDOLA ESTATE WINERY

Since you're in Hill Country, the state's wine-producing region, you should sample some of the local product. Started by PBS celeb chef Damian Mandola, the winery turns out delicious pours, like the viognier.

HEAR LIVE MUSIC ON SIXTH STREET

You can't visit the self-proclaimed "Live Music Capital of the World" without hearing some tunes. Along Sixth Street, Austin's entertainment district, you'll find bars and clubs with bands playing everything from rock to jazz.

GO SHOPPING ON SOCO

Instead of hitting up the same tired old stores in the mall, head to South Congress Avenue, which is lined with eclectic shops that sell one-of-a-kind goods. If you need some Texan footwear, visit Allens Boots, which carries more than 4,000 boots.

as a goat ranch in 1990, the zoo has grown to include more than 300 animals from more than 100 different species. African lions, Capuchin monkeys and miniature donkeys are just a few of the animals you can visit. There is also a petting zoo on the property where kids can get up close and feed the animals.

Admission: adults $8, seniors, students and miltary $6, children 2-12 $5. Daily 10 a.m.-6 p.m.

BALLET AUSTIN
501 W. Third St., Austin, 512-476-2163

In a city as alternative as Austin, there is little chance the resident dance company would limit itself to classical ballet. Ballet Austin mixes elegant tradition with modern innovation.

Admission: prices vary. October-May, showtimes vary.

BARTON CREEK GREENBELT
2201 Barton Springs Road, Austin, 512-472-1267; www.texasoutside.com

Hikers, rock climbers, and bikers get quite a workout on this 7½-mile urban trail. Sheer limestone walls up to 40 feet tall border the greenbelt, and they're perfect for scaling. If you can pull your own weight, the climbing is especially good at the Gus Fruh, Loop 360 and Spyglass access points along the trail.

Admission: free. Daily 5 a.m.-10 p.m.

BARTON SPRINGS POOL
2101 Barton Springs Road, Austin, 512-472-1267; www.ci.austin.tx.us

Within Zilker Park's 358 acres, you'll find one of Austin's coolest attractions, Barton Springs Pool. Three acres in size, the pool receives its 27 million gallons of watershed each day from underground springs that average 68 F year round.

Admission: adults $3, seniors $1, children 12-17 $2, children under 12 $1. Daily 5 a.m.-10 p.m.

BOB BULLOCK TEXAS STATE HISTORY MUSEUM
1800 N. Congress Ave., Austin, 512-936-8746, 866-369-7108; www.thestoryoftexas.com

Explore the three floors of this 34,000-square-foot Texas-size museum and you'll learn all you ever wanted to know about the Lone Star State. Through more than 700 artifacts and numerous interactive displays, you'll be transformed into a walking encyclopedia of Texas history. An IMAX theater is equipped with 2-D/3-D capabilities, and the Texas Spirit Theater rocks with special effects.

Admission: adults $7, seniors, military and students $6, children 5-18 $4, children under 5 free. Monday-Saturday 9 a.m.-6 p.m., Sunday noon-6 p.m.

ELISABET NEY MUSEUM
304 E. 44th St., Austin, 512-458-2255; www.ci.austin.tx.us

Few museums match the unique combination of frontierism and German Romanticism found here. Housed in the former studio of portrait sculptor Elisabet Ney, the museum puts more than 70 busts on display, including likenesses of such Texan heroes as Stephen F. Austin and Sam Houston.

Admission: free. Wednesday-Saturday 10 a.m.-5 p.m., Sunday noon-5 p.m.

FOREST CREEK GOLF CLUB

99 Twin Ridge Parkway, Round Rock, 512-388-2874; www.forestcreek.com

This 7,147-yard, par-72 gem is the finest public golf course in central Texas—which is a good enough reason to drive about 30 miles north of downtown Austin to visit it. Golf carts are equipped with global positioning systems, which tell the exact distance to the hole and alert golfers to hazards.

Admission: varies. Daily dawn-dusk.

FRENCH LEGATION MUSEUM

802 San Marcos St., Austin, 512-472-8180; www.frenchlegationmuseum.org

This circa-1841 building housed the charge d'affaires to the Republic of Texas. It features Creole architecture and furnishings. Take some time to wander through the well-manicured gardens and reconstructed carriage house.

Admission: adults $5, seniors $3, students $2. Tuesday-Sunday 1-5 p.m.

GOVERNOR'S MANSION

1010 Colorado St., Austin, 512-305-8400; www.txfgm.org

Serving as the official home of Texas governors since 1856, the Greek Revival-style mansion reigned as the fourth-oldest continuously occupied governor's residence in the country. In 2008, arson nearly destroyed the mansion, causing significant structural damage. The historic residence was empty at the time, and it underwent a major renovation. Tours are available.

HIGHLAND LAKES

325-388-4929; www.highlandlakes.com

Seven hydroelectric dams cross the Colorado River, creating a continuous series of lakes for nearly 150 miles upstream. Lake Buchanan and Lake Travis are the largest, but Town Lake and Lake Austin are easier to reach, as they are within the Austin city limits.

Admission: free. Daily.

LADY BIRD JOHNSON WILDFLOWER RESEARCH CENTER

4801 La Crosse Ave., Austin, 512-232-0100; www.wildflower.org

This native plant botanical garden of national renown began with a generous grant from Lady Bird Johnson, the former first lady, who added to her legacy by launching a national roadside beautification program in the 1960s. Now affiliated with the University of Texas at Austin, the 16 unique gardens incorporate courtyards, terraces, arbors and meadows, as well as an observation tower, a café, a gift store and a nature trail. In the springtime, the South Meadow transforms into a sea of color with wildflowers native to Central Texas.

Admission: adults $7, seniors and students $6, children 5-12 $3, children under 5 free. Mid-March-May, daily 9 a.m.-5:30 p.m.; June-mid-March, Tuesday-Saturday 9 a.m.-5:30 p.m., Sunday noon-5:30 p.m.

LYNDON BAINES JOHNSON LIBRARY & MUSEUM

2313 Red River, Austin, 512-721-0200; www.lbjlib.utexas.edu

Everything you wanted to know about the 36th president and more is in this expansive museum. Exhibits on Johnson's vision for a "Great Society," international affairs, his Oval Office, gifts given to heads of state, and a First Lady's Gallery are all permanent collections. There is also a retrospective on presidential history presented through memorabilia of political campaigns from Washington to Reagan. Visits to the reading room must be scheduled in advance, but allow access to private recordings of phone calls LBJ conducted on a variety of topics.

Admission: free. Daily 9 a.m.-5 p.m.

MANDOLA ESTATE WINERY
13308 FM 150 W., Driftwood, 512-858-1470; www.mandolawines.com

About 25 miles southwest of Austin, you will discover an imposing but elegant Tuscan-style winery and eatery. PBS celebrity chef Damian Mandola, co-founder of Carraba's and Damian's, "retired" five years ago and moved to Austin. Fast-forward to 2006, when state-of-the-art winery Mandola Estate Winery popped up on a perfectly framed piece of property near tiny Driftwood. The finest winery-restaurant in the state, Trattoria Lisina, followed a year later. With winemaker Mark Penna in place and Mandola at the helm, this breathtaking compound is the talk of Hill Country. A substantial and diversified menu awaits you at Trattoria Lisina, and standout wines served at the Estate tasting room next door include pinot grigio, viognier (a favorite, thanks to its lovely peach and apricot flavors), sangiovese, montepulciano, syrah and a dessert wine. Upcoming releases will include a slightly sweet moscato (with orange blossom and peach nuances), a dolcetto and a vermentino.

Monday 10 a.m.-6 p.m., Tuesday-Saturday 10 a.m.-10 p.m., Sunday 10 a.m.-9 p.m.

MCKINNEY FALLS STATE PARK
5808 McKinney Falls Parkway, Austin, 512-243-1643; www.tpwd.state.tx.us

Just a short drive from downtown, this 744-acre park in South Austin offers views of its namesake falls and activities such as fishing, hiking, camping, mountain biking, picnicking and swimming in Onion Creek. Keep your eyes open for armadillos, raccoons, white-tailed deer and other wildlife.

Admission: adults $5, children under 13 free. Daily 8 a.m.-10 p.m.

MEXIC-ARTE MUSEUM
419 Congress Ave., Austin, 512-480-9373; www.mexic-artemuseum.org

Focusing primarily on Mexican and Latino culture, this nonprofit arts organization has been exhibiting contemporary and historical artwork since 1984. The permanent collection showcases masks, paintings, prints and other mediums. On the Day of the Dead, a traditional Mexican holiday on November 1, the museum hosts a citywide celebration with live music, dancing and free entry.

Admission: adults $5, seniors and students $4, children under 12 $1. Monday-Thursday 10 a.m.-6 p.m., Friday-Saturday 10 a.m.-5 p.m., Sunday noon-5 p.m.

O. HENRY HOME AND MUSEUM
409 E. Fifth St., Austin, 512-472-1903; www.ci.austin.tx.us

This Victorian cottage was the residence of writer William Sydney Porter, more commonly known as O. Henry, from 1893 to 1895. The original furnishings remain, along with memorabilia from O. Henry's days in Austin. The O. Henry Pun-Off World Championships take place on the property every May and are worth a visit if you're in town.

Admission: free. Wednesday-Sunday noon-5 p.m.

SIXTH STREET

Southeast of the Capitol Complex on Sixth Street between Congress Avenue and Interstate 35, Austin, 512-974-2000; www.6street.com

In this entertainment district, sometimes compared to New Orleans' Bourbon Street, you'll hear everything from rock and hip-hop to soul and jazz in the many bars and nightclubs that line the streets. The east end of Sixth Street can get quite rowdy (especially on weekend nights), so head west if you're looking for a more low-key experience. The people-watching is a large part of the fun, and there is no better place to see the action than from Sixth Street's open-rooftop bars; get there early to secure a prime table.

STATE CAPITOL

1100 Congress Ave., Austin, 512-463-0063; www.capitol.state.tx.us

Texans think big, so it's no surprise that the state's 122-year-old capitol is the nation's largest statehouse, with nearly 18 acres of floor space. You can explore much of it on your own or take a guided tour that focuses on the building's architecture and prized contents. If the legislature is in session, take a seat in the Senate or House chamber and watch the political wrangling as lawmakers debate the issues of the day. The Capitol Complex Visitors Center (112 E. 11th St.) also offers changing historical and interactive exhibits.

Admission: free. Monday-Friday 7 a.m.-10 p.m., Saturday-Sunday 9 a.m.-8 p.m.

VELOWAY

Slaughter Creek Metropolitan Park, 6103 Slaughter Lane, Austin, 512-974-6700; www.veloway.com

Bicyclists and in-line skaters have this winding pathway all to themselves. No walkers, no joggers and of course, no cars are allowed on this paved asphalt loop, which stretches for just over three miles through more than 100 green acres of scenic parkland.

WAREHOUSE DISTRICT

West of Congress Avenue and South of Sixth Street, Austin, 512-474-5171, 800-926-2282; www.ci.austin.tx.us

Southwest of busy East Sixth Street, nightclubs and restaurants make this nine-block district yet another hot hangout. But here you'll party with mostly business professionals who prefer a more upscale scene. Live music is played nightly at Antone's (*213 W. Fifth St., 512-320-8424*), the city's best-known blues club; Bitter End B-Side (*311 Colorado St., 512-478-2462*) serves soft jazz mixed nicely with a martini.

Admission: varies. Showtimes vary.

ZILKER METROPOLITAN PARK

2100 Barton Springs Road, Austin, 512-472-4914; www.ci.austin.tx.us

This 351-acre park near downtown is the city's largest and most beloved. The main attraction is Barton Springs Pool, a 1,000-foot-long spring-fed watering hole. Swimming here is a chilling experience, with the water temperature averaging 68 degrees year-round. There's also a well-equipped playground, hike-and-bike trails, a botanical garden, a hillside theater, a nature center and a variety of athletic fields. The park has lovely picnic areas, so bring something tasty to chow on in the Texas outdoors.

Admission: free. Daily 5 a.m.-10 p.m.

HIGHLIGHT

WHY WAS AUSTIN DUBBED THE LIVE MUSIC CAPITAL OF THE WORLD?

Austinites claim their city as the "Live Music Capital of the World." Though that title may be self-applied, it's backed up by the city's rich tradition of supporting rock, country, folk, bluegrass and blues, and was cemented with the launch of the South by Southwest Music Festival (www.sxsw.com) in 1987. Though the week-long festival has grown to include film and multimedia presentations, the music portion attracts more than 1,500 bands and thousands of fans from all over each March. During the rest of the year, live music can be heard nightly at the clubs along Sixth Street, from blues hall Antone's to the recently rebuilt Art Deco Austin Music Hall.

Those who plan ahead can snag a ticket to a taping of Austin City Limits (www.austincitylimits.org), the acclaimed live performance program broadcast on PBS. It features some of the most cutting-edge bands in the rock, country, folk and alternative genres. A new stage was built in 2009, adding more seating and increasing the chances of gaining entrance to one of many popular performances. Or plan to visit during the Austin City Limits Music Festival (www.aclfestival.com), which takes place on 46-acres in Zilker Park over three days in October. More than 130 bands play on multiple stages and in the past have included Phish, Muse and The Eagles.

WHERE TO STAY

★★★BARTON CREEK RESORT & SPA
8212 Barton Club Drive, Austin, 512-329-4000, 800-329-4000; www.bartoncreek.com

The lure at this sprawling resort is the four 18-hole golf courses designed by legendary course architects Tom Fazio, Arnold Palmer and Ben Crenshaw. Those who choose to skip the links can spend their time secluded in the luxurious, oversized guest rooms, which feature powder rooms, plasma TVs and duvet-topped beds. The resort also has 11 tennis courts, a fitness center and spa. The Hill Country Dining Room, Barton Creek Lakeside restaurant and Austin Grill provide sustenance after a visit full of activity.

312 rooms. Restaurant, bar. Fitness center. Pool. Spa. Golf. Tennis. $251-350

★★★THE DRISKILL
604 Brazos St., Austin, 512-474-5911, 800-252-9367; www.driskillhotel.com

The Driskill has been an Austin landmark since it opened in 1886. The rooms and suites are in the original hotel and in the adjacent tower. The Driskill offers visitors the chance to experience the rich, dark ambiance of the historic rooms or the fresh, light colors of the Texas Hill Country-inspired tower rooms. Well-appointed business and fitness centers are among the perks here, and the Driskill Grill remains one of Austin's top restaurants.

189 rooms. Restaurant, bar. Business center. Fitness center. Spa. Pets accepted. $151-250

★★★★FOUR SEASONS HOTEL AUSTIN

98 San Jacinto Blvd., Austin, 512-478-4500, 800-819-5053; www.fourseasons.com

Located in the rolling hills of Austin overlooking Town Lake, the Four Seasons Hotel reflects its surroundings with cowhide-covered sofas and native pottery, cultivating a casual elegance filtered through Texas chic. Guest rooms feature luxuriously comfortable beds, plush terry robes and DVD players. Trio restaurant serves creative cuisine influenced by Texas standards and presented with contemporary flair. The Town Hill Lake hike-and-bike trail adjacent to the property delivers fresh air while the fitness center offers yoga classes and an outdoor pool.

291 rooms. Restaurant, bar. Business center. Fitness center. Pool. Spa. $251-350

★★★HILTON GARDEN INN AUSTIN DOWNTOWN

500 Interstate 35 N., Austin, 512-480-8181, 800-227-6963; www.hiltongardeninn.com

This full-service hotel caters to both leisure and business travelers. Rooms are decorated with contemporary furnishings and feature beds with down comforters. Opting for the executive club floor gives you access to the business center, a daily buffet breakfast, a cocktail hour and a CD player.

254 rooms. Restaurant, bar. Business center. Fitness center. Pool. $151-250

★★★HOTEL SAINT CECILIA

112 Academy Drive, Austin, 512-852-2400; www.hotelstcecilia.com

Tucked away on a side street off chic South Congress Avenue, this once Victorian bed and breakfast is a unique inn that is all about the finer things in life. From the luxe Hästens beds in every room (along with boasting rights as the only hotel in the U.S. to offer them) to the Geneva sound systems with turntables and iPod docks, and an impressive library showcasing vintage vinyl records, off-beat films and books of poetry, the property takes its name seriously; Saint Cecilia is the patron saint of music and poetry. Rivolta Carmignani cotton sheets, La Compagnie de Provence bath products, flat-screen TVs and a private outdoor 50-foot pool round out the unique experience.

14 rooms. Restaurant. Pool. Pets accepted. $351 and up

★★★HYATT REGENCY AUSTIN

208 Barton Springs Road, Austin, 512-477-1234, 800-633-7313; www.austin.hyatt.com

This contemporary hotel's location on Town Lake next to the Congress Avenue Bridge keeps rooms in demand. Each guest room features crisp, white-linen-swathed beds, flat-screen TVs and marble-tiled bathrooms. Business travelers enjoy the well-equipped meeting facilities, though the slick décor can feel a bit corporate. La Vista restaurant, with views of the city from the second floor of the hotel atrium, serves Tex-Mex-influenced cooking, including acclaimed fajitas.

448 rooms. Restaurant, bar. Business center. Fitness center. Pool. $151-250

★★★INTERCONTINENTAL HOTEL STEPHEN F. AUSTIN

701 Congress Ave., Austin, 512-457-8800; www.austin.intercontinental.com

This historic downtown Austin hotel is close to the city's best music venues on Sixth Street. Opening its doors in 1924, the landmark hotel has a warm and inviting lobby featuring a grand marble staircase. Guest rooms are decorated with dark mahogany furniture and stunning marble baths, and just in case you forget you are in Texas, details such as the Lone Star emblem on every headboard are there to remind you. Most rooms feature seating areas.

189 rooms. Restaurant, bar. Business center. Fitness center. Pool. Spa. $151-250

★★★LAKE AUSTIN SPA RESORT

1705 Quinlan Park Road, Austin, 512-372-7300, 800-847-5637; www.lakeaustin.com

Perched on a lake 30 minutes from downtown Austin, this resort blends the luxury of a top hotel with the amenities of a destination spa. Rooms come with deep Kohler soaking tubs, goose-down-topped beds and gas-burning fireplaces. The spa offers more than 100 treatments, as well as fitness classes from tai chi to spinning. The restaurant serves flavorful spa cuisine, complete with desserts like key lime pie. There is a minimum three-night stay.

40 rooms. Restaurant, bar. Fitness center. Pool. Spa. No children under 16. $351 and up

★★★THE MANSION AT JUDGES' HILL

1900 Rio Grande, Austin, 512-495-1800, 800-311-1619; www.judgeshill.com

Housed in a grand structure built as a private home at the turn of the 20th century, this boutique hotel features rooms filled with antiques from every period, canopied beds and original fireplaces. The venue is popular with Austin brides and grooms but also features a lounge and restaurant serving modern takes on classic recipes, such as roasted rack of lamb with mint risotto.

48 rooms. Restaurant, bar. Business center. Fitness center. Pets accepted. $251-350

★★★MARRIOTT AUSTIN NORTH

2600 La Frontera Blvd., Austin, 512-733-6767, 800-228-9290; www.marriott.com

With Dell as its neighbor, this outpost in the Marriott chain is a favorite of techies and tourists visiting Austin. Guest rooms come complete with down duvets and luxurious cotton linens. The River City Grille serves comfort food ranging from burgers to Buffalo wings, but also offers a health-conscious menu with options like miso salmon with bok choy and lemongrass broth.

295 rooms. Restaurant, bar. Business center. Fitness center. Pool. $61-150

★★★OMNI AUSTIN HOTEL

700 San Jacinto Blvd., Austin, 512-476-3700, 800-843-6664; www.omnihotels.com

With its downtown location and laundry list of must-have hotel amenities (free wireless Internet access, daily newspapers and fluffy bathrobes), this hotel is a safe bet for visitors to the Texas capital. Though guest rooms lack any distinct décor, they are spacious. Ask for an exterior room to enjoy a balcony that overlooks the skyline. The rooftop pool has views of downtown Austin while the Atrium Lounge is a popular spot for cocktails.

375 rooms. Restaurant, bar. Business center. Fitness center. Pool. $151-250

★★★OMNI AUSTIN SOUTHPARK

4140 Governor's Row, Austin, 512-448-2222, 800-843-6664; www.omnihotels.com

This contemporary hotel is close to the city's high-tech corridor, making it a top choice for business travelers. Since the property is slightly removed from downtown Austin, there is a resort-like feel in place with fountains at the entrance, an expansive marble lobby and sweeping views of the city skyline. The onsite Trinity Spa offers treatment packages like the "Texan," which includes a one-hour massage and hot towel wrap.

313 rooms. Restaurant, bar. Business center. Fitness center. Pool. Spa. $61-150

★★★RENAISSANCE HOTEL

9721 Arboretum Blvd., Austin, 512-343-2626, 800-468-3571; www.renaissancehotels.com

The newly renovated rooms at this hotel, located in the Arboretum Complex that houses specialty shops, cinemas and restaurants, are decorated in tones inspired by the colors of the wildflowers in the surrounding Hill Country. The lobby is aglow under a huge skylight and takes on a playful style with mobiles and giant chandeliers. The location—close to the area's high-tech companies—and amenities like the updated business and fitness centers make it a good choice for business travelers.

492 rooms. Restaurant, bar. Business center. Fitness center. Pool. Pets accepted. $151-250

WHERE TO EAT

★★★DRISKILL GRILL

604 Brazos St., Austin, 512-391-7162, 800-252-9367; www.driskillgrill.com

The hushed, clubby setting of this wood-paneled dining room sets the perfect tone for the elegant food prepared here by executive chef Josh Watkins. For you history buffs, it's rumored that Lyndon and Lady Bird Johnson had their first date here. Choose from a three-, six- or nine-course menu, with entrées such as olive oil-poached beef tenderloin or pan-roasted skate wing. Pastry chef Tony Sansalone flawlessly executes classics like lemon custard cake, dark and milk chocolate terrine and gaviato strawberry tart.

American. Dinner. Closed Sunday-Monday. Reservations recommended. Bar. $36-85

★★★FONDA SAN MIGUEL

2330 W. North Loop, Austin, 512-459-4121; www.fondasanmiguel.com

A pioneer in regional Mexican cooking, this hacienda has been famous for its food since 1976. Specialties include Gulf shrimp with salsa verde, enchiladas suizas and traditional chicken mole. The portions can be small considering the price, but the ingredients are always fresh and the service is impeccable. A superior wine list and a knockout brunch round out the experience.

Mexican. Dinner (Monday-Saturday), Sunday brunch. Closed for Sunday brunch in August. Reservations recommended. Bar. $16-35

★★★HUDSON'S ON THE BEND
3509 Ranch Road 620 N., Austin, 512-266-1369; www.hudsonsonthebend.com

Dining in Texas requires an adventurous spirit. An appetizer of diamondback rattlesnake cakes coiled on a pool of spicy chipotle cream is the kind of unusual, seriously spicy cuisine found at the Hill Country eatery Hudson's on the Bend. Chefs Jeff Blank and Robert Rhoades serve up dishes such as pecan wood-smoked duck breast with seared diver scallops and wild boar sweet potato hash and punctuate the experience with decadent desserts like caramel pecan pie dipped in chocolate.

Southwestern. Dinner. Reservations recommended. Outdoor seating. Bar. $36-85

★★★JEFFREY'S RESTAURANT & BAR
1204 W. Lynn St., Austin, 512-477-5584; www.jeffreysofaustin.com

Led by executive chef Deegan McClung, this longtime Austin favorite (in business for more than 35 years) features a sophisticated menu that hints at the restaurant's Texas location. Crispy fried oysters come accompanied by bacon royale and tangy tomato vinaigrette, while beef tenderloin is dressed with red peppers and remoulade.

American. Dinner. Reservations recommended. Bar. $36-85

★★★LOUIE'S 106
106 E. Sixth St., Austin, 512-476-1997; www.louies106.net

After more than 20 years, Louie's is still a favorite place for special occasions or a good hearty meal. The interior is a mishmash of dark woods, Frank Lloyd Wright-inspired architectural details and flamboyant oil paintings, but the bilevel space remains welcoming and comfortable. Wine flights are a popular way to try the more than 300-bottle selection and the menu includes inventive Mediterranean dishes, including maple-glazed rotisserie roasted duck with a white bean succotash and the signature "hot and crusty trout" with a mango chutney sambal sauce and pecan rice. A pianist entertains Wednesday, Thursday and Friday nights.

Mediterranean. Lunch (Monday-Friday), dinner. Bar. $36-85

WHICH AUSTIN RESTAURANTS HAVE THE BEST TEXAS-INSPIRED CUISINE?

Hudson's on the Bend: If you are looking for unique Southwestern fare, give Hudson's a go. The menu offers regional delicacies like diamondback rattlesnake cakes with spicy chipotle cream. And for dessert, there's chocolate-dipped pecan pie.

Jeffrey's Restaurant & Bar: This restaurant, a favorite haunt of locals, dishes out sophisticated American cuisine. But you can taste touches of Texas sprinkled in with items like fried oysters with bacon royale and tomato vinaigrette.

★★★RUTH'S CHRIS STEAK HOUSE

107 W. Sixth St., Austin, 512-477-7884, 800-544-0808; www.ruthschris-austin.com

Sports figures, musicians and celebrities have been spotted at this central Austin outpost of the national steakhouse chain. Specializing in custom-aged, Midwestern USDA Prime beef, the restaurant serves selections such as filet, New York strip, rib-eye and porterhouse. The menu also offers additional options, including salmon filet, veal chop and ahi tuna steak.

Steak. Dinner. Reservations recommended. Bar. $36-85

★★★TRIO

Four Seasons Hotel Austin, 98 San Jacinto Blvd., Austin, 512-685-8300;
www.fourseasons.com

TRIO, the signature restaurant of the Four Seasons Austin, has become a local favorite for its superlative Sunday brunch and for executive chef Elmar Prambs' fresh, seasonal, contemporary cuisine. At dinner, choose from dishes such as smoked Texas rib-eye or prosciutto-wrapped monkfish. Overlooking Lake Lady Bird, TRIO offers a stylish setting, whether dining indoors or out on the terrace. Ask award-winning sommelier Mark Sayre for a suggestion from the impressive wine list.

Contemporary American. Breakfast, lunch, dinner, Sunday brunch. Reservations recommended. Outdoor seating. Bar. $36-85

★★★WINK

1014 N. Lamar Blvd., Austin, 512-482-8868; www.winkrestaurant.com

Don't let the strip-mall location dissuade you. Wink is serious about its food and from where it comes. When fresh ingredients are not available at local farms and ranches, they are flown in from the coasts. The menu changes daily and dishes are simple and straightforward, allowing the natural essence of the ingredients to dominate the plate. Dishes might include seared halibut with Swiss chard and chive aioli or wagyu New York strip with fingerling potatoes and oyster mushrooms. The wine list is plentiful with more than 50 choices by the glass.

Contemporary American. Dinner. Closed Sunday. Reservations recommended. $36-85

SPA

★★★★THE SPA AT FOUR SEASONS AUSTIN

Four Seasons Hotel Austin, 98 San Jacinto Blvd., Austin, 512-685-8300;
www.fourseasons.com

Contemporary and colorful, this spa inside the Four Seasons Austin offers a full range of pampering treatments, including wraps, massages, facials and pedicures. Signature services include the Yellow Rose of Texas wrap, which begins with a lavender sea salt scrub, followed by a lavender-lemongrass body butter wrap and concludes with a head-to-toe massage. The men's treatment menu includes a natural spice body buff and a men's manicure complete with hand massage.

WHERE TO SHOP

ARBORETUM AT GREAT HILLS
10000 Research Blvd., Austin, 512-338-4437; www.simon.com

This 45-store suburban shopping center attracts an upscale crowd with familiar favorites such as Barnes & Noble, Bath & Body Works, Pottery Barn, Restoration Hardware, The Sharper Image and Tommy Bahama. Just across the street, a Saks Fifth Avenue anchors a smaller shopping center called the Arboretum Market. Don't miss Austin's legendary marble cow sculptures on display here.
Monday-Saturday 10 a.m.-9 p.m., Sunday noon-6 p.m.

SOUTH CONGRESS AVENUE SHOPPING
South Congress Avenue from Riverside Drive to Oltorf Street, Austin

Forget mainstream malls and come to the shopping area nicknamed "SoCo." One-of-a-kind stores with names like Lucy in Disguise, New Bohemia and Uncommon Objects sell everything from vintage clothes and kitschy antiques to 1950s furniture, Mexican imports and more. One SoCo landmark not to be missed is Allens Boots, which displays more than 4,000 boots and other Western wear. A few popular restaurants, such as Guero's Taco Bar, cater to hungry shoppers.

DALLAS

Far from its '80s-era television portrayal as a rough-and-tumble oil town, or a playground for cowboy hat-wearing oil tycoons' soapy shenanigans, Dallas is a well-dressed, sophisticated city that tends toward formality—folks dress to the nines for a night on the town, and there's nary an establishment without valet parking. It's also considered a financial and fashion capital—ExxonMobil, Texas Instruments, and AT&T are headquartered here; and Neiman Marcus' flagship has claimed a downtown address since 1907. Locals know that Dallas is defined by its neighborhoods—Deep Ellum's time-worn music venues, Highland Park's mansions and its historic upscale shopping center Highland Park Village, down-town's high-powered business district and Uptown's string of sports bars. Of course, there's the ever-growing Arts District, which in the past year has seen some major new players, including a theater designed by Rem Koolhaas and an opera house dreamt up by Pritzker Prize-winning architect Norman Foster.

A fleet of antique trolleys ferry visitors around town, and a 5.2-acre grassy expanse is under construction over Woodall Rogers Freeway—by 2012, it will seamlessly connect Uptown to the Arts District and provide some much-needed green space for urbanites on foot. The biggest venture under way is also one of the largest public works projects in history—the $2.2 billion Trinity River Project, which will beautify a 20-mile strand of nature within the city limits and plant two Santiago Calatrava-designed bridges over Dallas' Trinity River.

Despite the city's refined character, there's one place where civility goes out the window: the football field. The colossal new Cowboys Stadium is a towering reminder that even the most sophisticated city has to let loose and go wild sometimes.

HIGHLIGHTS

WHAT ARE DALLAS' TOP MUSEUMS?

DALLAS MUSEUM OF ART
Works by masters Degas, Monet and van Gogh are featured in the Dallas Museum of Art. Be sure to check out the noteworthy African, Asian and Pacific collections as well.

MEADOWS MUSEUM
This museum showcases one of the largest and most comprehensive collections of Spanish art outside of Spain. You'll see pieces from El Greco, Goya and Picasso.

MUSEUM OF NATURE & SCIENCE
The Science Place, the Dallas Museum of Natural History and the Dallas Children's Museum merged to create this science powerhouse for both parents and kids.

THE SIXTH FLOOR MUSEUM AT DEALEY PLAZA
Dallas was the site of President John F. Kennedy's assassination. This museum honors him with displays that look at his life, death and legacy.

WHAT TO SEE

AFRICAN AMERICAN MUSEUM
3536 Grand Ave., Dallas, 214-565-9026; www.aamdallas.org

This magnificent building of ivory-hued stone houses a library, research center and numerous permanent and visiting exhibits.

Admission: free. Tuesday-Friday noon-5 p.m., Saturday from 10 a.m.-5 p.m., Sunday 1-5 p.m.

ANGELIKA FILM CENTER & CAFÉ
5321 E. Mockingbird Lane, Dallas, 214-841-4713; www.angelikafilmcenter.com

If your taste in movies leans toward the avant-garde, then enjoy one of the Angelika's eight theaters, as its wall-to-wall screens showcase some of the most talked-about newly released foreign, independent and specialty films. A café and lounge draw a hip crowd to this movie house, which is in a trendy entertainment district. Ticket prices and showtimes vary, so see the website for details.

Monday-Thursday 10 a.m.-midnight, Friday-Saturday 10 a.m.-2 a.m.

DALLAS ARBORETUM GARDENS
8525 Garland Road, Dallas, 214-515-6500; www.dallasarboretum.org

Several themed gardens are situated on 66 acres, including a trial garden for research. Featured areas include the Jonsson Color Garden, the Palmer Fern Dell, the Sunken Gardens and the Lay Ornamental Garden. Also onsite are fountains, sculptures and two historic mansions.

Admission: free. Daily 9 a.m.-5 p.m.

DALLAS COWBOYS
Cowboys Stadium, 925 N. Collins St., Arlington; www.dallascowboys.com

The famed professional football team and its perhaps even more famous cheerleaders moved to this new stadium in 2009.

DALLAS FARMERS MARKET
1010 S. Pearl St., Dallas, 214-670-5880; www.dallasfarmersmarket.org

This is the area's largest outdoor market, located on 8½ acres in the southeast corner of downtown. The spacious facility accommodates up to 1,000 vendors who sell fruit, vegetables, meats, specialty items and flowers grown in Texas and elsewhere. You can also find pottery, furniture and handcrafted jewelry at the International Fair section of the market or sign up for a cooking class with some of the best chefs in Dallas.

Admission: free. Daily 8 a.m.-6 p.m.

DALLAS MAVERICKS
American Airlines Center, 2500 Victory Ave., Dallas, 214-747-6287; www.nba.com

This professional basketball team is owned by flamboyant businessman Mark Cuban.

DALLAS MUSEUM OF ART
1717 N. Harwood St., Dallas, 214-922-1200; www.dm-art.org

Paintings by masters such as Degas, Monet, Renoir and van Gogh are among the 22,000 pieces of artwork in this museum's permanent collection, with about 3,500 on display at any given time. Especially noteworthy are its African, Asian and Pacific collections, particularly objects from Africa and Indonesia, such as a rare Kongo power figure and an 11th-century bronze sculpture of the Hindu god Shiva Nataraja. Other galleries feature European, American and contemporary art. There is free admission on the first Tuesday of the month and Thursday evenings.

Admission: adults $10, seniors $7, students $5, children under 12 free. Tuesday-Wednesday, Friday-Sunday 11 a.m-5 p.m., Thursday 11 a.m.-9 p.m.

DALLAS SYMPHONY ORCHESTRA
Morton H. Meyerson Symphony Center, 2301 Flora St., Dallas, 214-692-0203; www.dallassymphony.com

This symphony began in 1900 with a 40-piece ensemble. Now, it's internationally renowned and plays at Carnegie Hall and around the world. Its home is the I.M. Pei-designed Meyerson Symphony Center Gallery. Classical programs are performed as well as pop, jazz, and country.

Admission: varies. September-May, showtimes vary.

DALLAS THEATER CENTER

3636 Turtle Creek Blvd., Dallas, 214-522-8499; www.dallastheatercenter.org

This professional theater, formed in 1959, occupies two performing spaces. The building at 3636 Turtle Creek Blvd., designed by Frank Lloyd Wright, houses the Kalita Humphreys Theater (approximately 500 seats) and at 2401 Flora St. is the Arts District Theater, which has flexible seating and staging arrangements.
Admission: varies. August-May, Tuesday-Sunday showtimes vary.

DALLAS WORLD AQUARIUM

1801 N. Griffin St., Dallas, 214-720-2224; www.dwazoo.com

More than 375 species of marine, freshwater and tropical fish, amphibians and reptiles are showcased at the aquarium.
Admission: adults $18.95, seniors $14.95, children 3-12 $10.95, children under 3 free. Daily 10 a.m.-5 p.m.

DALLAS ZOO

650 South R.L. Thornton Freeway, Dallas, 214-670-5656; www.dallaszoo.com

More than 1,400 mammals, reptiles and birds make their home on the 85-acre grounds of this city zoo. The 25-acre "Wilds of Africa" exhibit features a one-mile monorail ride, nature trail and African Plaza, where animals roam freely through six naturalistic habitats.
Admission: adults $10, seniors and children 3-11 $7, children under 3 free. Daily 9 a.m.-5 p.m.

DEEP ELLUM ENTERTAINMENT DISTRICT

Between Elm Street, Commerce Street, Oakland Avenue and Good Latimer Expressway, Dallas; www.deepellumtx.com

Starting in the 1920s, this was the area for the city's jazz, blues and art scenes. This urban village is a large cluster of renovated warehouses just west of downtown where popular restaurants do business right alongside live-music clubs, eclectic shops and art galleries.
Admission: free. Daily.

FAIR PARK DALLAS

1300 Robert B. Cullum Blvd., Dallas, 214-421-9600; www.fairpark.org

Comprising 277 landscaped acres lined with Art Deco buildings, Fair Park has numerous entertainment and cultural facilities. This is the site of the annual state fair, one of the world's largest expositions.
Admission: free. Daily.

HALL OF STATE

3939 Grand Ave., Dallas, 214-421-0281; www.hallofstate.com

This historic landmark is an excellent example of American Art Deco architecture. Murals, statuary and changing exhibits depict the history of Texas. The Research Center is in the East Texas Room, while the lower floor houses the Dallas Historical Society offices.
Admission: free. Monday-Saturday 9 a.m.-5 p.m., Sunday 1-5 p.m.

JOHN F. KENNEDY MEMORIAL PLAZA

Main and Market Streets, Dallas

A 50-foot monument, designed by Philip Johnson, was erected in 1969 and is situated 200 yards from the spot where President Kennedy was assassinated. *Admission: free. Daily.*

MCKINNEY AVENUE TRANSIT AUTHORITY
3153 Oak Grove, Dallas, 214-855-0006; www.mata.org

Four restored vintage electric trolley cars operate over a three-mile route, mainly along McKinney Avenue, which connects central Dallas (beginning at Ross Avenue and St. Paul Street) with McKinney Avenue's popular restaurants, night-clubs and shops. Some tracks date back 100 years to Dallas's original trolley system.

MEADOWS MUSEUM
Southern Methodist University, 5900 Bishop Blvd., Dallas, 214-768-2516; www.smu.edu

At this 66,000-square-foot art museum on the campus of Southern Methodist University, the focus is on one of the largest and most comprehensive collections of Spanish artwork beyond Spain's borders. The collection includes more than 750 pieces, with about 100 usually on display, from classic masters such as El Greco, Goya, Picasso and Velazquez.

Admission: adults $8, seniors $6, children under 12 free. Free Thursday 5-8 p.m. Tuesday-Saturday 10 a.m.-5 p.m., Thursday 10 a.m.-8 p.m., Sunday noon-5 p.m.

MUSEUM OF NATURE & SCIENCE
3535 Grand Ave., Dallas, 214-428-5555; www.natureandscience.org

This museum is the result of a 2006 conglomeration of Dallas's The Science Place museum, the Dallas Museum of Natural History and the Dallas Children's Museum. The complex includes an IMAX theater and planetarium, and has 50 different habitat exhibits showing the diverse plant and animal life of Texas. Fossil Hall guides visitors past animals of prehistoric Texas, including a reconstructed Trinity River mammoth from 20,000 years ago. There are also hands-on exhibits on energy, chemistry, physics and medical sciences. IMAX and planetarium tickets are not included with general admission.

Admission: adults $8.75, seniors, students and children 12-17 $7.75, children 3-11 $5.50. Monday-Saturday 10 a.m.-5 p.m., Sunday noon-5 p.m.

THE MUSIC HALL AT FAIR PARK
909 First Ave., Dallas, 214-565-1116; www.liveatthemusichall.com

Open since 1925, this music hall is the home of the Dallas Summer Musicals and hosts performances by the Dallas Opera and Fort Worth Dallas Ballet. Call for details; prices and showtimes vary.

OLD CITY PARK MUSEUM
1515 S. Harwood St., Dallas, 214-421-5141; www.oldcitypark.org

Lovely Victorian homes, turn-of-the-century commercial buildings, a school and a church are among the 38 historic structures that introduce visitors to how Dallas looked and how its citizens lived between 1840 and 1910. The museum, which also includes a working farm, is spread over 13 acres just south of downtown. Explore the grounds on your own or take the one-hour guided tour offered each afternoon at 1:30 p.m. (2:30 p.m. on Sunday).

Admission: adults $7, seniors $5, children 3-12 $4. Tuesday-Saturday 10 a.m.-4 p.m., Sunday noon-4 p.m.

THE SIXTH FLOOR MUSEUM AT DEALEY PLAZA

411 Elm St., Dallas, 214-747-6660; www.jfk.org

President John F. Kennedy was assassinated in Dallas more than 45 years ago on November 22, 1963. In a moving tribute to the fallen leader, this downtown museum helps visitors recall the president's life, death and legacy through artifacts, historic films, interpretive displays and photographs.

Admission: adults $13.50, senior and children 6-18 $12.50, children under 6 $3.50. Tuesday-Sunday 10 a.m.-6 p.m., Monday noon-6 p.m.

TEXAS RANGERS

Rangers Ballpark, 100 Ballpark Way, Arlington, 817-273-5222; www.texas.rangers.mlb.com

The games of this professional baseball team are played at Rangers Ballpark in Arlington.

VIKING MILESTONE CULINARY ARTS CENTER

4531 McKinney Ave., Dallas, 214-526-3942; www.vikingrange.com

Sharpen your skills with a cooking class at this upscale retail store, an affilliate of the Viking Range Corporation, manufacturer of high-end kitchen appliances. Learn from staff instructors and guest chefs who heat up ovens in the area's best restaurant kitchens. The daily instruction runs the gamut from soufflé workshops to ethnic weeknight dinners. Some classes are taught lecture-style with demonstrations; others are hands-on. Shop for utensils, cookware and cookbooks after class, or browse the appliance showroom.

Monday-Friday 10 a.m.-9 p.m., Saturday 9 a.m.-6 p.m., Sunday noon-6 p.m.

WHERE TO STAY

★★★THE ADOLPHUS

1321 Commerce St., Dallas, 214-742-8200, 800-221-9083; www.hoteladolphus.com

Adolphus Busch, of Anheuser-Busch fame, built this grand dame in 1912. Through the years, royalty and celebrities alike have experienced the hotel's baroque splendor. The elegant French Room still rates as one of the city's best restaurants. Antique furniture and paintings adorn the hotel's rooms and public spaces, and a proper afternoon tea is held in the lobby living room from September to July.

422 rooms. Restaurant, bar. Business center. Fitness center. $151-250

★★★THE FAIRMONT DALLAS

1717 N. Akard St., Dallas, 214-720-2020, 866-540-4427; www.fairmont.com

Walking distance from Dallas' best arts venues, this hotel also puts guests in proximity to the city's downtown business district. A renovation in 2007 bestowed rooms with pillow-top beds, flat-screen TVs and MP3 docking stations. The rooftop is home to an Olympic-size pool as well as an extensive vegetable and herb garden overseen by the hotel restaurant's chef. Floors 17 to 19 make up Fairmont Gold, a hotel within the hotel. The more upscale Fairmont Gold feels like a boutique property, with its own staff and a homey, uncrowded lounge where free breakfast and afternoon canapés are served.

551 rooms. Restaurant, bar. Business center. Fitness center. Pool. Pets accepted. $151-250

★★★HILTON ANATOLE HOTEL

2201 Stemmons Freeway, Dallas, 214-748-1200, 800-445-8667;
www.anatole.hilton.com

With seven bars and lounges, meeting space galore, an 80,000-square-foot indoor/outdoor fitness center, and five restaurants—including the much-lauded Nana, on the 27th floor—this hotel is itself a destination. There's also a private sculpture park with jogging trails, a fish pond and tennis courts, which are rarities for such a centrally located urban property.

1,606 rooms. Restaurant, bar. Business center. Fitness center. Pool. Spa. Tennis. $151-250

★★★HOTEL LUMEN

6101 Hillcrest Ave., Dallas, 214-219-2400, 800-908-1140;
www.hotellumen.com

Located within Dallas' leafy Park Cities neighborhood and steps from Southern Methodist University, this Kimpton property serves up all the amenities of a full-service hotel, plus a whole lot of pizzazz. Guests are greeted by Sigmund, the resident canine, and the hotel has the ability to illuminate its façade in 120 different colors. Rooms and suites, refreshed in 2010, have a contemporary masculine feel and sprawling glass-enclosed showers equipped with side showerheads. The onsite restaurant, Social, is a modern take on a traditional steakhouse.

52 rooms. Restaurant, bar. Fitness center. Pets accepted. $251-350

★★★HOTEL PALOMAR

5300 E. Mockingbird Lane, Dallas, 214-520-7969,
888-253-9030; www.hotelpalomar-dallas.com

Every Kimpton hotel is designed around a story—at this location, it's "Art in Motion," where design elements, visual art and architecture coalesce to create a highly refined place to stay. Decorated in multi-textured earth tones of mustard yellows and glossy chocolate browns, rooms exude glam sophistication, matched by the open-air infinity pool, yoga studio and much talked-about restaurant, Central 214. Some of the hotel's quirkier amenities include a goldfish companion upon request, art supplies in the minibar, and special "tall rooms" to accommodate statuesque guests.

198 rooms. Restaurant, bar. Business center. Fitness center. Pool. Spa. Pets accepted. $251-350

WHICH DALLAS HOTELS HAVE THE MOST UNIQUE DÉCOR?

Hotel St. Germain:
An arts and antiques lover restored this 1900 hotel, which explains the turn-of-century antiques from France and New Orleans that fill the rooms. You'll find dramatic canopy beds and beautiful chandeliers in these grand rooms.

The Joule, Dallas:
Rooms at the Joule are dressed in lacquered dark furniture, crisp white linens and brightly colored rugs and pillows.

The Stoneleigh Hotel:
The rooms in this hotel exude Art Deco chic with reproduced furniture and bathrooms that come with chrome fixtures and black and white Calcutta marble floors.

★★★HOTEL ST. GERMAIN

2516 Maple Ave., Dallas, 214-871-2516, 800-683-2516; www.hotelstgermain.com

Despite its location in buzzing Uptown, this bijou of an inn offers a secluded getaway in grand style. Built as a private residence in 1900, it was painstakingly restored in 1990 by Claire Heymenn, an art and antiques aficionado from Louisiana. Each of seven suites is individually decorated with turn-of-the-century antiques from France and New Orleans. You'll see towering canopy beds and dazzling chandeliers, and Bulgari amenities come standard in every bathroom. The hotel revels in Old World touches, like dinner menus encased in wax-sealed envelopes, a white-gloved butler offering champagne at arrival and a full breakfast—included in the cost of your stay—delivered to your door every morning on antique china. Come nightfall, dine by candlelight in a room overlooking the garden courtyard. Back at the Parisian-style champagne bar, choose from 40 bottles, and be sure to sample the housemade pâtés.

7 rooms. Restaurant, bar. Complimentary breakfast. Fitness center. Spa. Pets accepted. $251-350

★★★HOTEL ZAZA

2332 Leonard St., Dallas, 214-468-8399, 800-597-8399; www.hotelzaza.com

The hotel's bar—which, in warmer months, stretches out to the illuminated pool—is one of Uptown's hottest spots. The posh vibe continues in the guest rooms, where a dazzling array of rich fabrics and busy patterns make for a Vegas-meets-boudoir feel. A butler's pantry on every floor provides coffee in the morning, while ZaSpa offers an innovative menu of treatments.

153 rooms. Restaurant, bar. Fitness center. Pool. Spa. Pets accepted. $151-250

★★★HYATT REGENCY DALLAS

300 Reunion Blvd., Dallas, 214-651-1234, 800-633-7313; www.hyattregencydallas.com

This all-encompassing downtown hotel is home to Reunion Tower, the iconic sphere that has come to define the city's skyline. Take the elevator up to the 50th floor for Wolfgang Puck's Asian restaurant, Five Sixty. If you're there for business rather than pleasure, there's also 160,000 square feet of meeting space, and a fully staffed business center with the means to create everything from overhead transparencies to mass mailings.

1,122 rooms. Restaurant, bar. Business center. Fitness center. Pool. $151-250

★★★THE JOULE, DALLAS

1530 Main St., Dallas, 214-748-1300; www.starwoodhotels.com

You're immediately confronted by the scene upon entering this downtown hotel, opened in 2008 in the neo-Gothic former Dallas National Bank building. To your right—Charlie Palmer's restaurant, where patrons clad in cocktail dresses and sleek suits swirl martinis at the low-lit bar—to your left, a lobby draped in rich fabrics and dramatic patterns is also home to a giant gear wheel, a nod to the city's history in the energy biz (the hotel was named after a unit of energy). Rooms are just as trendy; they sport lacquered dark-wood furniture, stark white bedding, and bright accents like striped rugs and red throw pillows. Each comes with a stainless-steel martini-making kit and a phone with Neiman Marcus on speed dial. The stunning 10th-floor pool, partially cantilevered over the street below; an art collection that includes an Andy Warhol; and an onsite wine store with computerized ordering add to the sexy, modern, effect of this swank hotel.

150 rooms. Restaurant, bar. Business center. Fitness center. Pool. Spa. Pets accepted. $251-350

★★★RENAISSANCE DALLAS HOTEL

2222 N. Stemmons Freeway, Dallas, 214-631-2222, 800-811-8893; www.renaissancehotels.com

Housed in an elliptical-shaped tower adjacent to the Dallas Market Center, this hotel offers nicely appointed guest rooms and the requisite business amenities. A new 27th-floor lounge serves free breakfast and evening hors d'oeuvres to guests staying on club-level floors. If you can't snag a room on a club-level floor, try dining in the warmly decorated T-Bones Steakhouse or the casual Charisma.

514 rooms. Restaurant, bar. Business center. Fitness center. Pool. $151-250

★★★★THE RITZ-CARLTON, DALLAS

2121 McKinney Ave., Dallas, 214-922-0200; www.ritzcarlton.com

Situated in the heart of pedestrian-friendly Uptown, this elegant Regency-style building offers all the opulence you'd expect from a Ritz-Carlton. A marble-floored, chandeliered lobby with an impressive display of fresh flowers that changes every Thursday gives way to oversized salmon-hued guestrooms complete with Bulgari bath products. Suites, and rooms on the club level floor, are bathed in a pastel blue palette, which is jazzed up with aristocratic elements like chairs upholstered in gold floral fabric and techy perks like televisions built into the bathroom mirror. The hotel's Rattlesnake Bar, which is connected to outdoor, fireplace-equipped sitting areas, is one of the city's top spots to see and be seen. The drink of choice? Dean's Signature Margarita, of course. Arrive at 6 p.m. and meet the hotel's guacamologist—a chef prepares fresh guacamole on a cart and doles it out, along with mini margaritas to everyone in the lobby, bar and restaurant. The property also pampers guests with a terraced pool area, the award-winning Fearing's Restaurant and such thoughtful niceties as a free overnight shoeshine.

255 rooms. Restaurant, bar. Business center. Fitness center. Pool. Spa. Pets accepted. $351 and up

★★★ROSEWOOD CRESCENT HOTEL

400 Crescent Court, Dallas, 214-871-3200; www.crescentcourt.com

Located within the Crescent, an elegant clutch of mixed-use towers with facades of Indiana limestone, mansard roofs of cut slate and whimsical filigree trim—the hotel feels more like France than Uptown Dallas. Priceless antiques, artwork and Louis XIV tapestries decorate the public spaces, while spiral stair-cases add romance to suites. Rooms are clean and pretty, with marble sinks and muted tones. They come with genteel conveniences like a shoe horn and valet stand for your suit; some are brightened up with a green chaise lounge. The biggest draw here is a tossup between the award-winning spa, with aroma-therapy baths developed from ancient Balinese and Indonesian techniques, and the Dallas outpost of excellent Japanese eatery Nobu.

191 rooms. Restaurant, bar. Business center. Fitness center. Pool. Spa. Pets accepted. $351 and up

★★★★ROSEWOOD MANSION ON TURTLE CREEK

2821 Turtle Creek Blvd., Dallas, 214-559-2100, 888-767-3966; www.mansiononturtlecreek.com

Situated in the leafy residential area of Turtle Creek, with instant access to the city, this lovely hotel retains the ambience of a distinguished residence. It's elegant—but unfussy—and exquisitely epitomizes the city's sense of style. The lauded Mansion restaurant, set in the former home of cotton and oil magnate Sheppard King, features a low-lit wood-paneled bar with live jazz three nights a week. Renovated in February 2010, the larger-than-average rooms have a soft, luxurious feel with blond woods, crisp white linens emblazoned with the letter "M," sand-colored geometric-patterned carpet and dark-peach velvet sofas. French doors open to private balconies with views of downtown or the tree-lined street below, while the lobby sports a gleaming marble floor and hand-painted wallpaper.

143 rooms. Restaurant, bar. Business center. Fitness center. Pool. Spa. Pets accepted. $351 and up

★★★THE STONELEIGH HOTEL

2927 Maple Ave., Dallas, 214-871-7111; www.stoneleighhotel.com

Open since 1924, this stately Uptown hotel underwent a floor-to-ceiling overhaul in 2007 that restored it to its Beaux-Arts splendor. The lobby bar exudes Old World romance—on one wall, a worn red velvet banquette spires to the ceiling; several dainty beaded glass chandeliers hang above the bar. Rooms are a study in Art Deco, right down to the spot-on reproduction furniture and bathrooms equipped with gleaming chrome fixtures and black and white Calcutta marble floors. The 12th-floor penthouse, originally designed by famed interior designer Dorothy Draper and meticulously restored by one of her protégés, Carleton Varney, was built as living space for the hotel's first owner. It's full of secret passageways and storage spots and also has its own cozy library bar and a living room wrapped in 500-year-old wood panels. The Stoneleigh Spa, with a menu of signature treatments built upon traditional Ayurvedic methods—is a true retreat for relaxation and indulgence, while the hotel's Bolla Restaurant serves a creative menu of contemporary American and Italian fare.

170 rooms. Restaurant, bar. Business center. Fitness center. Pets accepted. $251-350

★★★W DALLAS-VICTORY

2440 Victory Park Lane, Dallas, 214-397-4100; www.starwoodhotels.com

Concertgoers and sports aficionados will appreciate this hotel's prime locale—right across the street from entertainment mecca American Airlines Center. The onsite Bliss Spa, Top Chef head judge Tom Colicchio's Craft restaurant, a fully shaded rooftop pool and a flashy nightclub make for an indulgent, fun-filled stay. If there's anything else you desire, just push the "Whenever/Whatever" button on your room phone, and your wish will be granted.

283 rooms. Restaurant, bar. Business center. Fitness center. Pool. Spa. Pets accepted. $251-350

★★★WARWICK MELROSE HOTEL DALLAS

3015 Oak Lawn Ave., Dallas, 214-521-5151, 800-635-7673; www.melrosehotel.com

Built in 1924, this inviting hotel has a timeless, elegant feel. All of its oversized rooms were renovated in spring 2009, and no two are alike—except for their European marble baths. Locals crowd into the cozy Library Bar to sip martinis, while the light-filled restaurant serves three spectacular meals a day.

184 rooms. Restaurant, bar. Fitness center. Pets accepted. $151-250

RECOMMENDED

ALOFT DALLAS DOWNTOWN
1033 Young St., Dallas, 214-761-0000, 877-462-5638; www.aloftdallasdowntown.com
The first location of this hip and affordable hotel brand to be built in an existing structure (a 1924 warehouse) is steps from Dallas' Convention Center. The bright, open-air lobby establishes the fun, communal vibe; there's a grab-and-go market of drinks and snacks, a pool table and a library of books and board games alongside the buzzing bar. The hotel adds nice touches: Rooms are simple and stylish, with picture windows, 14-foot ceilings, exposed brick walls and vintage-inspired analog alarm clocks; natty circular rattan loungers line the pool. Technology also rules—note the complimentary wireless and check-in/check-out computer consoles.
193 rooms. Bar. Fitness center. Pool. Pets accepted. $61-150

BELMONT HOTEL
901 Fort Worth Ave., Dallas, 214-393-2300, 866-870-8010; www.belmontdallas.com
This refurbished 1936 motel maintains a laid-back retro feel—think bowl-shaped patio chairs, original bathroom tiles and a deck bar that hosts local art exhibits. Situated on a hill just outside downtown, it also affords an incredible view. A new locavore restaurant, Smoke, opened in September 2009 with a menu full of house-cured meats and inventive takes on Texas classics.
68 rooms. Restaurant, bar. Fitness center. Pool. Pets accepted. $61-150

WHERE TO EAT

★★★★ABACUS
4511 McKinney Ave., Dallas, 214-559-3111; www.abacus-restaurant.com
Kent Rathbun is one of Dallas' most respected chefs, and Abacus is his gleaming crown jewel. Filled with modern furniture and serviced by an incredibly attentive staff, the bar and dining room exude an air of exclusivity. Tasteful, modern pops of color, like dramatic flowers in clear glass vases, keep it interesting. Lighting is soft and low, and the atmosphere is clean, professional and calm. The menu is global, but cohesive, with obvious touches of the South and Southwest, like the Serrano-jack cheese grits and the cumin-cured hanger steak sope. There's also a sushi menu, and, this being Dallas, a well-edited list of steaks. The signature lobster-scallion shooters—small fried lobster dumplings served in sake cups with a red chile and coconut sake sauce—are not to be missed.
International. Dinner. Closed Sunday. Reservations recommended. Bar. $86 and up

★★★AL BIERNAT'S
4217 Oak Lawn Ave., Dallas, 214-219-2201; www.albiernats.com
The downtown Highland Park neighborhood provides the perfect setting for one of Dallas' loveliest steak restaurants. The Kobe-style cut steak with a grill-charred crust and ruby interior is the menu's standout option. Lobster, lamb chops, à la carte sides and chocolate bread pudding round out the most favorable offerings. There is an extensive wine list of more than 600 selections.
American. Lunch (Monday-Friday), dinner, Sunday brunch. Reservations recommended. Outdoor seating. Bar. $36-85

WHAT ARE THE BEST AMERICAN RESTAURANTS IN DALLAS?

The Mansion Restaurant:
The upscale menu includes dishes like seared snapper and sea scallops with caramelized fennel and bouillabaisse jus and Maine lobster salad with tomato confit and caviar cream.

Nana:
Set inside the Hilton Anatole Hotel, this restaurant gets creative with its American cuisine. Tuna tartare come with wasabi ice cream and sesame tuile. Nana is one of Dallas' top culinary destinations.

★★★AURORA

4216 Oak Lawn Ave., Dallas, 214-528-9400; www.auroradallas.com

Mesmerizing food created by famed chef/owner Avner Samuel delights even the most demanding palates in this restaurant just outside Highland Park. Dishes such as warm egg custard infused with white truffles; diver scallops over chestnut-potato purée; roasted duck with duck confit and a sweet potato-roasted apple tart are all delicious.

American, Continental. Lunch (Monday-Friday), dinner. Closed Sunday. Reservations recommended. $36-85

★★★CAFÉ PACIFIC

24 Highland Park Village, Dallas, 214-526-1170; www.cafepacificdallas.com

Café Pacific has been a Dallas favorite for nearly 30 years, thanks to well-prepared, yet unpretentious dishes such as the chilled fruits de mer platter with lump crab meat, jumbo shrimp, lobster tail and Blue Point oysters. The halibut with papaya salsa can easily pair with a glass or bottle of wine from the extensive and well-selected list.

Seafood. Lunch (Monday-Saturday), dinner (Monday-Saturday), Sunday brunch. Outdoor seating. Bar. $36-85

★★★CAPITAL GRILLE

500 Crescent Court, Dallas, 214-303-0500; www.thecapitalgrille.com

This outpost of the national chain that specializes in steak dinners is decorated with rich dark wood and burgundy leather banquettes and located within the elegant Crescent Court complex in Uptown. Steaks dry-aged onsite are the main attraction, but fresh seafood, tender veal chops and flavorful lamb chops are other highlights.

American. Lunch (Monday-Friday), dinner. Reservations recommended. Bar. $36-85

★★★CHARLIE PALMER AT THE JOULE

The Joule, Dallas, 1530 Main St., Dallas, 214-261-4600; www.charliepalmer.com

This progressive American restaurant, helmed by celeb chef Charlie Palmer, puts a new spin on classic steakhouse fare. Expect dishes like poached black tiger shrimp in Bloody Mary vinaigrette, and plancha-seared mahi mahi with a ginger-tomato sauce. In a clever nod to Texas' growing status as a wind-energy producer, the warm, earth-tone interior features slowly spinning "turbines" overhead. To give it a cozier vibe, small white wall-mounted lamps dimly illuminate the dining room. If you liked a particular wine during dinner, head to the adjacent Next Vintage shop after your meal. The wine shop allows you to use the nifty touch-screen eWinebooks to peruse Palmer's eclectic collection of whites and reds.

American. Breakfast, lunch, dinner. Reservations recommended. Bar. $36-85

★★★CRAFT

W Dallas-Victory, 2440 Victory Park Lane, Dallas, 214-397-4111; www.craftrestaurant.com

Tucked inside the W Dallas, this Texas outpost of *Top Chef* judge Tom Colicchio's award-winning New York eatery takes ample advantage of the Lone Star State's agricultural bounty. Succulent meats from artisanal ranches, fresh-picked produce and day boat fish are served family-style beneath the glow of Craft's signature hanging filament bulbs atop handcrafted walnut tables. A handful of popular New York City dishes, including braised beef short ribs and hen-of-the-woods mushrooms, have gone west, finding a new home on the Dallas menu.

American. Breakfast, lunch, dinner. Reservations recommended. $36-85

★★★DEL FRISCO'S DOUBLE EAGLE STEAK HOUSE

5251 Spring Valley Road, Dallas, 972-490-9000; www.delfriscos.com

This steakhouse is ornately decorated with dark mahogany, marble and chandeliers. Prime beef is the star of the menu, while dishes such as sherry-rich mock turtle soup, thick-cut onion rings or four-layer lemon-cream cake add to the offerings.

American. Dinner. $16-35

★★★DRAGONFLY

Hotel ZaZa, 2332 Leonard St., Dallas, 214-550-9500; www.hotelzaza.com

One of Dallas' hippest nightspots is also a restaurant that serves dishes influenced by the flavors of Japan, Thailand, Vietnam, China and Morocco. Begin with the lamb chop lollipops or an order of ahi tuna tacos with mango relish. Other menu highlights include pot stickers stuffed with rock shrimp and laced with lobster butter over a crisp, cool salad of pear slices and watercress; black cod with a miso glaze; and a tagine of fish cooked with preserved lemons and garlic over a pillow of couscous.

International. Breakfast, lunch, dinner, brunch. Bar. $36-85

★★★★FEARING'S

The Ritz-Carlton, Dallas, 2121 McKinney Ave., Dallas, 214-922-4848; www.fearingsrestaurant.com

Often called "The Father of Southwest Cooking," chef Dean Fearing has instilled his eponymous eatery at the Ritz-Carlton, Dallas with dishes inspired by his grandmothers' love of Southern food and barbecue. Imbued with Texas taste enhancers like peppers, dried chilies, jícama and cilantro, signature dishes like the famous tortilla soup, barbecued shrimp tacos, and rib-eye mopped over mesquite don't disappoint. Choose among seven different seating options that range from The Gallery, with 18-foot-tall ceilings and light-backed honey onyx wall panels, to the decidedly causal, subtly Western Dean's Kitchen. Tables are set up around the action-packed kitchen, where you can watch the masters at work.

Southwestern. Breakfast, lunch (Monday-Saturday), dinner, Sunday brunch. Reservations recommended. Outdoor seating. Bar. $86 and up

★★★★THE FRENCH ROOM

Adolphus Hotel, 1321 Commerce St., Dallas, 214-742-8200; www.hoteladolphus.com

Located in the elegant Adolphus Hotel, The French Room has been one of Dallas' top destinations for an unforgettable meal since 1981. Inspired by the interiors of 18th-century European palaces, the dining room is unquestionably the city's most sumptuous—the walls and arched ceiling are covered with a rococo mural; bas-reliefs original to the hotel's 1912 construction have been beautifully restored; and the space is softly lit by hand-blown Murano glass chandeliers. Tuxedoed servers deliver a three-course prix fixe menu displaying classic French techniques, such as foie gras torchon, kalamata olive mousse-line, and braised short ribs with fork-mashed fingerlings, shaved truffle, and thyme natural jus. Try any of the playful desserts, such as the popcorn pot du crème with salted caramel ice cream or the slow-baked lemon meringue with sparkling lavender sorbet and mint oil.

French. Dinner. Closed Sunday-Monday. Jacket required. Bar. $86 and up

★★★LANDMARK

Warwick Melrose Hotel, 3015 Oak Lawn Ave., Dallas, 214-521-5151, 800-635-7673; www.melrosehotel.com

This warm, light-filled restaurant inside the historic Warwick Melrose Hotel offers a seven-course tasting menu available with or without wine pairings. Some of the unique offerings include the Hudson Valley foie gras parfait with slow-roasted Texas wild boar vin cotto and fig jam with sherry cream and the porcini-crusted aged strip loin "brick." The Library Bar features sophisticated bar food and cocktails backed by live piano performances.

American. Breakfast, lunch, dinner, late-night, Sunday brunch. Reservations recommended. Bar. $36-85

★★★LOCAL

2936 Elm St., Dallas, 214-752-7500; www.localdallas.com

Smart diners call well ahead to snag one of the 50 seats inside this sleek space in Deep Ellum. A study in understated refinement, Local is memorable for its creative use of seasonal fare. A simple salad of Texas strawberries and garden greens sprinkled with goat cheese and walnuts and drizzled balsamic provides a sustainable start. The entrées range from grilled Berkshire double pork chop with sautéed Texas greens to cornflake-panko-crusted sea bass with spring onion, English pea, and Meyer lemon risotto. Share the artisan cheese course or one of the clever desserts, like the cardamom-spiced cake doughnut holes by the dozen or half-dozen.

American. Dinner. Closed Sunday-Tuesday. Reservations recommended. Bar. $36-85

★★★★THE MANSION RESTAURANT

Rosewood Mansion on Turtle Creek, 2821 Turtle Creek Blvd., Dallas, 214-443-4747; www.mansiononturtlecreek.com

Built into the former home of cotton and oil magnate Sheppard King—note the ornate mantel over the fireplace and the intricate carved ceiling—this praiseworthy restaurant has been a Dallas favorite for 30 years. A meticulous renovation in 2008 injected the space with tasteful updated touches, like modern art from local artists and contemporary lighting. A new chef, Bruno Davaillon, took over in January 2010 to great fanfare and instilled the menu with modern French cuisine, keeping only one dish—the Mansion's famous tortilla soup. Test out some of the tasty new additions, including seared snapper and sea scallops with caramelized fennel and bouillabaisse jus, roasted Texas quail, Maine lobster salad with tomato confit and caviar cream.

American. Breakfast, lunch, dinner, Sunday brunch. Reservations recommended. Outdoor seating. Jacket required. $86 and up

★★★MORTON'S, THE STEAKHOUSE

501 Elm St., Dallas, 214-741-2277; www.mortons.com

Situated downtown, this branch of the Morton's chain is beloved for its animated signature tableside presentation of the menu's top dishes. Diners select their own cuts of meat at the table. Meals are made even heartier with a selection of the famously filling side dishes.

Steak. Dinner. Bar. $36-85

★★★★NANA

Hilton Anatole Hotel, 2201 Stemmons Freeway, Dallas, 214-761-7470; www.nanarestaurant.com

Nana, located on the 27th floor of the Hilton Anatole, is one of Dallas' top spots for inspired contemporary American cuisine. Chef Anthony Bombaci's whimsical creations include tuna tartare with wasabi ice cream and sesame tuile, pickled cucumber "spaghetti" with yogurt-lime sauce, and butternut squash and ginger sorbet. Awash in sophisticated, ivory tones and decorated with priceless Asian art from the private collection of Margaret and Trammel Crow, the room feels like a posh art gallery, especially when filled to capacity with its chic crowd of urban regulars.

American. Dinner. Reservations recommended. Bar. $36-85

★★★NEWPORT'S SEAFOOD

703 McKinney Ave., Dallas, 214-954-0220; www.newportsrestaurant.com

Tucked into the old Dallas Brewery & Bottling Works building, Newport's was one of the first restaurants to open in the West End. Although the setting is rustic, the menu surprises with dishes such as ahi tuna sashimi in a sake-soy sauce; pasta with calamari, shrimp, Greek olives, herbs and feta; and favorites like filet mignon with broiled lobster. Enjoy dinner with a background of live jazz on Saturday nights.

Seafood. Lunch (Monday-Friday), dinner. Bar. $36-85

★★★NICK AND SAM'S STEAK AND FISH

3008 Maple Ave., Dallas, 214-871-7444; www.nick-sams.com

This sophisticated Uptown restaurant is known for its exceptional steaks. Though the perfectly cooked bone-in rib-eyes need no adornment, the housemade steak sauce and horseradish cream are the perfect complements. The fish portion of the menu is substantial, featuring raw bar items alongside intriguing options such as fried lobster and green curry mussels. The restaurant has an award-winning wine list with a more-than-ample selection of pours by the glass.

American, steak. Dinner. Reservations recommended. Bar. $36-85

★★★PAPPAS BROS. STEAKHOUSE

10477 Lombardy Lane, Dallas, 214-366-2000; www.pappasbros.com

This busy restaurant serves a classically prepared steak house menu of prime aged beef and lobster. With an extensive wine list—more than 2,300 varieties—the options can be overwhelming. If you can't make up your mind, ask the waitstaff for a recommendation; the service is informed, attentive and accommodating.

Steak. Dinner. Closed Sunday. $36-85

★★★PYRAMID

The Fairmont Dallas, 1717 N. Akard St., Dallas, 214-720-2020; www.fairmont.com

A longtime downtown haunt, this elegant restaurant in the Fairmont hotel has evolved from a formal space for power lunches to a welcoming dining room that's just as appropriate for date night—thanks to a floor-to-ceiling redo in 2008. A new chef took over in early 2010, injecting the menu with a local focus. Some ingredients are even sourced from the hotel's expansive rooftop vegetable and herb garden, like the fruit and herbs for watermelon feta mint salad, and the berries that top the Texas spiced wine sorbet.

American. Breakfast, lunch, dinner, Sunday brunch. Reservations recommended. Children's menu. Bar. $36-85

★★★THE RESTAURANT AT HOTEL ST. GERMAIN

2516 Maple Ave., Dallas, 214-871-2516; www.hotelstgermain.com

The fixed-price, seven-course meal in the elegant dining room of the historic Hotel St. Germain is one of Dallas' most sought-after dining experiences. Expect perfectly executed French fare, like Jonah crab salad mousseline and beef tenderloin on pommes Anna with artichoke barigoule, served on antique china in the small, candlelit dining room ringed by hotel owner Claire Heymenn's collection of antique Limoges china and Waterford crystal.

French. Dinner. Closed Sunday-Monday. Reservations recommended. Outdoor seating. Jacket required. $86 and up

★★★RUTH'S CHRIS STEAK HOUSE

17840 Dallas Parkway, Dallas, 972-250-2244; www.ruthschris.com

This Dallas location of the national steakhouse chain offers a classic experience in a dining room decked out in masculine wood paneling. The menu features a wide selection of steaks, seafood and sides from Caesar salad to potatoes au gratin.

Steak. Dinner. Bar. $36-85

★★★SEVENTEEN SEVENTEEN

1717 Harwood St., Dallas, 214-922-1858; www.dm-art.org

Artful dishes worthy of this restaurant's Dallas Museum of Art location have made this eatery a favorite of fashionable diners. Start with a dish of tempura shrimp over baby greens dressed in a Thai vinaigrette and cradled in a crispy wonton basket. Sample an entrée quesadilla stuffed with smoked chicken and dabbed with a roasted tomatillo salsa, or try a pan-seared pork chop in a soy glaze over stir-fried rice in a baked acorn squash.

American. Lunch. Closed Sunday-Monday. Outdoor seating. Bar. $16-35

★★★STEEL

3102 Oak Lawn Ave., Dallas, 214-219-9908; www.steeldallas.com

Tucked into Uptown's Centrum Building, this restaurant attracts a fashionable crowd that comes for the sensational sushi, inspired Asian dishes and exotic wines. The red clam nigiri is superb, as is the Japanese ceviche of octopus, squid, clam and crab in a miso vinaigrette. Cooked dishes are worth a try, including the sea bass in miso and sake, and orange-infused Korean beef.

Pan-Asian. Lunch (Monday-Friday), dinner. Reservations recommended. Outdoor seating. Bar. $36-85

★★★★STEPHAN PYLES

1807 Ross Ave., Dallas, 214-580-7000; www.stephanpyles.com

Stephan Pyles has come a long way since his youth, when he rolled tamales at his family's truck stop. With several cookbooks and numerous accolades under his belt, Pyles uses his eponymous restaurant to showcase his elevated Southwestern cuisine. The dinner menu features imaginative dishes such as coriander-cured rack of lamb with Ecuadorian potato cake and cranberry mojo, but a meal here isn't complete without an order of ceviche. Among the eight varieties, go for the ahi tuna with jícama and grilled orange or the lobster with guayaba and avocado.

Southwestern. Lunch (Monday-Friday), dinner. Closed Sunday. Reservations recommended. Outdoor seating. Bar. $36-85

RECOMMENDED

ARCODORO & POMODORO

100 Crescent Court, Dallas, 214-871-1924; www.arcodoro.comsteel

A riveting menu of Italian and Sardinian specialties is served in a bright dining room or alfresco—on a stone-wall shaded patio—at this centrally located eatery, a standby since the late '80s. Go for the buffalo mozzarella and pesce al sale, a salt-crusted fish that changes daily, which are flown in each day from Europe.

Italian, Sardinian. Lunch (Monday-Friday), dinner, Saturday-Sunday brunch. Outdoor seating. Bar. $16-35

BOLSA

614 W. Davis St., Dallas, 214-367-9367; www.bolsadallas.com

This breezy locavore restaurant was a hit on the scene as soon it arrived in the burgeoning Oak Cliff neighborhood in 2009. Built into a former garage, the restaurant has tables set on smooth cement and huge windows behind the bar that are raised in warmer months to transform it into an outdoor space. The food echoes the simple space: Savory flatbread pizzas are topped with fresh arugula, braised short ribs are served with horseradish potatoes and there's even a Texas Clambake with littleneck clams, jalapeños and corn. The menu changes constantly, but few folks leave without ordering the bruschetta—four rows of seasonally varied takes on the classic Italian appetizer, like prosciutto and fig preserve; smoked salmon, pickled red onion, crème fraîche, and capers; and apple, Petit Basque cheese and toasted pine nuts.

Contemporary American. Lunch, dinner. Outdoor seating. Bar. $16-35

CENTRAL 214

Hotel Palomar Dallas, 5680 N. Central Expressway, Dallas, 214-443-9339; www.central214.com

Executive chef Blythe Beck of Naughty Kitchen fame runs the show at this low-lit modern dining room in the lobby of the Hotel Palomar. Expect a classic cocktail menu and inventive takes on Americana mainstays, like lamb chop lollipops, and shrimp and cayenne deviled eggs.

Contemporary American. Breakfast (Monday-Friday), lunch (Monday-Friday), dinner. Bar. $16-35

DISH

4123 Cedar Springs Road, Dallas, 214-522-3474; www.dish-dallas.com

A sleek, nightclub vibe dominates this Oak Lawn restaurant, which entered Dallas' dining scene in early 2010. The menu has plenty of options for sharing—flatbreads, crab dip, beef sliders—while entrées include everything from orecchiette to applewood-smoked bacon burgers. Pair dinner with something from the list of fanciful cocktails, some adorned with edible flowers. Try the Effen Good Cherry Lemonade, a blend of Effen cherry vodka and freshly squeezed lemon and lime juice.

Contemporary American. Brunch (Saturday-Sunday), lunch (Monday-Friday), dinner. Outdoor seating. Bar. $16-35

FIVE SIXTY

Hyatt Regency Dallas, 300 Reunion Blvd., Dallas, 214-741-5560

Fifty stories up inside the Hyatt Regency's iconic ball tower, Wolfgang Puck's new Japanese restaurant is named for its 560-foot elevation. The menu shows the influence of several Asian countries, with Indian spiced cauliflower soup as well as hamachi and tuna sashimi. Floor-to-ceiling windows afford an all-encompassing survey of the city, and you'll get a view of it all since the dining room completes a 360-degree rotation once every hour. Bottom line: You can't beat the views or the sushi.

Dinner. Reservations recommended. Bar. $16-35

HIBISCUS

2927 N. Henderson Ave., Dallas, 214-827-2927; www.hibiscusdallas.com

Hibiscus was one of the first new restaurants in the happening Knox-Henderson area five years ago, and Dallas' beautiful people flocked there. The neighborhood continues to transform into a dining destination, and Hibiscus remains on top—thanks to its luscious cocktails (go for the Hibiscus Cooler—bubbly champagne gently blended with watermelon purée and hibiscus tea), fabulously prepared entrées and enticing salads and small plates. Try the prosciutto-wrapped bobwhite quail, tenderloin tartare and baby greens topped with house-pickled asparagus and lemon-Parmesan vinaigrette.

Contemporary American. Dinner. Reservations recommended. Bar. $36-85.

RISE NO. 1

5360 W. Lovers Lane, Dallas, 214-366-9900; www.risesouffle.com

The menu is pretty straightforward at this homey Francophile respite. It's all soufflés, plus a handful of heartier entrées just to please the masses. But stick to what the restaurant does best and start with a savory soufflé, like the ham and

Gruyère, smoked salmon or truffle-infused mushroom. Then end with a sweet one, like the chocolate, Grand Marnier or praline pecan soufflé. Located in the Inwood Village shopping center, the eatery also serves wine flights and has an artisanal cheese cart.

French. Lunch, dinner. Outdoor seating. Bar. $16-35

SAMAR

2100 Ross Ave., Dallas, 214-922-9922; www.samarrestaurant.com

The latest venture from lauded local chef Stephan Pyles, this dreamy boudoir-inspired space is in Dallas' Arts District and specializes in small plates. The menu is divided into three sections—Spain, India and the Eastern Mediterranean. Stick to one region, or divide and conquer. If you choose a taste of Spain, order the almond gazpacho topped with guajillo chile oil and three "liquid grapes"; the croquetas del cangrejo, peekytoe crab fritters with celery-citrus salpicón; or the cerdo asado con manzanas, seared sous vide pork tenderloin with apples, saffron and vanilla. For Indian eats, try the Oyla Kandi Ka Machli, tandoor-roasted halibut served with eggplant pâté and coconut rice, and make a trip to the bread bar for naan fresh from a tandoor oven and several assorted chutneys.

Spanish, Indian, Mediterranean. Lunch (Monday-Friday), dinner. $16-35

SCREEN DOOR

1722 Routh St., Dallas, 214-720-9111; www.screendoordallas.com

Homemade, slow-roasted and locally harvested are the tenets to which this gracious new restaurant adheres. Located in One Arts Plaza, a brand-new multi-use development abutting the Arts District, it's Southern cuisine at its most sophisticated. But the restaurant doesn't sacrifice soulful Southern favorites in favor of sophistication; classics like chicken and waffles, shrimp and grits, and fried green tomatoes are just the beginning.

Southern. Lunch (Monday-Friday), dinner (Monday-Saturday), Sunday brunch. $16-35

SHINSEI

7713 Inwood Road, Dallas, 214-352-0005; www.shinseirestaurant.com

Lynae Fearing and Tracy Rathbun, the wives of two of Dallas' most lauded chefs, dreamt up this chic sushi restaurant. Helmed by a jovial chef, the restaurant also offers a full menu of decadent, fully cooked entrées. The crispy calamari salad, served over a bed of fresh hearts of palm, mango and banana, is not to be missed.

Pan-Asian. Lunch (Friday), dinner. Closed Sunday. Bar. $16-35

YORK STREET

6047 Lewis St., Dallas, 214-826-0968; www.yorkstreetdallas.com

Any well-informed Dallasite will tell you that York Street is the place to experience one of the city's most memorable dinners. Executive chef Sharon Hage is praised locally for her changed-daily menu of simple, mouthwatering creations—like spring pea soup, deviled goose eggs, and slow-roasted ham with shell beans and crumbled cornbread—which she will gladly pair with your favorite bottle of wine at this BYOB.

Lunch (Wednesday), dinner. Closed Sunday-Monday. $16-35

SPA

★★★★THE RITZ-CARLTON SPA DALLAS

The Ritz-Carlton, Dallas, 2121 McKinney Ave., Dallas, 214-922-4820; www.ritzcarlton.com

You don't need a degree in mathematics to figure out that eight massaging hands afford infinitely more knot-soothing relief than the standard two-palmer. The Texas Eight-Hand Massage is just one of the items on The Ritz-Carlton Spa Dallas' expansive menu of feel-good treatments. The 12,000-square-foot retreat also boasts six exclusive Prada Beauty facial treatments in addition to couples' programs and executive distress day packages. For those just as concerned about the state of their figure as their epidermis, the spa also has a 24-hour fitness center.

WHERE TO SHOP

BISHOP ARTS DISTRICT

Bishop and Davis streets, Dallas; www.bishopartsdistrict.com

In Dallas' burgeoning Oak Cliff area, this compact area of shops and restaurants is quickly gaining speed. You'll find everything here: Bishop Street Market (*419 N. Bishop Ave.*) has an encyclopedic selection of unique greeting cards; Make (*313 N. Bishop Ave.*) is all crafts, from locally made scarves to handmade earrings; and The Soda Gallery (*408 N. Bishop Ave.*) carries the city's largest selection of rare, small-batch soda. At The Soda Gallery, savor a glass-bottled Dublin Dr. Pepper—made using the original recipe with good old cane sugar and none of that newfangled fructose corn syrup—which is still produced in Dublin, Texas, the oldest bottler of the iconic Southern soda. If you get hungry, there's a handful of sought-after restaurants nearby, such as upscale roadhouse Tillman's, debonair Hattie's and its sophisticated takes on Southern cuisine, and Eno's—for wine and wood-fired pizza. For a sweet ending, don't miss Dude, Sweet Chocolate (*408 W. Eighth St.*), where you can get handmade artisan treats like the Provencal, chocolate with dried pear, basil and rosemary salt.
Hours vary.

THE GALLERIA

LBJ Freeway at North Dallas Parkway, Dallas, 972-702-7100; www.galleriadallas.com

Style-conscious Dallas has a longstanding dispute over the city's best mall— The Galleria or NorthPark Center? Either way, it's a buyer's market. Anchored by Saks, Macy's and Nordstrom, the Galleria was designed to mimic the Galleria Vittorio Emanuele in Milan and has some 200 men's, women's and specialty stores, including the whimsical Betsey Johnson boutique and purse purveyor Dooney & Bourke. A glassy dome covers the central atrium, home to an ice-skating rink that's open year-round.
Monday-Saturday 10 a.m.-9 p.m., Sunday noon-6 p.m.

HIGHLAND PARK VILLAGE

Mockingbird Lane at Preston Road, Dallas; www.hpvillage.com

It's no surprise that the nation's first open-air shopping center is in one of Dallas' wealthiest zip codes. It's also no surprise that all its shops are found underneath the beautifully maintained clay roof in this navigable Mediterranean-style compound, now a National Historic Landmark. Established in 1931, Highland Park Village continues to serve Dallas' best-dressed with high-end boutiques like Carolina Herrera, Escada, Hermès and Jimmy Choo. Take advantage of the valet parking, and refuel between shop stops with a Mambo Taxi margarita at Mi Cocina restaurant.

Hours vary.

KNOX-HENDERSON

Interstate 75 and Knox Street-Henderson Avenue, Dallas

Just north of downtown, this pedestrian-friendly neighborhood of shops and restaurants has grown organically—and exponentially—over the past few years. The avenue is split in half by North Central Expressway (Interstate 75). Big-name retailers Pottery Barn, Crate & Barrel and Apple anchor the Knox side, while Henderson takes on a more localized feel. Well-curated antique shops and vintage clothing stores abound. You can pick up authentic Mexican wares like talavera pottery at La Mariposa (*2813 N. Hendson Ave.*), or nab souvenirs from around the world, such as vegetable-died Turkish textiles, at Another Time and Place (*2815 N. Henderson Ave.*). One of the most recent newcomers to the shopping destination, We Are 1976 (*1902 N. Henderson Ave.*), is a design store with wares that range from art books to cartoony Japanese bento boxes.

Hours vary.

NEIMAN MARCUS

1618 Main St., Dallas, 214-741-6911; www.neimanmarcus.com

The brand's downtown Dallas flagship has everything you need to fit into this dressed-up city. Take a break from shopping at the sixth-level fine dining restaurant, the Zodiac, or the street-level NM Fashion Café, which serves the store's famously delectable chocolate-chip cookies.

Monday-Saturday 10 a.m.-6 p.m., Thursday 10 a.m.-7 p.m.

NORTHPARK CENTER

Northwest Highway and Interstate 75, Dallas, 214-361-6345; www.northparkcenter.com

Dillard's, Macy's, Nordstrom, Neiman Marcus and Barneys New York make up the backbone of this three-story spread. The second-largest mall in Texas, it's built around a 1.4-acre grass-covered indoor park. A 48-foot-fall orange sculpture made of crisscrossed steal I-beams by Mark di Suvero is a towering presence. The artsy mall also features works by Frank Stella and Andy Warhol, so you get a dose of culture with your shopping. Included in the array of more than 235 stores are denim boutiques True Religion and Seven for All Mankind, as well as outposts from Louis Vuitton and Bottega Veneta.

Monday-Saturday 10 a.m.-9 p.m., Sunday noon-6 p.m.

PRAIRIES AND LAKES

This region is known mainly for Fort Worth, which is filled with museums and other cultural pursuits. But it's also home to Arlington, which boasts several entertainment centers, water parks and sports arenas, including Six Flags Over Texas, Hurricane Harbor, and Rangers Ballpark, Home of the Texas Rangers. The New Cowboys Stadium, which hosts the NFL team in season and was completed in 2009, is another must-see.

WHAT TO SEE

ARLINGTON
LEGENDS OF THE GAME OF BASEBALL MUSEUM
Ameriquest Field, 1000 Ballpark Way, Arlington, 817-273-5600;www.texas.rangers.mlb.com

This 24,000-square-foot museum showcases more than 140 baseball artifacts, bats, gloves, jerseys, trophies and memorabilia collected from legends such as Hank Aaron, Ty Cobb, Lou Gehrig and Babe Ruth. Other exhibits focus on the Rangers and their history in the league. In the Learning Center, interactive exhibits are a hit with younger fans. You can take a tour of the ballpark as well.

Admission: adults $12, seniors and students $10, children 4-18 $7, children under 4 free. April-September, game day 9 a.m.-7:30 p.m., non-game day, Monday-Saturday 9 a.m.-4 p.m., Sunday 11 a.m.-4 p.m.; October-March, Tuesday-Saturday 10 a.m.-4 p.m.

NEW COWBOYS STADIUM
Arlington, 972-785-5000; www.dallascowboys.com

After nearly four decades in Irving, the Dallas Cowboys have a new home in Arlington at New Cowboys Stadium. It boasts a retractable roof that can open or close in just 12 minutes, seats for 80,000 (with the capability to expand for up to 100,000) and two enormous viewing screens. Opened in 2009, the stadium is slated to host the 2011 Super Bowl.

Admission: varies. August-January.

RIVER LEGACY LIVING SCIENCE CENTER
703 NW Green Oaks Blvd., Arlington, 817-860-6752; www.riverlegacy.org

The center has hands-on exhibits depicting the thriving ecosystem along the Trinity River. Kids will enjoy the Living Science Center Field Investigations where they get a chance to search for different plant species and animals such as raccoons, owls and opossums. There are also running and bike paths and pedestrian bridges spanning the Trinity River.

Admission: free. Park: Tuesday-Saturday 5 a.m.-10 p.m. Science Center: Tuesday-Saturday 9 a.m.-5 p.m.

SIX FLAGS HURRICANE HARBOR
1800 E. Lamar Blvd., Arlington, 817-265-3356; www.sixflags.com

Cool off from the hot Texas sun at this waterpark, which includes more than 30 slides, tube rides and wave pools.

Admission: adults $24.99, children under 48 inches $19.99, children under 3 free. June-August, Sunday-Friday 10:30 a.m.-7 p.m., Saturday 10:30 a.m.-8 p.m.

HIGHLIGHTS

WHAT ARE THE REGION'S TOP MUSEUMS?

DR. PEPPER MUSEUM
If you're a big fan of this cinnamon-flavored soft drink, quench your thirst for knowledge about its origins by visiting this museum and its working turn-of-the-century soda fountain.

FORT WORTH MUSEUM OF SCIENCE & HISTORY
Peruse more than 100,000 artifacts on fossils, anthropology, geology, natural sciences and history at this interactive museum.

KIMBELL ART MUSEUM
The Kimbell showcases masterpieces by the likes of Cézanne, El Greco, Matisse, Monet and Picasso. But don't overlook the standout collection of Asian art.

LEGENDS OF THE GAME OF BASEBALL MUSEUM
Baseball fans will want to check out this museum, which features bats, gloves, jerseys and other memorabilia from stars like Hank Aaron and Babe Ruth.

SIX FLAGS OVER TEXAS
2201 Road to Six Flags St. E., Arlington, 817-640-8900; www.sixflags.com

This amusement park features more than 50 rides, live music, games and fairway foods. Those planning a visit mid-summer should come prepared for large crowds and serious Texas heat. Purchase tickets online for a discount. Hours vary by season so see the website for latest information.

Admission: adults $49.99, children under 48 inches $31.00, children under 3 free. Mid-June-mid-August, Sunday-Friday 10:30 a.m.-10 p.m., Saturday 10 a.m.-10 p.m.

BRENHAM
BLUE BELL CREAMERY
1101 S. Blue Bell Road, Brenham, 800-327-8135

Blue Bell brand ice cream has been perfecting its recipes since 1907 and is the third-best-selling ice cream maker in the United States, though it's only sold throughout the South. Tours include a scoop of ice cream.

Admission: adults $3, children 6-14 $2. Monday-Friday 10 a.m.-2:30 p.m.

PLEASANT HILL WINERY
1441 Salem Road, Brenham, 979-830-8463; www.pleasanthillwinery.com

Spend an afternoon sampling wines made of local grapes at the Pleasant Hill Winery. Tours are available and include tastings. There are also grape-stomping events that take place on weekends from mid-July to mid-August. Kids are invited to join in the festivities.

Admission: adults $3. Saturday 11 a.m.-6 p.m., Sunday noon-5 p.m.

BRYAN/COLLEGE STATION
MESSINA HOF WINE CELLARS
4545 Old Reliance Road, Bryan, 979-778-9463, 800-736-9463; www.messinahof.com

Paul and Merrill Bonarrigo opened this winery in 1977. They combined his family's Sicilian and her family's German traditions to make wines reflecting the characteristics of both countries. The Harvest Festival, a five-week harvesting of grapes in late summer, lets the public join in the fun of picking and stomping the grapes. A souvenir of the day is a "signed" T-shirt marked by your own grape-stained feet. Winery and vineyard tours are available with a lakeside picnic area.

Admission: adults $5. Monday-Saturday 10 a.m.-7 p.m., Sunday 11 a.m.-4 p.m.

MUSEUM AT THE GEORGE H.W. BUSH PRESIDENTIAL LIBRARY
1000 George Bush Drive W., College Station, 979-691-4000; bushlibrary.tamu.edu

The George Bush Presidential Library and Museum is on the West Campus of Texas A&M University. The museum contains approximately 60,000 historical objects from Bush's personal collection. The archives have more than 38 million pages of personal papers and official documents from Bush's vice presidency and presidency as well as personal records from his public career.

Admission: free. Monday-Saturday 9:30 a.m.-5 p.m., Sunday noon-5 p.m.

FORT WORTH
AMON CARTER MUSEUM
3501 Camp Bowie Blvd., Fort Worth, 817-738-1933; www.cartermuseum.org

This building designed by Philip Johnson houses a major collection of American paintings, photography and sculpture that includes works by Winslow Homer, Georgia O'Keeffe and Frederic Remington.

Admission: free. Tuesday-Saturday 10 a.m.-5 p.m., Sunday noon-5 p.m., also Thursday 10 a.m.-8 p.m.

BASS PERFORMANCE HALL
Fourth and Calhoun streets, Fort Worth, 817-212-4325, 877-212-4280; www.basshall.com

Opened in 1998, this $65 million masterpiece has been hailed as the last great hall built in the 20th century. It is home to the Van Cliburn International Piano Competition, the Fort Worth Symphony, the Fort Worth Opera and the Fort Worth/Dallas Ballet. National touring productions and special concerts are offered here as well.

Prices and showtimes vary.

BOTANIC GARDEN
3220 Botanic Garden Blvd., Fort Worth, 817-871-7686; www.fwbg.org

The garden contains more than 150,000 plants of 2,000 species. The grounds include a conservatory, rose gardens, a perennial garden and a trial garden, as well as an extensive Japanese garden with bridges, waterfalls and teahouses.

Admission: adults $3.50, seniors $3, children 4-12 $2, children under 4 free. Daily 8 a.m.-dusk.

BURGER'S LAKE

1200 Meandering Road, Fort Worth, 817-737-3414; www.burgerslake.com

Cool off in this old-fashioned swimming hole, a one-acre, spring-fed lake with a sandy bottom. Five diving boards, a 20-foot slide and a trapeze over the water keep both adults and kids happy. Lifeguards are on duty. The park also includes concession stands, picnic tables and grills.

Admission: $12, children under 7 free. Daily 9 a.m.-7 p.m.

FORT WORTH MUSEUM OF SCIENCE & HISTORY

1501 Montgomery St., Fort Worth, 817-255-9300, 888-255-9300; www.fortworthmuseum.org

The museum houses exhibits of 100,000 artifacts on fossils, anthropology, geology, natural sciences and history. There are interactive exhibits like "Dino Dig," which has young (and old) explorers on a dig for dinosaurs' bones and fossils. The bones range in size from 4 inches to 6 feet. Also at the museum is the Omni Theater, which screens 70-millimeter Omnimax films on an 80-foot projection dome. The Noble Planetarium presents shows on astronomy.

Admission: adults $14, seniors and children $10, children 1 and under free. Daily 10 a.m.-5 p.m.

FORT WORTH STOCKYARDS NATIONAL HISTORIC DISTRICT

130 E. Exchange Ave., Fort Worth, 817-625-9715; www.stockyardsstation.com

This lively district, listed on the National Register of Historic Places, celebrates all things Western in its 15 square blocks. Cheer on the bull riders at the rodeo and then go for a spin on the Lone Star State-size dance floor at Billy Bob's Texas, the world's largest honky-tonk. If you're lucky, a country star might be singing his or her hits on stage.

Admission: free. Daily.

FORT WORTH WATER GARDENS

1502 Commerce St., Fort Worth, 817-871-5755; www.fortworth.com

The Fort Worth Water Gardens is a beautiful oasis adjacent to the Fort Worth Convention Center. The terraced fountain was designed by architect Philip Johnson and is adorned with a variety of foliage and water cascades.

Admission: free. Daily.

FORT WORTH ZOO

1989 Colonial Parkway, Fort Worth, 817-759-7500; www.fortworthzoo.com

One of the zoo's exhibits, "Texas Wild!," is an 8-acre spectacle that's a zoological trek across the Lone Star State, introducing the local flora and fauna in six regions. The zoo is packed with interactive displays for children—kids can milk a simulated cow, climb in a beehive and more. Set on 68 acres, with more than 5,000 animals, this is one of only two U.S. zoos with all four great ape species in residence: bonobos, chimpanzees, gorillas and orangutans.

Admission: adults $12, seniors $7, children 3-12 $8, children under 3 free. March-mid-October, Saturday-Sunday 10 a.m.-6 p.m.; mid-October-mid-February, daily 10 a.m.-4 p.m.; mid-February-October, daily 10 a.m.-5 p.m.

KIMBELL ART MUSEUM
3333 Camp Bowie Blvd., Fort Worth, 817-332-8451; www.kimbellart.org

With is worldwide reputation for excellence, the Kimbell draws plenty of art lovers through its doors and into its 22,000 square feet of galleries, where innovative use of natural light enhances the viewing. The museum's 331-piece permanent collection spans from antiquity to the 20th century, with masterpieces by the likes of Cézanne, El Greco, Matisse, Monet, Picasso, Rembrandt and Velasquez. Few other museums in the region can match its Asian art, with standouts such as "Earth Spirit," an 8th-century Chinese Tang Dynasty sculpture. The Kimbell also showcases selected pieces of pre-Columbian and African art, as well as Greek, Roman, Egyptian and Near Eastern antiquities.

Admission: free. Tuesday-Thursday, Saturday 10 a.m.-5 p.m., Friday noon-8 p.m., Sunday noon-5 p.m.

MODERN ART MUSEUM OF FORT WORTH
3200 Darnell St., Fort Worth, 817-738-9215, 866-824-5566; www.mamfw.org

In December 2002, the museum packed up its belongings and moved to a stunning 153,000-square-foot facility with 53,000 square feet of galleries—five times more space than the previous location. The 2,600-piece permanent collection of post-World War II international art includes works by modern stars such as Francis Bacon and Andy Warhol. From the outside, the museum's five flat-roofed pavilions seemingly float in a 1½-acre pond.

Admission: adults $10, seniors and students $4, children under 13 free. Tuesday-Saturday 10 a.m.-5 p.m., Sunday 11 a.m.-5 p.m.

SUNDANCE SQUARE ENTERTAINMENT DISTRICT
201 Main St., Fort Worth; www.sundancesquare.com

This shopping, dining, art and entertainment district is laid out along brick streets and housed in renovated turn-of-the-century buildings. Markers along a self-guided walking tour commemorate historic locations and events. The 300 block of Main Street is part of the city's colorful history thanks to visits by Old West characters such as Butch Cassidy, the Sundance Kid, and Luke Short, an infamous Western gambler who gunned down the town's marshal in front of the White Elephant Saloon.

Admission: free. Daily.

TRINITY RIVER TRAILS
300 N. Main St., Fort Worth, 817-926-0006; www.trinitytrails.org

Go walking, biking, running or in-line skating along any of these scenic trails that border the Trinity River and stretch for 32 miles in various directions from downtown. The west route will take you through an especially serene, heavily wooded area about two miles from the central business district. Go southwest and pass through popular Trinity Park and the city's cultural district.

Admission: free. Daily.

WACO

DR. PEPPER MUSEUM

300 S. Fifth St., Waco, 254-757-1025; www.drpeppermuseum.com

Learn exactly how to "be a pepper" at the home of the cinnamon-flavored soda pop. A once-abandoned building now features exhibits on the world's oldest major soft drink, memorabilia and a working turn-of-the-century soda fountain. It is also the center for the W.W. Clements Free Enterprise Institute, whose mission is to educate on the economic system of America and uses the soft drink industry as its model.

Admission: adults $7, seniors $4, students and children $3. Monday-Saturday 10 a.m.-4:15 p.m., Sunday noon-4:15 p.m.

FORT FISHER PARK

100 Texas Ranger Trail, Waco, 254-750-8631; www.waco-texas.com

Located behind the Texas Ranger Museum and the Texas Sports Hall of Fame, Fort Fisher Park features 30 acres of sprawling shady trees and riverfront picnic spots perfect for an afternoon snooze.

Admission: free. Daily.

TEXAS RANGER HALL OF FAME AND MUSEUM

100 Texas Ranger Trail, Waco, 254-750-8631; www.texasranger.org

This Texas Ranger museum includes memorabilia, firearm exhibits and dioramas with wax figures depicting a more than 170-year history of Texas Rangers. Displays include the 20-minute film *Story of the Texas Rangers*, country Western art and a library.

Admission: adults $6, children 6-12 $3, children under 6 free. Daily 9 a.m.-4:30 p.m.

WHERE TO STAY

ARLINGTON

★★★HILTON ARLINGTON

2401 E. Lamar Blvd., Arlington, 817-640-3322, 800-445-8667; www.arlingtontx.hilton.com

This full-service hotel is convenient to the Dallas/Fort Worth Airport and shopping districts. Rooms are newly renovated and feature luxury bedding and alarm clocks with MP3 docks. The outdoor pool and Jacuzzi help guests beat the heat. Whether you're going to the Rangers ballpark or Six Flags, a complimentary shuttle will take you to many of Arlington's top attractions.

308 rooms. Restaurant, bar. Business center. Fitness center. Pool. Pets accepted. $151-250

BRYAN/COLLEGE STATION

★★★HILTON COLLEGE STATION AND CONFERENCE CENTER

801 University Drive E., College Station, 979-693-7500, 800-774-1500; www.hiltoncs.com

This hotel and conference center is just two miles from Texas A&M and other area attractions. It often hosts university-related business and social events with its 27,000 square feet of meeting and ballroom space.

303 rooms. Restaurant, bar. Fitness center. Pool. Pets accepted. $61-150

WHAT ARE THE BEST BOUTIQUE HOTELS IN FORT WORTH?

The Ashton Hotel:
You'll feel right at home at this cozy hotel. It offers sophisticated guest rooms, with Frette linens, claw-foot whirlpool tubs, 12-foot ceilings and deep mahogany furniture.

Stockyards Hotel:
This Fort Worth hotel, which dates back to the 1900s, embraces its Stockyard roots and goes for a Western design motif. The lobby is filled with deep browns and leather, and the saloon uses saddles in place of barstools.

FORT WORTH

★★★THE ASHTON HOTEL

610 Main St., Fort Worth, 817-332-0100, 866-327-4866;
www.theashtonhotel.com

Small, intimate and upscale best describes this boutique hotel, which occupies a historic downtown 1915 building. All of its guest rooms have king-size beds with Italian Frette linens, duvets and down pillows. Some rooms have claw-foot whirlpool tubs, 12-foot ceilings and views of Main Street. Custom-designed mahogany furniture helps give the entire hotel a rich, inviting look. Sample the contemporary American cuisine dished out in Café Ashton; small groups of up to 20 can book the Wine Cellar for private dining.

39 rooms. Restaurant, bar. Fitness center. Pets accepted. $251-350

★★★DALLAS/FT. WORTH HOTEL & GOLF CLUB AT CHAMPIONS CIRCLE

3300 Championship Parkway, Fort Worth, 817-961-0800,
866-348-3984; www.marriott.com

Located just 15 miles from downtown Fort Worth, this hotel offers a blend of style and service. The championship 18-hole golf course was designed by Jay Morrish. The state-of-the-art exercise facilities and Creekside Café, with its contemporary American menu, are just a few of the amenities.

286 rooms. Restaurant, bar. Business center. Fitness center. Pool. Golf. $151-250

★★★RENAISSANCE FORT WORTH WORTHINGTON HOTEL

200 Main St., Fort Worth, 817-870-1000, 888-236-2427;
www.renaissancehotels.com

This newly renovated hotel is close to Sundance Square and local attractions such as Texas Stadium and the Kimbell Art Museum. With a spacious lobby and modern feel, the hotel features décor with Western accents.

504 rooms. Restaurant, bar. Business center. Fitness center. Pool. Pets accepted. Tennis. $151-250

★★★STOCKYARDS HOTEL

109 E. Exchange Ave., Fort Worth, 817-625-6427, 800-423-8471;
www.stockyardshotel.com

Located in Fort Worth's Stockyards, this hotel dates to the early 1900s, when it catered to businessmen and ranchers in town for the booming livestock market. Guest rooms have Western and Native American-influenced décor, including the "mountain man room." Instead of a traditional lobby bar, there is Booger Reds Saloon, where saddles serve as barstools.

52 rooms. Restaurant, bar. Pets accepted. $151-250

IRVING
★★★★FOUR SEASONS RESORT AND CLUB DALLAS AT LAS COLINAS
4150 N. MacArthur Blvd., Irving, 972-717-0700, 800-332-3442; www.fourseasons.com

The Four Seasons Resort and Club Dallas at Las Colinas is only moments from downtown Dallas, yet it feels a million miles away. Set on 400 secluded, rolling acres, the resort is a sports paradise. The Tournament Players Course is an 18-hole, par-70 course measuring 7,166 yards from the championship tees. It recently received an extensive redesign, now offering a new layout, designed to be challenging and inviting for both professional and recreational golfers. The resort also offers three outdoor pools, one indoor pool and a children's pool, while the Sports Club's spa offers a variety of massages and treatments. The elegant guest rooms are spacious and decorated in soothing, muted tones. They feature small balconies or patios that overlook the golf courses or the surrounding Cottonwood Valley.

397 rooms. Restaurant, bar. Business center. Fitness center. Pool. Spa. Pets accepted. Golf. Tennis. $351 and up

★★★OMNI MANDALAY HOTEL
221 E. Las Colinas Blvd., Irving, 972-556-0800, 800-843-6664; www.omnihotels.com

This full-service, Spanish-style hotel is in upscale Las Colinas, tucked away on 5 acres fronting Lake Carolyn in a peaceful suburban setting. Rich, sophisticated décor defines this hotel, which has its own fitness center and lakeside pool.

421 rooms. Restaurant, bar. Business center. Fitness center. Pool. Pets accepted. $151-250

WACO
★★★HILTON WACO
113 S. University Parks Drive, Waco, 254-754-8484, 800-234-5244; www.hilton.com

This hotel is conveniently located downtown and close to the convention center. The hotel overlooks the Brazos River. An onsite fitness center, restaurant and pool are some of the featured amenities.

196 rooms. Restaurant, bar. Business center. Fitness center. Pool. Tennis. Pets accepted. $151-250

WHERE TO EAT

ARLINGTON
★★★CACHAREL
2221 E. Lamar Blvd., Arlington, 817-640-9981; www.cacharel.net

Located on the ninth floor of the Brookhollow Tower Two building and just 15 minutes from downtown Dallas or Fort Worth, this inviting country French restaurant features panoramic views of Arlington. Pale pink tablecloths and fresh flowers add to the charm of the restaurant, as do the classic entrées like duck breast with cassis sauce. The almond tulip with black raspberry truffle ice cream and fresh berries is worth all the extra calories.

French. Lunch (Monday-Friday), dinner. Closed Sunday. Reservations recommended. Children's menu. Bar. $36-85

BRENHAM

★★★★★THE INN AT DOS BRISAS BRENHAM

10000 Champion Drive, Washington, 979-277-7750;
www.dosbrisas.com

There is definitely rest for the weary at the lovely Inn at Dos Brisas, set in the picturesque Texas countryside. This peaceful place reminds you that rustic relaxation doesn't have to lack sophisticated comforts. Served with flair in the elegant dining room, the masterful gourmet creations are sourced from the inn's own organic gardens. The haute cuisine includes dishes such as poached pheasant with black-eyed pea cassoulet and chilled lobster with Texas Rio star grapefruit. The extensive wine list includes more than 3,500 different varieties.

American. Lunch (Saturday), dinner (Thursday-Sunday), Sunday brunch. Reservations recommended. Jacket required. $36-85

FORT WORTH

★★★MICHAELS RESTAURANT & ANCHO CHILE BAR

3413 W. Seventh St., Fort Worth, 817-877-3413;
www.michaelscuisine.com

This local favorite in the cultural district of Fort Worth serves up contemporary ranch cuisine. The menu features dishes such as pecan-crusted goat cheese chicken, ranch lamb chops and pan-seared beef tenderloin. The cigar-friendly Ancho Chile Bar offers a bar menu in a relaxed atmosphere.

Southwestern. Lunch, dinner. Closed Sunday. Outdoor seating. Bar. $16-35

IRVING

★★★CAFÉ ON THE GREEN

Four Seasons Resort and Club Dallas at Las Colinas,
4150 N. MacArthur Blvd., Irving, 972-717-0700;
www.fourseasons.com

Sleek, cool and refined, this restaurant within the Four Seasons Resort offers a unique dining experience. The Asian-influenced dishes include griddled Dungeness crab cake with a sweet and smoky sauce, curried mango-orange soup with lump crab and blackened tuna steak with mango-cilantro chutney. Spa menu choices help virtuous diners stick with dieting programs.

American. Breakfast (Saturday-Sunday), lunch (Saturday-Sunday), dinner, Sunday brunch. Bar. $36-85

★★★VIA REAL
4020 N. MacArthur Blvd., Irving, 972-650-9001; www.viareal.com

Situated adjacent to the Four Seasons Las Colinas Resort, this popular family-owned restaurant serves Mexican and Southwestern cuisine in a comfortable atmosphere. The upscale Santa Fe style décor creates an authentic experience.
Mexican, Southwestern. Lunch, dinner, late-night. Reservations recommended. Children's menu. Bar. $16-35

SPA

IRVING
★★★★THE SPA & SALON AT THE FOUR SEASONS RESORT AND CLUB DALLAS AT LAS COLINAS
Four Seasons Resort and Club Dallas at Las Colinas, 4150 N. MacArthur Blvd., Irving, 972-717-0700, 800-332-3442; www.fourseasons.com

Texas may seem like a place where bigger is always better, but at this spa, it's the little things that count. Cool water and frosty, Texas-appropriate root beers are offered upon check-in. While relaxing during a detoxifying pumpkin enzyme facial, the therapist delivers a hand and arm massage. The spa menu also features a thoughtful collection of therapies designed just for men, including the gentlemen's hot towel facial. The Texas two-step treatment features a smoothing blue corn body polish followed by stimulating massage with sagebrush to soothe muscle soreness.

SAN ANTONIO

This beautiful old city has been under the rule of six flags: France, Spain, Mexico, the Republic of Texas, the Confederate States of America and the United States of America. The many different influences are still felt today. What started as a Native American village grew when Mission San Antonio de Valero (the Alamo) was founded by Friar Antonio de San Buenaventura Olivares in May, 1718, near the San Antonio River. Four more missions were built along the river during the next 13 years. In 1836, 189 Texans gathered at the Alamo for a 13-day standoff against General Antonio Lopez de Santa Anna, the President of Mexico, and his 5,000 men. Almost all the Texans died, but the battle was a turning point in the Texas Revolution. Today, the city has evolved into a modern, prosperous town that is the eighth largest in Texas.

WHAT TO SEE

THE ALAMO
300 Alamo Plaza, San Antonio, 210-225-1391; www.thealamo.org

The Alamo has come to symbolize courage for the cause of liberty. Here, a small band of Texans, including legendary figures such as James Bowie, Davy Crockett and William B. Travis, held out for 13 days against the centrist army of General Santa Anna. Although the Alamo fell on the morning of March 6, 1836, the legacy of the courageous Alamo Defenders lives on with its rally cry, "Remember the Alamo!" Today, there are more than 2.5 million people who

HIGHLIGHTS

WHAT ARE THE TOP THINGS TO DO IN SAN ANTONIO?

REMEMBER THE ALAMO
Join the 2.5 million people who visit this historic site each year. It was at this spot that a band of Texans held out against the army of General Santa Anna.

CHECK OUT CASCADE CAVERNS PARK
This 105-acre underground cavern has remarkable rock formations as well as a 100-foot waterfall, the highlight of the guided tour.

GO SHOPPING AT MARKET SQUARE
Browse the three blocks of shops and art galleries in Market Square. You can find Southwestern arts and crafts and a host of other souvenirs.

WALK THE PASEP DEL RIO
The River Walk's busy two-mile stretch is one of San Antonio's biggest tourist attractions. Sidewalk cafés and roving mariachi bands make it a festive spot.

visit each year. Located on Alamo Plaza in downtown San Antonio, its three buildings span 300 years of history.
Admission: free. Monday-Saturday 9 a.m.-5:30 p.m., Sunday 10 a.m.-5:30 p.m.

BRACKENRIDGE PARK
3910 N. Saint Mary's St., San Antonio, 210-207-6700
This 340-acre park has picnicking, a playground, athletic fields, golf, a carousel, a miniature train and pedal boats. If you're looking to get in a little exercise, there are well-surfaced jogging trails here. Within the park are Japanese Tea Gardens, the San Antonio Zoo and the Witte Museum.
Admission: free. Daily dawn-dusk.

BUCKHORN SALOON AND MUSEUM
318 E. Houston St., San Antonio, 210-247-4000; www.buckhornmuseum.com
Housing more than 4,000 items, this museum has a vast collection of animal horns, Old Tex (a stuffed Lonestar steer) and displays of animals and

memorabilia. The saloon, with its century-old bar, has live entertainment. Browse the museum shop, which is billed as "the world's oddest store."

Admission: $11.50. June-August, daily 10 a.m.-6 p.m.; September-May, daily 10 a.m.-5 p.m.

CASCADE CAVERNS PARK

226 Cascade Caverns Road, Boerne, 830-755-8080; www.cascadecaverns.com

Located on a 105-acre park is this water-formed underground cavern with spectacular rock formations. A special feature of this natural attraction is a 100-foot underground waterfall, viewed as the grand finale of a 45-minute guided tour.

Admission: adults $11, children 5-11 $7, children under 5 free. June-August, daily 10 a.m.-5 p.m.; September-May, daily 10 a.m.-4 p.m.

FORT SAM HOUSTON MUSEUM AND NATIONAL HISTORIC LANDMARK

3600 Fort Sam, San Antonio, 210-221-1211

Fort Sam Houston is headquarters for both the U.S. Fifth Army and Brooke Army Medical Center. The museum depicts the history of the fort and the U.S. Army in this region from 1845 to the present. Exhibits of uniforms, equipment and photographs detail the growth of the post and events that occurred here. More than 900 historic structures on the base represent the era between 1876 and 1935; the historic quadrangle once detained Geronimo and his renegade Apaches.

Admission: free. Wednesday-Sunday 10 a.m.-4 p.m.

LA VILLITA HISTORIC ARTS VILLAGE

418 Villita St., San Antonio, 210-207-8610; www.lavillita.com

This 250-year-old Spanish settlement was reconstructed in 1939 to preserve its unique buildings. There are several art galleries, shops and restaurants. The village also includes the unique Arneson River Theatre, which has the audience seated on one side of the river and the stage on the other.

Admission: free. Daily 10 a.m.-6 p.m.

MARKET SQUARE

514 W. Commerce St., San Antonio, 210-207-8600; www.marketsquaresa.com

Dating to the late 1890s, San Antonio's Market Square is a colorful, three-block district of shops, restaurants and art galleries, including El Mercado, the largest Mexican market in the United States. Shoppers can browse more than 80 stores offering Southwestern arts and crafts and worldwide imports. The Square hosts 14 different festivals throughout the year, ranging from Dia de los Muertos (Day of the Dead) to Freedom Fest, a Mexican-flavored Independence Day celebration. The Square's best-known restaurant is Mi Tierra, famous since the 1940s for its authentic Mexican cuisine.

MCNAY ART MUSEUM

6000 N. New Braunfels Ave., San Antonio, 210-824-5368; www.mcnayart.org

This was the first Texas museum for modern art established by the endowment of the extensive art collection and former residence of Marion Koogler McNay. The collection includes Gothic and Medieval art donated by the Oppenheimer family; late 19th- and 20th-century American and European paintings by classic masters such as Van Gogh, Gauguin and Cézanne along with modern painters Jackson Pollock and Jasper Johns; sculpture; graphic arts; rare books;

architecture and fine arts.

Admission: adults $8, seniors, military and students $5, children under 12 free. Tuesday-Wednesday, Friday 10 a.m.-4 p.m., Thursday 10 a.m.-9 p.m., Saturday 10 a.m.-5 p.m., Sunday noon-5 p.m.

PASEO DEL RIO (RIVER WALK)

www.thesanantonioriverwalk.com

The two-mile River Walk runs along the meandering San Antonio River and is lined with shops, galleries, hotels, popular nightspots and many sidewalk cafés. As the city's main tourist draw, the River Walk is often bustling with mariachi bands, river taxis and tours, and outdoor dining. Other stretches of the path are quiet and peaceful with public benches. The stone paths are a full story below street level so the River Walk is a fantastic way to feel removed from the commotion of the city.

SAN ANTONIO BOTANICAL GARDENS

555 Funston Place, San Antonio, 210-207-3250; www.sabot.org

This park comprises 33 acres of formal Japanese, rose and herb gardens, wildflower meadows and a climate-controlled conservatory with five glass exhibition greenhouses. There is a "touch and smell" garden for the visually impaired and a large collection of native Texas vegetation. Tours of the conservatory are self-guided.

Admission: adults $7, seniors, military and students $5, children 3-13 $4, children under 3 free. Daily 9 a.m.-5 p.m.

SAN ANTONIO MISSIONS NATIONAL HISTORICAL PARK

2202 Roosevelt Ave., San Antonio, 210-932-1001; www.nps.gov

San Antonio's four Spanish-colonial missions are administered by the National Park Service and have exhibits, talks and cultural demonstrations. Parishes within the missions are still active. Mission Concepción (*807 Mission Road, 210-534-1540*) is one of the best-preserved missions in Texas and the oldest unrestored stone mission church in the country. Mission Espada (*10040 Espada Road, 210-627-2021*) has had its friary and chapel restored. Mission San José (*6701 San José Drive, 210-932-1001*) is famous for its carvings and masonry. Mission San Juan (*9101 Graf Road, 210-534-0749*) was the center for this self-sufficient community with Native American artisans and farmers establishing a trade network.

Admission: free. Daily 9 a.m.-5 p.m.

SAN ANTONIO MUSEUM OF ART

200 W. Jones Ave., San Antonio, 210-978-8100; www.samuseum.org

An art museum in a former brewery? It works, especially given the beauty of this 1884 brick structure. Opened in 1981, this art museum is known for its Greek and Roman collection, Asian art, Latin American and folk art and American paintings. The latter collection includes landscapes and portraits dating from the colonial period to the early 20th century. The Nelson A. Rockefeller Center for Latin American Art includes pre-Columbian, Spanish-colonial and Latin American folk art. Other exhibits include Egyptian antiquities, ancient glass, classical sculpture and more. If all this culture makes you hungry, a cafe is onsite.

Admission: adults $8, seniors $7, students and military $5, children 4-11 $3, children under 4 free. Tuesday 10 a.m.-9 p.m., Wednesday-Saturday 10 a.m.-5 p.m., Sunday noon-6 p.m.

SAN ANTONIO SYMPHONY
222 E. Houston St., San Antonio, 210-554-1010; www.sasymphony.org

Making music accessible to many tastes, the San Antonio Symphony offers a 39-week season (September-May) with more than 100 concerts, 26 pop concerts, 32 classical concerts and special interactive Sunday events geared to children. There are also nine seasonal events, including holiday performances of *The Nutcracker* and on New Year's Eve, *Night in Old Vienna*. Concerts are performed at the Majestic, a restored theater crafted in Spanish Mission, Baroque and Mediterranean styles in downtown San Antonio.

Admission: prices vary. Showtimes vary.

SAN ANTONIO ZOO
3903 N. Saint Mary's St., San Antonio, 210-734-7184; www.sazoo-aq.org

Get up close with more than 40 lories—colorful medium-sized parrots from Australia—at the zoo's Lory Landing. The friendly birds range in color from scarlet and green to royal blue and fiery orange and are so social that they often flock close to visitors, landing on shoulders and even the occasional head. Beyond birds, you can visit more than 3,500 animals of 750 species here, making this one of the largest zoos in the United States. At the African Hill—a microcosm of life as it might be encountered on the African plains—look for ostriches, zebras, giraffes, cranes, ducks, gazelles and antelopes. The lushly planted Amazonian exhibit is a hit with more than 30 species of tropical animals, including venomous reptiles, tamarins and marmosets.

Admission: adults $10, military $9, seniors and children 3-11 $8, children under 3 free. Daily 9 a.m.-5 p.m.

SEAWORLD SAN ANTONIO
10500 SeaWorld Drive, San Antonio, 210-523-3000, 800-700-7786; www.seaworld.com

The world's largest marine life adventure park and family entertainment venue, SeaWorld San Antonio includes four parks within its 250 acres. There are animal attractions, rides, slides, and shows ranging from "The Steel Eel" (billed as the Southwest's first hypercoaster) to "Fools with Tools," a comic sea lion adventure poking fun at do-it-yourself types. You can pat Atlantic bottlenose dolphins, feed sea lions and seals, and observe killer whale behaviors. SeaWorld's "Viva!" show combines the fluid movement of synchronized swimmers, professional high divers and aerialists with the antics of Pacific white-sided dolphins and beluga whales. For a 3-D experience, head to the Sea Star Theater.

Admission: adults $54.99, children $46.99. Hours vary.

SIX FLAGS FIESTA TEXAS
17000 IH-10 West, San Antonio, 210-697-5050, 800-473-4378; www.sixflags.com

A 200-acre amusement park dramatically set in a former limestone quarry boasts four themed areas—Spassburg (German), Los Festivales (Hispanic), Crackaxle Canyon (Western) and Rockville (1950s)—all around a central Texas square.

Features include an aeroflight thrill attraction, an early 1900s-style carousel and Kinderspielplatz, a large space devoted to rides and games for young kids.

Admission: adults $49.99, children $34.99, children under 3 free. Hours vary by season.

WITTE MUSEUM

3801 Broadway, San Antonio, 210-357-1900;
www.wittemuseum.org

Founded in 1926, this museum features exhibits in history, science and the humanities, along with nationally traveling exhibits. Some standouts include the 2,000-year-old mummy and the H-E-B Science Treehouse, which is a four-level interactive exhibit devoted to hands-on learning about science.

Admission: adults $8, seniors and military $7, children $6. Monday, Wednesday-Saturday 10 a.m.-5 p.m., Tuesday 10 a.m.- 8 p.m., Sunday noon-5 p.m.

WHERE TO STAY

★★★EMILY MORGAN HOTEL

705 E. Houston St., San Antonio, 210-225-5100; www.emilymorganhotel.com

You can't get any closer to The Alamo (without holing up inside) than the Emily Morgan Hotel. Located right next door, the large picture windows in many of the rooms give a clear shot straight into the historic grounds. Guest rooms have been recently renovated to exude a modern charm with neutral tones and dark mahogany furnishings. The rooftop outdoor pool is small, but adequate for a quick dip.

177 rooms. Restaurant, bar. Fitness center. Pool. Pets accepted. $151-250

★★★THE FAIRMOUNT HOTEL

401 S. Alamo St., San Antonio, 210-224-8800, 877-365-0500;
www.thefairmounthotel-sanantonio.com

This Victorian hotel was built in 1906 and is across the street from the city's convention center. Rooms are elegantly decorated with period furniture and modern luxuries like flat-screen TVs. Guests and their pets are greeted by the hotel's resident canine, a rescued Labrador named Luke Tips. For an afternoon cocktail, head to the Wine Bar, where there are more than 23 wines by the glass from which to choose.

37 rooms. Restaurant, bar. Business center. Fitness center. Pets accepted. $61-150

★★★HAVANA RIVERWALK INN

1015 Navarro St., San Antonio, 210-222-2008, 888-224-2008;
www.havanariverwalkinn.com

Housed in an Italianate villa built in 1914, this small, charming inn has rooms decorated with antique iron canopy beds, exposed-brick walls and plantation shutters. It also has modern amenities such as data ports and Internet. The onsite bar, Club Cohiba, is the perfect spot for sampling Latin-inspired tapas or sipping one of the signature martinis.

28 rooms. Restaurant, bar. Complimentary breakfast. No children under 14. $151-250

★★★HILTON PALACIO DEL RIO

200 S. Alamo St., San Antonio, 210-222-1400, 800-445-8667; www.palaciodelrio.hilton.com

Conveniently located on the River Walk and close to the Alamo, this hotel offers a balcony in each room with views of the city. The Hilton has three restaurants, and on Friday and Saturday nights live music is played at the Ibiza Patio Restaurant and Bar.

482 rooms. Restaurant, bar. Business center. Fitness center. Pool. Pets accepted. $151-250

★★★HOTEL CONTESSA

306 W. Market St., San Antonio, 210-229-9222, 866-435-0900; www.thehotelcontessa.com

This 12-story property overlooking the River Walk carries a Mediterranean theme throughout its guest rooms and lobby. The multilevel atrium lobby is open and inviting. Guest rooms include oversized baths, flat-screen televisions and richly colored furnishings. Las Ramblas is the perfect spot to grab a cocktail and people-watch, or tie on your dancing shoes and join the professional ballroom salsa dancers who give lessons the second Thursday of each month.

265 rooms. Restaurant, bar. Business center. Fitness center. Pool. Spa. Pets accepted. $151-250

★★★HOTEL VALENCIA RIVERWALK

150 E. Houston St., San Antonio, 210-227-9700, 866-842-0100; www.hotelvalencia.com

The contemporary hotel is on the doorstep of the historic River Walk. The guest rooms were designed with sleek luxury in mind, boasting signature linens, custom-made beds and interior design by Dodd Mitchell. The modern style is continued in the Vbar, where seating is offered on leather bar stools or small lounge areas. Sip cocktails before heading over to Citrus, the hotel's restaurant.

213 rooms. Restaurant, bar. Fitness center. $151-250

★★★HYATT REGENCY HILL COUNTRY RESORT & SPA

9800 Hyatt Resort Drive, San Antonio, 210-647-1234, 888-591-1234; www.hillcountry.hyatt.com

This secluded resort is in woodlands across from SeaWorld. This former ranch has a cozy lobby with a large wood-burning fireplace, a wood porch and spacious, comfortably appointed rooms. Kids can try out the seasonal youth spa while adults visit the swimming pool, spa and nature trails.

500 rooms. Restaurant, bar. Business center. Fitness center. Pool. Spa. Beach. Golf. Tennis. $151-250

WHAT ARE SOME OF THE BEST HISTORICAL HOTELS IN SAN ANTONIO?

Menger Hotel:
At this historic hotel, which sits next to the Alamo, Teddy Roosevelt sat at the bar and recruited his Rough Riders team for the Spanish-American War.

The Mokara Hotel & Spa:
Although it looks like a luxury hotel, the Mokara has its own Old West history. The hotel building used to house a saddlery.

★★★HYATT REGENCY SAN ANTONIO

123 Losoya St., San Antonio, 210-222-1234, 800-633-7313; www.hyatt.com

This River Walk hotel has been updated with sleek, contemporary décor. Rooms have down-duvet-topped beds, stereos with iPod docking stations and large workspaces. The fitness center features cutting-edge equipment.

632 rooms. Restaurant, bar. Business center. Fitness center. Pool. $151-250

★★★MARRIOTT PLAZA SAN ANTONIO

555 S. Alamo St., San Antonio, 210-229-1000, 800-421-1172; www.plazasa.com

The fountains, courtyards and gardens of this hotel are a pleasant surprise in this downtown San Antonio location. The more adventurous can explore the historic district by foot or complimentary bicycle.

251 rooms. Restaurant, bar. Business center. Fitness center. Pool. Pets accepted. $151-250

★★★MENGER HOTEL

204 Alamo Plaza, San Antonio, 210-223-4361, 800-345-9285; www.mengerhotel.com

This hotel was built in 1859 and is a historic landmark located next door to the Alamo. There is a 19th-century wing with Victorian-style guest rooms. You can enjoy a drink in the bar where Teddy Roosevelt recruited his Rough Riders for the Spanish-American War.

316 rooms. Restaurant, bar. Fitness center. Pool. Spa. $61-150

★★★★THE MOKARA HOTEL & SPA

212 W. Crockett St., San Antonio, 210-396-5800, 866-605-1212; www.mokarahotels.com

This property, housed in a building that once served as a saddlery, provides plush accommodations and a world-class spa. Guest rooms and suites are handsomely appointed with iron four-poster beds, colonial furnishings and distinctive local artwork. The rooftop pool is a relaxing spot with great views, and the adjacent café serves breakfast and lunch. Ostra, the hotel's signature restaurant, spotlights international seafood in a dazzling contemporary space. The Mokara Spa is an urban oasis complete with a state-of-the-art fitness facility, classes and a comprehensive, nature-inspired treatment menu.

99 rooms. Restaurant, bar. Fitness center. Pool. Spa. Pets accepted. $351 and up

★★★OMNI LA MANSIÓN DEL RIO

112 College St., San Antonio, 210-518-1000, 800-292-7300; www.omnihotels.com

Built in 1852 and housed in a former boys' school, the Omni La Mansión del Rio is a Spanish colonial treasure. Guest rooms are appropriately decorated in the Spanish-colonial style with beamed ceilings and exposed-brick walls. The Las Canarias Restaurant is a popular spot, both for its intimate setting and its creative contemporary menu.

338 rooms. Restaurant, bar. Business center. Fitness center. Pool. Pets accepted. $151-250

★★★OMNI SAN ANTONIO HOTEL

9821 Colonnade Blvd., San Antonio, 210-691-8888, 800-843-6664; www.omnihotels.com

Rooms at this hotel have unobstructed views of downtown and the Texas Hill Country. The Omni Kids program features suitcases filled with games and books, a goodie bag upon check-in and menu choices prepared expressly for children. Guest rooms are technologically outfitted with video checkout, Nintendo gaming systems and individual climate control.

326 rooms. Restaurant, bar. Business center. Fitness center. Pool. Pets accepted. $61-150

★★★RADISSON HILL COUNTRY RESORT & SPA

9800 Westover Hills Blvd., San Antonio, 210-509-9800, 800-333-3333; www.radisson.com

This San Antonio resort sits on 27 acres of rolling hills with views of the Texas Hill Country. Close to SeaWorld and other local attractions, it's a popular choice for families. Guest rooms are updated and spacious. The resort has a full-service spa, well-equipped fitness center, a playground and a basketball court.

227 rooms. Restaurant, bar. Business center. Fitness center. Pool. Spa. $151-250

★★★SHERATON GUNTER HOTEL SAN ANTONIO

205 E. Houston St., San Antonio, 210-227-3241, 888-999-2089; www.starwoodhotels.com

This hotel, built in 1909, is a small jewel decorated with Texan style. The hotel is only a short stroll away from the River Walk. Guest rooms on the Club Level include complimentary continental breakfast, afternoon hors d'oeuvres and a comfortable lounge.

322 rooms. Restaurant, bar. Business center. Fitness center. Pool. Pets accepted. $61-150

★★★THE ST. ANTHONY HOTEL

300 E. Travis St., San Antonio, 210-227-4392, 877-999-3223; www.wyndham.com

This landmark property, built in 1909, is famous for its ornate, elegant lobby, which features a central staircase, crown molding, historic photos and oil paintings. The hotel is within walking distance to the Alamo and the River Walk, as well as numerous shops and restaurants. Many guest rooms feature four-poster beds and multiple closets.

350 rooms. Restaurant, bar. Business center. Fitness center. Pool. $151-250

★★★THE WESTIN LA CANTERA RESORT

16641 La Cantera Parkway, San Antonio, 210-558-6500, 800-937-8461;
www.westinlacantera.com

Located on one of the highest points above San Antonio, this 300-acre resort has views of the city and the hills of the countryside. The red-tile roof and stucco walls are a tribute to the region's Spanish heritage, while the interior is pure Southwest. The resort houses the Castle Rock Health Club and Spa, 36 holes of championship golf and a golf academy. The Lost Quarry Pools has multiple freshwater pools, a children's pool and whirlpool. Families can end the night with roasted s'mores by the fire pit.

508 rooms. Restaurant, bar. Business center. Fitness center. Pool. Spa. Golf. Tennis. $151-250

★★★THE WESTIN RIVERWALK HOTEL

420 W. Market St., San Antonio, 210-224-6500, 800-937-8461; www.westin.com

This modern hotel is on the River Walk. Local shops and restaurants are within steps of the front door. Afternoon tea is served daily in the lobby. The hotel welcomes pets (up to 50 pounds) with bowls, a pet bed, treats and a gift kit.

473 rooms. Restaurant, bar. Business center. Fitness center. Pool. Pets accepted. $151-250

WHERE TO EAT

★★★ANAQUA GRILL

555 S. Alamo St., San Antonio, 210-229-1000, 800-421-1172; www.marriott.com

Immediately south of downtown in the Plaza San Antonio Hotel, this elegant restaurant features an Old World-style courtyard with resident peacocks and pheasants. Starters include pan-seared calamari and lamb chop lollipops, while entrées offered include grilled salmon or prime tenderloin.

American. Breakfast, lunch, dinner, late-night, brunch. Outdoor seating. Children's menu. Bar. $16-35

★★★ANTLERS LODGE

9800 Hyatt Resort Drive, San Antonio, 210-647-1234; www.hillcountry.hyatt.com

This lovely gourmet dining room at the Hyatt Regency Hill Country features modern Texas cooking using fresh ingredients. The restaurant gets its name from the impressive antler chandelier, which features 500 pairs of naturally shed antlers. A cozy fireplace, elegant wood furnishings, open kitchen and sweeping views of the golf course complete the lodge atmosphere.

American. Dinner. Reservations recommended. Children's menu. Bar. $36-85

★★★BIGA ON THE BANKS

203 S. St. Mary's St., San Antonio, 210-225-0722; www.biga.com

Contemporary and inviting, this downtown showplace offers what might be considered the most sought-after meal in San Antonio. Dishes include seared Hudson Valley foie gras on a maple waffle with black trumpet mushrooms and grapefruit-duck glaze, and Axis venison with a goat cheese strudel. Ask about Table 31, which provides a kitchen view and a special tasting menu.

American. Dinner, Sunday brunch. Reservations recommended. Outdoor seating. Children's menu. Bar. $36-85

★★★FIG TREE

515 Villita St., San Antonio, 210-224-1976; www.figtreerestaurant.com

Located in the La Villita Historic District, this elegant restaurant has a cozy atmosphere. Specialties include mint-crusted lamb rack, tournedos Rossini with Perigourdine sauce and yellowfin tuna. The outdoor terrace, with views of the San Antonio River, is a relaxing spot to dine in nice weather.

American. Dinner. Reservations recommended. Outdoor seating. $36-85

★★★FRANCESCA'S AT SUNSET

16641 La Cantera Parkway, San Antonio, 210-558-6500; www.westinlacantera.com

Located in the Westin La Cantera Resort (which sits atop an abandoned limestone rock quarry), this elegant restaurant is decorated in a Spanish-colonial style. Outdoor seating with views of the Texas Hill Country is available. The lobster enchilada is delicious, as are the sweet-corn-dusted jumbo crab cakes.

Southwestern. Dinner. Closed Sunday-Monday. Reservations recommended. Outdoor seating. Children's menu. Bar. $36-85

★★★LAS CANARIAS
112 College St., San Antonio, 210-518-1063, 800-292-7300;
www.omnihotels.com

This three-tiered restaurant is full of Spanish-colonial charm. For a treat, experience a specially designed three-course meal while drifting along the San Antonio River on board the Las Canarias riverboat.

American. Breakfast, lunch, dinner, Sunday brunch. Reservations recommended. Outdoor seating. Children's menu. Bar. $36-85

★★★MORTON'S, THE STEAKHOUSE
849 E. Commerce St., San Antonio, 210-228-0700;
www.mortons.com

Although it may seem like Texas has more than its fair share of steak houses, this national chain can compete with the best of them. There are also several seafood selections and a good variety of side dishes.

Steak. Dinner. Reservations recommended. Bar. $36-85

★★★OSTRA
212 W. Crockett St., San Antonio, 210-396-5817;
www.mokarahotels.com

Situated within the Mokara Hotel, this upscale seafood restaurant mixes modern décor with friendly Texas service to create a top-notch dining experience. If you're looking to splurge, opt for the chilled shellfish tower from the raw bar, which is packed with everything from oysters to shrimp and lump crab. If noshing on seafood isn't your thing, try the vegetable fricassée. The wine list is expansive with many options by the glass.

Seafood. Breakfast, lunch, dinner. Reservations recommended. Outdoor seating. Children's menu. Bar. $36-85

★★★RUTH'S CHRIS STEAK HOUSE
7720 Jones Maltsberger Road, San Antonio, 210-821-5051;
www.ruthschris.com

This outpost of the New Orleans-based chain is near the convention center. The restaurant is known for its choice cuts of steak and attentive service. If you're not in the mood for beef, seafood is another good option as it's brought in fresh daily.

Seafood, steak. Dinner, late-night. Reservations recommended. Bar. $36-85

WHICH SAN ANTONIO RESTAURANT PROVIDES THE MOST UNUSUAL DINING EXPERIENCE?

When you dine at **Las Canarias**, you can choose to have your meal by land or sea, so to speak. The American restaurant has a brick-and-mortar location on College Street, but it also has a riverboat that floats along the San Antonio River and serves three-course dinners.

SPAS

★★★★THE MOKARA SPA

212 W. Crockett St., San Antonio, 210-396-5840, 800-830-1500; www.mokarahotels.com

Feminine without being frilly, this spa has a cool, fresh décor and a menu of treatments that spotlights natural, essential oil-based products. Signature body treatments include gentle citrus scrubs, mesquite scrubs and purple sage salt glows, along with mesquite clay body wraps, aloe skin quenchers, and avocado lime blossom scalp and body treatments. The Mokara Restoration massage begins with a Spanish rosemary rubdown and is followed by the application of yucca, a plant beloved by Native Americans for its healing properties. Men are particularly pampered here, with a special menu that includes clarifying back treatments and rescue facials.

HOUSTON

Often called "the most air-conditioned city in America," Houston gets the title for its frequent AC use to combat the year-round warm weather. But it's especially true during the hot, sticky summers, when the dials are turned up to full blast. Aside from its lack of a cold climate, the city offers a vast landscape of opportunity for tourists. As the fourth-largest city in the country, Houston has something for everyone, including the Museum District, the state-of-the-art Minute Maid ballpark, NASA headquarters of Mission Control, the Houston Zoo, Discovery Green and the newly constructed Hobby Center, which attracts countless world-class musical productions.

Houston's image stretches well beyond the rodeo and justly famous Texas barbecue, making it equally attractive not only for foodies but families and business travelers. Besides the historical and dazzling contemporary architecture, the charm of the city lies in the design itself. There are no formal zoning regulations, so you might find a high-end French restaurant in a strip mall next to a school.

It may all sound incongruous, but there is true beauty to experience in Houston's urban jungle. Just walk though Hermann Park's soothing Japanese Gardens, head to the Bayou Bend and bliss out in the romantic flower-lined landscape, or drive through River Oaks, coveted neighborhood to the rich, and ogle the amazing mansions. Aside from horrendous traffic and sizzling summer temperatures, the Bayou City is ideal for its millions of visitors seeking variety—whether it be shopping, art gallery hopping or dining—in a diverse cultural melting pot.

WHAT TO SEE

BAYOU BEND COLLECTION AND GARDENS

1 Westcott St., Houston, 713-639-7750; www.mfah.org/bayoubend

Garden enthusiasts and decorative arts buffs will appreciate the 14-acre Bayou Bend, the former home of Houston philanthropist Ima Hogg. The mansion now houses the Museum of Fine Arts and its 5,000-object American decorative arts collection. There is furniture designed by John Townsend and John Henry

HIGHLIGHTS

WHAT ARE HOUSTON'S TOP MUSEUMS?

CHILDREN'S MUSEUM OF HOUSTON
Kids will get all caught up in the interactive displays at this children's museum.
They'll be able to explore an Oaxacan village and play in bubbles.

JOHN P. MCGOVERN MUSEUM OF HEALTH AND MEDICAL SERVICES
All ages will be intrigued by this health museum's offerings. See what a clogged
artery or vocal chord really look like.

MENIL COLLECTION
The Menil is considered one of the most outstanding private collections in the
world. It includes contemporary, surrealistic and prehistoric art and antiquities.
Works by masters like Rene Magritte are also on display.

Belter, paintings by John Singleton Copley and Charles Willson Peale and silver
by Paul Revere. Outside, garden tours take you past regional plants and topiaries
shaped to resemble native Texas animals. No children under 10 are allowed.
*Admission: adults $10, seniors and students $8.50, children 10-17 $5. Guided tours, Tuesday-
Friday 10-11 a.m. and 1-2:45 p.m., Saturday 10-11:15 a.m.; audio tours, Saturday-Sunday
1-5 p.m. Closed August.*

BYZANTINE FRESCO CHAPEL MUSEUM
4011 Yupon St., Houston, 713-521-3990; www.menil.org
The story of how the only intact Byzantine frescoes came to be housed in
Houston is a dramatic one. Back in the 1980s, thieves stole the frescoes from a
chapel near Lysi in the Turkish-occupied section of the island of Cyprus. Hoping
to sell the works piece by piece, the thieves cut them up and smuggled them off of
the island. A curator from the Menil Foundation heard about it and rescued the
frescoes. The foundation then spent two years carefully restoring the paintings.
In gratitude, the Church of Cyprus made a long-term loan of the frescoes, which
are displayed in a building custom designed by Francois de Menil.
Admission: free. Wednesday-Sunday 11 a.m.-6 p.m.

CHILDREN'S MUSEUM OF HOUSTON

1500 Binz St., Houston, 713-522-1138; www.cmhouston.org

Kids can explore an Oaxacan village, get up to their elbows in bubbles, play cashier in a real-life grocery store and participate in dozens of hands-on activities that promote creative thinking and learning. Weekend visitors are treated to storytellers, musicians, magicians and dancers who perform in the museum's 164-seat auditorium.

Admission: adults and children $8, seniors and military personnel $7, children under one free. June-August, Monday-Saturday 10 a.m.-6 p.m., also Thursday 10 a.m.-8 p.m., Sunday noon-6 p.m.; September-May, Tuesday-Saturday 10 a.m.-6 p.m., also Thursday 10 a.m.-8 p.m., Sunday noon-6 p.m.

CONTEMPORARY ARTS MUSEUM

5216 Montrose Blvd., Houston, 713-284-8250; www.camh.org

This museum has rotating exhibits by international and regional artists, including paintings, sculpture, photography and media.

Admission: free. Tuesday-Saturday 10 a.m.-5 p.m., also Thursday 10 a.m.-9 p.m., Sunday noon-5 p.m.

GEORGE RANCH HISTORICAL PARK

10215 FM 762, Richmond, 281-343-0218; www.georgeranch.org

The George Foundation set aside 480 of its 23,000 acres of ranch and farmlands to create a park illustrating 100 years of Texas' past. Costumed interpreters teach visitors what it was like to be a colonial pioneer struggling to make it on a stock farm. There are also Old West cattle drives, chuckwagons, cattle camps and a glimpse at Victorian Texas at the 1890s Davis House.

Admission: adults $9, seniors $8, children 5-15 $5, children under 5 free. Tuesday-Saturday 9 a.m.-5 p.m.

HERMANN PARK CONSERVANCY

6201 A Golf Course Drive, Houston, 713-524-5876; www.hermannpark.org

This space was named after businessman and philanthropist George Hermann. Within its borders are the Garden Center, a Japanese garden with a tea house designed by Ken Nakajima, and the Miller Outdoor Theatre, which stages free summer music, ballet and theater productions.

Admission: free. Daily 6 a.m.-11 p.m.

HOUSTON ARBORETUM AND NATURE CENTER

4501 Woodway, Houston, 713-681-8433; www.houstonarboretum.org

This site is a 155-acre nonprofit nature sanctuary for the protection of native trees, shrubs and wildlife. The center includes five miles of nature trails. Guided tours are available.

Admission: free. Daily 8:30 a.m.-6 p.m.

HOUSTON ASTROS

Minute Maid Park, 501 Crawford St., Houston, 800-278-7672; www.houston.astros.mlb.com

Houston's professional baseball team plays at the city's Minute Maid Park.

HOUSTON BALLET

501 Texas Ave., Houston, 713-227-2787, 800-828-2787; www.houstonballet.org

Hailed as one of the nation's best ballet companies, the Houston Ballet produces an extensive repertoire of works including 19th-century classics such as *The Nutcracker, Swan Lake* and *Don Quixote,* as well as new works by contemporary choreographers, including Trey McIntyre, Stanton Welch and Natalie Weir. The company performs at the Wortham Theater Center in downtown Houston.

Admission: varies. September-June, showtimes vary.

HOUSTON GRAND OPERA

Wortham Theater Center, 550 Prairie St., Houston, 713-228-6737, 800-828-2787; www.houstongrandopera.org

This opera company celebrated its 50th season in 2010. Each season includes performances of major productions featuring international stars.

Admission: varies. September-June, showtimes vary.

HOUSTON MUSEUM OF NATURAL SCIENCE

1 Hermann Circle Drive, Houston, 713-639-4629; www.hmns.org

This museum is also home to the Burke Baker Planetarium, the Wortham IMAX Theatre, the Cockrell Butterfly Center and three floors of natural science halls and exhibits. Most popular is the Hall of Paleontology, which features dinosaur and Egyptian artifacts. Other exhibits include vast displays of gems and minerals, a 100,000-specimen dried insect collection and Native American artifacts. The Welch Chemistry Hall and the Fondren Discovery Place include hands-on interactive displays and a live demonstration theater. Planetarium, IMAX and Butterfly Center tickets are available for an additional cost.

Admission: adults $15, seniors, students and children 3-11 $10, children under 3 free. June-mid-October, Monday-Saturday 9 a.m.-9 p.m., Sunday 11 a.m.-9 p.m.; Mid-October-June, Monday-Saturday 9 a.m.-5 p.m., also Tuesday 9 .m.-8 p.m., Sunday 11 a.m.-5 p.m.

HOUSTON ROCKETS

Toyota Center, 1510 Polk St., Houston, 713-627-3865; www.nba.com

The city's professional basketball team shoots hoops at the Toyota Center.

HOUSTON TEXANS

2 Reliant Park, Houston, 832-667-2000 www.houstontexans.com

After losing their team to Nashville in 1995, Houston went seven years without pro football before the Texans' launch season in 2002. You can see the team in action at Reliant Stadium, the first NFL stadium with a retractable roof.

HOUSTON ZOO

1513 N. MacGregor Drive, Houston, 713-533-6500; www.houstonzoo.org

Founded in 1922, this zoo houses a vampire bat colony, reptile and primate houses, a hippopotamus building, an alligator display, a gorilla habitat, an education center and more. There is also a 3-acre discovery zoo with separate petting areas.

Admission: adults $10, seniors and children 2-11 $6. March-October, daily 9 a.m.-7 p.m.; November-February, daily 9 a.m.-6 p.m.

JOHN P. MCGOVERN MUSEUM OF HEALTH AND MEDICAL SCIENCE

1515 Hermann Drive, Houston, 713-521-1515; www.mhms.org

A 22-foot-long backbone with ribs descending from the ceiling, a 10-foot-tall walk-through brain and a 27-foot long intestine—the sheer novelty of the exhibits at the McGovern Museum of Health and Medical Science make it a must-see for all ages. There are also exhibits that let you look down the throat at vocal chords in action, or see what a clogged artery really looks like.

Admission: adults $8, seniors and children 3-12 $6. Tuesday-Saturday 9 a.m.-5 p.m., Sunday noon-5 p.m.

MENIL COLLECTION

1515 Sul Ross St., Houston, 713-525-9400; www.menil.org

Considered one of the most outstanding private art collections in the world, the Menil is housed in this museum designed by Italian architect Renzo Piano. The collection includes contemporary, surrealistic and prehistoric art and antiquities. It counts works by such varied masters as Vincent Van Gogh, Rene Magritte, Cy Twombly, Cindy Sherman and Francis Bacon among its holdings. It houses more than 400 photographic prints selected specially for the museum by Henri Cartier-Bresson himself.

Admission: free. Wednesday-Sunday 11 a.m.-7 p.m.

MUSEUM OF FINE ARTS

1001 Bissonnet St., Houston, 713-639-7300; www.mfah.org

You could spend days viewing the museum's vast collections, housed in six locations. There are more than 45,000 artworks on display representing the major civilizations of Europe, Asia, North and South America and Africa. Traveling exhibits rotate in and out, sharing focus with special exhibits drawn from the museum's permanent collection. The MFAHs two house museums, Bayou Bend Collection and Gardens (American works) and Rienzi (European works), are well worth the trip.

Admission: adults $7, seniors and children 6-18 $3.50, children under 6 free. Tuesday-Wednesday 10 a.m.-5 p.m., Thursday 10 a.m.-9 p.m., Friday-Saturday 10 a.m.-7 p.m., Sunday 12:15-7 p.m.

OLD MARKET SQUARE

301 Milam St., Houston, 713-845-1000

This square is the site of the city's first commerical center and dates to the early 1800s. A redevelopment project features a central plaza and sidewalks paved with collages of paving material taken from old Houston buildings. Photos commemorating the city's history are reproduced on porcelain-enameled panels decorating benches in the square.

Daily.

ROTHKO CHAPEL

1409 Sul Ross St., Houston, 713-524-9839; www.rothkochapel.org

This octagonal chapel houses canvases of the late Mark Rothko, the Russian-born painter. Rothko was commissioned by art patrons to build the chapel and given complete control over the aesthetic experience, creating 14 paintings especially for this space. Also on the grounds are a reflecting pool and the Broken Obelisk, a sculpture by Barnett Newman dedicated to Martin Luther King, Jr.

Admission: free. Daily 10 a.m.-6 p.m.

SAM HOUSTON PARK

1100 Bagby St., Houston, 713-655-1912; www.heritagesociety.org

A haven of quiet and green in the midst of downtown Houston, this park includes eight historic structures dating from 1823 to 1905. Heritage Society-guided tours of the buildings give a glimpse into the life and times of the Houstonians who lived here. Buildings range from a cedar log cabin believed to be the oldest surviving structure in the county to St. John Church, a country parish relocated here. Soak up more history at the park's free Heritage Society Museum, where exhibits range from 19th-century paintings to priceless pieces of early Texas furniture to an exact replica of a general store from Egypt, Texas.

Admission: free. Tuesday-Saturday 10 a.m.-4 p.m., Sunday 1-4 p.m.

SAM HOUSTON RACE PARK

7575 N. Sam Houston Parkway W., Houston, 281-807-8700, 800-807-7223; www.shrp.com

Thoroughbreds, American quarter horses and Arabians draw crowds at this racetrack. The park offers 10 races nightly throughout its season, which runs from fall through spring. Track amenities include the Winner's Circle restaurant, featuring fine dining for 750 in a multitiered seating arrangement.

Admission: varies. Hours vary.

SPACE CENTER HOUSTON

1601 NASA Parkway, Houston, 281-244-2100; www.spacecenter.org

Designed by Disney, Space Center Houston brings space travel down to earth. Interactive exhibits depict how astronauts perform complicated tasks such as landing the space shuttle, retrieving satellites and using the Manned Maneuvering Unit, and what it's like to eat and shower in space. Kids can ride across the moon in a Lunar Rover, perform experiments and command a space shuttle. Tram tours to Johnson Space Center depart every half hour. Admission fees are half-price if purchased online.

Admission: adults $19.95, seniors $18.95, children 4-11 $15.95. June, Monday-Friday 10 a.m.-7 p.m.; July, Monday-Friday 9 a.m.-7 p.m.; August, Monday-Friday 10 a.m.-5 p.m., Saturday-Sunday 10 a.m.-7 p.m.; September-May, Monday-Friday 10 a.m.-5 p.m., Saturday-Sunday 10 a.m.-7 p.m.

TRADER'S VILLAGE

7979 N. Eldridge Road, Houston, 281-890-5500; www.tradersvillage.com

Billed as a Texas-sized marketplace, Traders Village opened in 1989 and has become the largest flea market on the Texas Gulf Coast. Besides shopping, there is camping, an RV park, rides, games and concessions. Special events range from barbecue and chili cook-offs to square dancing and bluegrass festivals.

Admission: free. Saturday-Sunday 9 a.m.-6 p.m.

WHERE TO STAY

★★★ALDEN HOUSTON

1117 Prairie St., Houston, 832-205-8800, 877-348-8800; www.aldenhotels.com

This mod downtown boutique hotel is known for its hospitality, which makes guests feel instantly pampered. With its proximity to the legal, business and theater districts as well as the Houston Astros' ballpark, the hotel is in the heart of the city. After a long day, it's easy to fall into the sumptuous beds fitted with luxury linens and pillow-top mattresses and watch one of the free DVDs on the flat-screen TV. Equally pleasing are the granite-walled bathrooms with oversized tubs and soothing Aveda products. If planning a special event, the veranda is a spectacular setting with views of downtown. The hotel gets extra points for its intimate restaurant, *17, featuring regional American cuisine in a seductive red-accented dining room, and a+ bar and grille, a lighter and more relaxed option that offers a hip loungey scene.

97 rooms. Restaurant, bar. Business center. Fitness center. Pets accepted. $150-250

★★★CROWNE PLAZA, BROOKHOLLOW

12801 Northwest Freeway, Houston, 713-462-9977, 800-826-1606; www.cphoustontx.com

Have you ever arrived to your hotel room after a long day of travel and just craved silence? Then the Crowne Plaza might be the right hotel for you. On floors known as quiet zones, no maintenance or housekeeping is performed from 9 p.m. to 10 a.m. for your convenience. To further enhance your peaceful experience, you can reserve a private patio by the pool, which also gives you access to the outdoor sundeck, sauna and exercise room. Once you're ready to play, the Galleria shopping, Sam Houston Raceway and many more attractions are nearby. Spacious rooms include work desks with ergonomic chairs and plush bedding.

294 rooms. Restaurant, bar. Business center. Fitness center. Pool. Pets accepted. $61-150

★★★DOUBLETREE HOTEL HOUSTON-ALLEN CENTER

400 Dallas St., Houston, 713-759-0202, 800-222-8733; www.doubletreehotels.com

This newly renovated Doubletree not only has a prime location in pedestrian-friendly downtown Houston, but it connects via sky bridges to the Allen Center and Heritage Plaza office buildings. Guest rooms in serene Mediterranean shades of cool blue and peachy coral sport floor-to-ceiling windows, which provide a striking view of the city from any angle. Amenities include flat-screen TVs, big work areas and duvet-topped beds, making it an inviting place to return to following a long day. Trofi Restaurant offers regional selections as well as classic foods that keep Doubletree guests coming back. If you seek a quick nosh or relaxing drink, check out the lobby lounge, ideal for a mid-afternoon break from sightseeing.

350 rooms. Restaurant, bar. Business center. Fitness center. Pets accepted. $151-250

★★★DOUBLETREE HOTEL HOUSTON INTERCONTINENTAL AIRPORT

15747 John F. Kennedy Blvd., Houston, 281-987-1234, 800-222-8733;
www.doublehotelstree.com

Located within minutes of the George Bush Intercontinental Airport, this newly remodeled, contemporary Doubletree provides an oasis for those looking to take a step back from the bustling city. It is also near the Beltway and Interstate 45, in case you need to make a dash into the bright lights of the city. Stick to the elegantly understated hotel and there are plenty of amenities available to keep you busy. For golf lovers, there are several courses close to the hotel (just ask the concierge to set you up) and Oakley's Restaurant is always cooking up regional Texas classics.

313 rooms. Restaurant, bar. Business center. Fitness center. Pool. $151-250

★★★★FOUR SEASONS HOTEL HOUSTON

1300 Lamar St., Houston, 713-650-1300, 800-332-3442; www.fourseasons.com

Despite downtown competition, the Four Seasons still stands out as the hotel with the highest standards, making it a favorite among discriminating dignitaries, VIPs and celebrity travelers. Everything about the 20-story hotel is big, including the elegant guest rooms washed in clean white and neutral hues with rich fabrics and a mix of traditional and contemporary décor. Extra-large bay windows showcase dazzling views of the skyline and pool. Signature Four Season beds fashioned with high-quality linens ensure a night of sublime comfort, and the irresistible turndown treats left on your pillow nightly guarantee sweet dreams. Don't oversleep; you'll want to plant yourself in the recently renovated outdoor pool area with new cabanas and bar, or the fitness center and spa. The lobby lounge is the go-to spot for cocktails and appetizers, but for more substantial fare, head to Quattro. The signature restaurant, which serves modern Italian cuisine, is a feast for the senses. Book the chef's table with a peek into the gleaming kitchen for a special group occasion.

404 rooms. Restaurant, bar. Business center. Fitness center. Pool. Spa. Pets accepted. $251-350

★★★HILTON AMERICAS-HOUSTON HOTEL & CONVENTION CENTER

1600 Lamar St., Houston, 713-739-8000, 800-445-8667; www.hilton.com

As the largest convention hotel in Houston, the 24-story Hilton Americas is adjacent to the George R. Brown Convention Center, so it is constantly booked with business visitors. Expect sprawling state-of-the-art event spaces but also a striking ambiance that is pleasant for leisurely stays. Guest room appointments include lush pillow-top mattresses, down pillows and high-thread-count linens along with Crabtree & Evelyn La Source bath amenities. After a day at work, conventioneers can have dinner at Spencer's for Steak and Chops with two intimate dining choices, including a stunning glassed-enclosed wine room. For something quick and casual, The Café and the Lobby Bar are convenient. The hotel has a clean and sleek feel with soaring ceilings, bold light fixtures and plenty of room—and we mean plenty—to wander or lose yourself after those long days of being cooped up in meetings.

1,203 rooms. Restaurant, bar. Business center. Fitness center. Pool. Spa. Pets accepted. $151-250

★★★HILTON HOUSTON NASA CLEAR LAKE
3000 NASA Parkway, Houston, 281-333-9300, 800-445-8667; www.hilton.com

The recently remodeled Hilton Houston NASA Clear Lake offers all the amenities of city life in a suburban atmosphere. It even offers an outer-space atmosphere, since the NASA/Johnson Space Center and Space Center Houston are across the street from the Hilton. This hotel is also close to both Houston and Galveston Island, giving you the opportunity to check out urban life and the beach. Anticipate guest rooms with panoramic views of the lake; newly updated features like wide-screen HDTVs in the guest rooms provide the hotel with a welcoming touch.

243 rooms. Restaurant, bar. Business center. Fitness center. Pool. $61-150

★★★HILTON HOUSTON PLAZA/MEDICAL CENTER
6633 Travis St., Houston, 713-313-4000, 800-445-8667; www.hilton.com

Talk about a prime location. This hotel is near medical centers, the gorgeous grounds of Rice University, the convention center, museums and Minute Maid ballpark. So instead of struggling with how to manage your time in this sprawling city, you get to see it all and much of it within walking distance. In the hotel, there's a heated outdoor pool and jogging track and views from each guest room of the pretty tree-lined neighborhood around the university. The hotel also features the Garden Court restaurant and Shamrock bar.

186 rooms. Restaurant, bar. Business center. Fitness center. Pool. $61-150

★★★HOTEL DEREK
2525 W. Loop S., Houston, 713-961-3000, 866-292-4100; www.hotelderek.com

This isn't your parents' hotel. Modernists adore the boutique hotel for its hip look and feel with a sleek yet cozy lobby and long cool marble-topped Valentino Vin Bar. Its terrific contemporary Italian restaurant, Valentino, is an outpost of the flagship restaurant founded by restaurateur Piero Selvaggio, one of the modern fathers of Italian cuisine in America. Guests are ferried about town in the hotel's stretch SUV, nicknamed the "Derek Mobile," a righteous choice for this tricky location smack-dab in the center of inner-loop Galleria traffic. The loft-like rooms and suites are contemporary in design and are outfitted with flat-screen TVs, CD and DVD players and plush bedding—luxurious places that you don't want to leave in the morning.

314 rooms. Restaurant, bar. Business center. Fitness center. Pool. Spa. Pets accepted. $151-250

★★★★HOTEL GRANDUCA
1080 Uptown Park Blvd., Houston, 713-418-1000, 888-472-6382; www.granducahouston.com

Travel to Italy without taking out a passport when staying at this luxurious full-service hotel. From its stunning terra cotta exterior to its warm, inviting interior design complete with cozy fireplaces, the lovely space blends Old World style with new world amenities. Hotel Granduca may feel like a secluded resort with its manicured grounds and serene ambiance, but this hotel is in Houston's Uptown Park, a walkable outdoor shopping center channeling a little slice of Europe. Despite the location, it feels so private that you might just spot a celebrity hiding away. The comfortable rooms have original Italian art, plush beds draped in luxury linens and flat-screen high-definition TVs. The amenities, from chauffeur service to personal trainers to a heated outdoor pool, are expansive, and the polished staff makes staying here a pleasure. The veranda, conservatory and clubroom are among the many spots to dine. The signature restaurant, Ristorante Cavour, serves northern Italian food.

126 rooms. Restaurant, bar. Business center. Fitness center. Pool. $151-250

★★★HOTEL ICON

220 Main St., Houston, 713-224-4266, 800-970-4266; www.hotelicon.com

This dramatic, rambling historic building in downtown Houston was built in 1911 and is housed in the former Union Bank. Rooms are decked out in Victorian-inspired wall coverings, lush fabrics in sunny gold and pale blue and one-of-a-kind retro fixtures. Each lofty guest room is unique, so you might find an antique claw-foot tub in one and a Jacuzzi tub in another, similar to an elegant European B&B or inn. The fine onsite restaurant, Voice, serves food with regional influences and has an extensive basement wine vault. The sophisticated Asian-style Voice Lounge is a hot setting for sampling a signature drink, like the Tea House, a mix of green tea vodka, lemongrass and peach tea.

135 rooms. Restaurant, bar. Business center. Fitness center. Spa. $151-250

★★★HOTEL INDIGO

5160 Hidalgo St., Houston, 713-621-8988, 800-864-8165; www.hotelindigo.com

Some seek refuge when they travel, while others seek retail. If shopping is your bag, Hotel Indigo is your place. Across the street from Houston's famed Galleria shopping complex, the Hotel Indigo pampers its guests after a long day of exercising their credit cards. Nautical colors and bright aquatic hues of purple and green punctuate the public and private spaces. The rooms and suites feature playful décor with mood-lifting murals and blue-and-white-striped bedding and sparkling white bed frames. Kick back at the casual European-style café and lounge/bar.

131 rooms. Restaurant, bar. Fitness center. Pool. Pets accepted. $151-250

WHAT ARE THE MOST LUXURIOUS HOTELS IN HOUSTON?

Four Seasons Hotel Houston:
It's all about the details at the Four Seasons. The small things—treats on your pillow during the turndown service and rooms with large bay windows overlooking the skyline and pool—add up to a great hotel.

Hotel Granduca:
The Italian-inspired Hotel Granduca offers great service with that personal touch. Trainers will help you work on your fitness and chauffeurs will be on hand to escort you around town.

St. Regis Hotel, Houston:
Live the high life while staying at the St. Regis. The hotel provides butler service where someone will come and unpack or pack for you, deliver your morning coffee or have your shoes shined.

★★★THE HOUSTONIAN HOTEL, CLUB & SPA
111 N. Post Oak Lane, Houston, 713-680-2626, 800-231-2759; www.houstonian.com

An urban retreat within the city, The Houstonian strives to lavish luxury on its guests. Remodeled in 2008, rooms have floor-to-ceiling windows that showcase the tranquil wooded grounds. Access to the Houstonian Golf Club and the Houstonian Club—considered one of the finest private fitness facilities in the country—is complimentary. From the rock-climbing wall to boxing, yoga and martial arts classes, exercise here sure beats the usual hotel-gym treadmill. Trellis, the new spa, has a gorgeous Mediterranean-style exterior and a beautiful garden. Facial, body and hair-salon treatments are available along with an indoor saltwater float pool and well-equipped locker rooms with a Jacuzzi and steam room. This is an ideal setting for accommodating weddings and their guests, but there's no need for a special occasion to visit. The Houstonian is ready to treat you like a VIP any day of the week.

287 rooms. Restaurant, bar. Business center. Fitness center. Pool. Spa. Golf. Tennis. $251-350

★★★HYATT REGENCY HOUSTON
1200 Louisiana St., Houston, 713-654-1234, 800-233-1234; www.hyatt.com

This 30-story atrium hotel is downtown but magically provides a quiet retreat from all the bustle of the city. Nearby you'll find the convention center, the theater district and Bayou Place, a massive shopping, entertainment and restaurant venue. Head's up sports fans: Minute Maid Park and the Toyota Center are also around the corner, and Shula's Steakhouse, created by pro football Hall of Fame coach Don Shula, is in the hotel. For those cruising out of downtown, the METRO LightRail can get you there quickly to enjoy the Museum District, The Zoo, Medical Center and Reliant Park.

947 rooms. Restaurant, bar. Business center. Fitness center. Pool. $61-150

★★★INN AT THE BALLPARK
1520 Texas Ave., Houston, 713-228-1520, 866-406-1520; www.innattheballpark.com

A true baseball lover could never go wrong here. Steeped in a rich history, the downtown inn is right across the street from Minute Maid Park, home to the Houston Astros. In 2004, this 12-story complex was remodeled and reopened to the public with a nostalgic baseball theme. Don't let the sporty gimmick fool you; this hotel is luxurious. Guest rooms are handsome and tastefully decorated with timeless furnishings like plush leather chairs and ottomans appealing to a more masculine clientele. The open atrium allows for amazing city views, which seem to go on for miles and miles. For a treat, take a few steps over to Vic & Anthony's Steak House for a lavish dinner and award-winning wines.

201 rooms. Restaurant, bar. Business center. Fitness center. $151-250

★★★INTERCONTINENTAL HOTEL HOUSTON
2222 W. Loop S., Houston, 713-627-7600, 800-496-7621; www.intercontinental.com

Located in Uptown near the Galleria shopping mall, this hotel is also convenient to Memorial Park, golf courses and jogging trails and within minutes of the medical district and downtown Houston. The enormous hotel has a comfortable lobby for socializing or just reading the complimentary newspaper. If you want to relax outdoors, there's a roof deck, swimming pool and whirlpool. Guest rooms are simple, clean and comfortable, if a bit dated.

485 rooms. Restaurant, bar. Business center. Fitness center. Pool. $151-250

★★★JW MARRIOTT HOTEL HOUSTON

5150 Westheimer Road, Houston, 713-961-1500, 800-228-9290; www.marriott.com

With more than 40,000 square feet of renovated meeting and function space, the 23-story JW Marriott wins high marks for its business-friendly services and good location. Situated in the heart of Houston's Galleria/Uptown area, the hotel is an ideal base for those exploring the myriad shops and restaurants outside the front doors. In fact, you won't need to rent a car if you stay here, since you're within walking distance of 200 stores and restaurants. The roomy guest rooms outfitted in eye-opening orange shades feature work stations, high-definition TVs and comfortable bedding with down comforters and cotton linens.

514 rooms. Restaurant, bar. Business center. Fitness center. Pool. $151-250

★★★LA COLOMBE D'OR HOTEL

3410 Montrose Blvd., Houston, 713-524-7999; www.lacolombedor.com

If you love the feel of Europe and hate hotel chains, this is the place for you. Known as the Fondren Mansion, this is a true Texas landmark. And while everything is bigger in Texas, La Colombe d'Or is the world's smallest luxury hotel. This Prairie-style mansion, flanked with towering palm trees, was built in 1923 by Walter Fondren, the founder of Humble Oil (now known as Exxon). There are five rooms in the mansion and nine townhouses surrounding a New Orleans-style courtyard. Each guest room is uniquely decorated in a southern French style. Stop by the intimate library lounge for a nightcap.

14 rooms. Restaurant, bar. Pets accepted. $151-250

★★★LANCASTER HOTEL

701 Texas Ave., Houston, 713-228-9500, 800-231-0336; www.thelancaster.com

Situated in Houston's downtown theater district, this historic hotel is within walking distance of area businesses and cultural attractions. Everything from Discovery Green, Bayou Place, The Downtown Aquarium, Jones Hall, the Hobby Center and endless other activities are just around the corner. Opened in 1926 and handed down through several owners, the Lancaster still feels like an exclusive private club with its jewel-toned walls and pristine European furnishings. Elegant guest rooms feature marble vanities and dark wood two-poster beds with feather pillows and down-filled duvets. The flavors of the Gulf Coast are celebrated at Bistro Lancaster, the hotel's stylish and popular after-theater haunt.

93 rooms. Restaurant, bar. Business center. Fitness center. $151-250

★★★MAGNOLIA HOTEL HOUSTON

1100 Texas Ave., Houston, 713-221-0011, 888-915-1110; www.magnoliahotelhouston.com

This hotel is the only one in Houston with a rooftop pool and Jacuzzi for those who want to see but don't want to be seen. Located downtown, the boutique hotel is only minutes from Minute Maid Park, the Toyota Center, the symphony and many area attractions. The décor is modern and warm with a glamorous appeal. Contemporary rooms include plush bedding, executive work spaces, and spacious marble bathrooms with oversized tubs.

314 rooms. Restaurant, bar. Complimentary breakfast. Fitness center. Pool. Pets accepted. $151-250

★★★MARRIOTT HOUSTON MEDICAL CENTER
6580 Fannin St., Houston, 713-796-0080, 800-228-9290; www.marriott.com

This hotel, which has a newly refurbished lobby, is ideal for guests who need to visit the Texas Medical Center. An air-conditioned walkway connects the property to the medical center, which is a welcome relief when it comes to the grueling Texas heat. It's also adjacent to Rice University, which offers several lovely walking paths that take you into the surrounding neighborhood with some of the city's oldest and prettiest homes. It's only minutes from downtown Houston and many attractions, such as the Museum District, are just a short stroll away. Most rooms have a city view and are elegantly appointed with a spacious work desk and luxurious bedding primped with a flurry of pillows.

247 rooms. Restaurant, bar. Business center. Fitness center. Pool. Pets accepted. $251-350

★★★OMNI HOUSTON HOTEL
4 Riverway, Houston, 713-871-8181, 800-843-6664; www.omnihotels.com

The Omni Houston occupies an enviable location in the upscale Post Oak/Galleria neighborhood. With well-manicured grounds and beautiful views, Omni shows its signature eloquence everywhere. In the lobby, you'll find cascading waterfalls, an inviting and relaxing welcome to the property. NOE is the hotel's restaurant serving contemporary American cuisine with a French accent, and The Black Swan is a fine place for a cocktail. New to the hotel are Mokara, a full-service spa, and Ceron Salon, which has a loyal following of local socialites. A well-equipped gym, tennis and basketball courts and the nearby jogging trails of Hershey Park are waiting for fitness fiends.

378 rooms. Restaurant, bar. Business center. Fitness center. Pool. Pets accepted. Tennis. $251-350

★★★RENAISSANCE HOUSTON HOTEL
6 Greenway Plaza E., Houston, 713-629-1200, 888-236-2427; www.marriott.com

This hotel is in the Greenway Plaza Corporate complex steps away from your business meeting or luncheon. Speaking of lunch, don't miss posh landmark Tony's, which moved to Greenway in the late '90s. When you need a break from work, explore the Upper Kirby district with its eclectic shops and mom-and-pop eateries or do some shopping in nearby River Oaks, Houston's wealthiest area, where there are several chic cafés from which to choose. The décor of the Renaissance is modern with spacious, chic guest rooms featuring skyline views and plush bedding. Edloe's lobby lounge is a stylish stop for one of the 15 specialty tequilas or the signature cocktail, the Texas mojito. Expect a light, seasonal menu of Texas-American cuisine. There's also a Starbucks in the lobby for those early-morning meetings.

388 rooms. Restaurant, bar. Business center. Fitness center. Pool. Pets accepted. $251-350

★★★SHERATON SUITES HOUSTON
2400 W. Loop S., Houston, 713-586-2444, 866-716-8134; www.sheratonsuiteshouston.com

One block north of the Galleria, this Uptown all-suites hotel will make you feel right at home without breaking the bank. With easy access to all of Houston's major attractions, you can easily hop on the freeway loop to explore Houston. This is also a favorite property for meetings and events, as there's plentiful meeting spaces conveniently located on the ground floor. The contemporary guest suites have complimentary wireless access, refrigerators and new pillow-top beds. If you bring your pet, he'll get his own Sheraton Sweet Sleeper dog bed. The hotel is home to Omaha Steakhouse, if you're looking to grab a hearty Texas meal.

281 rooms. Restaurant, bar. Business center. Fitness center. Pool. Pets accepted. $104-189

★★★★ST. REGIS HOTEL, HOUSTON

1919 Briar Oaks Lane, Houston, 713-840-7600, 877-787-3447; www.stregis.com/houston

The St. Regis, a small luxury hotel, is nothing like any chain hotel you'll find here. Set in Houston's tony River Oaks section, it not only has a prime location but it feels exclusive the minute you drive up to the glamorous building with a tree-shaded circular drive and assiduous valet attendants. Attention to detail is the key. Interiors paved with marble flooring are always polished to a high gloss, and staff members assist with doors, shopping bags or fetch bottles of water for you. Rooms are styled with rich mahogany furnishings, including grand pillow-top beds with plush leather headboards; luxe bathrooms are stocked with Remède bath products. The climate-controlled outdoor pool is ideal for lounging, while the Tea Lounge offers a more formal affair with its special afternoon tea service complete with finger sandwiches, petit fours, scones with Devonshire cream and champagne (reservations recommended). Quality seafood and steaks combined with a classy, secluded aura make for a memorable in-house dining experience at Remington Restaurant.

232 rooms. Restaurant, bar. Business center. Fitness center. Pool. Spa. Pets accepted. $251-350

★★★THE WESTIN GALLERIA HOUSTON

5060 W. Alabama, Houston, 713-960-8100, 800-937-8461; www.westin.com

Step into the Westin from the noise and street traffic of the populated Galleria/Post Oak area and your troubles seem to melt away. With soothing music and the signature white tea scent exuding from botanical arrangements, the Westin offers a hidden oasis in the city. When you need to get back to civilization, its location within the Galleria shopping mall provides quick foot access to more than 350 shops, including Tiffany, Neiman Marcus and Macy's in addition to small boutiques. Memorial Park, golfing, tennis and jogging trails are all nearby. Spacious rooms, which feature the signature Heavenly bed and bath, are comfortable and stylish with contemporary light-cherry-wood furnishings and most have balconies. The hotel lobby features several sitting areas in case you need a quick break from all of the hubbub outside.

453 rooms. Restaurant, bar. Business center. Pool. Pets accepted. $151-250

★★★THE WESTIN OAKS

5011 Westheimer Road, Houston, 713-960-8100, 888-627-8514; www.westin.com

The Westin sits in a good spot. Shopping enthusiasts will appreciate its location on the northeast corner of the Galleria Mall. Business travelers will like that it's in the heart of it all, which makes it ideal for any conference. Both will like the three distinct restaurants that meet your needs at any time of the day, whether you need a quick bite before a meeting or to refuel after a long day of shopping. Contemporary furnishings and décor lend some style to the hotel.

406 rooms. Restaurants, bar. Pool. Pets accepted. $151-250

★★★THE WOODLANDS RESORT & CONFERENCE CENTER

2301 N. Millbend Drive, The Woodlands, 281-367-1100, 800-433-2624; www.woodlandsresort.com

Surrounded by natural forest, this resort offers a secluded location, yet it's only 30 minutes from downtown Houston. The towering green trees and beautifully manicured lawns set the scene for a relaxing rustic getaway. With a full-service spa and restaurants at your disposal, this all-inclusive oasis makes it hard to leave for the big city. Two golf courses, a tennis center, 120 miles of nature trails and a pool area with water slides are among the attractions on the property. Most of the guest rooms have views of the wooded environs with all the extra comforts and high-tech conveniences expected from a fine hotel.

490 rooms. Restaurant, bar. Business center. Fitness center. Pool. Spa. Golf. Tennis. $151-250

★★★WOODLANDS WATERWAY MARRIOTT HOTEL

1601 Lake Robbins Drive, The Woodlands, 281-367-9797, 800-228-9290; www.marriott.com

This hotel, in one of Houston's fastest-growing suburbs, is ideal for business conventions. There is a sky bridge that connects the hotel to the Cynthia Woods Mitchell Pavilion, an open-air music venue, making this a great vacation spot as well. Whether you're headed into the city for business or pleasure, downtown Houston is only a 30-minute trip. The hotel has two restaurants, Aqua Lounge and Ristorante Tuscany, while several other eateries are nearby. In your room, you'll get wonderful vistas of the Woodlands and its waterway. A restful night's sleep is ensured with Marriott Revive bedding stacked high with a flurry of pillows and quality linens. Upgraded showerheads, Bath and Body Works aromatherapy amenities and the Starbucks in the lobby will help you get your morning off to a good start.

345 rooms. Restaurant, bar. Business center. Fitness center. Pool. $151-250

RECOMMENDED

CROWNE PLAZA, NORTH GREENSPOINT

425 N. Sam Houston Parkway E., Houston, 281-445-9000; www.ichotelsgroup.com

Formerly The Sofitel, the newly renovated Crowne Plaza has a more modern streamlined look and luxurious feel. The new lobby reflects a chic Texas theme with hardwood floors and cow-skin-covered chairs and rugs. Conveniently located near George Bush Intercontinental Airport, the hotel especially appeals to business travelers who have easy access to the Greenspoint business district (The Woodlands) and complimentary airport shuttle service. Stylishly remodeled guest rooms in earthy moss green have oversized workstations and plasma TVs. Though if you spend extra for the club-level rooms, you'll get free continental breakfast in the concierge area, evening cocktails and appetizers. The casual in-house restaurant Grille 425 repeatedly gets raves for its modern American cuisine and cocktails in the bar.

331 rooms. Restaurant, bar. Business center. Fitness center. Pool. Pets accepted. $61-150

HOTEL SORELLA

CityCentre, 800 W. Sam Houston Parkway N., Houston, 713-973-1601, 866-842-0100; www.hotelsorella-citycentre.com

Built in 2009 by the Valencia group, this ultra-hip hotel anchors the new west side CityCentre shopping and residential complex. The sprawling stylish public areas paved in glass are decorated with furnishings in cream, chocolate brown, bold chartreuse and purple with stained hardwood floors and contemporary art. A dreamy rooftop pool with pivoted cabanas and bright pillows overlooks the shopping center with multiple restaurants and lush green spaces. Spacious guest rooms are spare and artsy in gold, green and burgundy shades with floor-to-ceiling windows and sheer gossamer curtains revealing natural light. There are also custom-designed beds with plush linens and walk-in showers with apothecary bath goodies. Throw in the eclectic Monnalisa bar and New Orleans-inspired Bistro Alex restaurant inclusive of the property, and what's not to love?

224 rooms. Restaurant, bar. Business center. Fitness center. Pool. $151-250

LOVETT INN BED AND BREAKFAST

501 Lovett Blvd., Houston, 713-522-5224, 800-779-5224; www.lovettinn.com

This bed and breakfast that shares the same name as the country star has built its own fan base since 1989. The sunny colored Colonial-style house, constructed in 1923 by Houston Mayor Joseph Hutcheson, sits on a tree-lined boulevard in the eclectic Montrose neighborhood near the museum district and is within walking distance of restaurants, shopping and clubs. Guest rooms are in the main building and the carriage house and feature balconies, whirlpool tubs and sitting rooms. Many of the bedrooms are decorated in period antiques with four-poster beds.

10 rooms. Pool. Pets accepted. $61-150

SARA'S BED AND BREAKFAST INN

941 Heights Blvd., Houston, 713-868-1130, 800-593-1130; www.saras.com

Ever want to step into the movie *Gone with the Wind*? Then a stay in Sara's fully restored Queen Anne mansion in the Historic Heights just might make you feel like Scarlett. An innkeeper lives on the property, though not in the home; guests receive a key for the house and one for the room that'll allow you to come and go as you please. The Southern-tinged hotel is strictly historical, but the rooms are fully stocked with the latest technology. This house may be old, but it doesn't show its age; the inn beams with clean white and neutral tones, making it a sophisticated destination for corporate events, parties and retreats as well.

11 rooms. Complimentary breakfast. No children under 11. $61-150

WHERE TO EAT

★★★AMÉRICAS

1800 Post Oak Blvd., Houston, 713-961-1492; www.cordua.com

Eclectic New World cuisine with North, South and Central American influences is served in this exotic restaurant, which has a fantasy-like impressionistic design by architect Jordan Mozer. As for the menu, chef-owner Michael Cordua and son David entice with a stream of culinary surprises, like soft-shell crawfish taquitos; pork fillet with corn tomalito, grilled shrimp and crabmeat; or the chicken crusted with plantain chips over black bean sauce. Cordua's signature churrassco, a flavorful grilled beef tenderloin with chimichurri sauce, continues to be a menu favorite, and don't miss the voluptuous coconut ice cream. There's a second location in the Woodlands and the Américas River Oaks spot recently opened in fall 2010.

Latin American. Lunch, dinner (Monday-Saturday), Sunday brunch. Reservations recommended. Children's menu. Bar. $16-35

★★★THE CAPITAL GRILLE

5365 Westheimer Road, Houston, 713-623-4600; www.thecapitalgrill.com

For over-the-top steakhouse excess, there's nothing like the spacious Capital Grille, which many describe as a "man's restaurant" because of its opulent, clubby décor. Oriental rugs, velvet-covered armchairs, gorgeous oversized light fixtures, polished dark woods and hunting trophies on the walls set the tone for decadence. Prepare for excellent dry-aged certified Angus beef and the freshest of seafood along with an award-winning wine list. Veal chops, lamb rib chops, and the roasted cremini, portobello, shiitake and oyster mushroom mélange are highly recommended dishes.

Steak. Dinner. Reservations recommended. Bar. $36-85

★★★LA COLOMBE D'OR

3410 Montrose Blvd., Houston, 713-524-7999; www.lacolombedorhouston.com

With its unique setting in the historic Fondren Mansion, the restaurant in the La Colombe d'Or—the world's smallest luxury hotel—is perfect for a special occasion or romantic evening. For a brief moment you feel like you are in Europe surrounded by antiques, period art and pretty views of the rose garden. The fine dining menu adds a Texas twist to modern southern French cuisine, featuring wild game and other ever-changing exotic delicacies.

American, French. Lunch (Monday-Friday), dinner. Closed Sunday. Reservations recommended. Outdoor seating. Bar. $36-85

★★★LA GRIGLIA

2002 W. Gray St., Houston, 713-526-4700; www.lagrigliarestaurant.com

This colorful and bustling Italian restaurant paved in whimsical murals and mosaics is true to its name, which means "the grill." Seafood specialties, pasta, pizza and rotisserie-roasted chicken are prepared on cavernous wood-burning grills, sending a fragrant aroma wafting through the dining rooms. Or order a more serious entrée of roasted wild boar chop or grilled yellowfin tuna with tomatoes and shiitakes. The River Oaks crowd makes for an animated bar scene with lots of happy-hour cheer.

Italian. Lunch (Monday-Friday), dinner. Reservations recommended. Outdoor seating. Bar. $16-35.

★★★MARK'S AMERICAN CUISINE

1658 Westheimer Road, Houston, 713-523-3800, 800-523-3800; www.marks1658.com

Mark's is a romantic and usually remarkable dining experience. The first thing you'll notice is the striking décor in this former 1920s church, with high-vaulted ceilings and hand-painted deco walls. Veteran chef Mark Cox's seasonal menus reflect what's fresh and trendy; they are so fresh that selections usually change twice a day. Memorable entrées include roasted Alaskan halibut over squash tasso risotto, maple leaf duck and grilled veal medallions. Hallelujah to the many surprising off-the-wall dishes, the lauded wine list and the jovial crowd.

Contemporary American. Lunch (Monday-Friday), dinner. Reservations recommended. Outdoor seating. Bar. $16-35

★★★MASRAFF'S

1753 Post Oak Blvd., Houston, 713-355-1975; www.masraffs.com

This new chic location near the Galleria boasts an impressive elevated fireplace, floor-to-ceiling windows and two patios with a 60-foot-long illuminated waterfall (also note the innovative restrooms with automatic doors). Masraff's is well-known for fresh American cuisine with a touch of southern Europe. Menu favorites include the crab salad, seared foie gras with pears and coveted steak tartare. A live jazz brunch jams on Sundays.

Contemporary American. Lunch (Monday-Friday), dinner (Mon-Saturday), late-night, Sunday brunch. Reservations recommended. Outdoor seating. Bar. $16-35

★★★MORTON'S THE STEAKHOUSE

5000 Westheimer Road, Houston, 713-629-1946; www.mortons.com

Morton's in Houston delivers an elegant steakhouse atmosphere and gorgeous steaks—a place that you would be proud to take your mother or an important client. The polished waitstaff guides diners through the menu offerings with a tableside presentation of the cuts of meat, sides and live lobsters, the latter of which are on display in the tanks. The recently remodeled lounge is handsome with warm woods, a spacious bar and a bird's-eye view of twinkling Post Oak Boulevard below. A second location is downtown near the theater district.

Steak, seafood. Dinner. Bar. $36-85

★★★NOÉ

Omni Houston Hotel, 4 Riverway, Houston, 713-871-8177, 800-843-6664; www.noerestaurant.com

Noé is an upscale dining spot with a dedicated following. The innovative, contemporary cuisine with French flavors borders on the exotic—try the cured Tasmanian salmon, wild Gulf shrimp with wasabi ketchup or the panko-crusted jumbo crab mac and cheese. Brunch is a lavish event with custom crêpe stations and anything else you could possibly crave.

Contemporary American. Dinner, Sunday brunch. Reservations recommended. Bar. $16-35

★★★OLIVETTE

Houstonian Hotel, 111 N. Post Oak Lane, Houston, 713-685-6713; www.houstonian.com

This serene restaurant inside the Houstonian Hotel, with views of lush green towering trees, serves innovative American fare with a delicious Mediterranean bent. The seasonally changing menu includes braised veal ravioli and potato gnocchi with butternut squash and wild mushrooms.

French, Mediterranean. Breakfast, lunch, dinner, Saturday-Sunday brunch. Bar. $16-35

★★★PAPPAS BROS. STEAKHOUSE

5839 Westheimer Road, Houston, 713-780-7352; www.pappasbros.com

Old-fashioned elegance defines this steakhouse with a classic menu of the finest wet- and dry-aged Angus beef, generous sides and an extensive wine list with more than 500 entries. The local Pappas family never fails to provide excellent service, and guests living the good life never fail to return for more. The handsome dark-paneled space is lined with stylish booths outfitted with real retro telephones and larger tables for those frequent and lively parties. Do expect a dessert conundrum: Will it be the pucker-inducing, tart Key lime pie or the housemade peanut butter moon pie? The tab can soar into the stratosphere, but it's worth it if you're trying to impress someone. Piano entertainment is provided nightly in the cozy, dimly lit bar.

Steak. Dinner. Closed Sunday. Reservations recommended. Children's menu. Bar. $36-85

★★★POST OAK GRILL RESTAURANT AND BAR

1415 S. Post Oak Lane, Houston, 713-993-9966; www.postoakgrill.com

Chef Polo Becerra's distinctive menu offers a combination of steak, fresh seafood, pasta and huge salads. Popular entrées include fragrant roasted rosemary chicken and grilled Gulf red snapper. French doors, painted murals and auburn wood tones set the scene in this contemporary, always-bustling restaurant in the Galleria area.

Contemporary American, seafood. Lunch, dinner. Closed Sunday. Reservations recommended. Bar. $16-35

★★★★QUATTRO

Four Seasons Hotel Houston, 1300 Lamar St., Houston, 713-650-1300; www.fourseasons.com

Contemporary Italian-American food is the focus at Quattro, the chic restaurant in the Four Seasons Hotel Houston. The kitchen uses local, seasonal ingredients and offers a roster of daily specials. The architectural presentation of the food is as visually alluring as the dining space, which attracts foodies, downtown business diners and visiting celebrities. To sample a little bit of everything, head there for the lavish Sunday brunch spread, with carving stations, antipasti, salads and desserts to die for.

American, Italian. Breakfast, lunch, dinner, Sunday brunch. Reservations recommended. Children's menu. Bar. $16-35

★★★RAINBOW LODGE

2011 Ella Blvd., Houston, 713-861-8666, 866-861-8666; www.rainbow-lodge.com

Housed in a 100-year-old log cabin, Rainbow Lodge cooks up wild game and fresh seafood, but puts the meats in eclectic contemporary dishes designed for epicures. Try the nilgai antelope, the cast-iron-seared grilled snapper or the distinctive mixed grill of venison, game sausage, Texas quail and wild boar chop. The rustic interior features hunting and fishing collectibles, a stone fireplace and a working garden with fresh vegetables, herbs and citrus that are used in the kitchen.

Contemporary American. Lunch (Monday-Friday), dinner, Sunday brunch. Closed Monday. Reservations recommended. Outdoor seating. Bar. $16-35

★★★RUTH'S CHRIS STEAK HOUSE

6213 Richmond Ave., Houston, 713-789-2333, 800-544-0808; www.ruthschris.com

Thick-cut fillets, rib-eyes and New York strips are among the meaty dishes at this branch of the national steak house chain. Ruth's has a reputation for cooking steaks exactly as ordered, but the menu also includes plenty of grilled seafood, chicken, pork and generous salads doused in rich housemade dressings. While the food will satisfy you, the ambiance at this particular location could use some updating.

Steak. Dinner. Reservations recommended. Bar. $36-85

★★★TONY'S
3755 Richmond Ave., Houston, 713-622-6778; www.tonyshouston.com

Tony Vallone's place has become the de facto dining room of the city's fabulous and famous. The airy, sleek space filled with contemporary art is matched by an avant-garde, European-style menu showcasing Italian roots with premium seasonal ingredients. The changing menu includes selections such as crunchy risotto-crusted black cod, roasted squab and zucchini blossoms stuffed with crab, shrimp and lobster. During the hot Texas summer, order the spanking-fresh, slightly spicy chilled gazpacho with shrimp. Expect polished service and a well-edited wine list.

Italian, contemporary American. Lunch (Monday-Friday), dinner, late-night. Closed Sunday. Bar. $36-85

RECOMMENDED

BRENNAN'S OF HOUSTON
3300 Smith St., Houston, 713-522-9711; www.brennanshouston.com

Legendary New Orleans classic dining is back, as the shrine to Creole cuisine has been fully restored after fire damage a few years ago. This beautiful historic 1930s restaurant still charms with its many French doors, exposed brick and lovely patio with live oaks and a splashing fountain. From the minute the valet opens your door until you exit after ending a leisurely meal with a gratis praline, the service is cordial and polished. Brennan's kitchen explores the vast spectrum of Creole's evolution in the Bayou City with dishes such as classic turtle soup, blue crab and leek bread pudding, and mesquite-honey-lacquered bobwhite quail. Expect variations on traditional ingredients, such as barbecue crawfish shortcake with buttermilk biscuits and St. Arnold's beer aioli. Don't dare pass up the gorgeous towering and tart lemon meringue pie with blueberry coulis.

Creole, Contemporary American. Lunch (Monday-Friday), dinner, Saturday-Sunday brunch. Reservations recommended. Outdoor seating. Bar. $16-35

DAMARCO
1520 Westheimer Road, Houston, 713-807-8857; www.damarcohouston.com

Tucked inside a peaceful, sunny renovated Montrose bungalow, talented chef-owner Marco Wiles' restaurant serves some of the best Italian food in Houston. Dishes like artichoke alla giudea, mushroom trifolati gnocchi and smoky lamb chops scottadito reflect the true cuisine of the chef's homeland in northern Italy. Tempting seasonal options are many. Try the sweet corn ravioli with lobster, seabass with grapefruit and vinegar or housemade pappardelle with rabbit. Servers are knowledgeable about the all-Italian wine list, which is as irresistible as the food.

Italian. Lunch (Tuesday-Friday), dinner. Closed Sunday and Monday. Reservations recommended. $16-35

FLEMING'S PRIME STEAKHOUSE & WINE BAR
2405 W. Alabama St., Houston, 713-520-5959; www.flemingssteakhouse.com

Nationally renowned for its USDA prime beef, Fleming's is equally celebrated for its award-winning wine program that features 100 pours by the glass. The sprawling, romantically lit dining room appeals to both ladies and men, and the open kitchen provides a fun show to watch. Big appetites should order the Texas-sized 24-ounce porterhouse steak. There's also a Town & Country location near the Memorial suburb and one in the Woodlands.

Steak. Dinner. Bar. $36-85.

THE GROVE

1611 Lamar St., Houston, 713-337-7321; www.thegrovehouston.com

Some people call this sprawling restaurant anchoring Discovery Green a version of Manhattan's iconic Tavern on the Green. The Schiller Del Grande restaurant group went all-out on the design with high ceilings, glass red brick and soothing lime accents. A second level overlooking the downtown city park soars above the trees with a rooftop garden and The Treehouse, a cool place to wait for your table or have a cocktail and an appetizer. The menu, created by renowned chef Robert Del Grande and overseen by executive chef Ryan Pera, revolves around rotisserie specialties, seafood and steaks prepared with regional flair. Pulled pork on tiny corn cakes, mesquite smoked quail and deviled eggs with fiery fish sauce are fine starters. The best bets for entrées include char-grilled skirt steak with tomatillo and jalapeños, soft-shell crab tacos, Hill Country venison and marinated black cod. Come back for the down-home Sunday supper.

Contemporary American. Lunch, dinner. Bar. $16-35

IBIZA FOOD & WINE BAR

450 Louisiana St., Houston, 713-524-0004; www.ibizafoodandwinebar.com

Ibiza offers a rich mix of Spanish, French and Mediterranean cuisines that appeal with large portions, reasonable prices and deft culinary treatments by chef-owner Charles Clark. The mouth waters thinking about the braised lamb shank with Spanish mint oil, the seabass with mango essence or the Sunday paella. There's a hip, noisy crowd and cosmopolitan aura among the dining room and outside patio as rolling bar carts are brought tableside to prepare premium cocktails.

Mediterranean. Lunch (Tuesday-Friday), dinner. Closed Monday. Outdoor seating. Bar. $16-35

RDG + BAR ANNIE

1800 Post Oak Blvd., Houston, 713-840-111; www.rdgbarannie.com

Formerly Café Annie, this upscale restaurant by local celebrity-chef Robert Del Grande has moved into its new modern home in Boulevard Place. The sizable, multilevel space wrapped in glass is dramatic with décor in hues of purple, chartreuse and moss; there's also a terrace beautifully set with low tables and lounges. Del Grande's revised concept offers innovative Southwestern cuisine, but now there are three menus to choose from that vary from casual bites to full entrées. Go for the Asian nachos made with yellowtail sashimi with avocado and ginger, slow-cooked beef rib enchiladas, crisp-skinned wood-grilled squab or the handmade Gulf shrimp burger. There's a buzzy vibe at the restaurant, and the beautiful people dine there to rub shoulders with, well, more beautiful people.

Contemporary American, Southwestern. Lunch, dinner, Sunday brunch. Bar. $16-35

SPA

★★★★TRELLIS, THE SPA AT THE HOUSTONIAN

The Houstonian Hotel, Club and Spa, 111 N. Post Oak Lane, Houston, 713-685-6790, 800-378-4010; www.trellisspa.com

Popular with hotel guests and locals alike, this Mediterranean-style spa focuses on beauty and well-being by offering a variety of European-inspired treatments. Relax with a Swedish, stone or aromatic massage. Active contouring helps reduce unwanted cellulite, while the body bronzing treatment adds a healthy glow to skin. Whether you choose a body wrap that invigorates and detoxifies or a unique treatment that soothes aching legs, you are treating yourself to a much deserved pampering.

WHERE TO SHOP

THE CHOCOLATE BAR

1835 W. Alabama St., Houston, 713-520-8599; 2521 University Blvd., Houston, 713-520-8888; www.theoriginalchocolatebar.com

This purple palace of chocolate, a Houston original, channels a Willy Wonka fantasy. Every chocolate concoction you can think up is at this shop, from fresh fruit covered in chocolate to chocolate breakfast cereals. Along with an area dedicated to an assortment of chocolate candy in every shape and a section of daily made chocolate-dipped treats like pretzels or nuts, the store offers 20 different types of chocolate cake—yes, 20. Even in sweltering Texas, it's hard to pass up the decadent hot chocolate.

Monday-Thursday 10 a.m.-10 p.m., Friday-Saturday 10 a.m.-midnight, Sunday noon-10 p.m.

CITYCENTRE

800 W. Sam Houston Parkway N., Houston, 713-629-5200; www.citycentrehouston.com

Stylish CityCentre is Houston's newest mixed-use urban development on the west side of town. Situated on 37 acres, it lives up to its name of being a city all on its own. Luxurious lofts, apartments and office space share the grass-covered grounds with Houston's new avant-garde Hotel Sorella, in addition to several notable independent restaurants, retailers and national eateries. Head there to shop in Republic of Couture, Anthropologie and Sur La Table. When you get hungry, check out Straits, a striking modern Asian-fusion restaurant with outdoor cabana-style seating, or Creole-American Bistro Alex, from the famed Brennan's restaurant family.

Hours vary.

THE GALLERIA

5085 Westheimer Road, Houston, 713-622-0663; www.simon.com

If you're looking for the preeminent place to shop while in Houston, the Galleria has no equal. Visited by 24 million people a year, this shopping metropolis is anchored by four of the most luxurious department stores: Neiman Marcus, Saks Fifth Avenue, Macy's, Barneys New York and Nordstrom. But there's a lot more on offer; the Galleria is the fourth-largest mall in America, boasting 375 stores and restaurants. If you get tired of shopping, mosey downstairs to Polar Ice, the mall's huge indoor ice-skating rink. On a hot Houston day, it's the perfect spot to cool off.

Monday-Saturday 10 a.m.-9 p.m., Sunday 11 a.m.-7 p.m. Store hours may differ from mall hours.

HIGHLAND VILLAGE

4055 Westheimer Road, Houston, 713-850-3100; www.shophighlandvillage.com

Ever-growing since its inception in 1957, Highland Village is an upscale shopping oasis dotted with towering palm trees on one of Houston's busiest boulevards. Fine boutiques, national retailers and restaurants fill the two-level complex. For women, there is no rival to luxury independent boutique Tootsies, which provides a pampering and high-end shopping experience in an airy, contemporary space. Other favorites include Cole Haan, Kiehl's, Anthropologie and Williams-Sonoma. Hungry? Choose a coveted window seat overlooking the boulevard at stunning RA Sushi or a cozy bar table at bustling Escalantes Mexican cantina. Every Saturday, rain or shine, Highland Village hosts a farmers' market with fresh local produce and other giftable gourmet items for sale.

Hours vary.

MEMORIAL CITY MALL

303 Memorial City, Houston, 713-464-8640;
www.memorialcitymall.com

Of all the shopping centers in Houston, Memorial City Mall may be the least flashy, but it is not one to miss. While it doesn't exude the splash of high-end stores, this mall offers a family-friendly atmosphere mixed with affordable shopping. As you peruse go-to stores like Macy's, Dillard's, Sears, JCPenney and Target, admire the mall's European-inspired architecture. When your feet start hurting, catch a flick at the 16-screen Cinemark movie theater.

Monday-Saturday 10 a.m.-9 p.m., Sunday noon-6 p.m.

RICE VILLAGE

2500 Rice Blvd., Houston, 713-524-8084;
www.ricevillageonline.com

Located within blocks of Rice University, The Village—as it's known to the natives—is composed of more than 300 shops within a 16-block range. This beloved outdoor shopping destination dates back to the 1930s, when it only had a handful of shops, but much of it still retains a small-town English village look. Parking can be a nightmare, but everything is within easy walking distance. Establishments range from independent cafés and international restaurants to specialty boutiques and chain stores like Banana Republic or Eddie Bauer. One shop that you must visit is Lot 8, a women's boutique owned by Chloe Dao, the season-two winner of *Project Runway*. While Rice Village is family-friendly during the day, it has great nightlife for the over-21 crowd. Many of the bars have shaded outdoor patios, so after a long day you can grab a drink and watch stars shine over Texas.

Hours vary.

THE SHOPS AT HOUSTON CENTER

1200 McKinney St., Houston, 713-759-1442; www.shopsathc.com

When nasty weather prevents you from hitting the outdoor malls, try the Shops at Houston Center. Part of a larger complex consisting of office space and living space, this mall was created for comfort with its sky bridges and underground pedestrian tunnels so you can stay dry and cool in transit. It contains a diverse demographic of stores, including Jos. A. Bank Clothiers, Hogan's Jewelers, Eyewear Express and Dress Barn along with quick on-the-go eateries like Salata, Ninfa's Express and Sarku Japan. Massa's Seafood is one of the upscale restaurants with a longtime following. The mall's somewhat small multilevel parking garage gives it an edge, since downtown Houston parking can be a headache.

Hours vary.

UPTOWN PARK

Uptown Park (at Interstate 610) and Post Oak boulevards, Houston, 713-840-8474; www.uptownparkhouston.com

As Houston's newest outdoor shopping mall, charming Uptown Park blends Southern Texas style with European elegance. Offering a variety of stores, restaurants and services, this mall attracts shoppers looking for boutiques like M Penner Houston or the fine Paul Cater Jewels for special-occasion gifts. There are also several salons, spas and even a dental office. After shopping, grab a glass of wine at The Tasting Room, an expansive wine bar. Or for a sweet ending, visit Crave Cupcakes, a sleek contemporary bakery that bakes some of the best cupcakes in town.

Hours vary.

GULF COAST

The Gulf Coast, known for its great beaches and wildlife, has seen more than its share of problems, with Hurricanes Katrina, Rita and Ike ravaging its shores and the BP oil spill polluting its waters. But the region somehow manages to overcome its obstacles and carry on. It still remains a nice place to visit. Corpus Christi is a popular vacation spot, with miles of sandy beaches along the Gulf of Mexico. Galveston, an island directly off Texas's northeastern shores of the Gulf of Mexico, offers 32 miles of sandy beaches, fishing piers, deep-sea fishing and cool breezes off the Gulf.

Aside from the beachy locales, you'll find places like Glen Rose. Recognized as the "Dinosaur Capital of Texas," Glen Rose boasts a prehistoric past. Tracks in the area's limestone riverbeds reveal that dinosaurs inhabited this region more than 100 million years prior. Kingsville also provides land-locked fun. It's the home of King Ranch, one of the world's largest privately owned ranches.

WHAT TO SEE

CORPUS CHRISTI
ART MUSEUM OF SOUTH TEXAS
1902 N. Shoreline, Corpus Christi, 361-825-3500; www.stia.org

Built by internationally renowned architect Philip Johnson, the Art Museum of South Texas is as much a work of art as the paintings inside. While the permanent collection spans a wide variety of styles and mediums, the museum's most comprehensive groupings are works by Texas artists and contemporary art. Large-scale abstract paintings by Texas modernist Dorothy Hood are displayed in the Singer Gallery and photographs by Houston-based artist Michele Wambaugh are featured in the Historical Gallery. Traveling exhibits change every few months.

Admission: adults $6, seniors and military $4, students $2, children under 12 free. Tuesday-Saturday, 10 a.m.-5 p.m., Sunday 1-5 p.m.

ASIAN CULTURES MUSEUM AND EDUCATIONAL CENTER
1809 N. Chaparral St., Corpus Christi, 361-882-2641; www.asianculturesmuseum.org

Best known for its collection of more than 2,800 Hakata dolls, Corpus Christi's Asian Cultural Museum is one of five such museums in the United States. Founded in 1974, the museum includes Noh theater masks, opera costumes, Chinese porcelain and lacquerware. A 5-foot bronze Amida Buddha and rickshaw are two of the most popular attractions. The Educational Center holds classes ranging from origami and calligraphy to flower arrangement.

Admission: adults $5, students $3, children $2. Tuesday-Saturday 10 a.m.-5 p.m.

CORPUS CHRISTI MUSEUM OF SCIENCE & HISTORY
1900 N. Chaparral St., Corpus Christi, 361-826-4667; www.ccmuseum.com

The main attractions at this museum are the reproductions of the Pinta and Santa Maria, crafted in Spain in 1993 to commemorate the 500th anniversary of Columbus' voyages. Guided tours of the ships, which were built using the same materials that 15th-century shipbuilders would have used, are offered every hour on the half hour. Equally compelling are the collections inside the museum, such as Texas's marine archaeology, a history collection with 28,000 items representing the history and culture of South Texas, an interactive kids section and exhibits featuring reptiles and shells of the area.

Admission: adults $11.50, seniors and military $9, children 5-12 $6, children under 5 free. Tuesday-Saturday 10 a.m.-5 p.m., Sunday noon-5 p.m.

GREAT TEXAS COASTAL BIRDING TRAIL
Corpus Christi, 800-792-1112; www.tpwd.state.tx.us

Spoonbills and egrets, plovers and terns—Texas is a bird-watchers paradise, with more species than any other state. Seventy-five percent of these birds can be viewed along the Texas Gulf Coast. The trail is divided into three parts: upper, lower and central. While in Corpus Christi, visit the Mustang Island loop of the trail, which starts with a free ferry ride across the bay to Port Aransas (watch for bottle-nosed dolphins and brown pelicans on the way over) and proceeds south down the island.

Admission: free. Daily.

HIGHLIGHTS

WHAT ARE THE TOP THINGS TO DO ON THE GULF COAST?

SEE A SHOW AT THE GRAND 1894 OPERA HOUSE

Located in Galveston, The Grand 1894 Opera House is listed in the National Register of Historic Places and is one of the few remaining theaters of its era in Texas. The extraordinary theater hosts national touring shows and other performing arts year-round.

CHECK OUT SOME DINOSAUR TRACKS

Dinosaur Valley State Park, located northwest of Glen Rose, contains some of the most interesting and well-preserved dinosaur tracks in the world. The park includes two fiberglass dinosaur models—a 70-foot Apatosaurus and a 45-foot Tyrannosaurus Rex.

TEXAS STATE AQUARIUM

Corpus Christi Beach, 2710 N. Shore Line Blvd., Corpus Christi, 361-881-1200, 800-477-4853; www.texasstateaquarium.org

The aquarium has 10 major indoor and outdoor exhibit areas focusing on marine plant and animal life indigenous to the Gulf of Mexico. It features approximately 350,000 gallons of saltwater and more than 250 species of sea life.

Admission: adults $15.50, seniors and military $13.95, children 3-12 $10.50, children under 3 free. September-February, daily 9 a.m.-5 p.m.; March-August, daily 9 a.m.-6 p.m.

USS LEXINGTON MUSEUM IN THE BAY

2914 N. Shoreline Blvd., Corpus Christi, 361-888-4873, 800-523-9539; www.usslexington.com

Popularly known as the Blue Ghost or Lady Lex, the *USS Lexington* was the last World War II Essex Class aircraft carrier to remain in U.S. naval service. Decommissioned in 1991 and opened to the public in 1992 as a naval aviation museum, the ship, now permanently moored in Corpus Christi Bay, is an awe-inspiring 910 feet long (more than three football fields) and 16 decks high. The museum also holds memorabilia and artifacts that date from 1943 to 1991 and includes 19 vintage aircrafts, ranging from an F-14 Tomcat to an SBD-3 Dauntless. Visit the 44-foot-wide and three-story-tall Joe Jessel Mega Theater, the only large-format theater aboard a World War II aircraft carrier.

Admission: adults $12.95, seniors and military $10.95, children 4-12 $7.95, children under 4 free. June-August, daily 9 a.m.-6 p.m.; September-May, daily 9 a.m.-5 p.m.

GALVESTON

THE BISHOP'S PALACE

1402 Broadway, Galveston, 409-762-2475; www.galveston.com

The city's most celebrated landmark, this four-story stone Victorian mansion was built in 1886 and serves as an outstanding example of that period. It features marble, mosaics, stained- and jeweled-glass windows, a hand-carved stairwell and woodwork. Tours are available.

Admission: adults $10, students 6-18 $7, children under 6 free. June-August, Monday-Saturday 10 a.m.-4:30 p.m., Sunday noon-4 p.m.; September-May, daily noon-4:30 p.m.

GRAND 1894 OPERA HOUSE

2020 Postoffice St., Galveston, 409-765-1894, 800-821-1894; www.thegrand.com

The Grand is listed in the National Register of Historic Places and is one of the few remaining theaters of its era in Texas. As further recognition of its importance to the citizens of Texas, in 1993 the 73rd Texas Legislature proclaimed the Grand "The Official Opera House of Texas." The extraordinary theater hosts national touring shows and other performing arts year-round. Call or visit the website for performance details.

Admission: varies. Showtimes vary.

MOODY GARDENS AQUARIUM & RAINFOREST

1 Hope Blvd., Galveston, 800-582-4673; www.moodygardens.com

Rising from the edge of Galveston Island like three polished gems, the massive pyramid structures that house Moody Gardens Aquarium & Rainforest are architectural wonders. The 10-story glass Rainforest Pyramid includes thousands of tropical plants, exotic fish, birds and butterflies native to the rain forests of Africa, Asia, and the Americas. It also houses "Totally Frogs," the largest frog and toad collection in the country. With 1.5 million gallons of water, the Aquarium at Moody offers exhibits representing the North Pacific, South Pacific, Antarctic, and Caribbean regions with 8,000-plus specimens of marine life. The Discovery Pyramid focuses on science, with interactive demonstrations of science experiments and traveling exhibits. IMAX 3-D and Ridefilm theaters offer visual thrills, and the Garden's Palm Beach water park is a relaxing outdoor oasis.

Admission: varies. Sunday-Friday 10 a.m.-6 p.m., Saturday 10 a.m.-8 p.m.

GLEN ROSE

DINOSAUR VALLEY STATE PARK

Park Road 59, Glen Rose, 254-897-4588; www.tpwd.state.tx.us

Located northwest of Glen Rose, this more than 1,500-acre state park abuts the Paluxy River. Dinosaur Valley State Park contains some of the most interesting and well-preserved dinosaur tracks in the world. The tracks are in the riverbed, so call ahead to check river conditions. The park includes two fiberglass dinosaur models—a 70-foot Apatosaurus and a 45-foot Tyrannosaurus Rex. They were built for the 1964-1965 New York World's Fair Dinosaur Exhibit. Other available activities include camping, picnicking, hiking, mountain biking, river swimming and fishing.

Admission: adults $5, children under 13 free. Daily 8 a.m.-10 p.m.

FOSSIL RIM WILDLIFE CENTER
2299 CR 2008, Glen Rose, 254-897-2960; www.fossilrim.org

This 3,000-acre wildlife conservation center has more than 1,000 endangered, threatened and exotic animals. Breeding programs for endangered species include the white rhinoceros, Mexican wolf, red wolf, Grevy's zebra, Arabian oryx, scimitar-horned oryx, addax and cheetah. Jump aboard the 10-mile drive-through with animal sightings, a nature trail, a fossil area and a petting pasture. Roaming animals include giraffes, cheetahs, ostriches, zebras and rhinos. There is also an onsite restaurant and gift shop.

Admission: varies by season. Hours vary by season.

KINGSVILLE
KING RANCH
Highway 141 W., Kingsville, 361-592-8055, 800-333-5032; www.king-ranch.com

Texas visitors who want to have real-life encounters with cowboys, cattle and horses can do no better than make a visit to King Ranch, one of the oldest and largest working ranches in the United States. Larger than Rhode Island, the ranch sprawls over 825,000 acres of south Texas. Nature enthusiasts can choose from eight different tours of the vast acreage, ranging from half-day wildlife and bird-watching excursions to full-day birding tours and customized trips. Don't leave without checking out the saddle shop for everything from hunting gear to luggage. Reservations are required for tours.

Admission: varies. Daily.

WHERE TO STAY

CORPUS CHRISTI
★★★OMNI CORPUS CHRISTI HOTEL BAYFRONT TOWER
900 N. Shoreline Blvd., Corpus Christi, 361-887-1600, 800-843-6664; www.omnihotels.com

Gaze from a private balcony at the miles of sandy beaches just outside this bayfront hotel. More than 24,000 square feet of meeting space attracts groups, but the sailing, swimming and ocean fishing makes this a great leisure destination as well.

475 rooms. Restaurant, bar. Business center. Fitness center. Pool. Pets accepted. $151-250

★★★OMNI CORPUS CHRISTI HOTEL MARINA TOWER
707 N. Shoreline Blvd., Corpus Christi, 361-887-1600, 800-843-6664; www.omnihotels.com

Located in the downtown Seaside Marina on the Texas Coast, this hotel has an indoor and outdoor pool, a spa and an exercise facility. The hotel is conveniently situated only 15 minutes away from the airport.

346 rooms. Restaurant, bar. Business center. Fitness center. Pool. Pets accepted. $61-150

GALVESTON
★★★HILTON GALVESTON ISLAND RESORT
5400 Seawall Blvd., Galveston, 409-744-5000, 800-445-8667; www.galvestonhilton.com

On the 30 acres of the San Luis resort, this hotel offers attentive service, an airy lobby and a bar that overlooks the pool. Request a room with a view of the Gulf—all of which come with wireless access and in-room movies.

150 rooms. Restaurant, bar. Fitness center. Pool. $61-150

★★★SAN LUIS RESORT AND CONFERENCE CENTER

5222 Seawall Blvd., Galveston, 409-744-1500, 800-445-0090; www.sanluisresort.com

This hotel rests on a 22-acre island and has a heated pool with a swim-up bar and whirlpool, a full spa and more. Rooms have balconies overlooking the Gulf.

241 rooms. Restaurant, bar. Business center. Fitness center. Pool. Spa. Tennis. $151-250

★★★WYNDHAM HOTEL GALVEZ

2024 Seawall Blvd., Galveston, 409-765-7721, 800-996-3426; www.wyndham.com

Known as the "Queen of the Gulf" since it opened in 1911, this historic hotel has hosted its share of celebrities, such as Teddy Roosevelt, Frank Sinatra and Howard Hughes. Enjoy rooms with views of the Gulf; take a lap in the outdoor pool with swim-up bar; or ride horses along the beach.

226 rooms. Restaurant, bar. Business center. Fitness center. Pool. Beach. $61-150

★★★WYNDHAM TREMONT HOUSE HOTEL

2300 Ship Mechanic Row, Galveston, 409-763-0300, 800-996-3426; www.wyndham.com

Located in the center of the Strand, this landmark was restored to its original European grandeur. Famous Texan Sam Houston delivered his last public speech here. Enjoy the lobby with its four-story glass atrium, the rooftop terrace and afternoon tea.

119 rooms. Restaurant, bar. Fitness center. $151-250

GLEN ROSE

★★★ROUGH CREEK LODGE

5165 County Road 2013, Glen Rose, 254-965-3700, 800-864-4705; www.roughcreek.com

This luxury lodge offers a stylish escape. There's a cattle drive, guided fishing expeditions on one of the three private lakes and ranch tours. Enjoy spa services, lounge by the pool or take a private cooking lesson from the award-winning chef.

39 rooms. Restaurant, bar. Fitness center. Pool. Spa. Pets accepted. Tennis. $251-350

WELCOME TO UTAH

UTAH'S NATURAL DIVERSITY HAS MADE IT A STATE OF

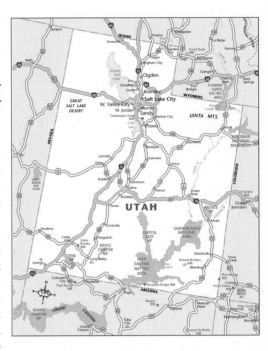

magnificent beauty, with more than 3,000 lakes, miles of mountains, acres of forests and large expanses of desert. In northern Utah, the grandeur of the Wasatch Range, one of the most rugged mountain ranges in the United States, cuts across the state north to south. The Uinta Range, capped by the white peaks of ancient glaciers, is the only major North American range that runs east to west. In the western third of the state is the Great Basin. Lake Bonneville extended over much of western Utah leaving behind the Great Salt Lake, Utah Lake and Sevier Lake. To the east and west extends the Red Plateau. This Red Rock country, renowned for its brilliant coloring and fantastic rock formations, is home to one of the largest concentrations of national parks and monuments. Utah is definitely the place for those who love the Western outdoors and can appreciate the awesome accomplishments of the pioneers who developed it.

This natural diversity created an environment inhospitable to early settlers. Although various groups explored much of the state, it took the determination and perseverance of a band of religious fugitives, members of the Church of Jesus Christ of Latter-Day Saints, to settle the land permanently. Brigham Young, leader of the Mormons, once remarked, "If there is a place on this earth that nobody else wants, that's the place I am hunting for." On July 24, 1847, on entering the forbidding land surrounding the Great Salt Lake, Young exclaimed, "This is the place!" The determined settlers immediately began to plow the unfriendly soil and build dams for irrigation. During 1847, as many as 1,637

HIGHLIGHTS

UTAH'S BEST ATTRACTIONS

BRYCE CANYON

See some of the best scenery Utah has to offer at this national park. The jagged, towering rocks change color when the sun's rays hit them at different angles. The Pink Cliffs are quite a sight.

PARK CITY

Each January, Park City becomes a celebrity hot spot when the Sundance Film Festival comes to town. Outside of the festival, people also flock to this resort town for its great skiing and outdoor sports.

SALT LAKE CITY

Salt Lake City is known for its Mormon sites, like the Mormon Temple and the Tabernacle. But the city also has a slew of other offerings, including Lagoon Amusement Park, the Utah Opera Company and Jazz basketball.

Mormons came to Utah, and by the time the railroad made its way here, more than 6,000 had settled in the state. Before his death in 1877, 30 years after entering the Salt Lake Valley, Brigham Young had directed the founding of more than 350 communities.

The LDS church undoubtedly had the greatest influence on the state, developing towns in an orderly fashion with wide streets, planting straight rows of poplar trees to provide wind breaks and introducing irrigation throughout the desert regions. But the church members were not the only settlers. In the latter part of the 19th century, the West's fabled pioneer era erupted. The gold rush of 1849 to 1850 sent gold seekers pouring through Utah on their way to California. The arrival of the Pony Express in Salt Lake City in 1860 brought more immigrants, and when the mining boom hit the state in the 1870s and 1880s, Utah's mining towns appeared almost overnight. In 1900, the population was 277,000. It now stands at more than 1.7 million, with more than 75 percent living within 50 miles of Salt Lake City. The LDS church continues to play an important role, and close to 60 percent of the state's population are members.

SALT LAKE CITY

Salt Lake City—with its 10-acre blocks, 132-foot-wide, tree-lined streets and mountains rising to the east and west—is one of the most beautifully planned cities in the country.

On a hill at the north end of State Street stands Utah's classic Capitol building. Three blocks south is Temple Square, with the famed Mormon Temple and Tabernacle. The adjacent block houses the headquarters of the Church of Jesus Christ of Latter-day Saints, whose members are commonly called Mormons.

Once a desert wilderness, Salt Lake City was built by Mormon settlers who sought refuge from religious persecution. Followers of Brigham Young arrived and named their new territory Deseret. In the early days, the Mormons began a variety of experiments in farming, industry and society, many of which were highly successful. Today, Salt Lake City is an industrious, businesslike city, a center for electronics, steel, missiles and a hundred other enterprises.

West of the city is the enormous Great Salt Lake, stretching 48 miles one way and 90 miles the other. It is less than 35 feet deep and between 15 and 20 percent salt—almost five times as salty as the ocean. You can't sink in the water—instead you'll just bob up and down. The lake is what remains of ancient Lake Bonneville, once 145 miles wide, 350 miles long and 1,000 feet deep. As Lake Bonneville's water evaporated over thousands of years, a large expanse of perfectly flat, solid salt was left. Today, the Bonneville Salt Flats stretch west almost to Nevada.

Salt Lake City was laid out in grid fashion, with Temple Square at the center. Most street names are coordinates on this grid: Fourth South Street is four blocks south of Temple Square, Seventh East is seven blocks east. These are written as 400 South and 700 East.

WHAT TO SEE

BRIGHAM YOUNG MONUMENT
Salt Lake City, Main and South Temple streets
This statue honoring the church leader was first seen at the Chicago World's Fair in 1893.

CLARK PLANETARIUM
110 S. 400 W., Salt Lake City, 801-456-7827; www.hansenplanetarium.net
The Hansen Dome Theatre and the IMAX Theatre are the two main attractions here. Free exhibits include images from the Hubble Space telescope and a fully functioning weather station.
Admission: free; prices for theatres vary. Monday-Wednesday 10:30 a.m.-8 p.m., Thursday 10:30 a.m.-9 p.m., Friday-Saturday 10:30 a.m.-11 p.m., Sunday 10:30 a.m.-6 p.m.

FAMILY HISTORY LIBRARY
35 N. West Temple St., Salt Lake City, 801-240-2584, 800-346-6044; www.familysearch.org
If you are looking to learn about your family tree, head to the Family History Library. This five-floor genealogical library is the largest such facility in the world.
Monday 8 a.m.-5 p.m., Tuesday-Saturday 8 a.m.-9 p.m.

HIGHLIGHTS

WHAT ARE THE TOP MORMON SITES?

EAT AT THE LION HOUSE
Lion House may seem like an ordinary home-style restaurant, but in fact, the mansion used to be the home of Brigham Young and his family.

TRY TO SNEAK A LISTEN AT THE TABERNACLE
The famous Mormon Tabernacle Choir sings in this house of worship, which is also known for its impressive organ, which boasts more than 11,500 pipes.

SEE THE MONUMENT AT THIS IS THE PLACE HERITAGE PARK
The park marks the spot where Mormon pioneers first entered the valley, and a large monument pays homage to Brigham Young's first words upon seeing the site.

TAKE A TOUR AT TEMPLE SQUARE
Salt Lake City's most popular tourist destination, 10-acre Temple Square is owned by the Church of Latter-day Saints. Head there for complimentary guided tours from the church.

GOVERNOR'S MANSION
603 E. South Temple St., Salt Lake City, 801-538-1005; www.utah.gov
Built by Thomas Kearns, a wealthy Utah senator in the early 1900s, this mansion is the official residence of the state's governor. It was painstakingly restored after a fire in 1993. President Theodore Roosevelt, a personal friend of Senator Kerns, dined here often.
June-September, Tuesday and Thursday 2-4 p.m.

INNSBROOK TOURS
Salt Lake City, 801-534-1001; www.saltlakecitytours.org
This is the best way to see all the famous sites in Salt Lake City. Pick-up begins at 9:15 a.m., and then you're off to see landmarks like the Mormon Tabernacle, the Salt Lake Temple and the Olympic Stadium and Village.
Daily.

LAGOON AMUSEMENT PARK, PIONEER VILLAGE AND WATER PARK

Salt Lake City, 17 miles north on Interstate 15, 800-748-5246; www.lagoonpark.com

Besides fun rides and waterslides, the village includes a re-creation of a 19th-century Utah town with stagecoach and steam-engine train rides. There are also camping sites and picnicking areas here.

Admission: adults $42.95, seniors and children $37.95, children 3 and under $27.95 (for rides). April-October, hours vary.

LIBERTY PARK

1300 South St., Salt Lake City, 801-972-7800; www.slcgov.com

This 100-acre park is Salt Lake's largest. Go for a run, play tennis or enjoy a picnic. There's a playground, and paddleboats are available in summer.

Park: daily 7 a.m.-10 p.m. Aviary: daily 9 a.m-6 p.m.; November-March, daily 9 a.m.-4:30 p.m.

LION HOUSE

63 E. South Temple St., Salt Lake City, 801-363-5466

Lion House was home to Brigham Young's family. Today the mansion houses a restaurant. Next door is another residence, Beehive House, which is open for tours.

Monday-Saturday 11 a.m.-8 p.m.

MAURICE ABRAVANEL CONCERT HALL

123 W. South Temple St., Salt Lake City, 801-355-2787; www.finearts.slco.org

Home to the Utah Symphony, this building is adorned with more than 12,000 square feet of 24-karat gold leaf and a mile of brass railing. It has been rated one of the best halls in the U.S. for acoustics. Free tours are available by appointment.

MOKI MAC RIVER EXPEDITIONS

6006 S. 1300 E., Salt Lake City, 801-268-6667, 800-284-7280; www.mokimac.com

This company offers one- to 14-day white-water rafting and canoeing trips on the Green and Colorado rivers. Check the website for the schedule.

MUSEUM OF CHURCH HISTORY AND ART

45 N. West Temple St., Salt Lake City, 801-240-4615; www.lds.org

Mormon temples may be off limits to the public, but you can head to this museum to learn more about the religion. Exhibits examine Latter-day Saints church history from 1820 to the present.

Admission: free. Monday-Friday 9 a.m.-9 p.m., Saturday-Sunday 10 a.m.-7 p.m.

PIONEER MEMORIAL MUSEUM

300 N. Main St., Salt Lake City, 801-532-6479; www.dupinternational.org

This extensive collection of pioneer relics includes a carriage house with exhibits relating to transportation, including Brigham Young's wagon and Pony Express items. One-hour guided tours by appointment.

Admission: free. Monday-Saturday 9 a.m.-5 p.m.; June-August, also Sunday 1-5 p.m.

RED BUTTE GARDEN AND ARBORETUM

300 Wakara Way, Salt Lake City, 801-581-4747; www.redbuttegarden.org

The arboretum includes more than 9,000 trees on 150 acres, representing 350 species. There's a conservatory on the grounds, and you can take self-guided tours. During the summer, there are special events.

Admission: adults $6, seniors and children 3-17 $4, children 2 and under free. May-August, daily 9 a.m.-9 p.m.; September, April, daily 9 a.m.-7:30 p.m.; October-mid-December, March, daily 9 a.m.-5 p.m.; January-February, Monday-Saturday 9 a.m.-5 p.m.

SOLITUDE RESORT

12000 Big Cottonwood Canyon, Salt Lake City, 801-534-1400; www.skisolitude.com

The resort offers three quads, one triple and four double chairlifts; a race-course; a patrol; a school; and rentals. The longest run goes for three miles with a vertical drop of 2,047 feet.

November-April, daily.

TEMPLE SQUARE

50 W. North Temple St., Salt Lake City, 801-240-1245, 800-537-9703; www.mormon.org

This 10-acre square is owned by the Church of Jesus Christ of Latter-day Saints. Two visitors' centers provide information, exhibits and guided tours.

TABERNACLE

50 W. North Temple St., Salt Lake City, 801-240-4150, 866-537-8457;
www.mormontabernaclechoir.org

The self-supporting roof, an elongated dome, is 250 feet long and 150 feet wide. The tabernacle organ has 11,623 pipes, ranging from 5/8 inch to 32 feet. The world-famous Tabernacle Choir may be heard at rehearsal (Thursday 8 p.m.) or at broadcast time (Sunday 9:30 a.m.).

Organ recitals: Monday-Saturday noon, Sunday afternoon.

THIS IS THE PLACE HERITAGE PARK

2601 E. Sunnyside Ave., Salt Lake City, 801-582-1847; www.thisistheplace.org

This historic park is at the mouth of Emigration Canyon, where Mormon pioneers first entered the valley, and includes Old Deseret Pioneer Village and This Is the Place Monument (1947), commemorating Brigham Young's words upon first seeing the Salt Lake City site. Hundreds of people on the monument depict pioneer life. Admission to the monument and visitor center, which includes an audio presentation and murals of the Mormon migration, is free.

Monument and grounds: daily, dawn-dusk. Visitor center: Monday-Saturday 9 a.m.-6 p.m. Village: late May-early September, Monday-Saturday 10 a.m.-6 p.m.

UTAH MUSEUM OF FINE ARTS

410 Campus Center Drive, Salt Lake City, 801-581-7332; www.umfa.utah.edu

Representations of artistic styles that range from Egyptian antiquities to contemporary American paintings are displayed here, as well as 19th-century French and American paintings and furniture.

Admission: adults $7, seniors and children 6-18 $5, children 5 and under free. Tuesday-Friday 10 a.m.-5 p.m., Wednesday 10 a.m.-8 p.m., Saturday-Sunday 11 a.m.-5 p.m.

UTAH MUSEUM OF NATURAL HISTORY
1390 E. Presidents Circle, Salt Lake City, 801-581-6927; www.umnh.utah.edu
The natural history museum shows exhibits of the Earth's natural wonders and honors Utah's native cultures.
Admission: adults $7, seniors and children 3-17 $3.50, children 2 and under free. Monday-Saturday 9:30 a.m.-5:30 p.m., Sunday noon-5 p.m. First Monday of every month until 8 p.m.

UTAH JAZZ (NBA)
EnergySolutions Arena, 301 W. South Temple, Salt Lake City, 801-325-2500; www.nba.com
The state's professional basketball team jazzes up EnergySolutions Arena.

UTAH OPERA COMPANY
123 W. South Temple, Salt Lake City, 801-533-5626; www.utahopera.org
Utah's premier opera company has been singing to the rafters since 1978. The company's past performances have included *Little Women* and *La Bohème*. *October-May.*

UTAH STARZZ (WNBA)
EnergySolutions Arena, 301 W. South Temple St., Salt Lake City, 801-355-3865; www.utah.com
Utah's professional women's basketball team calls EnergySolutions Arena its home base.

WASATCH-CACHE NATIONAL FOREST
125 S. State St., Salt Lake City, 801-236-3400; www.fs.fed.us
This wilderness area has alpine lakes, rugged peaks and several canyons. There's fishing, boating, deer and elk hunting, winter sports and camping.

WHEELER HISTORIC FARM
6351 S. 900 E. St., Salt Lake City, 801-264-2241; www.wheelerfarm.com
This living history farm on 75 acres depicts rural life from 1890 to1918 and includes a farmhouse, farm buildings, animals, crops and hay rides. You can feed the animals, gather eggs and milk cows. There is a small fee for various activities and events.
Monday-Saturday dawn-dusk.

ZCMI (ZION'S CO-OPERATIVE MERCANTILE INSTITUTION) CENTER
Main and South Temple, Salt Lake City
A department store established in 1868 by Brigham Young anchors this 85-store, enclosed downtown shopping mall.
Monday-Saturday.

WHERE TO STAY

★★★★THE GRAND AMERICA HOTEL
555 S. Main St., Salt Lake City, 801-258-6000, 800-621-4505; www.grandamerica.com
Set against the beautiful backdrop of the Wasatch Mountains, the Grand America is a tribute to Old World Europe. The guest rooms are classically French, with luxurious fabrics, fine art and Richelieu furniture. The spa offers a full menu of treatments, from massages to facials and body wraps, and includes a full-service salon. The hotel's Sunday brunch is a Salt Lake City institution,

with a sprawling buffet of breakfast dishes and a huge array of desserts.
775 rooms. Restaurant, bar. Pool. Spa. $251-350

★★HILTON SALT LAKE CITY CENTER

255 S. West Temple St., Salt Lake City, 801-328-2000; www.hilton.com

Located downtown, this large hotel caters to business travelers with updated rooms equipped with large work areas and wireless access. The fitness center includes first-rate cardio machines, a sauna and an indoor pool. The onsite restaurant serves grilled steaks and seafood, along with an expansive wine list.
499 rooms. Restaurant, bar. Pool. Spa. Pets accepted. $61-150

★★★HOTEL MONACO SALT LAKE CITY

15 W. 200 S., Salt Lake City, 801-595-0000, 877-294-9710; www.hotelmonaco.com

This hotel stands out for its contemporary décor and personalized services. Situated in downtown Salt Lake City, the refurbished 14-story landmark hotel has rooms with beds swathed in Frette linens. Those who are vertically endowed should book one of the tall rooms, which have eight-foot beds and heightened showerheads. Amenities include coffeemakers with Starbucks coffee, yoga programs—grab a mat from the basket and flip on the Yoga channel for some in-room poses—and gourmet minibars. If all you're missing is a travel companion, you can adopt a goldfish during your stay.
225 rooms. Restaurant, bar. Pets accepted. $61-150

★★LITTLE AMERICA HOTEL

500 S. Main St., Salt Lake City, 801-596-5700, 800-453-9450; www.littleamerica.com

This hotel offers a variety of accommodations. Rooms in the tower are decorated in rich French brocade fabrics and English wool carpets, and they offer large parlor areas with views of the city. There's also a separate dressing area and bathroom with an oval-shaped tub. Garden rooms are spacious and have private entrances. The hotel includes a large indoor pool and salon.
850 rooms. Restaurant, bar. Pool. Spa. $61-150

★★★MARRIOTT SALT LAKE CITY DOWNTOWN

75 S. West Temple St., Salt Lake City, 801-531-0800; www.marriott.com

Across from the Salt Palace Convention Center, this hotel caters to business travelers and is close to the airport and major ski resorts. Everything is on hand here, including a heated pool, fitness center and Starbucks.
514 rooms. Restaurant, bar. Business center. $151-250

★★★MARRIOTT SALT LAKE CITY-CITY CENTER

220 S. State St., Salt Lake City, 801-961-8700, 866-961-8700; www.marriott.com

Situated adjacent to the Gallivan Center, which hosts concerts in summer and skating in winter, this hotel is within walking distance to numerous restaurants and shops. The contemporary guest rooms are decorated in a relaxing palette and feature down comforters, large marble baths and views of either the city or the mountains. The hotel's restaurant, Piastra, serves up continental cuisine in a sophisticated setting.
359 rooms. Restaurant, bar. $61-150

★★★RADISSON HOTEL SALT LAKE CITY DOWNTOWN

215 W. S. Temple St., Salt Lake City, 801-531-7500, 800-333-3333; www.radisson.com

Sitting next to the Salt Palace Convention Center, this downtown hotel is at a good spot for those traveling on business. The rooms also help out worker bees by providing spacious desk areas with Herman Miller-designed ergonomic chairs and complimentary high-speed Internet access. When you need a break, visit the indoor pool, fitness center, sauna or whirlpool.

381 rooms. Restaurant, bar. Fitness center. Pool. Pets accepted. $61-150

WHERE TO EAT

★★★BAMBARA

202 S. Main St., Salt Lake City, 801-363-5454; www.bambara-slc.com

This chic contemporary American bistro housed in a former bank serves up creations based on whatever is fresh and seasonal. Entrées include seared halibut with sweet corn and crab hash, smoky bacon and green chili butter, and housemade angel hair pasta with Maine lobster, seared oyster mushrooms, basil and sweet corn butter.

American. Breakfast, lunch, dinner. Reservations recommended. Children's menu. $36-85

★★★FRESCO ITALIAN CAFE

1513 S. 1500 E., Salt Lake City, 801-486-1300;
www.frescoitaliancafe.com

A winding brick walkway lined with flowers leads the way to this neighborhood bistro, where you'll find a fireplace in winter and alfresco dining during the summer. Standout dishes include the chef's nightly risotto and freshly made herb gnocchi.

Italian. Dinner. Reservations recommended. Outdoor seating. $16-35

★★★LA CAILLE

9565 S. Wasatch Blvd., Little Cottonwood Canyon, 801-942-1751; www.lacaille.com

This country French chateau is surrounded by beautiful gardens populated by peacocks, llamas, ducks and a host of other exotic animals. The menu features innovative fare such as roasted rack of venison with a venison cabernet sauvignon glaze and lingonberries.

French. Dinner, Sunday brunch. Reservations recommended. Outdoor seating. Children's menu. Bar. $36-85

★★★LOG HAVEN

6451 E. Millcreek Canyon Road, Salt Lake City, 801-272-8255; www.log-haven.com

This rustic log mansion is one of Utah's most innovative restaurants. The fresh specialties change daily, but you might see chilled edamame soup with sake steamed clams, tomato coulis and lime aioli; grilled lamb lollipops with truffled potato salad, arugula and tarragon aioli; or tarragon-crusted sea scallops with English pea risotto, lemon-carrot butter and watermelon radish salad. The restaurant also has an extensive wine list.

International. Dinner. Reservations recommended. Outdoor seating. Bar. $36-85

WHAT ARE THE BEST OVERALL RESTAURANTS IN SALT LAKE CITY?

Log Haven:
Don't let this restaurant's rustic log exterior fool you. Log Haven serves some of the most innovative cuisine in the state. You can expect dishes like grilled lamb lollipops with truffled potato salad, arugula and tarragon aioli.

The New Yorker:
This restaurant has been turning out classic dishes since 1978, and it shouldn't stop anytime soon. The top steak house, tucked inside the New Yorker Hotel, offers traditional fare like bouillabaisse.

★★★METROPOLITAN
173 W. Broadway, Salt Lake City, 801-364-3472; www.themetropolitan.com

This restaurant specializes in contemporary American cuisine. Indulge in dishes such as mahi mahi with purple potatoes, peas, kumquat and lychee-lavender foam; or potato gnocchi with caramelized sunchokes, heirloom cauliflower and macadamia nut pesto. End with a soufflé, which comes in a variety of flavors, including spicy chocolate and kumquat.

American. Lunch, dinner. Closed Sunday. Bar. $36-85

★★★THE NEW YORKER
60 W. Market St., Salt Lake City, 801-363-0166; www.gastronomyinc.com

Recognized as one of Salt Lake's top dining spots since 1978, this elegant restaurant in the historic New York Hotel, serves traditional fare. The menu sticks to the classics, including bouillabaisse, grilled rib-eye with béarnaise sauce, and Caesar salad.

Steak. Lunch (Monday-Friday), dinner. Closed Sunday. Reservations recommended. Bar. $36-85

★★★TUSCANY
2832 E. 6200 S., Salt Lake City, 801-277-9919; www.tuscanyslc.com

This tremendously popular place maintains a high quality of service and offers authentic Tuscan fare while incorporating modern American culinary trends. Tasty items on the menu include risotto with sautéed sea scallops, bacon, sweet peas and basil with a carbonara Parmesan cream sauce; or steak with fresh-cut haystack potatoes.

Italian. Lunch, dinner, Sunday brunch. Outdoor seating. Bar. $36-85

WHERE TO SHOP

TROLLEY SQUARE
600 S. 700 East St., Salt Lake City, 801-521-9877; www.trolleysquare.com

This 10-acre complex of trolley barns has been converted into a shopping/dining center. You can shop at stores such as American Apparel, Pottery Barn, Brookstone and Williams Sonoma. Restaurants include The Old Spaghetti Factory, Green Street Social Club and others.

Monday-Saturday 10 a.m.-9 p.m., Sunday noon-5 p.m.

SALT LAKE CITY METRO AREA

While Salt Lake City is the big city in these parts, the metro area has its fair share of offerings. The most recognizable name is Park City, a four-season resort with skiing, snowboarding, golf, tennis, water sports and mountain biking. Celebs fill the city every year to attend the Sundance Film Festival. Speaking of Sundance, the popular ski resort of the same name is 30 miles south of Park City. Sundance, the resort, was purchased by Robert Redford in 1968 and is named after the role Redford played in the film *Butch Cassidy and the Sundance Kid*.

Provo is the state's third-largest city. It lies in the middle of a lush, green valley: to the north stands 12,008-foot Mount Timpanogos; to the south is the perpendicular face of the Wasatch Range; to the east Provo Peak rises 11,054 feet; and to the west lies Utah Lake, backed by more mountains. Provo is the headquarters of the Uinta National Forest, and many good boating, camping and hiking spots are nearby.

WHAT TO SEE

PARK CITY

BRIGHTON SKI RESORT
12601 E. Big Cottonwood Canyon Road, Brighton, 801-532-4731, 800-873-5512; www.skibrighton.com

The resort includes 16 high-speed quad, triple and double chairlifts; a gondola; a ski patrol; a school; rentals; and a restaurant, bar and lodge. The grounds have 155 trails.
Winter lift: daily 9 a.m.-4 p.m.

THE CANYONS
4000 The Canyons Resort Drive, Park City, 435-649-5400; www.thecanyons.com

This ski resort features 16 high-speed quad, triple and double chairlifts; a gondola; a ski patrol; a school; rentals; and a restaurant, bar and lodge. The Canyons has 155 trails.
Winter lift: daily 9 a.m.-4 p.m.

DEER VALLEY RESORT
2250 Deer Valley Drive S., Park City, 435-649-1000, 800-424-3337; www.deervalley.com

This exclusive resort has eight high-speed quads, eight triple and two double chairlifts; rentals; a patrol; a school; snowmaking; restaurants, a lounge, a lodge and a nursery. The number of tickets sold each day is limited, so buy early if you want to ski here—and meet your snowboarding friends later. Deer Valley is for skiers only. There's approximately 1,750 skiable acres. The vertical drop is 3,000 feet. Summer activities include mountain biking, hiking and horseback riding.

EGYPTIAN THEATRE
328 Main St., Park City, 435-649-9371; www.egyptiantheatrecompany.org

Originally built in 1926 as a silent movie and vaudeville house, this is now a year-round performing arts center with a semi-professional theater group.
Wednesday-Saturday; some performances other days.

HIGHLIGHTS

WHAT IS THERE TO DO ASIDE FROM SKIING?

GO BIRD WATCHING AT ROCKPORT STATE PARK
You can visit this 1,000-acre park and do some bird watching; you'll spy bald eagles and golden eagles here. In warm weather, go swimming, waterskiing, fishing or sail boating.

SKI JUMP AT UTAH WINTER SPORTS PARK
Take your skiing to the next level at this park, built for the 2002 Olympic Games. You can get lessons on recreational ski jumping and then spend two hours practicing your jumps.

DRIVE THROUGH UINTA NATIONAL FOREST
Take a drive through this national forest to see awe-inspiring views of vibrant landscapes, canyons and waterfalls.

KIMBALL ART CENTER
638 Park Ave., Park City, 435-649-8882; www.kimball-art.org
The art center features rotating exhibits in various media by local and regional artists.
Admission: free. Monday, Wednesday-Friday 10 a.m.-5 p.m., Saturday-Sunday noon-5 p.m.

PARK CITY MOUNTAIN RESORT
1310 Lowell Ave., Park City, 435-649-8111, 800-222-7275; www.pcski.com
The ski resort has a gondola; two quads, four doubles, five triples, and four six-passenger chairlifts; a patrol; a school; rentals; snowmaking; and restaurants, a cafeteria and a bar. The 3,300-acre area has 104 trails and 750 acres of open-bowl skiing. Lighted snowboarding is available.
Mid-November-mid-April, daily.

ROCKPORT STATE PARK
9040 N. Highway 302, Peoa, 435-336-2241; www.stateparks.utah.gov
This 1,000-acre park along the east side of Rockport Lake offers great opportunities for viewing wildlife, including bald eagles (winter) and golden eagles. There's also swimming, waterskiing, sailboarding, fishing and boating at the park. The grounds have a cross-country ski trail (six miles), camping and tent and trailer sites.
Daily.

UTAH WINTER SPORTS PARK
3419 Olympic Parkway, Park City, 435-658-4200; www.olyparks.com

Recreational ski jumping is available at this $25 million park built for the 2002 Olympic Winter Games. Lessons are offered, followed by a two-hour jumping session. An Olympic bobsled and luge track are available.

Wednesday-Sunday.

WHITE PINE TOURING CENTER
1790 Bonanza Drive, Park City, 435-649-8710; www.whitepinetouring.com

There are 12 miles of groomed cross-country trails, a school, rentals and guided tours at this center.

November-April, daily.

PROVO

HARRIS FINE ARTS CENTER
HFAC Campus Drive, Provo, 801-422-4322; cfac.byu.edu

The center includes periodic displays of rare instruments and music collections. Concert and theater performances are held here.

MUSEUM OF PEOPLES AND CULTURES
105 Allen Hall, Provo, 801-422-0020; mpc.byu.edu

The museum displays material from South America, the Near East and the Southwestern United States.

Admission: free. Monday, Wednesday, Friday 9-5 a.m., Tuesday, Thursday 9-7 a.m.

UINTA NATIONAL FOREST
88 W. and 100 N. Provo, 801-342-5100; www.fs.fed.us

Scenic drives through the forest give an unsurpassed view of colorful landscapes, canyons and waterfalls. You can do some stream and lake fishing, hunting for deer and elk, camping and picnicking. Reservations are accepted.

UTAH LAKE STATE PARK
4400 W. Center St., Provo, 801-375-0731; www.stateparks.utah.gov

The park is situated on the eastern shore of Utah Lake, a 150-square-mile, freshwater remnant of ancient Lake Bonneville that created the Great Salt Lake. The park offers fishing, boating (ramp, dock), ice skating, picnicking and camping.

Summer: daily 6 a.m.-10 p.m.; winter: 8 a.m.-5 p.m.

SNOWBIRD

SNOWBIRD SKI AND SUMMER RESORT
Highway 210, Snowbird, 801-933-2222, 800-232-9542; www.snowbird.com

Snowbird offers 89 runs on 2,500 acres—27 percent beginner, 38 percent intermediate, 35 percent advanced/expert. There are elevations of 7,800 to 11,000 feet. There are six double chairlifts, four high-speed quads and a 125-passenger aerial tram. A patrol, a school, rentals and four lodges are available. Night skiing and heli-skiing are permitted. Snowboarding, snowshoeing and ice skating are wintertime pursuits. Summer activities include rock climbing, hiking, mountain biking, tennis, tram rides and concerts.

Mid-November-early May, daily.

SUNDANCE

SUNDANCE SKI AREA

8841 N. Alpine Loop Road, Sundance, 801-225-4107, 800-892-1600; www.sundanceresort.com

There are three chairlifts, a rope tow, a patrol, a school, rentals, a warming hut and restaurants. The longest run is two miles with a vertical drop 2,150 feet. Cross-country trails are also on offer.

Late November-April, daily.

WHERE TO STAY

ALTA

★★★ALTA'S RUSTLER LODGE

10380 Highway 210, Alta, 801-742-2200, 888-532-2582; www.rustlerlodge.com

With its ski-in/ski-out access to all of Alta's lift base facilities and a full-service ski shop onsite, the Rustler Lodge is all about the slopes. A complimentary shuttle takes you wherever you want to go in Alta and Snowbird. The new business center offers wireless Internet access for those who need to get some work done between runs. The lodge also has a steam room and offers manicures, pedicures and other spa treatments. The children's programs will keep kids occupied.

85 rooms. Restaurant, bar. Closed May-October. Business center. Fitness center. Pool. Ski in/ski out. $251-350

MIDWAY

★★★THE BLUE BOAR INN

1235 Warm Springs Road, Midway, 435-654-1400, 888-650-1400; www.theblueboarinn.com

Decorated in a unique Austrian-influenced style, the guest rooms at this inn feature themes inspired by famous authors and poets. From the handmade willow bed of the Robert Frost room to the English cottage style of the William Butler Yeats, each room attempts to capture its namesake's distinctive personality. The restaurant serves fresh American cuisine.

12 rooms. Restaurant, bar. Complimentary breakfast. Business center. $151-250

★★★HOMESTEAD RESORT

700 N. Homestead Drive, Midway, 435-654-1102, 888-327-7220; www.homesteadresort.com

Surrounded by gardens and the Wasatch Mountains, this historic country resort on 200 acres features quaint cottages that make up the majority of the accommodations. Amenities include an Aveda spa, an adventure center with billiards, board games, a video library and a championship golf course. The resort also rents cross-country skis and snowshoes and provides transportation to nearby Deer Valley's Jordanelle Express Gondola.

144 rooms. Restaurant, bar. Business center. Pets accepted. Spa. Golf. Tennis. $151-250

★★★INN ON THE CREEK

375 Rainbow Lane, Midway, 435-654-0892, 800-654-0892; www.innoncreek.com

Picturesque landscaping and hot springs surround this full-service inn. Located at the base of the Wasatch Mountains in Heber Valley, the inn is near popular ski resorts and golf courses. Guests can choose from rooms in the main inn or luxury chalets. All are spacious and most rooms feature fireplaces and balconies or private decks. The inn's restaurant, which serves American-French cuisine, utilizes garden vegetables and herbs, and has an extensive wine selection.

40 rooms. Restaurant, bar. Pool. $151-250

PARK CITY

★★★THE CANYONS GRAND SUMMIT HOTEL

4000 The Canyons Resort Drive, Park City, 435-649-5400, 888-226-9667; www.thecanyons.com

This mountain lodge, one of three at the Canyons Resort, is set at the foot of Park City's ski slopes. Guest rooms, most of which have balconies and fireplaces, offer excellent views of the mountains and the valley below. If you need a break from skiing, check out the resort's Village Shops, where regularly scheduled concerts and other events are held. Summer brings warm-weather activities like horseback riding, hiking and fly-fishing and the gondola remains open for scenic rides.

358 rooms. Restaurant, bar. Spa. Ski in/ski out. Pool. $351 and up

★★★THE CHATEAUX AT SILVER LAKE

7815 E. Royal St., Park City, 435-658-9500, 800-453-3833; www.the-chateaux.com

Situated in the heart of Deer Valley Resort's Silver Lake Village, the Chateaux at Silver Lake offers guests a comfortable stay in an elegant and picturesque setting. Rooms are decorated with custom-designed furniture and feature pillow-top mattresses and feather beds, gas fireplaces and wet bars. The hotel also provides a full-service spa; heated, covered parking; free local shuttle service and winter sports equipment rentals.

95 rooms. Restaurant, bar. Business center. Fitness center. Pool. Spa. $351 and up

★★★CLUB LESPRI BOUTIQUE INN & SPA

1765 Sidewinder Drive, Park City, 435-645-9696; www.clublespri.com

The suites here all feature fireplaces, hand-carved furniture, custom beds, oversize tubs and full kitchens. The onsite spa offers a full range of massages, and two restaurants serve steaks and more in an upscale setting.

10 rooms. Restaurant, bar. Fitness center. Spa. $251-350

★★★GOLDENER HIRSCH INN

7570 Royal St. E., Park City, 435-649-7770, 800-252-3373; www.goldenerhirschinn.com

Warm and inviting, this ski resort blends the services of a large hotel with the charm of a bed and breakfast. The romantic guest rooms and suites have warm colors and hand-painted furniture. All-day dining and après-ski service are available at the hotel's Austrian-themed restaurant.

20 rooms. Restaurant, bar. Complimentary breakfast. Ski in/ski out. Closed mid-April-early June, early October-early December. $351 and up

★★★HOTEL PARK CITY

2001 Park Ave., Park City, 435-200-2000, 888-999-0098; www.hotelparkcity.com

This all-suite resort pampers its guests. The amenities are top notch, from triple-head showers and jetted tubs to Bose audio systems and Bulgari bath products. The suites have a residential feel with cozy fireplaces and traditional alpine-style furnishings. Set at the base of the Wasatch Mountains, this hotel has a scenic location that's ideal for skiers.

100 rooms. Restaurant, bar. Pool. Spa. Golf. Ski in/ski out. $151-250

★★★PARK CITY MARRIOTT

1895 Sidewinder Drive, Park City, 435-649-2900, 800-234-9003; www.marriott.com

This newly renovated hotel is a mile from downtown Park City and the historic Main Street. Take the complimentary shuttle to Utah Olympic Park, outlet stores and old Main Street. Starbucks fans will find a coffee kiosk in the lobby, as well as rental ski equipment and bicycles.

191 rooms. Restaurant, bar. Business center. Pool. Pets accepted. $151-250

★★★★★STEIN ERIKSEN LODGE

7700 Stein Way, Park City, 435-649-3700, 800-453-1302; www.steinlodge.com

Situated mid-mountain at Utah's Deer Valley ski resort, this Scandinavian resort calls a magnificent alpine setting home. Heated sidewalks and walkways keep you toasty, while the ski valet service takes care of all your needs on the slopes. The dining at Glitretind is outstanding, and the Sunday brunch is a local favorite. Be sure to try the housemade chocolates from executive pastry chef Raymond Lammers in the Chocolate Atelier, where the gourmet treats are made. The fireplace and inviting ambience of the Troll Hallen Lounge make it a cozy spot for après-ski or light fare. Rooms are all distinctive and feature jetted tubs; suites have gourmet kitchens and stone fireplaces.

180 rooms. Restaurant, bar. Business center. Fitness center. Pool. Spa. Ski in/ski out. $351 and up

★★★★THE ST. REGIS DEER CREST RESORT

2300 Deer Valley Drive East, Park City, 435-940-5700; www.starwoodhotels.com/stregis

Located in Deer Valley, just outside of Park City, this ski in/ski out resort offers immediate access to Deer Valley's renowned skiing. The 181 well-appointed and luxurious guest rooms or 67 suites offer unparalleled views of the surrounding range. Be sure to visit the incredible split-level infinity swimming pool. If snuggling up in your room is what your after, the cozy fireplaces provide all the warmth you need but open the door to your balcony and let the fresh mountain air in. The alluring Remède Spa offers a welcome respite to a hard day on the slopes. The hotel's signature restaurant J&G Grill is famed New York chef Jean-Georges Vongerichten's take on his greatest hits repurposed for the elegant mountainside setting. If you are an early riser, stop by the intimate Library for complimentary hot beverages and a glance at the daily paper for the day's weather and snow fall before heading to the mountain.

181 rooms. Restaurant, bar. Business center. Fitness center. Pool. Spa. Ski in/ski out. $351 and up

SUNDANCE

★★★SUNDANCE RESORT

8841 N. Alpine Loop Road, Sundance, 801-225-4107, 877-831-6224; www.sundanceresort.com

This resort offers standard rooms, studios and cottages, all of which, like the resort itself, are intended to blend in with the surrounding landscape. All of the rooms feature natural wood and Native American accents; most have fireplaces and private decks. The resort also provides fine dining and endless recreation, from artist workshops to nature programs. The general store is so popular that a mail-order catalog has been designed. A superb spa completes the well-rounded experience available at this unique resort.

110 rooms. Restaurant, bar. Fitness center. Spa. Ski in/ski out. $251-350

RECOMMENDED

WALDORF ASTORIA PARK CITY
2100 W. Frostwood Blvd., Park City, 435-647-5500; www.waldorfastoria.com

This beautiful property, located near The Canyons ski area with ski in/ski out access via a free lift brings a dose of luxury to laidback Park City. Inside the upscale rustic interior is rooms with full kitchens, working fireplaces and super views of the slopes outside. The onsite outpost of San Francisco's Spruce restaurant serves up refined American fare, while the 16,000 square foot Golden Door Spa has treatments to soothe sore muscles. The onsite ski shop provides all the equipment you'll need to hit the slopes in a flash.

175 rooms. Restaurant, bar. Pool. Spa. Ski in/ski out. $351 and up

PROVO

★★★PROVO MARRIOTT HOTEL AND CONFERENCE CENTER
101 W. 100 North, Provo, 801-377-4700, 800-777-7144; www.marriott.com

Nearby attractions include two shopping malls, as well as the Seven Peaks Water Park and Ice Rink, where the ice hockey competition and practices for the 2002 Winter Olympics were held. The comfortable rooms feature views of the Wasatch Mountains, duvet-topped beds and flat-screen TVs.

330 rooms. Restaurant, bar. Business center. Fitness center. Pool. $151-250

WHERE TO EAT

MIDWAY

★★★THE BLUE BOAR INN RESTAURANT
The Blue Boar Inn, 1235 Warm Springs Road, Midway, 435-654-1400, 888-650-1400; www.theblueboarinn.com

This charming Tyrolean chalet offers some of the best contemporary American cuisine in Utah. The menu changes periodically to capture the best produce and fresh seafood available, but you might see entrées like herb-crusted salmon with roasted fingerling potatoes, spring vegetables and a roasted red bell pepper sauce or braised lamb shank with pine nut couscous, spring vegetables, white wine and tomato sauce.

American. Lunch, dinner, Sunday brunch. Outdoor seating. Bar. $36-85

★★★FANNY'S GRILL
Homestead Resort, 700 N. Homestead Drive, Midway, 435-654-1102, 800-327-7220; www.homesteadresort.com

Dine on Western cuisine like sirloin and country-fried steaks and hearty side dishes in an elegant country setting, either inside the dining room by the fireplace or outside on the deck, with beautiful views of the valley. The outdoor patio is a comfortable spot to dine in warm weather.

American. Breakfast, lunch, dinner. Outdoor seating. Children's menu. Bar. $16-35

WHICH PARK CITY RESTAURANTS HAVE THE BEST CONTEMPORARY AMERICAN FOOD?

Glitretind Restaurant:
This restaurant resides in the excellent Stein Eriksen Lodge. The food is as good as its chic surroundings, with succulent dishes like Berkshire pork porterhouse with pecan grits, baby beans, watermelon and bourbon sauce.

Riverhorse on Main:
The casual, bustling Riverhorse is a favorite among the ski crowd. But delicious American fare like macadamia-crusted halibut and poached lobster tail will appeal to all palates.

PARK CITY

★★★THE CABIN
The Canyons Grand Summit Hotel, 4000 The Canyons Resort Drive, Park City, 435-649-8060; www.thecanyons.com
This upscale restaurant at the Canyons Grand Summit Hotel has rustic décor and a friendly staff. The restaurant serves dishes from an eclectic Western menu, including buffalo tenderloin, lamb osso buco and its signature crispy trout.
American. Breakfast, lunch, dinner. Children's menu. Bar. $36-85

★★★CHIMAYO
368 Main St., Park City, 435-649-6222; www.chimayorestaurant.com
Tucked on Main Street in downtown Park City, this restaurant serves creative Southwestern cuisine. Dishes include scallops wrapped in wild boar bacon and served with a tortilla tomato casserole with salsa verde and seared trout fajitas. A fireplace enhances the warm, colorful atmosphere.
Southwestern. Dinner. Reservations recommended. Children's menu. $36-85

★★★★GLITRETIND RESTAURANT
Stein Eriksen Lodge, 7700 Stein Way, Park City, 435-645-6455; www.steinlodge.com
Executive chef Zane Holmquist prepares acclaimed contemporary American cuisine at this restaurant inside the Stein Eriksen Lodge. Try the Berkshire pork porterhouse with pecan grits, baby beans, watermelon and bourbon sauce; or the filet of Colorado beef with smoked blue cheese, fingerling potatoes, peas and veal jus. The wine selection is managed by sommelier Cara Schwindt and includes more than 750 types of wine that total more than 10,000 bottles. The restaurant also provides a wide selection of dessert and after-dinner drinks, including a wide range of single-malt Scotch, bourbon, cognac and brandy.
American. Breakfast, lunch, dinner, Sunday brunch. Reservations recommended. Outdoor seating. Children's menu. Bar. $36-85

★★★GRAPPA
151 Main St., Park City, 435-645-0636; www.grapparestaurant.com
Nestled inside a former boarding house on Park City's historic Main Street, this upscale restaurant offers dining on three levels. Many of the dishes feature fresh herbs and flowers plucked from the adjacent gardens, such as the salmon encrusted in horseradish, garlic, herbed breadcrumbs and chopped shallots with

housemade fettuccine, mushrooms, tomatoes and sherry-butter sauce.

Italian. Dinner. Outdoor seating. Children's menu. $36-85

★★★J&G GRILL

The St. Regis Deer Crest Resort, 2300 Deer Valley Drive East, Park City, 435-940-5760; www. jggrilldeercrest.com

With restaurants around the world, Jean-Georges Vongerichten has an extended repertoire to choose from and that is exactly what he did for the elegantly casual J&G Grill. A long communal table, elegant but rustic stone walls, a fireplace and unique light fixtures highlight the space where the views might be the best design attribute. Open for lunch and dinner daily, the Grill serves dishes ranging from rice cracker crusted tuna to signature black truffle with fontina cheese pizza to short ribs. An appealing selection of side dishes rounds out the menu. If you have a sweet tooth, the salted caramel sundae is the perfect ending to your day of skiing and fun.

American. Breakfast, lunch, dinner. Reservations recommended. $36-85

★★★★RIVERHORSE ON MAIN

540 Main St., Park City, 435-649-3536;
www.riverhorsegroup.com

Even ski bunnies (and bums) must eat, and when they do, they come to Riverhorse on Main, a bustling scene. Located in the renovated historic Masonic Hall on Main Street, this modern restaurant, with dark woods, soft candlelight and fresh flowers offers lots of fun, Asian-inspired eats, such as chicken satay, shrimp potstickers, crispy duck salad, macadamia-crusted halibut, poached lobster tail and grilled rack of lamb. While the dress code is informal, reservations are a must.

American. Dinner. Reservations recommended. Outdoor seating. Children's menu. $36-85

SUNDANCE

★★★THE TREE ROOM

Sundance Resort, 8841 N. Alpine Loop Road, Sundance, 801-223-4200, 866-627-8313;
www.sundanceresort.com

Located at the base of the Sundance ski lift, this restaurant's two-story windows offer views of the rugged mountains and surrounding wilderness. The upscale yet casual room is filled with beautiful displays of Native American dolls and pottery. The sophisticated contemporary American cuisine includes wild game, steaks and seafood, prepared with herbs and vegetables from the resort's own organic gardens.

American. Dinner. Closed Sunday-Monday. Bar. $36-85

SPAS

PARK CITY

★★★★THE SPA AT STEIN ERIKSEN LODGE

Stein Eriksen Lodge, 7700 Stein Way, Park City, 435-649-3700; www.steinlodge.com

The Spa at Stein Eriksen Lodge was designed to appeal to guests needing remedies for sore and tired muscles after skiing, or those affected by the resort's high altitude. All spa services come with complimentary use of the fitness center, steam room, sauna, whirlpool and relaxation room. Aromatic and exhilarating treatments refresh and renew at this European-style spa, where Vichy showers are de rigueur. The extensive massage menu includes Swedish, deep tissue, aromatic, stone, reflexology and a special rubdown for mothers-to-be. In-room massages are available for additional privacy.

★★★★REMÈDE SPA, THE ST. REGIS DEER CREST RESORT

The St. Regis Deer Crest Resort, 2300 Deer Valley Drive East, Park City, 435-940-5830; www.starwoodhotels.com/stregis

This spacious 14,000-square-foot spa fills two levels of the hotel and has a soothing atmosphere that reflects the natural colors and elements of the beautiful mountain setting. The most unusual feature is an intriguing reflecting pool that brings the outside in. A grand spiral staircase adds an architectural element and naturally leads to the private treatment rooms. Indulge yourself with the Deer Crest healing ritual that includes an exfoliation, body wrap and facial as well as a scalp massage and a paraffin treatment for both the hands and the feet. Couples can secure one of the two private suites and enjoy pre- or post-treatment relaxation time on the private heated patio just outside their suites. There is also a 3,000-square-foot fitness center as well as fitness and yoga classes, in case you didn't get your workout on the slopes.

WHERE TO SHOP

PARK CITY
TANGER FACTORY OUTLET

6699 N. Landmark Drive, Park City, 435-645-7078, 866-665-8681; www.tangeroutlet.com

Get discounted deals at Tanger Factory Outlet. The more than 45 outlet stores here include Gap, Calin Klein, Polo Ralph Lauren, Ann Taylor, Banana Republic, Nike and Eddie Bauer.

Monday-Saturday 10 a.m.-9 p.m, Sunday 11 a.m.-6 p.m.

SOUTHERN UTAH

This region of Utah is filled with majestic scenery, from spectacular canyons to shimmering waters. There's Bryce Canyon, Zion National Park and Lake Powell, the second largest man-made lake in the United States, with more than 1,900 miles of shoreline. If you love the great outdoors, Southern Utah is a great destination.

WHAT TO SEE

BRYCE CANYON NATIONAL PARK
BRYCE CANYON

Bryce Canyon; www.nps.gov

This 56-square-mile area of colorful, fantastic cliffs was created by millions of years of erosion. Towering rocks worn down into odd, sculptured shapes stand grouped in striking sequences. The Paiute, who once lived nearby, called this "the place where red rocks stand like men in a bowl-shaped canyon." Although labeled as a canyon, Bryce is actually a series of "breaks" in 12 large amphitheaters—some plunging as deep as 1,000 feet into the multicolored limestone. The formations appear to change color as the sunlight strikes from different

HIGHLIGHTS

WHAT ARE THE TOP THINGS TO DO IN SOUTHERN UTAH?

CHECK OUT BRYCE CANYON
This 56-square-mile area of colorful, fantastic cliffs created by millions of years of erosion is a spectacular sight.

SPEND THE DAY AT ZION NATIONAL PARK
Take a long hike on one of the many trails. The park's spectacular canyons and enormous rock formations are the result of powerful upheavals of the earth and erosion by flowing water and frost.

angles and seem incandescent in the late afternoon. The famous Pink Cliffs were carved from the Claron Formation; shades of red, orange, white, gray, purple, brown and soft yellow appear in the strata. The park road follows 17 miles along the eastern edge of the Paunsaugunt Plateau, where the natural amphitheaters are spread out below. Plateaus covered with evergreens and valleys filled with sagebrush stretch into the distance. Camping is available at the North Campground (year-round), east of park headquarters; Sunset Campground, two miles south of park headquarters.
Fourteen-day limit at both sites; fireplaces, picnic tables, restrooms, water available.

CEDAR CITY
DIXIE NATIONAL FOREST
1789 N. Wedgewood Lane, Cedar City, 435-865-3700; www.fs.fed.us
This 2-million-acre forest provides opportunities for camping, fishing, hiking, mountain biking and winter sports.
Daily.

IRON MISSION STATE PARK
635 N. Main, Cedar City, 435-586-9290; www.stateparks.utah.gov
The museum at the park is dedicated to the first pioneer iron foundry west of the Rockies and features an extensive collection of horse-drawn vehicles and wagons from Utah pioneer days.
Daily.

KANAB
CORAL PINK SAND DUNES STATE PARK
Yellow jacket and Hancock Roads, Kanab, 435-648-2800; www.stateparks.utah.gov
The park includes six square miles of very colorful, windswept sand hills. Hiking,

picnicking, tent and trailer sites are all available. Off-highway vehicles are allowed.
Daily.

LAKE POWELL

BOAT TRIPS ON LAKE POWELL
Bullfrog Marina, Highway 276, Lake Powell, 435-684-3000; www.lakepowell.com

Trips include the two-hour Canyon Explorer tour and the half-day and all-day
Rainbow Bridge tours. Due to the current level of the lake, these tours involve
a one-mile hike to see the monument. You can also take wilderness float trips
and rent houseboats and powerboats. Reservations are advised.
Daily.

MOAB

ADRIFT ADVENTURES
378 N. Main St., Moab, 435-259-8594, 800-874-4483; www.adrift.net

This outfitter offers oar, paddle and motorized trips that range from one to
seven days. Jeep tours and horseback rides are also offered.
Early April-late October.

CANYON VOYAGES ADVENTURE COMPANY
211 N. Main St., Moab, 435-259-6007, 800-733-6007; www.canyonvoyages.com

Choose among kayaking, white-water rafting, canoeing, biking or four-wheel
drive tours.
Early April-October.

CANYONLANDS BY NIGHT
1861 S. Highway 191, Moab, 435-259-2628, 800-394-9978; www.canyonlandsbynight.com

The two-hour boat trip with sound-and-light presentation highlights the history
of area. April-mid-October, daily, leaves at sundown, weather permitting.
Reservations required.

DAN O'LAURIE CANYON COUNTRY MUSEUM
118 E. Center St., Moab, 435-259-7985; www.discovermoab.com

See exhibits on local history, archaeology, geology, uranium and minerals of the
area. Walking tour information is also provided.
Admission: free. March-October, Monday-Friday 10 a.m.-6 p.m., Saturday noon-6 p.m.;
November-February, Monday-Friday 10 a.m.-3 p.m., Saturday noon-5 p.m.

HOLE 'N THE ROCK
11037 S. Highway 191, Moab, 435-686-2250; www.moab-utah.com

See a 5,000-square-foot home carved into huge sandstone rock. The site also
has a picnic area with stone tables and benches.
Tours: daily 8 a.m.-dusk.

PACK CREEK RANCH TRAIL RIDES
La Sal Mountain Loop Road, Moab, 435-259-5505; www.packcreekranch.com

Go horseback riding through the foothills of the La Sal Mountains. Guided
tours are offered for small groups; reservations are required.
March-October; upon availability.

REDTAIL AVIATION SCENIC AIR TOURS
North Highway 191, Moab, 435-259-7421, 800-842-9251; www.moab-utah.com

Get a bird's-eye view of Moab's beautiful scenery. This tour offers flights over Canyonlands National Park and various other tours.

Daily.

RIM TOURS
1233 S. Highway 191, Moab, 435-259-5223, 800-626-7335; www.rimtours.com

Guided mountain bike tours lead you through canyon country and the Colorado Rockies. Vehicle support is available for camping tours.

Daily and overnight trips; combination bicycle/river trips available.

SHERI GRIFFITH RIVER EXPEDITIONS
2231 S. Highway 191, Moab, 435-259-8229, 800-332-2439; www.griffithexp.com

Take your pick and ride oar boats, motorized rafts, paddleboats or an inflatable kayak for one- to five-day trips. Instruction is available.

May-October.

TAG-A-LONG EXPEDITIONS
452 N. Main St., Moab, 435-259-8946, 800-453-3292; www.tagalong.com

Choose from one- to seven-day white-water rafting trips on the Green and Colorado rivers; jet boat trips on the Colorado River; and jet boat trips and four-wheel-drive tours into Canyonlands National Park. Winter four-wheel drive tours are given November to February. One-day jet boat trips with cultural performing arts programs are offered part of the year as well.

April-mid-October.

TEX'S RIVERWAYS
691 N. 500 W., Moab, 435-259-5101; www.texsriverways.com

Take a flatwater canoe trips for four to 10 days. Confluence pick-ups are available.

March-October.

ZION NATIONAL PARK
RIVER RAFTING
Dinosaur National Monument, Zion, 435-781-7700; www.nps.gov

Go rafting down the Green and Yampa rivers. You need an advanced permit from the National Park Service or to go, with concession-operated guided float trips.

PARK TRAILS
Zion, 435-772-3256; www.nps.gov

These trails lead to otherwise inaccessible areas, including the Narrows (walls of this canyon are 2,000 feet high and as little as 50 feet apart at the stream), the Hanging Gardens of Zion, Weeping Rock and the Emerald Pools. Trails range from half-mile trips to day-long treks, some requiring great stamina. The paths in less-traveled areas should not be undertaken without first obtaining information from a park ranger. Backcountry permits are required for travel through the Virgin River Narrows and other canyons, and on all overnight trips.

ZION NATIONAL PARK
Zion; www.nps.gov

The spectacular canyons and enormous rock formations in this 147,551-acre national park are the result of powerful upheavals of the earth and erosion by flowing water and frost. Considered the grandfather of Utah's national parks, Zion is one of the nation's oldest and one of the state's widest with large sections that are virtually inaccessible.

WHERE TO STAY

CANYON POINT
★★★AMANGIRI
1 Kayenta Road, Canyon Point, 435-675-3999; www.amanresorts.com

Located in the Four Corners region—where Utah, Colorado, New Mexico and Arizona meet—this mountain retreat is a stunner, and a destination in itself. Tucked into a protected valley with sweeping views of the dramatic landscape, the resort was designed to complement its surroundings (cement buildings were dyed to match the rock). Guests arrive via a winding road that descends into the valley. The swimming pool is the focal point. Located right off the main pavilion, the pool was built around rock and includes king size day beds. Suites have white stone floors (which are heated in cooler months) and concrete walls, and sleek furnishing include white sofas and timber cabinets. Bathrooms feature twin rain showers and soaking tubs with views of the surrounding landscape. Pool suites boast a private plunge pool and a private sky terrace complete with a daybed. This being an Aman Resort (only their second in North America), activities are unique. Care to explore the area with an archaeologist or geologist? They'll set that up for you. Other activities include hiking, horseback riding, rock climbing, hot air ballooning, helicopter flights and boating on Lake Powell. Be sure to check out the Aman Spa, which features many unique amenities, including the Water Pavilion, which includes an outdoor heated step pool and a relaxing lounge.

34 suites/villas. Restaurant, bar. Spa. Pool. Fitness Center. $351 and up

MOAB
★★★SORREL RIVER RANCH RESORT & SPA
Highway 128, Moab, 435-259-4642, 877-359-2715; www.sorrelriver.com

Set in a dramatic landscape of red rock formations, this full-service resort is just 30 minutes from Arches National Park. Many of the Western-themed guest rooms, all of which have kitchenettes, overlook the Colorado River. Family loft suites are available and fireplaces and jetted hydrotherapy tubs are found in the deluxe suites. Also offered are horseback tours, tennis and a spa. After a busy day, enjoy an upscale meal at the Sorrel River Grill.

59 rooms. Restaurant. Spa. Tennis. $151-250

INDEX

ARIZONA

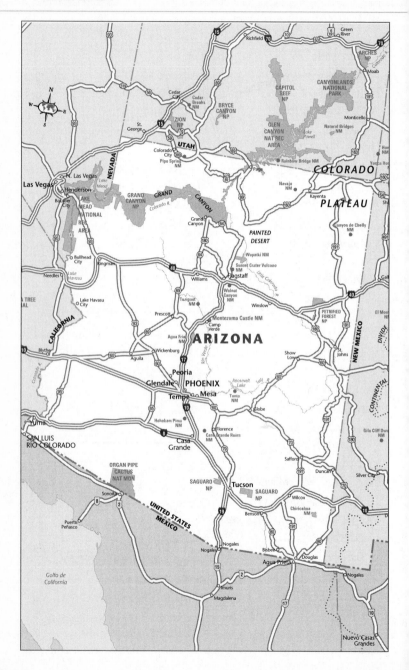

NEVADA

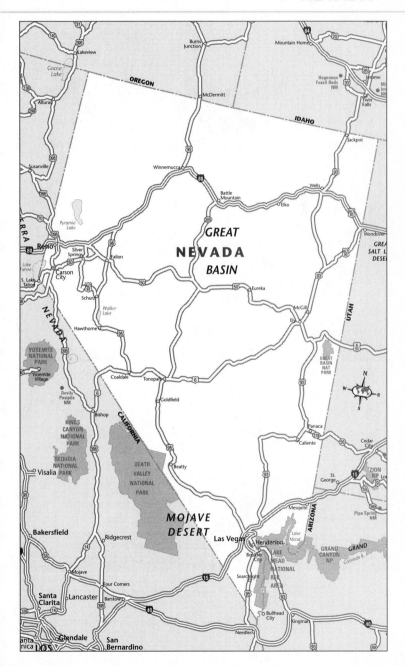

COLORADO

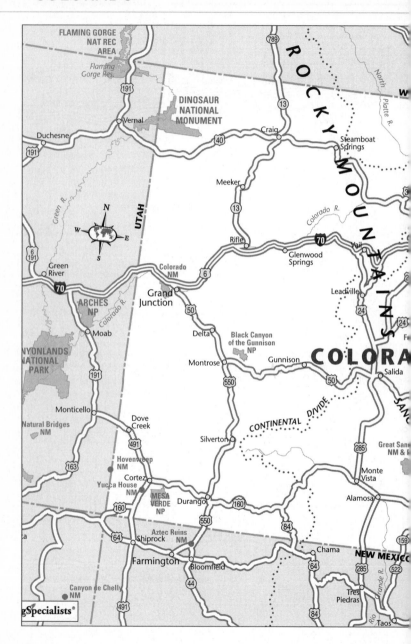

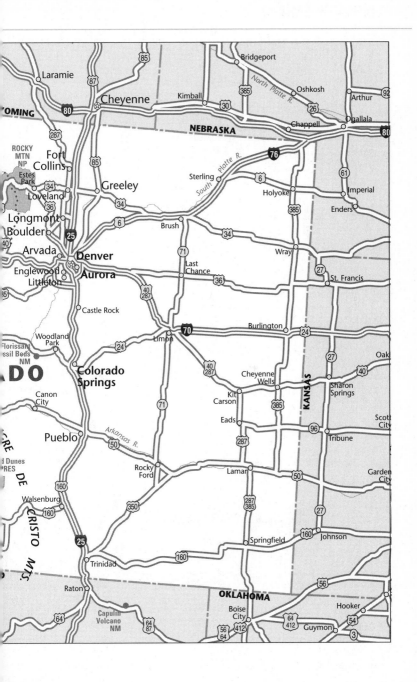

NEW MEXICO

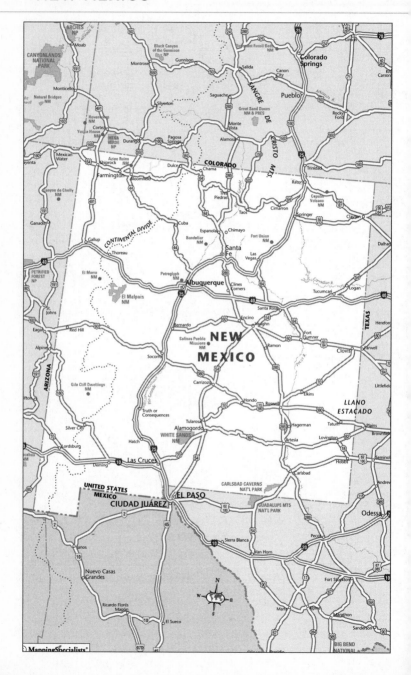

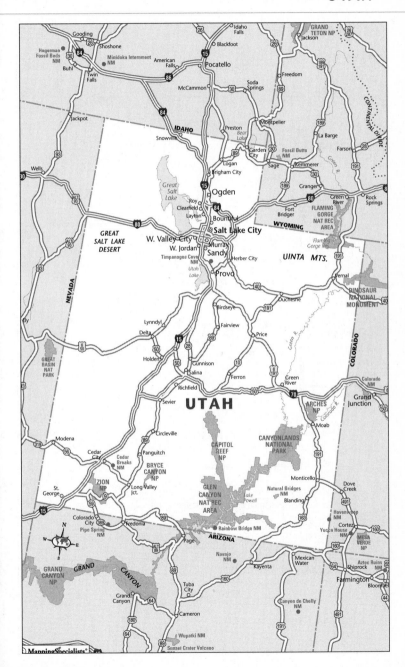

TEXAS

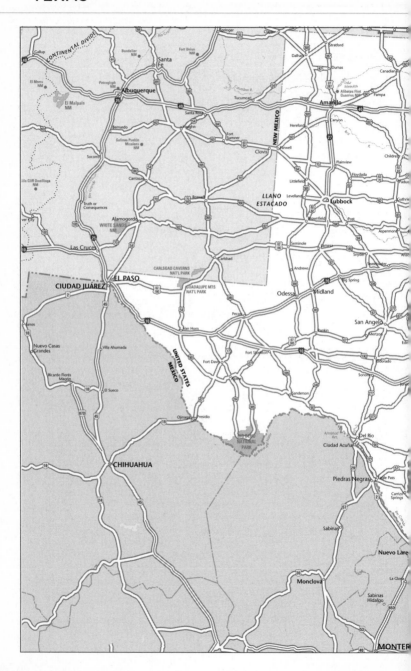